P9-BZL-127

Reading in the Secondary Schools

Reading in the Secondary Schools

M. JERRY WEISS
JERSEY CITY STATE COLLEGE

THE ODYSSEY PRESS, INC. · *New York*

Printed in the United States of America

A 0 9 8 7 6 5 4 3 2

TO

Helen and Max

Acknowledgments

Acknowledgment is made to the following sources for permission to quote copyright or original material:

To The International Reading Association for permission to quote the following articles from the IRA *Proceedings:* "Why Many Children and Youth Are Retarded in Reading," by Anne McKillop (1956); "Implications of Research for Teaching Reading in a Changing Society," by Miriam Aronow (1959); "Enlisting Faculty-Wide Co-operation for Improvement of Reading Skills in Senior High School," by Marshall Covert (1957); "Improving the Quality of Reading Instruction throughout a School System," by Earle W. Wiltse (1956); "How Can We Secure Parent Co-operation?" by Nancy Larrick (1956); "Setting College-Bound Students into Orbit," by Phillip Shaw (1959); "Mass Media and the Interests of High School Youth," by Charles G. Spiegler (1957); "Developing Critical Reading as a Basic Skill," by Roma Gans (1957); "Helping Students to Read Scientific Material," by Homer L. J. Carter (1958); "Science," by Mary K. Eakin (1958). To *The Reading Teacher* for "Reading Inventories for Classroom Use," by Marjorie Seddon Johnson (September, 1960), and "Clinical Diagnosis in the Classroom," by George D. Spache (September, 1960).

To The University of Chicago Press for "Principles for Selecting Methods and Materials to Promote Growth in Reading," by Marvin D. Glock, in *Promoting Maximal Reading Growth Among Able Learners* (December, 1954); "Relationship of Mass Media to Reading Interests," by Paul A. Wagner in *Developing Permanent Interest in Reading* (December, 1956); "Using Radio and Television in Grades Seven through Nine," by David V. Curtis in *Developing Permanent Interest in Reading* (December, 1956); "Problems Met When Reading Critically in Grades Seven to Ten," by Charles B. Huelsman, Jr., in *Promoting Maturity in Interpreting What is Read* (November,

1951); "Interpreting Materials in Arithmetic and Mathematics in Grades Seven to Fourteen," by Kenneth B. Henderson in *Improving Reading in All Curriculum Areas* (November, 1952); "Materials for the Unit Plan in Social Studies," by Jean Fair in *Materials for Reading* (December, 1957). To the Office of Education Bulletin, 1957, No. 10, *Improving Reading in the Junior High School*, for "What Experiences, Activities, and Materials Are Helpful in a Developmental Reading Program?" by Paul Witty; "The Problem of Reading Instruction in Mathematics," by John R. Clark; "What Are the Responsibilities of Social Studies Teachers for Teaching Reading?" by Mabel Rudisill. To *Teachers College Record*, May, 1960, for "Contributions of Reading to Personal Development," by David H. Russell.

To *The English Journal* for "Reading for Therapy," by Dorothy Bratton (September, 1957); "Improving the Reading of Academically Untalented Students," by Edwin Mingoia (January, 1960); "What Is a Good Unit in English?" by Richard S. Alm (September, 1960); "About Successful Reading Programs," by Margaret J. Early (October, 1957). To *The Bulletin of the National Association of Secondary School Principals* for "Reading for the Gifted in the Secondary School," (October, 1955); "Teaching Essential Reading Skills," (February, 1950); "Campaigning to Get Students to Read," by Dwight L. Burton (September, 1955); "Semantics in the Secondary School," by Richard Corbin (September, 1955). To *Journal of National Association of Women Deans and Counselors*, for "Reading Ability and High School Drop-Outs," by Ruth C. Penty (October, 1959). To George E. Murphy for his article, "Some Start with Comics." To E. Elona Sochor for her article, "Comprehension in the Reading Program." To *Kansas Studies in Education* for "Reading Skills and Methods of Teaching Them," (February, 1960).

To *The High School Journal* for "Teaching Reading in Science Classes," by Ruth Strang (October, 1955), and "Improving Comprehension of Mathematics," by Mary C. Austin (November, 1955). To *The Journal of Developmental Reading* for "Teaching Reading, an Essential Part of Teaching English," by Ruth Strang (October, 1957). To *The Illinois English Bulletin* for "How Can We Help Students Enjoy Literature?" by Joseph Mersand (October, 1959), and "Reading in the Junior High School," by Mary Clifford (May, 1957). To Cordelia Smith for her aid in compiling the "College Preparatory Reading List."

Contents

Part One. Teaching Begins with a Philosophy

Part Two. Groundwork for a Reading Program

Part Three. The Program and the Student

Part Four. Student Motivation

Part Five. Developing Reading Skills

Part Six. Teaching Reading in the Content Fields

SCIENCE

ENGLISH

MATHEMATICS

SOCIAL STUDIES

Part Seven. Examples of Secondary School Reading Programs

Part Eight. The Effectiveness of a Reading Program

Introduction

Ever since I began teaching English in a small rural Virginia high school in 1949, I have been concerned about the growing number of secondary school students who cannot or do not read as well as they might or who do not find personal values and pleasure through reading.

During the intervening years, a great number of publications — including James B. Conant's reports, *The American High School Today* and *A Memorandum to School Boards: Education in the Junior High School Years* — have warned teachers and administrators in the secondary school to place greater emphasis on reading. Several states, such as Pennsylvania, have added remedial or developmental reading, or both, to the junior high school curriculum.

However, the various publications have not always indicated how adequate reading programs for *each* child can be developed. This book is an attempt to present the ideas teachers and professors have offered for effective programs.

Part One of the book presents the over-all philosophy of reading. Reading is more than the mere mastery of skills. There are many causes for students' deficiencies in reading.

Part Two argues that reading is every teacher's job. No one person can carry the program. Parents need to understand the program and to cooperate in developing it.

Part Three emphasizes the role of reading as a personal experience. It suggests ways of handling the problem of individual differences. This means pin-pointing the needs of a child and providing individual or small-group (if several children have the same interests and needs) instruction and activities.

Part Four deals with motivation through printed sources and other forms of mass media. Ways of recognizing and building on student interests are described.

Parts Five and Six show ways that reading skills can be vastly improved, both generally and in specific content fields. Suggestions are given for developing critical reading. Organizing content matter around unit themes seems to be a particularly effective method of providing for the individual interests and reading levels of students.

Part Seven offers some guideposts for developing and conducting reading programs on the secondary level.

Part Eight discusses ideas basic to evaluating the effectiveness of an all-school, all-faculty reading program.

A bibliography of professional publications and materials useful in a secondary school reading program follows the chapter on evaluation.

This entire book is built on the belief that effective teaching must contribute to the development of the total student and that the teacher must therefore understand and make use of the student's existing reading patterns and patterns of general experience. Every teacher needs to start where the individual student is and, by providing the most appropriate materials and instruction, help that student to develop to his maximum potential. Through such instruction, a student may soon find that reading is a constant source of meaning and value for him.

M. J. W.

Reading in the Secondary Schools

PART ONE

Teaching Begins with a Philosophy

1. A Personal Approach to Reading Instruction

M. Jerry Weiss

A number of years ago a good friend of mine confessed with some discouragement and chagrin that his daughter was having difficulty in the private school in which she was enrolled. The principal had written him that although Mary's IQ was above average she was in need of remedial instruction in reading and that the school had added special reading sessions to her curriculum. Would I go over the problem with Mary when she came home for the Christmas vacation?

Mary, it turned out, was an alert, well-spoken, and lovely girl, and she soon gave me her confidence. She was not surprised when I broached the subject of remedial reading. She knew very well that her grades were slipping and that she found it difficult to concentrate on her studies. She did not, in fact, enjoy reading.

Was she deficient in basic reading skills? At my office I put her through a series of tests. She was relaxed and in good humor and scored well in all categories. The difficulty was obviously elsewhere, but what was it? Was it primarily a matter of attitude?

Mary's father was in publishing and had long filled his home with books and reading. But where he himself enjoyed reading he assumed that he could force a similar enjoyment upon his children. If Mary wanted to attend a movie, have a date, buy a record, choose a new dress, or go to a party, first of all she had to read a book and pass an oral examination upon its contents. When she passed the test the privilege was granted, and this was the way it had been year in and year out. Finally, without really realizing it, she had rebelled. Since Mary's problem did involve her attitude, the way back to reading enjoyment was obviously intricate and personal.

Following my experience with her, I have encountered the problem a number of times, and the conviction that it must be met with individualized instruction has been confirmed repeatedly.

For the teacher, though, another problem remains. As long as there is only one student, the teacher's method is almost inevitably individualized. But a teacher is commonly expected to instruct a group of students simultaneously, to conduct a "class." Should he now reduce his teaching to a least common denominator and ignore his conviction that each student has a set of problems all his own? The following experience was useful to me in pointing toward the answer.

I was teaching a required class in sophomore English in Defiance, Ohio. Dutifully, I began the course with a discussion of the nature of reading and writing, only to discover that many of the students had read hardly anything beyond the assignments imposed by high school teachers and that they were taking my course only because it was required, not because they enjoyed literature. I was shocked to discover that there were college students to whom "the wonderful world of books" was no more wonderful than a rubble heap.

The first step, clearly, was to make a sober analysis of my students' attitudes, their varying abilities, their backgrounds, and their previous experience in reading. Through conferences with individual students I learned that many of them had had very limited reading opportunities, coming from rural areas where library facilities were meager and from homes where books were considered unimportant. Few intended to become English teachers, and few anticipated taking any further English courses. Time and again it was said, "If I can get through this course I can get through the rest without trouble." Unless I managed to stir their interest, their time with me was obviously going to be wasted.

I asked the students to tell me what they actually did enjoy. So few of the answers centered upon the textbook that I tossed it out and substituted special reading assignments which not only satisfied the requirements of the course but also corresponded to the students' various interests. The librarian was most cooperative in ferreting out useful books, and I arranged for paperbound titles to be stocked by the bookstore so that students could build up personal libraries and increase their reading at home.

The change in the level of classroom interest was astonishing. Students who were reading books on a similar topic presented panel discussions, with the rest of the class participating in what often became lively debates on the significance of the events or the merits of the ideas which the various authors offered. Every student read, and every student contributed to class discussion. Some made dioramas of scenes and characters from the books, short stories, poems, or plays they had read. Some adapted short stories or poems as plays. Two boys designed and built a detailed Elizabethan theater of balsa wood and explained how Shakespeare's *Henry IV* might have been staged. Another group caught a frog and on slides recorded the hilarious history of "The Celebrated Jumping Frog." Instead of dreading sophomore English, my students now came to look forward to class sessions with excitement. I, in turn, had become a "listener" rather than a "lecturer," and my function as a guide accordingly became less obtrusive.

Under the right conditions, apparently, all of my students could and would read, although — particularly at first — they felt abashed when faced with the need for critical judgment and often turned to stock attitudes for their opinions of the characters about whom they read. One group discussing Robert Anderson's *Tea and Sympathy* turned vehemently on one of the characters who, without proof, had been accused of homosexuality. For my students, more careful weighing of evidence and the broadening of perception and sympathy might come with more diverse reading and a continuously deepening process of evaluation, but now their prejudice took the form of a generalized principle. "If you're different, that's tough. Find your own kind." It did not occur to them immediately that each of them was different — physically, mentally, emotionally, and even culturally — and that even the greatest differences between individuals and groups involve gradations more often than sharp distinctions. We began to read heavily in material which illustrated the great diversity in human beings and social groups and developed, almost without knowing it, a unit on "The Individual in Society." In contact with controversial issues — politics, prejudice, persecution — my students gradually began to feel responsible for forming their own opinions. At the same time, since we were dealing with literary matter, they began to extend their self-reliance into the areas of literary criticism. With their new sense of independence, they often asked, "Why didn't we get this opportunity in high school? Why couldn't we use this same approach in all subjects? Why can't we go on finding things out for ourselves?"

True, many great writers were never discussed in our class and inferior writers might be substituted, but at least prevailing attitudes were changed and the door to great writing was never closed. In that course, students encountered research techniques, were introduced to literary criticism, and found that literature held reservoirs of excitement when explored in depth. Old attitudes were shaken and uprooted, and a number of students went on to other English courses by their own choice.

For the members of my class the result was a discovery of pleasures they did not know existed. For me, the result was a conviction that all my teaching from that time on would have to be adjusted to permit each student to find, on his own terms, the strength and attraction of reading. I would have to take him from where he was, not from where I assumed he should be.

I knew that the problem was fundamental and continuous and have met it again and again in teaching English and reading at secondary and college levels. Each time the door opens for a new class, I know that the young people who enter bring with them a wealth of different backgrounds and experience. They have not read the same books, been to the same places, or shared the same recreations or serious pursuits. Their interests vary. Their abilities are uneven. Nor do they all have the same needs.

Each student is unique and has something of his own to offer to the learning process. Each has some base upon which the teacher can help to build. Accordingly, it is the function of the teacher to find out what that base is and to use it as a point of departure in developing the basic reading skills through individualized instruction. The goal of the program is a mastery of all the reading skills so that every student can read with ease and pleasure, but, in view of the individual differences I have mentioned, the order and timing of various phases of instruction must be varied from one student to another. In the elementary classroom, not every child is ready for phonics on the second day of the thirty-fourth week. On the other hand, if a group of children are ready for help in the same skills, "skill-group" instruction is the most practical approach. For the teacher this means not only an absolutely thorough familiarity with the necessary skills and with the methods for achieving them but also a constant checking on the progress of the individual student, whether that student is a child or an adult.

I have been speaking of basic skills. It may be well to comment upon them separately:

Word recognition, word attack, the meaning of a word in a specific context. The resourcefulness of the teacher is at a premium in arousing a student's interest in developing his vocabulary. Crossword puzzles and such word games as Scrabble, applied at various levels of difficulty, can draw heavily on the student's existing vocabulary and also lead to use of the dictionary in the search for new words. Many teachers suggest special projects on word origins for certain students who can grasp the excitement of discovering that words have lives of their own and are not merely mechanical counters to be fitted onto a grammatical pegboard. Techniques and materials will vary from teacher to teacher and from student to student. When it is appropriate in a given case, the teacher will introduce phonics, configuration, structural analysis, etc.

Comprehension. This skill is more general than the preceding one and involves understanding and retaining main ideas and supporting details. Comprehending the main ideas of a biology unit is quite different from comprehending the main ideas of a history unit. The student needs to develop comprehension in all content-area subjects and should maintain a check on his own comprehension ability in each of the major subjects he is taking.

Speed. Many students come for help in this skill alone. Fairly often, and not without some seriousness, they make such complaints as the following: "I want to read my chemistry faster because I don't like it. If I can read it faster, I won't dislike it so long." Whatever the student's real or ostensible motive, the teacher helps him adjust his speed according to the purpose for which he is reading in a particular instance, the type of material being read, and the degree of difficulty he has in comprehending what he is reading. Speed reading is not a panacea for all reading difficulties. I have, in fact, had to warn students to use caution in increasing their speed.

For a student who has read very little, the first step is to provide him with reading materials which are both simple and interesting. As his familiarity with reading techniques improves, he can move on to more complex material. As a motivational device I find reading machines less effective than a full array of books, magazines, etc., covering a broad range of subject matter. Consequently, I use the machines sparingly.

For speed, as well as the mastery of other reading skills, I myself use workbooks to provide drill material. But no student has a workbook for himself. He is not required to fill out an entire series of pages whether he needs them or not. Instead, the workbooks are cut up and filed according to the type of drill material each page offers. If it appears that Max, say, needs help in skimming, I first go over the techniques of skimming with him and make sure that he understands the purpose of such a skill. Then I go to the file labeled "Skimming," pull out a few pages for him to practice on, and turn him loose. I find this system is both effective and economical.

Other general areas. These include reading for the following purposes: to follow directions, to interpret, to make inferences, to summarize and draw conclusions, to analyze ideas critically, to locate specific information quickly and accurately, to use reference materials, to know the parts of a book, to develop effective study habits, and to understand such specialized materials as maps, charts, tables, and diagrams. It is important to provide practice in the content subjects so that the student will see the need for mastering these specialized skills. The practice material can often be taken from the textbooks and specific assignments a student receives in his subjects.

The teaching of reading, as I have already implied in the preceding pages, is not concerned solely with the development of basic reading skills, important as they are, since none of these skills operates in a vacuum. If a person reads, he encounters subject matter. Whatever he learns from that subject matter changes him as a person: it can enlarge his range of ideas, quicken his emotions, broaden his tolerance, sharpen his perception and appreciation of art, deepen his sense of moral order and public responsibility — and it can do the reverse. The reading teacher, like any teacher, has a responsibility for pointing his students in the direction of fulfillment of their best and greatest potentialities. He is, inevitably, concerned with the student as a whole person. In the reading program, he wants each person in his charge to become sensitive to the values of language as a vital part of life, as a constant communication between civilization and himself. The student thus comes to see the multitude of purposes for which men have put their thought into writing. He sees how, from the time when writing first came into being, language has recorded human accomplishment. He learns to respect the miracle of written symbols and understands that the scientist and the historian use them differently and that he, in turn, must read the scientist and the historian differently. He learns that some meanings are more variable than others, and that two people reading the same passage might well have a different understanding of its contents.

As they continue to read, students realize that language is not merely an instrument for communication. When my English students — at my suggestion — discuss the familiar quotation, "The pen is mightier than the sword," they show that they recognize language as a force which has changed the course of history and deeply influenced the lives of men. They discuss how, from generation to generation, language has kept ideas alive in people, has passed along the forms of literature for their use and enjoyment, has given them knowledge of the past, has preserved the earlier scientific discoveries upon which the later scientist can build a greater understanding of the physical universe. Some students find their own purposes — and even answers to their own problems — expressed in biographies and novels.

But we cannot expect students to reach depth of understanding unless they are encouraged to read and unless they have freedom in a wealth of reading material presenting many different points of view. If they read enough, under these conditions, they will continue to read more, and they will begin to be selective in their reading choices. A discriminating taste for permanent reading comes from the free exploration of books, newspapers, magazines, journals, and so on — not from the demands of a teacher's reading list which is forgotten or ignored when the teacher is no longer around.

The point is worth stressing. Many of the people who belong to book clubs do so because they have not learned to select books on their own. Many students, with a sense of shame at not knowing what to read, have asked me, "What do you recommend, Doc?" Every year, high schools turn out thousands of students who, having studied *Silas Marner* as sophomores and *David Copperfield* as juniors and having handed in their monthly book reports, stop reading on graduation day.

One recent high school graduate, coming to Penn State for a

summer course in reading improvement, confessed he had read only one major book in his lifetime — *A Tale of Two Cities*. He liked it but hadn't read any more because he was "too busy doing other things." How did he get by in class? He listened, took good notes, and parrotted back the teacher's own comments. Book reports? He made liberal use of digests of great (and therefore acceptable) books. "Of course, I always made a few mistakes so the teacher would be convinced it was my work." Another teen-age friend of mine had a tape recorder on which he recorded panel discussions of books which occurred on a weekly radio program. Abbreviating the panel discussions, he turned them into book reports and was consistently praised by his unwitting teacher. Neither of these students had crossed the threshold into "active" reading.

We cannot force a child — or an adult — to read. At best, we can help him with his skills and offer him an opportunity to explore, helping him here and there to find books which he can handle and which are personally satisfying because his own ideas and experiences connect with those of the writer. Moreover, the younger the reader the more important it is for him to have an opportunity to express the experience he has found in his reading. Through various projects — dramatic, artistic, written, oral — we can help develop readers who will do something with their reading: discuss ideas, form ideas of their own. Reading to answer questions is not enough. The reader must go on to examine and evaluate his own reactions.

The critical reader is one who reads actively and widely. It is he who will learn that history is more than a succession of dates and names, that social and political dangers must be understood before they can be combatted effectively, that the techniques of propaganda are recognizable, that if he is to maintain his personal values and the values of his culture in a complex and threatening age he will need sharpness of perception and the greatest range of knowledge he can absorb. He, more than most, is apt to become an alert, sensitive, and constructive citizen.

Until now, I have omitted one extremely important ingredient in the success of a reading program. If the objective of a reading program is to develop active and selective readers, critical and creative readers, readers who are sensitive to the values of language, readers who have mastered the basic skills and can apply them readily to all types of reading assignments, readers who find pleasure in reading and will continue to read throughout their lifetimes, then it should be apparent that reading instruction and programming cannot be left to the responsibility of the reading instructor alone. It is the responsibility of the entire school faculty.

For a time I was teaching reading and English at the Rhodes School in New York City and had an opportunity to work closely with all of the staff, including the guidance counselor. I sent reports to every teacher on the students with whom I was working, and we developed assignments and special-credit projects which students could do under my direction. The assignments were very elaborate and covered every subject in the curriculum.

Content-area teachers provided ideas and materials for the students to use. For French we chose to investigate the contributions of great French scientists, artists, writers, musicians, and statesmen and devised research projects which entailed digging up details and reading widely in the library. For algebra we selected pages of statement problems and went over them again and again to help the students understand the nature of such statements, which in turn improved their handling of the problems themselves. For biology we studied the lives of great biologists, read reports on antibiotics and the nature of cancer, posed research problems, and checked the latest magazines and scientific journals for recent information. In social studies we tried to analyze a current problem (such as integration in the South), economic and governmental problems in a foreign country, the history of unions, etc. The list of projects and activities was extensive. After I had checked each project, it was turned over to the subject teacher for comment and grading.

Knowing that I was trying to help students handle special content subjects more effectively, the entire faculty cooperated wholeheartedly and offered many valuable suggestions. Several teachers scheduled special-help classes to supplement work done in the regular period and in my class. The administration, in turn, provided additional compensation for those teachers who offered extra Saturday sessions to their students. Without such general interest and cooperation, the entire program would have been much less successful.

The attitudes of the students themselves changed drastically with such encouragement. They were enthusiastic over the opportunity to bring up their grades and get extra help. They could choose subjects which really interested them, explore these subjects deeply, and gain recognition for their efforts. They were frankly delighted to see so many teachers actively interested in helping them. For each of them, the meaning of the reading program came to life.

Students read as many as ten books every six weeks. Since they were free to select books from the classroom or school libraries, or to bring in books from outside, we naturally had a variety of mysteries and a few *Peyton Place*s and *Blackboard Jungle*s. I learned not to judge these books or their readers too hastily, realizing that I was being tested. We discussed the controversial works, and when it appeared that I was not shocked at the choices, my students began to regard me as a sincere and interested teacher and turned to other sources for their reading pleasure. They opened up to me with their problems and gave my suggestions serious consideration. They readily shared ideas during our frequent book talks; everyone wanted to discuss his book. As the year rolled on, we set up advanced reading programs as electives. And these were children who had once thought they were "stupid" and "illiterate." Not all of them were college material, but most of them would leave Rhodes better equipped to face their world and themselves.

For me, the experience at Rhodes helped to round out the conception of an effective reading program:

1. Reading instruction must aim at individual students, taking into account their different backgrounds, abilities, and interests.

2. Flexibility of instruction depends upon the availability of a wide range of reading materials of all kinds and on all sorts of subjects. In an effective program much of the initiative passes to the student and the teacher's role changes to that of a guide, a "listener," a resource person, a critic.

3. Reading instruction means paying attention not only to the basic skills of reading but also to the general end which education should serve; the widening of the student's intellectual, emotional, and moral horizons.

4. Reading instruction is completely successful only when the student has acquired the habit of active, continuous reading and can read with ease in all of the subject areas which, by necessity or choice, he faces.

5. The reading program is not the product of one teacher but demands the involvement of the entire faculty and administration in a whole-hearted and single-minded concentration on drawing the best possible work out of each student.

It is my firm conviction that the old, standardized classroom — with its standardized texts, standardized teachers, and standardized students — may provide for educational quantity; but it is the fresh teacher, with a philosophy of experimentation and a genuine love for the individual mind and person, who will, ultimately, provide for educational quality.

2. Why Many Children and Youth Are Retarded in Reading

Anne McKillop

"Retarded in reading" is a phrase that frightens parents and embarrasses youngsters. What does it mean and why is it being applied to so many youngsters and teenagers today?

"Retarded in reading" means different things to different people. To some it means that a child is still reading a primer when all the other children in his class are reading a first-grade reader. To some it means that he obtained a test score a year, or a year and a half, or two years below the national norms. To others it means that "he is not reading up to his ability." To still others it means that he is not reading as well as he needs to in order to meet the demands put upon him. If we consider retardation to mean the inability to read as well as one might under certain desirable conditions, or if we think of the ever increasing demands for reading faced by citizens today, most adults could be considered retarded in reading.

Because of this uncertainty about the meaning of retardation and because of the limitations of tests, it does not seem wise to set up an arbitrary criterion for retardation. Differences in abilities or in developmental patterns make the process of learning to read too subtle to set up neat categories; and tests, at best, are crude tools which must be used with imagination and caution. A rigid criterion of retardation is not necessary. It is relatively easy to pick out those youngsters who are severely handicapped in school by their inability to read, and whose lack of ability in reading is out of line with their other abilities. Why are they having so much trouble?

Instead of seeking an answer to this question in a listing of the various environmental and personal characteristics that have been found to be associated with difficulty in learning to read, the answer can be found in an analysis of the nature of the reading process. From this analysis one can deduce the reasons why some children learn to read easily while others struggle with the process. It should be remembered, too, that there is seldom only *one* cause; usually there are several working together.

Reading Is a Complex Perceptual Task

First of all, reading is a complex perceptual task. It involves the ability to make fine visual discriminations; to focus clearly on relatively small stimuli; to progress in a rigidly patterned sequence from left to right and from one line to the next; to take in large "eyefuls" at a glance; and, perhaps most difficult of all, to pick out certain words for emphasis, to know which ones to skip, which to note carefully. The complexity of the task was made vivid to me a few weeks ago when I participated with friends in a Seder, the Jewish passover ceremony. The *Haggadah* was in Hebrew; others at the table could read it; I could not. The symbols all looked alike to me. In my attempt to follow, I was constantly losing the place, starting on the wrong page and on the wrong side of the page. Later in the week I listened with sympathy to a six-year-old read from his reader.

Since reading is a complex perceptual task, youngsters will learn it most easily if by experience and endowment they are equipped to perceive verbal symbols accurately and quickly. Anything which might interfere with quick accurate perception of symbols may prove a handicap. Poor vision is an example. Within broad limits, the human eye is capable of amazing accommodations so that words may be seen clearly, but fatigue and distaste for the reading process may ensue.

Another interfering factor may be hearing loss which will certainly prove a handicap in learning to read by the usual methods. Most common, however, is lack of auditory discrimination. This lack of ability to hear the differences between sounds may have nothing to do with hearing loss, but may be related closely to the kind of English the child has heard at home and in his community. If, for example, he has grown up where a dialect is spoken, the language at school may sound almost as different as if it were a foreign tongue.

There are many things which we do not know about the perceptual abilities and skills involved in reading, especially in the beginning stages. We do know these abilities and skills are important.

Reading Is an Abstract Task

A second characteristic of the reading task is that it is abstract. It involves the capacity to make generalizations, to apply knowledge learned in one situation to another, to see relationships not only between word parts but also between ideas. It is reasonable to expect that the slow learner, the child who is not so bright as the others, will have difficulty learning to read. He is handicapped in several ways. He does not catch on as quickly as the others; he needs more repetitions; he probably has a more limited vocabulary; he may have poorer speech patterns.

Most teachers expect that the slow learner, the child with an IQ on an individually administered intelligence test of 75 or 80, will have difficulty with reading. They are less likely to recognize that other children may also have trouble with the abstract aspects of reading. Difficulty is especially likely to arise if the teaching method relies heavily on abstract generalizations, or if the child is already under one or more handicaps.

Reading Is Learned

Another characteristic of the reading process is that it is learned. No one was born able to read. Even those bright youngsters who seem to have taught themselves to read did a lot of practicing with letters, sounds, words and pictures before they could put it all together into reading. As with many other skills, much can be learned about reading without formal instruction; but also, as with many other skills, much of this learning may be inefficient and even detrimental to a highly skilled performance. Good teaching can be an important factor in the acquisition of a high degree of reading skill; and conversely, poor teaching can be a severe handicap.

Many youngsters have not learned to read because they have not been taught. A child may have missed a great deal of school, have changed schools many times, or had many different teachers in any one year. The class may have been too large; the program too poorly organized. In the upper grades many of the more subtle reading skills such as skimming, picking out main ideas, selecting the important points to remember, may never have been demonstrated, analyzed, or practiced.

A youngster may have been exposed to enough teaching, but he may have failed to learn. The method, the materials, or the teacher may have been unimaginative, rigid, and unsuited to this child. His experiences may have been so limited that he has an inadequate fund of meanings; he may not see the connection between reading in school and anything that goes on in real life; he may not even see the relationship between the different parts of a reading program. Instruction in phonics may have been something quite apart from his reading. He may have been preoccupied with his own affairs. He may have been bored or fearful in school.

Even under the most desirable conditions, learning requires effort and concentration. If a youngster sees no use for this skill, he may fail to learn. Reading seems very important to teachers, but to many youngsters it is a rather silly business. It may be that the people the child knows and loves do little reading and they get along quite well. Why should he learn? He may be unable to concentrate on reading because he is so busy concentrating on other matters of more concern to him.

One youngster said, "My eyes go on, but my mind goes away — to my past." An eight-year-old put it this way, "Some days I'm just in a bad mood and I can't do anything. I still have a nightmare in my system."

Reading Is an Interpersonal Experience

Reading is a complex perceptual task; it does require the ability to think abstractly; it must be learned; but there is more to it than this. Reading is an interpersonal experience. It involves a relationship between the reader and the author. It is essentially a form of communication. Communication may fail because the individual does not know the language or because he does not care to communicate. A child may not know the language of reading if he does not see it as important or if he does not understand the task. He may not want to communicate if he is fearful or angry.

He may be fearful if he is sure he is "no good," if he is convinced that he cannot do this difficult thing, cannot learn to read. One child expressed his reaction vividly when his teacher asked what he did when he came to a word he did not understand. "It feels bad inside," was his response. How can we expect him to remember to break a word into syllables, to sound out each part, or even to use a context clue when his energies are tied up in "feeling bad"? A child who feels he is not really competent will feel even less competent before such an important and difficult task as reading.

The child may also be fearful of making mistakes, a necessary part of learning to read. This involves "taking a chance," "giving it a try." The six-year-old must take a chance on a word — for example, is it "and" or "said"? The teenager must take a chance on the main idea of the paragraph. No child ever learned to read without taking these chances and without being wrong sometimes. And yet to some children "taking a chance" seems dangerous — you could be wrong and being wrong is bad, and being bad is dangerous because you might lose the affection and respect of those you love.

Being afraid to try may take other forms. Some children feel that success achieved without effort, without making any mistakes, is the only kind that counts in proving your worth. For them to try at all is almost equivalent to failure. Unless you get it "first shot," it is a failure. These children cannot really study; they either get it at once or they don't try, and they don't try because they are so afraid of being wrong. Related to this is the tendency to put forth the minimum effort — to study hardly at all and get a B. Then the student feels, "If I got a B with that little work, look what would happen if I worked!" But he never does because he might prove to himself and others what he fears — that he couldn't really do it.

The unrealistic goals of some children are part of the picture of fear as a barrier to communication. There is the child who will read only seventh-grade books, nothing else; he must learn all at once without effort. This desire for magic seems to reflect a deep fear of trying and failing. A child may have to learn to fail before he can succeed. He has to be able to try, to take a chance on a relationship with the printed word and thus on a relationship with a person. He can only risk this attempt at relationship when he has had satisfying relationships with real people.

Another aspect of taking a chance or trying involves curiosity and zest for exploring and learning. Reading is the key to finding out about the world. Of course, we assume that the child is curious, that he wants to find out, wants to explore this new and exciting world, wants to learn about toads, and rockets and knights of old. This desire to explore, this curiosity seems to be an essential condition for learning to read. A child starts out with eager curiosity, but sometimes he loses it. He may have asked too many questions until adults told him to keep quiet. He may have asked questions at inappropriate times, about the wrong subjects. He may have explored too enthusiastically and been constantly warned about getting hurt. Parents may have let him know their embarrassment over his questions; they may have been abrupt, or may have laughed or may have given him untrue answers. He has become resigned to the feeling that questions don't have answers. He may have learned to feel that it isn't safe to be curious and actively exploratory — you might get hurt, or people might get angry with you. He is afraid of his own curiosity because it seems to lead to trouble. In this way he is afraid to enter into the communication process, to ask questions of the authors.

The fear of being wrong is the other side of the individual's desire to be always right and perfect. Many children have not learned to differentiate between being partly wrong and being all wrong. An eight-year-old reads "massacred" for "murdered." We say he is wrong and do not give him credit for having kept the sense of the story and been almost right. He may feel that no one credits him with his attempts to use previous knowledge, that we aren't interested in how the story turns out. Often he gives up.

In addition to being afraid of mistakes, a child may be afraid of success. This sounds impossible, but success to a child may be something to be avoided and failure something to be sought. The child who feels "bad," "wicked" or "guilty," may feel that he does not deserve success, that failure is his just punishment, that he has no right to communicate with others. Sometimes failure in reading represents a form of self-punishment.

A youngster may not wish to enter into the interpersonal experience of reading if he is angry. He may be angry at grown-ups. He may see them as people to be outwitted. One nine-year-old memorized the location of all the type bars of the typewriter rather than learn touch typing. He was outwitting the teacher! Another eighth-grade youngster said about a hated teacher, "I don't like her; she don't like me. I ain't goin' to do no work at all." It is true — this a cut-off-your-nose-to-spite-your-face technique, but it is one that children often use. Thus, failure to learn to read becomes a child's secret weapon, one he is not fully aware of using but which he may use, nonetheless, with telling effect.

A youngster may be angry, too, because he feels smothered, feels that he has no life of his own, that others would take over his life if he would let them. This may, of course, be true. Parents may have made all the decisions for him and may have fed off him emotionally, taking his achievement as their own so that he may feel he has no say in his own life. However, he must retain some autonomy and he can do it in the area of reading. Here he is boss. Perhaps he can maintain this self-integrity only by not reading. He will willingly pay the high cost of adult and peer disapproval, of inability to find out about interesting things, rather than give up his own right to determine his life, rather than capitulate to the enemy.

It is possible for a child to be so angry that he is afraid of his own anger, the roots of which are to be found in his early experiences. He has to keep a tight hold on himself or else anger would come out in violent form. Reading involves being active, making an aggressive attack on the page and this may be too much for him. He cannot do this lest his aggression get out of bounds. He dare not communicate if he is too angry.

A child's reading is as truly an expression of all that he is as his way of walking or talking, as his interests or his friendships. Anything which influences him may influence his reading. His general health, for example, or his rate of basal metabolism; his inability to attend to the task at hand, or his identification with a non-reading hero. There is seldom only one reason why any child does not read easily. It is more often a series of difficulties with one serving as the straw that broke the camel's back. Many children, for example, miss a good deal of school, need glasses, don't hear very well, and yet learn to read easily; while comparatively short absences, or a slight visual or auditory handicap may disrupt the performance of others. It is not the objective situation that is important. It is what it means to the child.

Why Reading Causes So Much Trouble

One more question remains. Why reading? Why don't any of the other tool subjects cause so much trouble? No one knows the answer, but what we know about the reading process provides some clues. Reading is the most personal and least structured of the forms of communication which depend upon printed symbols. Spelling may involve more specifically perceptual abilities and skills; arithmetic is less personal. In none of the other tool subjects do one's feelings about people and about communicating with them enter in so clearly.

Then, reading often symbolizes growing up in our society. We say to children, "Wait until you get big enough to read for yourself." Visitors to the home of a seven-year-old often ask, "Can you read yet?" The youngster soon comes to see that this is an unusually important skill, one which takes a long step toward grown-upness. This is fine if the youngster wants to grow up, but if he doesn't, and there are a few who do not, he cannot afford to learn to read. Most children cannot verbalize their fears about growing up, but one little girl said, "I don't want to learn to read. I don't want to be a mommy. I want to be a little girl. Little girls can't read." The other tool subjects do not carry this symbolic meaning.

Reading, too, is considered an unusually important skill in our society. Some of this pre-eminence is based on reality. A person who cannot read finds many doors closed in his face. But the anxiety of parents and teachers goes beyond the realistic. It is as if reading symbolizes success to the child and his parents. If he learns to read easily, it appears that his success in school and life is assured, if he fails, then, as one mother put it, "He can't never be nothing but a no-good." The mother of a three-year-old called to ask for tutoring for her child. She said, "I want her to get a good start and not be one of those retarded readers." Anything upon which so much depends is bound to be fraught with difficulty.

Why are so many children and teenagers retarded in reading? For as many reasons as there are children.

3. Implications of Research for Teaching Reading in a Changing Society

Miriam Aronow

Throughout the years, more has been written and more research has been conducted about reading than about any other subject of interest to educators. In this regard, the last few years have been no exception. I have no intention of reviewing here all the research in reading, nor even the research of the recent past. *The Reading Teacher*, the *English Journal*, February issues of the *Journal of Educational Research*, and other periodicals and publications have devoted many pages to such summaries. What I shall try to do is to indicate some recent approaches in research that seem to have good potentialities for reading instruction, and to suggest what these potentialities might be.

Some Trends in Current Research

Three Trends in Reading Experimentation:

1. I note that more attention is being given to the reader himself. Research is being conducted, for example, to learn what a good reader is like, what he does when he reads, what skills he uses in critical reading.

2. Reading is now being treated more as a thinking process. In many investigations, and certainly in many of the articles being written on reading, the first premise is that reading is thinking.

3. I see flexible ways that are being employed to permit students to express their thinking in reading situations. There seems to be

less dependence in the basic research on multiple-choice items, as a way of getting evidence on thinking-in-reading. Individual interviews are being conducted in which thinking is recorded and later studied and analyzed. Open-end questions are being utilized. Introspective and retrospective reports are being gathered.

In classrooms, teachers are allowing students to differ in the forms and materials they use in expressing their ideas about what they read. Oral book reviews are taking place in which individuals share their reading experiences with other group members. Book-reporting is becoming less formalized. The term *book report* is losing its traditional connotation. It is coming to mean a simple record of books read, with students differing in the number and kind. The term *book review* is being used to designate not what a book report used to mean, but what a book review really means in adult terms — a piece of creative writing which the writer fashions to his own taste.

Significance of the Trends

The trends I have observed are important: the emphasis on the reader, the stress on reading as a thinking process, the drive to get at and facilitate the expression of children's actual thinking-in-reading. They are important for the future improvement both of basic research and of classroom practice.

But more important for the present discussion is this: a clear identification of the reader's role in reading can help to clarify the teacher's role in reading instruction. Actually, when the student reads, only he and the author are involved. Reading is a highly personal and intimate meeting with an author. Where does the teacher fit in? The teacher seems to stand outside, someplace between the student and the author. The teacher's role seems to be to promote and facilitate the meeting of student and author, to guide the student in such a meeting, to see that it is fruitful.

Some Suggestions for Developing Independent Thinking-in-Reading

A few suggestions are listed to show how instruction may be geared so that students will know how to handle printed matter efficiently.

Let students think in reading situations. Note that I said *let* them think, not *make* them. Give students a chance first.

Given a little more time and appropriate opportunities to direct their own reading, thinking, and learning, students can accomplish more than we generally think they can. This is exactly the practice they need for a society that will be changing at an ever increasing pace — opportunities to think, read, and learn by themselves.

Give students every opportunity possible to select their own reading materials so that, with guidance, they will develop the standards for the selection of materials for various purposes. Arrange opportunities for the free oral discussion of ideas found in printed matter so that students will be helped to acquire the functional standards they need for selecting and using authors' ideas and for judging when their own ideas are good enough to be expressed and fought for.

Students should be helped to learn different approaches to different types of materials, and different approaches to the same type of material, depending on the purpose. Arrange situations that will require students, on their own, to select the best approach. Give them practice in switching approaches.

Increased attention needs to be given to the questions employed in reading activities, for questions affect the reader-author relationship. A question represents the beginning of an idea. Teacher questions are, of course, essential. They help to check on thinking. They help to guide and stimulate thinking.

Some of these questions may, however, not be necessary to the student for his thinking-in-reading. They may even disturb the reader-author relationship. Every unneeded question is an opportunity lost for a student to start an idea on his own. From an overabundance of teachers' questions, students may get the impression that the main purpose in reading is to answer questions. A superfluity of questions — oral and written — may give the student the feeling that he should not start his own thinking with printed matter. Without adequate opportunity to organize his own thinking while reading, he may become dependent on others for determining what ideas he is to have while reading.

Finally, teachers should help students have the equipment they need for critical thinking, including critical thinking with printed matter. Children must have knowledge for critical thinking. They must have values, principles, and ideals. They need also standards of beauty, ethics and morality, and an understanding of logic and the nature of proof. Teachers can help students acquire this equipment.

But if critical thinking with printed matter is to be *self-initiated*, these things must be so dynamically acquired that, when touched on by an author, the standard or ideal itself serves to goad the student into action. Capitalize on children's natural needs, desires, and abilities to work out problems, to evaluate and to think, and critical reading will follow naturally.

4. Contributions of Reading to Personal Development

David H. Russell

In his autobiography, *Safe Conduct*, Boris Pasternak says that the biography of a poet is found in what happens to those who read him. What *does* happen to a reader?

We read at four levels. At the first level we are largely concerned with the association of printed words with their sounds. In some school situations children are drilled in word-calling — "barking at words" without much attention to meaning. At the second level we read for literal meanings. We get the facts or we follow explicit directions. Such reading may have many functional values for the child finding out about India or for the suburbanite engaged in a week-end do-it-yourself project.

The other two levels of reading are more complex. At the third level we interpret what we read. That is, we go beyond the literal comprehension of the fact or the main idea to read between the lines. We draw some conclusion of our own from the passage — we envisage or predict or infer. Sometimes we reflect on the author's point of view or the relation of the material to other things we know — we evaluate or analyze critically. But we also read at a fourth level or depth. Sometimes the passage takes us beyond thoughtful analysis or critical review to a more stirring experience. We feel "the shock of recognition." We recognize a new or an important idea in the actions, characters, or values described. The impact of the material is such that we receive fresh insight into our own or others' lives. In our reading we are changed, a little, as persons.

Most reading is done at the second, literal level, and most of the writing and research in the field of reading have had to do with the first two levels. We know a lot about word perception, the teaching of phonics, and ways of developing comprehension of the printed page. Such activities make many contributions to the individual. The young child enjoys his new-found skill of working out new words, and the world's work and its week-end hobbies involve the use of much factual reading matter contributing to knowledge and skill. Reading has always been one of the individual's most important resources for gaining knowledge. Granted a modicum of reading skill in the individual, books and libraries are storehouses of information for him. Thus, reading at the second level may have many influences on personal development, as in increasing skill in making model airplanes or in preparing a traveler in Spain to get the most out of direct experiences in a foreign country. The main branch of the Berkeley Public Library has approximately 375 books whose titles begin with the words "How to ———," starting with *How to Abandon Ship* and including *How to Live with Children.* Reading at the second level can be a big help to us!

At the third level, we are not so sure of our ground as we are when concerned with word recognition or literal comprehension. A feature of recent research, however, has been considerable work on critical and creative reading abilities. In a recent study at the University of California, for example, Clark [4] [1] developed twenty-three lessons in reading to predict beyond the given facts and tested some ways of teaching these in the classroom. He found that tests of reading to predict were relatively independent of vocabulary and comprehension. In going from literal comprehension to personal interpretation as in prediction a reader puts more of himself into his reading. He thinks beyond the line of print. The perceptual process is the stimulus to many kinds of thinking — to drawing analogies, to checking a writer's point of view, or to beginning an attack on a personal problem. As suggested below, more work needs to be done in exploring this process of thoughtful reaction to an author's ideas.

It is at the fourth level, however, that our knowledge is slight and our needs are great, and so it is with effects of reading on individuals that this discussion is chiefly concerned. Can Pasternak or other poets influence us deeply? Do we really have *Books That Changed the World*, as the optimistic title of one publication suggests? Can a book, story, or poem change one person, much less the world? Can reading have the effect Lincoln believed it could have when he first met Harriet Beecher Stowe? On that occasion he said, "Is this the little woman whose book made such a great war?" In a world of television, radio, comic books, parents, and teachers, can a book be an experience which changes the nature of reality for the young reader? In the words of Ciardi, can it make him "quietly passionate" about an idea or a cause? Or can a book help

[1] Figures in brackets refer to bibliographical items at the end of this article.

a person to the self-insight attributed to a man who, seeing his neighbor going by in a new pink Cadillac, said, "There, but for me, go I!" Can a book fill a boy with courage or help him find himself? Or is this too much to ask, even of great literature? Reading may be useful at all four levels, but somehow this fourth level seems the most tantalizing and important of all.

Some Possible Effects of Reading

The kind of reading that we do affects the contribution of the reading matter to our development. In the primary school grades so much of the effort goes into the first level — into the mechanics of reading, into getting the words right, toward following the sequence of the writer's thought — that the chance of added dividends is unlikely. Similarly, in the later grades, the poor reader, or the child deciphering material much too difficult for him, has little opportunity or stimulus to interpret a story or to find materials meaningful to his larger concerns or problems. Piekarz [11] has shown that when children are unable to read a passage with reasonable ease they have fewer reactions to it, with many more responses at the literal-meaning level than at the implied-meaning or evaluation level.

Accordingly, the time and effort given to the making of fluent, skillful readers at the elementary and secondary school levels may be worth while, not only in terms of specific aspects of reading skill but also because such reading is a basis for operation at the two higher levels of reading. Children need word-attack skills and ability to follow directions, not because they are merely going to read words or to follow directions blindly, but so that, having clearly recognized words or accurately interpreted directions, they can then go to the meanings behind the words and, if necessary, to questions about the validity of the directions.

Such an interpretation of reading is not a derogation of reading skills. Many children and adolescents work very hard to attain word recognition skills and the ability to grasp the literal meaning of a paragraph, passage, or chapter. Indeed, success in these matters may make a contribution to personal development beyond that of the facts read because of the "nothing succeeds like success" formula. The child who learns to read skillfully not only pleases his parents but contributes positively to his self-concept. The converse is even clearer. The child who has reading difficulties at the first two levels may have emotional and personality problems associated with his reading. The primary causation may not be so important as the *fact* that reading difficulties are affecting his total development adversely.

When poor readers have not achieved fluency in reading they must have help. For these pupils various types of remedial programs have been developed in schools.

For young children, one aid to fluency is to have their parents and teachers read stories to them, more complex stories than they can read for themselves. For their own first reading practice there seems no reason why children should not begin on easy, graded materials developed in light of many of the things we know about the psychology of learning. In the preschool and early primary years, children can be challenged and helped to reach higher levels of reading by the ideas in the stories read to them.

An example of such reading-listening situations affecting total development is given in a recent master's thesis by Webster [21]. She found in a group of eighty first-graders that thirty-five expressed fear of the dark and five indicated fear of dogs. Accordingly, in groups of seven children, she read to and discussed with the children five stories dealing positively with the dark and with dogs — stories such as Margaret Wise Brown's *A Child's Good Night Book* and Ruth Dixon's *Three Little Puppies.* Three months later, an impartial judge agreed with Webster's analysis of interviews: twenty-nine out of the thirty-five children had, it seemed, reduced their fear of the dark and all five of the children had lost most of their fear of dogs. Such a study needs verification with more careful controls, but it suggests that, for young children, the "read-to" situation may affect a child's emotional development.

As a child develops the ability to read for himself some books and stories of merit, the second level of reading flourishes. He finds out not only the secret of the lost treasure but something of the lives of early Americans or something about woolgrowing in Patagonia or in Queensland. The purpose of many books, newspapers, and magazines is to inform. We live in a difficult period of man's history, and the problems which beset us demand our best knowledge and efforts. Therefore, we read for main ideas, for facts, for following a sequence of events, for seeing relationships, and for arriving at conclusions.

Teachers of English at the secondary school and college level have not always considered such reading part of their domain. Of course they must also be concerned with the third and fourth reading levels of interpretation and with the impact of great literature. The value of the information contained in a book has little or nothing to do with its value as literature. One level is concerned with getting a fact right and clear, the other is concerned with some basic human expression or need. One makes for grasp of the immediate, the other, as Bernard Berenson remarked of great pictures, makes for the enhancement of life. Most of our school texts are written and should be used at the level of accurate comprehension. I believe the problem is not "either-or" and that the teacher of English must be concerned with both kinds of reading. Skill at the first two levels seems to be basic to achievement at the third and fourth levels. But it is in the realm of imaginative literature that we usually get to the third and fourth levels of reading. It is here that writing is intrepid in its approach to problems, ingenious in its solution of difficulties, in a way that the child or adolescent cannot achieve by himself. It is at these levels that reading can operate in depth and make its greatest contribution to individual development.

Fortunately, some research evidence is beginning to be accumulated about reading at the third level of interpretation of printed materials. May I quickly suggest a variety of findings. (*a*) Most children do not seem to respond to some of the commoner literary devices such as metaphor or personification before they are in their teens [23]. (*b*) Children's interpretations are influenced by their attitudes and expectancies toward what they are reading, by their previous "set" in the reading situation [5]. (*c*) When asked to respond to short stories, adolescents give interpretational reactions as a dominant type of response; other categories of response, in order of frequency, are narrational, associational, self-involvement, literary judgment, and prescriptive judgment [19]. (*d*) Responses to a piece of literature are largely an individual matter. Children and youth with different experiences, personalities, and needs see different things in the same character, story, or poem — and one interpretation may be just as "true" or "honest" as the other. Consequently, teachers of reading and literature should beware of looking for the one "correct" interpretation [14]. (*e*) With adolescents, literary judgments and emotional involvements vary inversely. In other words, children and adolescents tend to suspend objectivity when emotionally involved [19]. (*f*) The most common emotional involvements of adolescents in fiction seem to be "happiness binding" (the desire for a happy ending) and insistence upon certainty in interpretation [19]. These half-dozen statements can be extended in a consideration of the process of interpretation. Perhaps the samples are enough to show that we are beginning to accumulate some research evidence about some of the psychological factors which are involved in interpretation, whether of a good story in a third reader, a chapter or poem in a high school anthology, or an individual example of an author's work.

Unfortunately, the evidence about effects at the fourth level of reading is sparse. Perhaps it will always be shaky in the scientific sense and we shall always have to rely in part on individual testimony regarding the effects of books or literature. Down through the generations great and good men have testified to the influence of a book or books in their lives. The Greeks believed in the effect of literature on the growing boy, and Plato wrote in *The Republic*, ". . . we should do our utmost that the first stories that they hear should be so composed as to bring the fairest lessons of virtue to their ears." Much later, Stephen Vincent Benét wrote, "Books are not men and yet they are alive." Luther Burbank, the great horticulturist, testified that his whole life was changed by reading one book, *The Origin of the Species*. But the testimony of these and other men and women, interesting in itself, does not constitute evidence in the scientific sense. What about the individual's readiness for change? What about other supporting or conflicting influences in classroom, home, or community? Can a biography of sacrifice and social service influence a twelve-year-old girl for whose parents the good life consists of cocktail parties and Las Vegas week ends? If we as teachers are trying to influence the ideas and lives of young people through literature, we need to know much more about the role of the individual himself, the content of the materials, the total situation in which the reading takes place, and the overt reactions to be expected in speaking, writing, and action [14].

To some teachers such analysis of the four factors influencing the impact of reading on the individual makes the whole process needlessly complex. Not every teacher of reading in the fourth grade or of literature in the tenth grade can take time to know individual children and materials in such intimate fashion, nor can they easily arrange maximum environmental conditions for reading to affect individual development. Perhaps the problem is still one for research rather than classroom practice, and yet somehow the two must be combined. All elementary and secondary teachers of literature know that some pieces are more effective than others with a group but may not have tried to discover the reason. Why does one story "hit" a group of ten-year-olds or another, a group of fifteen-year-olds "just right"? What kind of matching of material and reader can a teacher accomplish? How can this be individualized at the secondary as well as the elementary school level? What are maximal conditions when "boy meets book"?

The evidence that reading affects lives is largely confined to the subjective, individual testimony illustrated above and to some reports of bibliotherapy in individual case studies [8, 15, 17, 24].

Studies by Russell [12], Smith [18], and Weingarten [22] have attempted to get at the effects of reading by requesting direct reports of them from teachers and from elementary and secondary school students. Such reports may all be too optimistic because of the desire of students to give congenial answers but they do suggest that the effects of reading may be widespread and sometimes profound. The present scattered findings can be substantiated or refuted by further research. Perhaps at the moment the teacher can only adopt the optimistic view that there are certain things that are true even if not experimentally verified. Perhaps such a faith is needed if one is to teach literature well. The possibilities are so vast that this article concludes with a few more examples of research explorations in unmapped territory.

Research on Interpretation

In addition to the investigation by Squire cited above and the studies supporting the six conclusions stated earlier, some careful investigations have been made of the interpretive process in reading. These date back at least to 1919, when Thorndike [20] published his classical study of ways children misinterpret paragraphs. One reason for flagrant errors in interpreting a factual passage he attributed to the overpotency of certain words. He said, "The mind is assailed as it were by every word in the paragraph. It must select, repress, soften, emphasize, correlate and organize, all under the influence of the right mental set or purpose or demand." This statement was explored further by Hinze [9] in a recent doctoral study at the University of California. She was interested in the cluster of associations the reader may have with certain words as explored by Jenkins, by Osgood and others. She first selected two passages, one factual (about scientific discoveries) and one emotionally charged (part of a Kafka story). Before the students saw these passages they were asked, in interview, to associate all the words they could with certain individual words from the two selections and to rate the words as positive or negative associations. Later, the students read each passage and interpreted its meaning. Hinze found clear evidence that when students had consistent emotional responses to the words in the passage, that is, all positive or all negative reactions, they tended to interpret the paragraphs objectively or "correctly," but when some of their emotional responses to the individual words were opposed to the dominant association, that is, when they had "conflict words," they had trouble giving a clear interpretation of the passage. Conflict words, in contrast to unidirectional words, caused significantly greater misinterpretation of the affective materials.

Some other investigations have given clues to the kinds of interpretation a teacher can expect. In a study [23] in England, the subject of the work was found to be most important for young children. Before they were twelve they made judgments about the ethical intention of the writer, and after twelve there emerged some feeling for "literary quality" as shown in structure and the aptness of simile or metaphor. In an American study, Harris [6] analyzed students' responses to literature into four types: translating; summarizing; inferring tone, mood, and intent; and relating technique and meaning. He devised tests of seven specific recognition skills but found on factor analysis of results that one general factor was adequate to account for the intercorrelations of the test results. This suggested that comprehension of literary materials may be a general function.

A study by Groff [5], however, emphasized the factors of individuality and attitude in interpreting paragraphs. He found that as a child reads critically, his interpretations are influenced by his attitude toward the content type of material read and his attitude toward reading as a school activity. In a factor analysis of scores on twenty-seven variables Bauer [2] found that achievement in reading was positively related to two variables, "self-expressiveness" and "drive for achievement," but negatively related to social adjustment and absence of excessive fears. Personality factors may influence reading behavior.

Another unpublished study of interpretation is that of Scribner [16], who found wide differences in the interpretation of poems by students, teachers of English, and literary critics. These differences are not great in the interpretation of relatively clear-cut poems such as Robert Frost's "The Road Not Taken." Even here, however, in a group of eighteen-year-olds, Scribner got such divergent interpretations of the main theme as

> The necessity of making decisions in life.
> The idea that one road may be better than the other.
> The idea that it is important to think for yourself and make your own decisions.
> He took the less travelled road.

These may seem varied responses from a group of eighteen-year-olds to a relatively simple poem, but Scribner found that variety in interpretation becomes much greater for the more "difficult" or ambiguous poem such as Blake's "Tiger," both in the student group itself and in terms of differences among students, teachers, and critics.

Why do students interpret a poem, story, or novel differently?

We have already suggested one group of causes in the student or reader — his reading ability, his background of experience, his attitude and expectancies, his needs perhaps. The second group of causes lies in the piece of literature itself. As Hinze found, an overlap in these two occurs in the reader's associations with the individual words. It also occurs in the pupil's sensory perception of a poem or other piece of imaginative writing — his response to images in seeing, hearing, feeling, or even smelling. The piece of literature itself may affect the reader's interpretation through the arrangement or pattern; for example, the rhyme scheme or the use of onomatopoeia.

Finally, there is the symbolization in the story or poem. At the elementary level the lion is the symbol of courage, a flag of nationality, and Loki of trouble and mischief among the gods. With older children, we begin to get values attached to symbols. Some things are true and good, as motherhood, and some wrong or unworthy, as cowardice. Studies of school reading texts by Anderson [1] and by Child [3], of children's biographies by McConnell [10], and of best-selling fiction by Harvey [7] are examples of analyses of content of reading materials which *may* influence a reader. Thus the reader himself and the content of the material, particularly the symbolic content, may influence interpretation.

This research report is sketchy, and necessarily so. Most of it consists of spot checks instead of long-term studies of the effects of reading. We need to know much more about both cross-sectional and longitudinal aspects of each of the four factors influencing interpretation and personal development through reading. Since the days of the *New England Primer* we have had the feeling that, somehow, reading can help create a virtuous life. Almost three hundred years after the *Primer* perhaps the goal is still a good one.

References

1. Anderson, Paul S. *McGuffey* vs. *the Moderns in Character Training*. Phi Delta Kappan, 38:53–58, November, 1956.
2. Bauer, Edith B. *The Interrelatedness of Personality and Achievement in Reading*. Doctoral dissertation, University of California, Berkeley, 1956.
3. Child, Irwin L., and others. *Children's Textbooks and Personality Development: An Exploration in the Social Psychology of Education.* Psychological Monographs, 60, No. 3, 1946, 54 p.
4. Clark, Charles M. *Teaching Sixth-Grade Students to Make Predictions from Reading Materials*. Doctoral dissertation, University of California, Berkeley, 1958.
5. Groff, Patrick J. *Children's Attitudes Toward Reading and Their Critical*

Reading Abilities in Four Content-Type Materials. Doctoral dissertation, University of California, Berkeley, 1955.

6. Harris, Chester W. *Measurement of Comprehension of Literature.* School Review, 56:280–89, 332–43, May, June, 1948.
7. Harvey, John. *The Content Characteristics of Best-Selling Novels.* Public Opinion Quarterly, 17:91–114, 1953.
8. Herminghaus, Earl G. *The Effect of Bibliotherapy on the Attitudes and Personal and Social Adjustment of a Group of Elementary School Children.* Doctoral dissertation, Washington University, 1954.
9. Hinze, Helen A. *The Individual's Word Associations and His Interpretation of Prose Paragraphs.* Doctoral dissertation, University of California, Berkeley, 1959.
10. McConnell, Gaither A. *An Analysis of Biographical Literature for Children.* Doctoral dissertation, University of California, Berkeley, 1952.
11. Piekarz, Josephine A. *Getting Meaning from Reading.* Elementary School Journal, 56:303–9, March, 1956.
12. Russell, David H. *Teachers' Memories and Opinions of Children's Literature.* Elementary English, 26:475–82, December, 1949.
13. Russell, David H. *Personal Values in Reading.* The Reading Teacher, 12:3–9, October, 1958.
14. Russell, David H. *Some Research on the Impact of Reading.* English Journal, 47:398–413, October, 1958.
15. Russell, David H., and Shrodes, Caroline. *Contributions of Research in Bibliotherapy to the Language Arts Program.* School Review, 58:335–42, 411–20, September, October, 1950.
16. Scribner, Marion. *Responses of Students, Teachers and Critics to Selected Poems.* In manuscript, University of California, Berkeley.
17. Shrodes, Caroline. *Bibliotherapy: A Theoretical and Clinical-Experimental Study.* Doctoral dissertation, University of California, Berkeley, 1949.
18. Smith, Nila B. *Some Effects of Reading on Children.* Elementary English, 25:271–78, May, 1948.
19. Squire, James R. *The Responses of Adolescents to Literature Involving Selected Experiences in Personal Development.* Doctoral dissertation, University of California, Berkeley, 1956.
20. Thorndike, Edward L. *Reading as Reasoning: A Study of Mistakes in Paragraph Reading.* Journal of Educational Psychology, 8:323–32, June, 1917.
21. Webster, W. Jane. *Some Effects of Stories on the Reduction of Fears of First Grade Children.* M. A. Seminar Study, University of California, Berkeley, 1960.
22. Weingarten, Samuel. *Developmental Values in Voluntary Reading.* School Review, 62:222–30, April, 1954.
23. Williams, E. D., Winter, L., and Woods, J. K. *Tests of Literary Appreciation.* British Journal of Educational Psychology, 8:265–84, November, 1938.
24. Witty, Paul A. *Promoting Growth and Development Through Reading.* Elementary English, 27:493–500, December, 1950.

PART TWO

Groundwork for a Reading Program

5. Enlisting Faculty-Wide Co-operation for Improvement of Reading Skills in Senior High School

Marshall Covert

As we well know, poor readers in the high school present a vexing problem. Helping them all read better calls for a greater effort than a single reading teacher can produce. He must have the active assistance of the subject teachers as well. What are some ways in which the reading teacher can awaken the subject teachers' interest in helping with the problem, and acquaint them with what they can do to help?

The remarks here focus upon the poor reader; however, by extension, they can be applied to a general reading improvement program reaching every student.[1]

[1] With respect to the school that does not maintain a reading program, an excellent example of how a comprehensive program might be implanted is discussed by W. E. Compbell, "Reading Can Be Improved," *The Bulletin of the National Association of Secondary-School Principals*, XL (November, 1956), 42–48.

Communicating with the Teachers

Without a certain degree of publicity, it is conceivable that some teachers would not be informed of the reading program within their own school. A good beginning in stimulating their interest in helping the poor readers is to acquaint the teachers with the organization of the existing reading program, its scope, and the limitations imposed by its isolation from the general curriculum.

In a tactful manner, the teachers should be reminded that the purpose of education is to create independent learners; as good reading achievement is the primary tool of learning, fostering good reading habits in his students is an intrinsic part of a teacher's function. They should be made aware — those who are not — that as a student progresses in school, his reading tasks necessarily become more difficult; while increasing maturity brings new awareness and insight, these may lie fallow because of reading disability.

Determining Interest

After these early overtures, the next step is to determine the degree of faculty interest and enthusiasm for the reading teacher's ideas. This can be discovered through the use of an appropriate questionnaire: What are the teachers doing about the teaching of reading within their classrooms? Are they acquainted with the reading test scores of their students? Would they like to learn more about the techniques and materials used by the reading teacher?

The typical high school teacher is alert to ideas which might improve his teaching, and he is well aware of the importance of good reading skills to success in his course. If he is approached properly, the typical teacher will gladly co-operate in the general effort to help solve the problem presented by the poor readers.

In-Service Training

There are various ways of further stimulating activity among the teachers to learn what they might do. Establishing a reading committee is an excellent beginning. Composed, say, of one teacher from each academic department, the committee's function would be to plan a means of informing the subject teachers of procedures they could adopt for helping the poor readers in their classes. This planning might result in an in-service program or seminar, which could be held the last period of each school day during released time (providing incentive for teacher attendance).

Inviting interested elementary school teachers to the seminar would provide some continuity in the development of reading skills. These teachers, moreover, could contribute to the success of the in-service training by discussing their experience with grouping students for optimal teaching, and by outlining or demonstrating the methods they have found successful in working with poor readers.

Primarily, the training program — workshop, seminar, teacher conferences — should be designed to equip the subject teachers with practical suggestions. The reading teacher must be able to conduct the meetings so as to give the teachers an understanding of reading problems, to show them the materials they can use to help bring improvement of reading, to give the teachers confidence in using reading techniques, and to indicate that they will not sacrifice any part of their teaching time by giving attention to the reading problems of their students.

Areas of Emphasis

Early in the training it would be wise to discuss the reasons for the low motivation of poor readers. Somewhere along the educational line, these students were neglected and consequently failed to succeed in learning to read well. One of the important things that the subject teacher can do is to obtain the reading test scores of his students; the reading teacher can show him how to interpret the data and to diagnose reading disabilities. This leads to a better understanding of the poor readers and will help the subject teacher know how to section his classes for better teaching.

Often poor reading achievement is correlated with poor understanding of the broad concepts of a subject. Limited experience of students does not yield the proper background for good intellectual development. Somehow the teachers must try to supply this background. Audio-visual aids, demonstrations, informal discussions, field trips, supplementary assignments of easy materials, and project planning are some of the means for giving poor readers better insight into the specific subject matter to be learned.[2]

Next, and in order to nurture an improved attitude in the poor reader, the teachers should learn about the materials they can use. The reading teacher can give them information about workbooks, free and inexpensive materials, adapted stories, and other published materials for use with the poor or reluctant reader. Materials

[2] For a discussion of the importance of teaching concepts and for a review of the topic discussed here, see "Improvement of Reading in Colleges and Secondary Schools," *The North Central Association Quarterly*, XXXI (October, 1956), 199–208; prepared by the Subcommittee on the Improvement of Reading, of the Commission on Research and Service.

could be borrowed from the reading room and an exchange system set up between classes of the same department. A section of the school library could be reserved, containing high-interest, low-level reading matter; and a small library could be established in the classroom, containing simple reference works and supplementary readings of interesting sidelights of the teacher's subject.

A variety of workbooks and adapted materials could be demonstrated to the subject teachers to give them an idea of the things they could use in their teaching. Filmstrips illustrating study habits, dictionary skills, word attack, structural analysis of words and other aspects of basic reading skills should be examined. The teachers should learn how to adapt materials from various sources for specific uses in their teaching.

Then, to give the teachers confidence in using new techniques and materials, they should be informed that there is no cloak of mystery surrounding the teaching of reading. It takes no special lore to make students word conscious, to require that they learn the new words they encounter in their assignments, to insist upon good use of the dictionary, to show them good library usage, to outline basic study habits, to make supplementary reading assignments in fiction, to supply the right book for the reluctant reader, to encourage wide and abundant reading. With experience the subject teacher will gain confidence in his ability to do a worthwhile job of teaching reading.

Finally, to indicate to the teachers that they can find time for teaching reading skills, they might be reminded that they fail to teach well if they fail to help their students become better readers of their subject matter. For example, the typical poor reader tends to procrastinate in doing his home assignments; he approaches his work in a desultory fashion; he repeats his reading several times (this is the only way he feels he can understand it); and he comes to class with his work ill-prepared and only vaguely understood.

How much better if the teacher had spent a little time in teaching some basic things about study habits: that the students should always study at the same time and in the same place; that they should establish a purpose for their reading; that the assignment should be skimmed over quickly before intensive reading (for pre-comprehension and in order to be able to relate the small unit to the large); that they should ask questions as they read and record the answers to these questions in their own words; and that they should review their notes periodically in preparation for their examinations. If the students could be taught to practice these habits, they would be much better prepared and classroom work would proceed much faster.

Conclusion

Improvement of reading skills in the high school requires a concerted effort on the part of the subject teachers within their classrooms using appropriate techniques and materials. The effort will bring improvement. The logical person to provide the leadership is the reading teacher.

But the subject teacher generally can do a better job of teaching reading than the reading teacher. Reading instruction within the regular classroom is more meaningful to a student than the same instruction in the reading room; in the classroom what he is taught has an immediate reference to his school work. And much of the work of the teachers could be incorporated into their regular teaching without sacrifice of subject-matter teaching. Far from weakening their standards, they will find, ultimately, that they have raised them. And the co-operating teachers will have the satisfaction of realizing that they are doing a better job of teaching their subject.

6. Improving the Quality of Reading Instruction Throughout a School System

Earle W. Wiltse

As society becomes more complex, the problems of school administration increase in geometric ratio. The modern school administrator must discharge a series of responsibilities that is exceedingly broad and all-inclusive. Some of these responsibilities are urgent and spectacular. Because of their nature, they usually get first consideration by the superintendent of schools while equally important but less glamorous responsibilities are postponed. The bulging school population and the presence of obsolete school buildings are examples of the spectacular. Before there can be reading instruction, there must be housing. School buildings require bond issues. There never is enough money to provide the facilities that are needed. It is necessary to devote a large amount of time to the study of ways to provide comfortable learning spaces adequately heated, properly lighted, and equipped with modern furniture. This must be done with too few inflated dollars, and even these dollars are hard to come by. All this must be done with an eye to the future so flexibility is emphasized. The school housing shortage will continue to be a pressing problem for at least a decade of the foreseeable future.

Coupled with the school building shortage, there is a pronounced lack of well-qualified teachers. It seems that the number of qualified teachers coming from our colleges is on the wane. This acute problem promises to take an undue portion of the school administrator's time for the next ten or fifteen years — again reducing the attention which he can give to problems of classroom instruction. This critical situation has made it necessary to study such problems as better salaries for teachers, improving conditions under which teachers work, orienting new teachers and keeping the good teachers we already have.

But these are not the only problems that require the attention of the busy school administrator. He must keep abreast of the times. This requires more meetings and more time for travel, study and reflective thinking.

As these and many other administrative problems compete for the attention of the conscientious school administrator, some of his less newsworthy but equally important duties are likely to be neglected. Improvement of the quality of reading instruction throughout the school system is one example.

Suggestions for Reading Improvement

Administrators and supervisors who are anxious to improve the quality of reading instruction usually follow certain guiding principles. The list suggested in this paper is not all-inclusive. The principles are implemented one way in one school system and in an entirely different way in another. Controlling factors include size of community, number of personnel, availability of specialists, administrative organization and the amount of time building principals have for this type of work. In the time allotted for this discussion, I want to suggest four basic principles which may be helpful in improving the quality of reading instruction in our schools.

1. *The reading program in the modern school should facilitate continuous growth from the kindergarten through the twelfth grade.* Reading instruction begins with the readiness program in the kindergarten. While

children are not actually taught to read in the kindergarten, the program at this level is designed to develop the kindergarten child socially, mentally, emotionally and physically so that when he enters the first grade he will be mature enough to start the actual reading process. The administrator understands the importance of rhythm and the relation of music to reading readiness. He makes it administratively possible for kindergarten children to have many real experiences. He is careful that children have a sound basis of instruction in beginning reading. This requires teachers trained in the techniques of accurate word recognition and vocabulary development. Children also need to get meaning from the printed page. To become independent readers, children require basic instruction that involves phonics. Since the English language is not a phonetic language, the good reader should be acquainted with a variety of ways of recognizing and analyzing words.

He knows that reading instruction does not stop in the third grade — or the sixth — or the ninth. Reading is a gradual process of growth. Therefore, the school administrator must be alert to the need of reading improvement at all levels, including the junior and senior high schools. The program should be designed so as to stretch the ability of the best readers as well as to remedy the defects of the poorest. While remedial classes may be necessary for the children whose abilities are found to be so low as to require special attention, the reading program should also challenge reading ability of students in all areas and at all levels.

This implies that there are certain abilities that can best be developed in the subject-matter areas where they are needed. The science and mathematics teachers, for example, should know what they are and should plan their reading so as to develop these abilities in their science classes. Other reading skills can best be developed in social studies, still others in shop. Teachers at all levels should be concerned about the speed with which their children read and with the degree of comprehension that is developed. Pupils in a school having an effective reading program will be able to "shift gears" during the reading process. There are certain types of material that require slow, meticulous, painstaking reading; whereas at other times the individual must emphasize speed.

2. *There should be a systematic program for professional stimulation, study and teacher growth.* The problem of maintaining a sensitized staff, alert to the need for reading improvement at all levels, is a challenging one. Children make the greatest reading progress in school systems where the teaching staff is working together as a unit with clearly established goals.

Alert teachers are interested in the recommendations of the authorities in the field of reading. Therefore, they want an adequate professional library. This library should contain books of such authors as Betts, Bond, Gates, Gray, McKee, Witty, and Monroe. But books are not enough. Principals and supervisors will find it necessary to motivate teachers to study the materials that are available. In one school, a reading committee in each staff is responsible for two building meeting programs during the year. Recent magazine articles and books on reading improvement are presented and discussed at these meetings.

Teachers in another school study the tabulated results of standardized tests under the guidance of the Director of Research. After the results are thoroughly understood, they are used by the teachers in planning reading programs for each elementary-school child.

In another community, 27 secondary-school teachers recently attended reading workshops in institutions of higher learning in widely scattered geographic areas where they took courses in modern techniques of reading instruction. Needless to say, these individuals brought back with them the benefit of stimulation of their summer study. These people served as leaders in the reading improvement program throughout the entire school year. The Board of Education paid part of the summer-school expense of the teachers.

Pre-school and post-school workshops on reading improvement are growing in number. These workshops are especially helpful to secondary-school teachers. In the first place, many secondary-school teachers do not know how to adjust their teaching to the needs of poor readers in high school. Many are just as helpless in challenging the brilliant students. Elementary teachers in one pre-opening workshop explained to the secondary teachers how reading is taught. In turn, the secondary teachers told the elementary people about the reading deficiencies of high school pupils. After the exchange of ideas, a feeling of mutual respect existed which was not apparent before.

Reading improvement is getting increasing attention from national, regional, and local co-operative study councils. An example is the Associated Public School Systems. This organization includes 200 schools, widely scattered throughout the United States. Through national and regional meetings, administrators and teams of supervisors and teachers meet to exchange information on effective practices and to discuss mutual problems. Reading is one of the topics often listed for discussion at the conferences. Through the pages of *Know-How Magazine*,[1] teachers of member

[1] *Know-How Magazine* is published quarterly by the Associated Public School Systems, 525 West 120th Street, New York City.

schools assist each other by exchanging their best practices. Thus, the best practice of each school may become the common possession of all schools.

In September, 1954, the Nebraska Co-operative School Study Council, consisting of 71 member schools, decided to embark upon a two-year program of reading improvement at the secondary level. The first year of endeavor was limited to two areas of improvement — speed and comprehension. Member schools administered a machine-scored, standardized reading test in all sophomore classes in October. During the year, the Council scheduled conferences on reading improvement. Classroom teachers attended the sessions. At one such conference, teachers saw demonstrations of a wide variety of visual aids, including reading materials, the Iowa and Harvard films, the tachistoscope, and other mechanical devices for improving reading speed. Some schools purchased this equipment for use mainly as a motivating device.

At Grand Island Senior High School last year, the vice-principal met with all of the teachers early in the school year for the purpose of discussing reading problems and deciding how best to improve reading speed and comprehension among high school students.

After two staff meetings, during which the teachers analyzed the results of standardized reading tests and identified reading improvement practices that are already being stressed, the staff was organized into "buzz" sessions by subject-matter areas. This was done to determine how best to devote five minutes daily to reading improvement in regular classes. The "buzz" sessions resulted in the accumulation of a series of reading-improvement techniques that might be used throughout the year. In the first place, all teachers agreed that vocabulary development is extremely important. Plans were made for vocabulary improvement in each subject-matter area. However, special stress was also placed upon this matter in mathematics classes and in shops. Social-studies teachers decided to emphasize outlining, using the method of outlining which had been presented to students in regular English classes. English teachers agreed to work five minutes a day in each class on techniques for improving reading mechanics, such as increasing eye span and reducing regressive movements. Science teachers decided to stress the importance of careful, slow, and meticulous reading which is necessary in learning to follow directions. Latin and Spanish teachers agreed to stress root words in English which are derived from foreign languages.

3. *A well-rounded school improvement program requires the provision of an abundance of reading materials.* No longer are children taught to

read out of just one book. The modern reading improvement program requires the provision of a wide variety of reading materials. This material should be of such variety that part of it can be read by the poorest reader in a given group. It should appeal to the interests of boys as well as girls. There should be well-illustrated books on science, athletics, history, geography, and literature. In the interest of economy, reading materials should be catalogued and should be managed so that children will receive the maximum benefit out of the minimum number of dollars appropriated for the purchase of reading materials.

One Nebraska administrator recently told me, "I may not know too much about how a first-grade teacher should be teaching reading, but there is one thing I can do. As an administrator, I can furnish teachers and children with a wealth of reading matter." In many schools, the greatest single thing the administrator could do to improve reading is to increase the textbook and library budget. Children cannot be expected to learn to read in schools where the budget for reading materials has been curtailed to the vanishing point.

Well-organized libraries are basic to an adequate reading program. This calls for teachers and librarians trained in library science. Much remains to be done by people with vision if libraries in our schools are to become the true reading centers that they should be.

4. *School administration should attempt to speed up the acceptance and use of the findings of research in reading.* It has been said that a period of 50 years is required to secure wide acceptance of new ideas in education. This is too long a waiting period. It does not happen in any field outside of education. If fifty years were required to secure general use of penicillin in the treatment of disease, some of us in this room would not be alive today. School administrators are faced with the responsibility of speeding up the spread of best practices so that the good work of our best teachers becomes the common possession of all our teachers.

Many school systems throughout the United States have tried to speed up the use of best practices within local school systems by making it easy for teachers to exchange them. In Grand Island, Nebraska, one vehicle that is used for the exchange of best practices is a four-page lithographed bulletin entitled *Gee I Know-How.* This bulletin is printed four times a year, at a cost of 15½¢ per copy for 400 copies, by an editorial board composed of classroom teachers. One representative in each school collects best practices from that school building and submits them to the editorial board. A committee of three teachers is released one-half day every other month to select and edit practices for publication.

Periodically, the entire issue of *Gee I Know-How* is devoted to reading. The last such issue is Volume V, Number IV, published in May of last year. An attempt is made to select contributions from all levels from kindergarten through senior high school. The contributions are brief and tersely written.

This little device is a simple, inexpensive technique which may be used by any school for improving the teaching techniques of teachers in service. The cost is negligible in comparison with the value received.

A committee of our teachers has just finished preparation of a fifty-frame colored filmstrip entitled *The Teaching of Beginning Reading*. A script accompanies the film which explains to lower-grade teachers how our best teachers go about teaching reading in the first grade. Materials, teachers, classrooms and children in the film are all local. We also expect to show the film to Parent-Teacher Associations and service clubs to explain beginning reading to parents and taxpayers.

Another method of exchanging best practices is to encourage reading teachers to visit classrooms of other reading teachers within the building or within the system. Much good can result also from inter-system visitation. With proper pre-planning and follow-up, this type of in-service improvement demonstrates better reading methods for teachers who are seeking them.

Summary

Reading improvement requires administrative leadership which recognizes the importance of reading growth as a continuous process, beginning in the kindergarten and continuing through the secondary school and into college. Democratic leadership will involve the entire staff of teachers in a vigorous program attack upon the reading problems at all levels and in all areas. Educational leaders must find new ways of speeding up the spread of best reading practices and of keeping the public informed. Greatest progress in reading takes place in those communities where pupils, teachers and the administrative staff work together on a program that is highly motivated and well understood by all.

7. How Can We Secure Parent Co-operation?

Nancy Larrick

Ten years ago when television was in its infancy, there were many who predicted that reading would be crowded out by the new medium. "Television will keep the children glued to the screen," they said. "Youngsters will never read. Libraries might as well close up, and publishers might as well go out of business." These prophets of gloom were so logical in their reasoning that many thought of the television set as the big bad monster that might devour the first of the Three R's and remove it from our culture altogether.

Actually, what has happened? The sale of children's books has more than doubled in the past five years. Public librarians report increased use of children's books, and school libraries have more than quadrupled their purchase of books for young readers.

Does this mean that television has failed to influence its young audience to the degree that was predicted? Not at all. For librarians tell us over and over that children are asking for books which have been mentioned on television or they are coming with questions that have been only partially answered by television. When Disney produced Davy Crockett, the libraries and bookshops were swept bare of everything pertaining to the hero of the wild frontier. Booksellers and publishers find that mention of almost any book on television will increase sales to a remarkable degree. As one librarian put it, "If we could only know in advance about these programs, we could stock the books and be ready for would-be readers." From reports like this, it would seem that there has seldom been anything to equal television as a means of motivating and guiding children's reading.

Influence of the Home

It is in the home that youngsters are seeing television. Here they are being introduced to new worlds of music, drama, science and folk tale. Here they are talking over their favorite programs, comparing this week's production with last week's, and evaluating programs in the effort to influence the family choice of TV channels. The very fact that this kind of motivation is leading to a search for appropriate books and to further reading is evidence of the influence which the home is having on children's reading.

There seems to be little doubt that parental influence on children's reading is tremendous. It may be a constructive influence which encourages a time to read aloud and discuss stories and books. Or it may be a negative influence which makes reading seem unimportant or even undesirable. It may be a creative influence that encourages the child to look up information about the snakes that were shown on *Zoo Parade* or it may be a deadening influence that dampens the curiosity such a television program can generate.

Yet there is everything to indicate that parents are interested in their children's reading. They want them to learn to read and to read well. The popularity of the Flesch book and the syndicated articles from that book show that parents want to help. It also shows that many of them are sadly misinformed about present-day methods of teaching children to read.

What Parents Are Interested In

What are parents thinking about their children's reading? What do they want information about? What are they worried about? In an effort to find answers to such questions as these, I made a survey last year of parents of middle-grade children in one community. We listed the name and address of every eighth child in grades four, five, and six and then visited his parents in the home to try to determine their interests, apprehensions, and perhaps anxieties about their children's reading. To encourage complete frankness, we promised no names would be recorded.

What those parents had to say was extremely interesting and, I believe, significant for all of us who are concerned with children's reading.

After we had explained the purpose of the interview, we asked the parent to tell us just how well he thought his child was getting along in reading — "In your opinion is his progress in reading Excellent, Good, Fair, or Poor?" 63.6 per cent of the parents felt that their children were making excellent or good progress in their reading. Only 8.3 per cent felt their children were making poor progress.

Next we presented four big questions and asked parents to tell us which ones they were most concerned about, most interested in.

The four questions and the per cent of parents who indicated that question was of major interest were as follows:

1. How is reading taught in school today? 19.2%
2. How can parents help their children learn to read better? 20.8%
3. How can parents help their children learn to enjoy reading more? 35.2%
4. What books and magazines should parents recommend to their children? 24.8%

Thus, 40 per cent of the parents indicated their chief interest is in how reading is taught and how they themselves can help increase reading skills. Sixty per cent indicated they are more interested in increasing reading pleasures and in learning how to guide children in their choice of reading matter.

We went on to more specific queries under each of these four big questions, asking parents to tell us which of these sub-questions had troubled them. Under the first question "How is reading taught in school today?" almost half of the parents expressed concern over the following queries:

Why don't children learn their ABCs before they start to read?
Why is one child slower in learning to read than another?
Why do they promote a child from one grade to the next when he is behind in his reading?
Do they still teach reading by the sound of the letters? When?

At several points, we asked parents what further questions they had and what additional problems have given them concern. Many of them volunteered further comments or questions. Among these a number voiced concern over what they called "the old system" and "the new system" of teaching reading. At a conference held with the interviewers immediately after the survey was completed, the interviewers were eager to tell more about parents' concern over what they felt to be the failure to teach phonics (variously referred to as syllable-division, the ABC method, and sounding) as a part of reading. According to interviewers, these parents seemed to feel that there are two mutually exclusive ways of teaching reading: (1) By sight which was invariably called the "new" or "progressive" method and (2) by sounding the letters and syllables (phonics) which they call the "old" method. Interviewers agreed that a large proportion of the parents felt the "old" method is preferable to the "new" and is sadly neglected today. They reported no comment that would indicate parents understood the two "systems" might be used simultaneously, one supplementing the other.

When we got to those questions which 60 per cent of the parents had said were of greatest interest to them — "How can I help my child enjoy his reading?" and "What books and magazines should I recommend?" — we found parents were full of comments and queries. Almost every parent said he felt the surest way to increase a child's reading enjoyment is to help him find books that interest him. Next is to encourage him to talk about the things he reads. Reading aloud in the family is a practice endorsed by over half of these parents, although many admitted they seldom got around to it in their own homes.

When it came to the last question — "What books and magazines should I recommend to my child?" — parents showed a tragic need and eagerness for guidance. Many frankly admitted they never recommended any books to their children. About half of those replying to this question said they recommended only those books they had read as children. Less than a fourth of the parents recalled reading any review of children's books or seeing lists of recommended children's books.

By strange coincidence another survey was being made at about the time this study was underway. I am referring to the study of children's reading interests made under the direction of Shores and Rudman at the University of Illinois for Spencer Press, an affiliate of Sears, Roebuck.[1] In this survey, questionnaires were completed by over 6,000 children, parents, teachers and librarians. One interesting point revealed by this study is that children more readily accept the book recommendations of parents than those of teachers or librarians. Yet the parents we interviewed seemed to be groping for help in naming book recommendations. Apparently the ones whose voices carry the greatest weight hardly know what words to utter!

In our survey, interviewers expressed great concern over the oft-repeated comment of parents to the effect that "teachers have told us to keep hands off and leave reading to them." All interviewers reported that again and again parents showed they were "afraid" to go to the school with their questions, were "afraid to help their child with reading."

Efforts to Tell Parents About the Reading Program

Despite these reports, we know that many school systems have made a concerted effort to tell parents about the reading program. In Indianapolis a series of television programs was directed to the

[1] J. Harlan Shores and Herbert C. Rudman. "Reading Interests and Informational Needs of Children in Grades Four to Eight." Mimeographed Report, 1954.

parents to explain how reading is taught in school today and why. The Minneapolis Board of Education has issued a series of pamphlets which are sent home to the parents of youngsters at various grade levels. In Richland, Washington, a questionnaire was sent into the home of every elementary-school child to try to find out what questions parents would like to ask about the reading program. Then a pamphlet was prepared to answer those questions and was sent to each home.

In countless communities, classroom teachers have acquainted parents with information about the reading program and have enlisted parent co-operation. Individual conferences at school or in the home have been very effective for talking over specific questions. Group discussion has been valuable in explaining the way reading is taught, what materials are being used, and how parents can aid and abet the teacher.

What We Want Parents to Understand About the Teaching of Reading

What do we want to have parents understand about the teaching of reading? It seems to me that one of the first points we want to get across is that *reading is understanding*. And to understand, the reader must bring ideas to the printed page. Therefore every kind of activity that broadens the child's experience can contribute to his interest in reading and his skills in reading. A visit to a hatchery and inspection of an incubator tray will give a child new ideas to talk about and later to read and write about. His acquaintance with the sound and meaning of new words learned at the hatchery will help him with his reading.

Equally broadening experiences are often gained through television. Disneyland takes its 12 million viewers to the Living Desert, for example. Interests are aroused. New words and new concepts are developed. Curiosity is stirred. Here is ideal motivation for reading, motivation which the parent can help to capitalize on if he has learned the relation of such experiences to reading.

In many situations, the school is giving children firsthand experiences that relate to their reading. But the connection with reading is sometimes missed by parents unless teachers have explained how these experiences give meaning and interest to reading.

The second big point that I believe we must get over to parents is the idea that a child must *want* to read — no one can make him unless he is willing. If he is interested in a subject, he will often push himself a little harder to read about that subject. One important part of the reading program, then, is to develop children's interests. If his current interest springs from a television program being watched at home in the evening or over the week end, the parent can encourage that interest through conversation and discussion and through help in locating reading matter related to the topic of interest.

Third, I would like to help parents understand that children grow and develop at different rates. It is only normal and healthy that they should begin to read at different times and that they should progress at different rates. Pressure from adults will not speed up some children's reading any more than it speeded up their walking or talking.

Fourth, reading goes on all the time, not just during the so-called reading lesson. Street and traffic signs, supermarket shelves, pantry labels, and television commercials give constant practice in reading and some incentive to read. Yet these reading experiences are usually outside of school when the parent is more apt to be on the spot than the classroom teacher. The parent can give valuable help if he knows how to utilize these reading materials effectively.

How Can the Teacher Make the Most of the Parents' Help?

In addition to cementing warm, friendly relations with the parent, the teacher can take certain specific steps which will bring the home into effective participation in the reading program.

One important way is to encourage reading aloud in the home. Before a child can read, he will enjoy having some grown-up read to him and then talking over the story and the pictures. After he is able to read independently, he will enjoy the opportunity to share his reading with others. From experiences such as these, he will not only gain practice in reading, but he will develop the feeling that reading is an adventure that brings delight to all ages.

If the child is encouraged to take home stories and books, parents will see the kind of things he is reading at school and will thus become acquainted with samples of the very beautiful and appealing literature available for children.

As a further means of showing parents what books are available, it is often effective to set up a book exhibit at the school or in the neighborhood library. If children have time to explore such an exhibit in advance, they are usually good guides for their parents, showing them the books which they have read, those which they want to read, and those which they would like to own.

In one elementary school in a small town in Virginia, each teacher has encouraged her youngsters to prepare a short list of favorite books at intervals throughout the past school year. The lists are compiled in each classroom, then duplicated by the children to take home as reminders for themselves and their parents. Many parents have expressed appreciation for these lists, and the increase in children's reading has been outstanding.

Probably the most important job of all is to encourage parents to come to school with queries and comments about their children's reading. A mother's report of what her Henry is reading at home, or what he has to say about reading, may help the teacher in her work at school. And the teacher may smooth out an anxiety that could have grown into a harmful pressure on Henry at home.

But whatever the question brought up by the parent, the teacher has a definite responsibility, I believe, to answer with complete honesty and sincerity. Certainly, it will be neither politic nor profitable for the child if the teacher gives a "hands-off" treatment to the parent who wants to know and wants to help.

In Conclusion

To be truly effective, the reading program must go far beyond the classroom. How children read and what they read will be affected by their life and their interests outside of school. All the time, parents and the home environment are influencing children's attitudes toward reading and their skill in reading. It may be a positive, constructive influence. Or it may be a negative influence that pressures the slow reader and pokes fun at the steady reader. Whether the parents' influence is a positive one or not will depend in part on the extent to which we have enlisted their co-operation in the total reading program.

8. Reading Inventories for Classroom Use

Marjorie Seddon Johnson

Good teaching is dependent on understanding of those to be taught. Planning for reading instruction is, therefore, impossible without thorough investigation of each pupil's present level of achievement, his capacity for achievement, and his specific strengths and weaknesses. The classroom teacher must make an evaluation, in all of these areas, of each pupil in his group. He can accomplish this task most efficiently through the use of informal inventories.

Nature of Informal Inventories

Standardized tests rate an individual's performance as compared to the performance of others. By contrast, an informal inventory appraises the individual's level of competence on a particular job without reference to what others do. It is designed to determine how well *he* can do the job. Materials of known difficulty are used to find out if he can or cannot read them adequately. Inventories can be administered on an individual or a group basis. For general classroom use the group inventory is most desirable, except for those pupils whose status cannot be appraised adequately without a complete clinical inventory. For them, the evaluation may depend on an individual word recognition test and reading inventory.

In either case, the child reads material at known levels and responds to questions designed to measure his understanding of what he has read. When group procedures are used, material at one level only is usually employed for each test. When an individual inventory is administered, materials at successively higher levels are read until the pupil reaches the point at which he can no longer function adequately. In both cases specific abilities can be evaluated at the same time that information is obtained on the appropriate difficulty level of materials for independent reading, instruction, and listening activities. Getting all this information through group inventory techniques may require a number of sessions with reading at various levels. However, with either procedure the teacher has an opportunity to determine levels and needs in the only logical way — by seeing how the pupil functions in an actual reading situation.

Purposes

If instruction has the object of helping the child improve his performance, it must begin at his present functioning level. The first purpose of the inventory, therefore, is to find the correct level for instruction. Does the particular pupil need to begin work at primer, third reader, sixth level? Where is the point at which he has needs which require instructional help and at which he can profit from it?

Not all work which the child does should be dependent on instructional aid. He should have opportunities to apply the abilities he has acquired, to function under his own direction, and to practice so that he can develop a more facile performance. All of this must be done at a level where he can achieve virtual perfection without assistance. A second purpose of the inventory, then, is to determine the highest level at which the individual can read well on his own, his independent level.

Reading ability is not an entity, but rather a composite of a large number of specific abilities. Improvements in reading performance, therefore, can be brought about only as the individual gains greater grasp of needed abilities. Before plans can be made to help a pupil, the teacher must determine what causes him trouble, etc. A third purpose of the inventory is to get this information on each child's specific assets and liabilities in the total picture of his reading ability.

Many factors, in addition to the language and thinking abilities, influence the child's performance in reading. How well is he able to attend and concentrate? What does he expect to get from reading? How does he respond to ideas presented by others? How much background of information and experience does he have to bring to the reading? How efficiently does he use his background? A fourth purpose of the inventory is to find answers to these and other related questions.

Procedures

For evaluating in group situations, the first step is to make an estimate of the possible instructional level of each child. Many kinds of data can be gotten from cumulative records, former teachers, and observations of daily performance. From these sources comes the information on which the hypothesis about instructional levels is made. Perhaps in a sixth-grade class, for instance, a teacher decides tentatively that he may have one group ready for instruction at fourth level, another at fifth, a third at sixth, and a fourth somewhere above sixth. In addition, he feels that four of his pupils are quite far below the others in achievement, but is uncertain about definite levels.

He might proceed by selecting a good piece of reading material at sixth level and preparing himself thoroughly for using it as an inventory. This preparation would include all of the attention to vocabulary, word recognition problems, thinking abilities, etc., which would be given to a piece of material to be used for an instructional reading activity. When his preparation is complete, he is ready to begin the inventory for those whose instructional levels are approximately at sixth reader.

When this group is assembled for the inventory, the over-all plan for the activity will vary little from that for any good instructional reading activity. The differences lie in matters of emphasis. The objective is not to teach, but rather to find out if this material would be suitable for teaching. The basic question to be answered for each pupil is this: "Can he profit from instruction in this material?" Each phase of the reading activity, therefore, must be slanted toward evaluation. Actual teaching would be done only to see how well various individuals can respond to instruction given at this level. Thus any instruction given in the inventory situation is actually for purposes of further evaluation.

During the readiness or preparatory period of the group inventory the teacher may use a variety of techniques and materials. His objectives are the following: to evaluate the pupils' background of relevant experiences and their ability to use these experiences, to see how many relevant concepts they have at their disposal, to determine whether or not they have a grasp of the vocabulary used in this material to express essential concepts, to evaluate their ability to perform whatever thinking processes are involved in understanding the selection, and to determine the degree of interest they show. These same objectives guide the evaluative phase of an instructional directed reading activity. In both inventory and instructional activity these objectives will be achieved only if the teacher allows freedom for the pupils to reveal themselves — their interests, concepts, vocabulary, experiences, thinking abilities, attention, etc. As the teacher guides the activity he must not become the dispenser of information, the judge of ideas presented. He may stimulate group discussion through use of what he knows about the children's backgrounds, materials read previously, pictures accompanying the material to be read currently, concrete objects rich in stimulus value, or countless other things related to the chosen material.

In the inventory no attempt would be made to fill all the discovered gaps. For some of the pupils taking the inventory, deficiencies in experience, vocabulary, concepts, or thinking abilities, for instance, might be so severe that instruction in this material would be impossible. For them the essential question has already been answered — sixth reader is too high for instruction. Depending on the total classroom situation at the moment, they might be dropped from the reading inventory to go on with some other activity or continue in it even though no more evaluation of their performance at this level is necessary. If they continue, the teacher is obligated to see that it is not a frustrating experience for them and that their inability to function is not evident to all to a debilitating degree.

For those pupils who seem able to proceed with the material the preparatory phase would continue with some developmental work. Clarification or development of concepts, introduction of essential vocabulary, guidance in thinking processes, etc., might be undertaken. Students would be guided toward the establishment of purposes for reading. All this would be done to further the evaluation — to see how well they can profit from this help and apply it during the rest of the reading activity.

Once the preparation has been completed and purposes for reading established, the second phase of the activity begins. Pupils read the material silently to satisfy the purposes they set up. Now the teacher has an opportunity to observe their performance. Some may proceed with no difficulty — reading at an acceptable rate, reflecting their understanding in their expressions, stopping when they have achieved what they set out to do. Others may exhibit various symptoms of difficulty — frowning, lip movement, finger pointing, requesting frequent help, and many others. Some may take an inordinate amount of time as they struggle along. All the things the teacher sees and hears during this silent reading period will become part of the data on which he bases his final evaluation. If pupils want to ask questions, he will be available. From the questions they ask and the comments they make to him he may discover a great deal about the strengths and weaknesses in their performance.

When the silent reading has been completed, group discussion will focus on the purposes established for reading. Here the teacher will have an opportunity to discover how well various individuals satisfied these purposes. Rereading, both oral and silent, may occur spontaneously or be done on request. Appraisal can be made of oral reading performance, ability to locate information, ability to determine relevancy of ideas, etc. Questions other than those raised in the original purposes can be asked to allow for more nearly complete evaluation of each individual's understanding of the material and his handling of the word recognition problems.

By the time the preparatory phase, silent reading, discussion, and rereading have been completed, the teacher should have clear evidence of each child's ability or inability to profit from instruction at this level. About those who can function adequately with his instructional aid, he should have a great deal of additional information. He may have noted that one had difficulty getting meaning from a context clue expressed in an appositional phrase. Another may have needed help with handling the *ti* element in words like *partial*. A third may have had trouble with two vowels together when they are in two separate syllables. A fourth may have trouble with a sequence based on order of importance. In other words, the teacher may have discovered a great deal about the specific needs of these pupils he is going to instruct at sixth level. At the same time, he undoubtedly learned much on the positive side as he observed the things they were able to do well and the readiness they had for additional learnings.

About those who handled everything independently, spontaneously, and virtually perfectly at sixth level, the teacher may know only that he must check them at a higher level. He has not seen their needs because they are not evident at the independent level. About those for whom this material was much too difficult, he may know little more than that he must check them at a lower level. He could not appraise their skills and abilities because they were in so much trouble that they were unable to apply even those they had. Evaluation of specific needs would have to wait for the inventory at the instructional level.

During succeeding periods the same procedures would be followed with other groups and other materials. Those for whom sixth reader materials had been too difficult might become part of groups being checked at fourth or fifth. Those for whom sixth had been too easy might be checked at seventh or eighth. Even after all the group inventories are completed, additional information might be needed on some pupils. It would be to these that individual inventories would be administered. This might well mean making special arrangements outside the classroom setting.

Materials

For both group and individual inventories materials must be ones of known difficulty level. Each piece of material should be a meaningful unit, not a disjointed portion of a longer selection. It should offer the possibility of evaluating important skills and abilities. It should not be material with which the pupil is already familiar.

Many types of material can be used. Selections from basal readers, graded texts in the content areas, "news papers" designed for pupil use — all these and many others are among the choices. For the group inventory in the classroom one might well use selections from the very texts being considered for use. In this way a direct answer can be gotten to the immediate question — "Is *this book* suitable instruction material for *this child?*"

If a science teacher wants to determine his pupils' instructional levels for science work, he needs good science material for his inventory. The question, however, might be this: "What level should this child be using for his light, recreational reading?" In that case, the inventory should be done with story-type material.

In other words, the material must be pertinent to the purpose for which the evaluation is being made.

Summary

Reading needs can be diagnosed only through observation of reading performance. Instruction can be planned effectively only on the basis of such diagnostic study. Through group reading activities conducted with the stress on evaluation the good classroom teacher can determine appropriate levels for independent and instructional work. Having found the right level for instruction, he can appraise each child's strengths and weaknesses and plan to meet his needs. All this can be accomplished with classroom materials by any alert, sensitive teacher who knows his pupils, knows a reading program, and knows his materials for the informal inventory.

9. Clinical Diagnosis in the Classroom

George D. Spache

Before actual diagnosis of reading problems can be undertaken in the classroom, a clear-cut definition of the problem is essential. What is a severely retarded reader? How much retardation must be present to justify intensive remedial work? When can we say that a pupil really needs such help? We must have certain definite criteria in mind if we are to avoid dissipating those few hours the average teacher has to devote to her retarded readers.

For these reasons we offer the following definition: "An individual who is retarded in a number of reading skills by one year or more, if in the primary grades, or by two years or more if older, below that reading level necessary for full participation in the reading tasks of his age or socio-economic group may be considered a case of reading disability. It is assumed that he has had normal opportunities for schooling, and that he has continued to show this degree of retardation below his estimated capacity despite corrective efforts extending over a period of months" (*11*).

This definition eliminates wasted motion in diagnosis and remediation of pupils who: (1) show trouble with a single reading skill, such as rate, (2) are functioning on a reading level which permits them to participate reasonably well in school or their society, (3) are illiterate because of lack of schooling, (4) have shown temporary difficulty which will probably respond to classroom corrective efforts, or (5) are achieving at a level reasonably close to their estimated capacities.

Rigorous application of this definition of reading disability results in a selection of those pupils in whom a real reading handicap exists. Complete clinical diagnosis would be attempted only with these pupils. Children with simple reading problems, identified in the course of applying these criteria, would not be diagnosed. Instead these problems would be attacked by classroom adjustments such as changes in reading materials, small group instruction, change in grade placement, intensive training in a specific skill, or the use of more realistic academic standards.

Preliminary steps to reading diagnosis would include the administration of group tests of reading and intelligence. The reading test should yield separate scores in at least the three areas of rate, vocabulary and comprehension so that the breadth of the reading difficulty may be determined. A supplementary test of phonic and word-attack skills such as the *Doren* (*6*), the *Roswell-Chall* (*9*), the Committee on Diagnostic Reading Tests *Word Attack*, *Silent Test* (*5*), or the *Silent Reading Diagnostic Tests* (*1*) would sample other important reading abilities.

The intelligence test should, of course, be free from the influence of the pupil's reading skills and therefore involve little or no reading. The non-language section of the *California Mental Maturity* (*3*), the *Revised Beta Examination* (*8*), the *Chicago Non-Verbal* (*4*), or portions of the *SRA Primary Mental Abilities* (*10*) are suitable. These can readily be administered by the classroom teacher.

Since the intelligence test results are only a crude guide to the reading capacities of the pupil, we prefer to estimate capacity by a formal or informal measure of listening, or auditory comprehension. This test, in our opinion, provides a better reflection of the pupil's language and socio-economic opportunities than the intelligence test. The *Brown-Carlsen Listening Comprehension* (*2*) or the *Silent and Auditory Comprehension* of the Committee on Diagnostic Reading Tests (*5*) may be used, or an informal test such as that described later.

These preliminary tests would differentiate severely retarded readers from those needing corrective efforts. The test scores would show the degree of retardation in comparison with capacity, and the extent of retardation in various skills. These facts when considered in relation to the school history would identify pupils in need of careful diagnosis.

Diagnostic Steps

Physical factors. Although they are not frequently a major cause of reading disability, certain physical factors must be explored. Information regarding significant variation in nutrition, hearing, metabolism, chronic ailments and general physical development may be obtained from the records of the school nurse or family physician. Unfortunately, vision tests done by these medical personnel are often completely inadequate for reading diagnosis. All too often, only tests of visual acuity at twenty feet are given, and the results are irrelevant to vision at reading distance. In these instances teachers should refer pupils to a local optometrist for complete vision testing. In those cases of reading disability in which the physical factors seem important, the teacher can secure some advice from medical and optometric advisers regarding the adjustment of the remedial program to the pupil's handicaps.

Personality. Most of the effective personality tests require more training for their interpretation than the average teacher possesses. For this reason teachers are well advised to depend upon observational and interview techniques and their knowledge of child development and personality dynamics, while they are learning more about the technical testing of personality. Teachers should attempt to have pupils talk or write about (1) their feelings about reading, (2) the values (if any) they find in reading, and (3) their needs and interests that could be appealed to through reading. The teacher will try to understand what part reading plays in the child's self-concept, how he evaluates himself as a reader, and what reading success means to him now and in the future.

Patterns of attitudes toward reading and, therefore, of reading development are established in children as early as the end of the first grade, as recent studies show. These attitudes often explain why a pupil feels he cannot succeed in reading, or they may actually determine how he reads. For example, the child may read haltingly because of anxiety, lack of self-confidence, or distaste for reading, while the older pupil may read slowly for these same reasons and also because of neurotic perfectionism, rigidity, or ingrained habit. In other words, before we can attempt to correct the pupil's reading performances, we must try to understand how these reflect his ideas about himself and reading.

Insights into the poor reader's self-concept and his emotionalized attitudes toward reading cannot be quickly and completely obtained by a single formal personality test, even in the hands of a psychologist. Careful observation of the pupil's behavior, comments and reactions to reading on numerous occasions are necessary. His spontaneous conversation and stories of his relationships with school and teachers will provide additional clues. Among older pupils, an autobiography of reading experiences, or compositions on such topics as their ambitions, unpleasant experiences in school, most enjoyable book, etc., provide leads which may be followed up by teacher-pupil discussion.

Sociological factors. Reading is as much a sociological process as it is a psychological or personal one. The reading habits of the pupil reflect the attitudes of the family, the community, and even the school. Therefore, before we can expect to help the poor reader perform at what we consider a normal level, we must understand what is normal for his environmental setting. What are the attitudes of his parents toward his reading? What part does reading play in the family's leisure-time activities? Has his schooling gone beyond mechanical instruction in reading to reading as a useful, pleasant activity? What shall our goals for this child's future uses of reading be, in view of these environmental facts? We should certainly attempt to improve the status symbols of breadth of reading, verbal fluency, reading tastes and interests. But we must recognize that these must be realistically related to the probable uses of reading for this child now and in the future in his environmental setting.

Choice of teaching approach. One aspect often neglected in diagnosis of reading problems is an objective determination of the pupil's aptitude for learning by various instructional methods. The decision to use the visual, phonic, or kinesthetic method, or some combination of these, is frequently based simply on the teacher's preference for the method. In fact, if we read the remedial literature, quite often there doesn't seem to have been any question of this point, for the pupil is given remedial training by the same visual method under which he has previously failed.

The nonreader's or the primary reader's ability to profit from these various teaching approaches can be evaluated by the classroom teacher. The Learning Methods Test (7) will accomplish this distinction for individuals or small groups. Briefly, the test consists of a series of four trial lessons in word recognition, each taught by a different method. By the use of comparable words in each lesson, and by the simple testing of actual learning at the end of the lesson and after one day, the appropriate method for each pupil may be discovered. Some pupils do not show significantly greater learning aptitude for any one method. But, on the other hand, many pupils do exhibit a strong tendency in this series of simple trial lessons which any teacher can conduct.

Informal tests. In addition to the facts obtained from the group reading tests mentioned earlier, the teacher will undoubtedly desire information regarding other reading skills. This testing may well be accomplished by informal, teacher-constructed instruments, since few commercial tests are available for assessment of abilities in the content fields or in study skills.

For reading in the content fields, a series of graded selections can be used to estimate silent reading comprehension levels and rate of reading. A parallel set of passages will function for the measurement of listening, or auditory comprehension in this same area. Auditory comprehension level will reveal the pupil's potential for reading in this field, or the possibility of improvement from remedial training. Knowledge of the technical vocabulary of a content field may be sampled by a test constructed with the aid of the glossary of the text. A test of matching definition to one of a group of words is simpler to construct than one of synonyms.

Some teachers will wish to supplement the group reading test by informal tests of the pupil's skills in basal reading materials. Dr. Nila B. Smith has recently made available a series of graded selections for primary levels for this type of testing.[1] The selections permit the evaluation of literal comprehension, interpretation, phonic attack, and vocabulary. A similar informal reading inventory is available for the second to sixth grade levels in Emmett A. Bett's *Handbook on Corrective Reading*.[2] This latter series includes measures of level in basal materials, word recognition, and hearing comprehension.

A few teachers will wish to explore study skills, particularly with older pupils. They may wish to evaluate the pupil's abilities in locating information, as in library skills, use of the dictionary, map reading, and the reading of tables, charts and diagrams. Or evaluation of skill in organizing information may seem desirable, as in outlining, summarizing and note-taking. Still other study skills of significance in retaining and using information that may be sampled are: memorizing, preparing reports, and the act of studying a chapter. With a little ingenuity, informal tests can be devised which provide a functional evaluation of these various study skills.

[1] *Graded Selection for Informal Reading Diagnosis.* New York: New York University Press, 1959.

[2] Chicago: Wheeler, 1956.

Strictly speaking, these informal tests of content field reading, study skills, and reading in basal materials are not clinical diagnosis. Such tests are more likely to be distributed through the course of the remedial program rather than being concentrated at the time of diagnosis. But these evaluations are an integral part of the diagnostic process of discovering how the pupil functions in all types of reading tasks. Moreover, because of their informality and obvious relationship to the pupil's work, they are much more realistic and meaningful to the pupil. Since they parallel the daily reading tasks the pupil is attempting, the results lend themselves to pointed teacher-pupil discussion, and thus to more complete understanding of the pupil's reading and study practices.

References

1. Bond, G. L., and Hoyt, C. J. *Silent Reading Diagnostic Tests*. Chicago: Lyons and Carnahan, 1955.
2. *Brown-Carlsen Listening Comprehension Test*. New York: World Book.
3. *California Mental Maturity Tests*. Los Angeles: California Test Bureau.
4. *Chicago Non-Verbal Examination*. New York: Psychological Corporation.
5. Committee on Diagnostic Reading Tests, *Word Attack*, *Silent Test* and *Silent and Auditory Comprehension Test*. New York: The Committee.
6. *Doren Diagnostic Reading Test*. Philadelphia: Educational Test Bureau.
7. Mills, Robert E. *The Learning Methods Test*. 319 S.E. 6th Street, Fort Lauderdale, Florida: The Author.
8. *Revised Beta Examination*. New York: Psychological Corporation.
9. *Roswell-Chall Diagnostic Test of Word Analysis Skills*. Box 258, Cooper Station, New York: Essay Press.
10. *S.R.A. Primary Mental Abilities Test*. Chicago: Science Research Associates.
11. Spache, George D. *Toward Better Reading*. Champaign: Garrard Press, 1960.

10. What Experiences, Activities, and Materials Are Helpful in a Developmental Reading Program?

Paul Witty

There has been, during the past 5 years, much criticism of reading instruction in our schools. Some of the criticism is justified despite the fact that studies show clearly that our schools are doing an effective job in teaching reading — better perhaps than during any period in the past. And this outcome is being obtained today despite mounting enrollments and the distracting influence of TV and related pursuits which bid for pupils' leisure. There is evidence, too, that many children and youth are reading widely. For example, *Business Week* (1) reports: "Actually book sales have been moving up. . . . And for those who worry about 'Why Johnny can't read,' children's books have skyrocketed even more." [1] However, a great need exists in junior and senior high schools today for the provision of experiences in reading of high interest and of a sufficiently diversified nature to meet the needs of the various reading classes.

There is encouraging evidence that attempts to improve the reading ability of high school students are generally successful and that many poor readers are now learning to read effectively. In a recently published book, Elizabeth Simpson describes a number of newly developed and highly successful programs (2). Moreover, there is a growing tendency in our junior and senior high schools to initiate developmental reading programs designed to satisfy students' interests and meet their needs, and hence to lead them to enjoy reading and to read widely.

Characteristics of a Developmental Reading Program (3)

A developmental reading program seeks to provide opportunities for students to cultivate reading skills throughout the full range of

[1] Bibliographical references are listed on page 68 at the end of this article.

education, including the junior and senior high school and, when necessary, in college. Also, the developmental approach recognizes various purposes and needs for reading. Some needs relate to common attainments or "developmental tasks" on which happiness and adjustment depend. Other needs which are highly personal are significant for individual adjustment. Although some needs are, of course, temporary and transient, others constitute the basis for long-range objectives to be satisfied at different times. A developmental program seeks to evaluate such needs and to plan for their fulfillment in the most beneficial manner.

A developmental program, however, depends on other experiences and activities operating in association with reading; it does not rely on reading as the sole basis for satisfying human needs. Adequate satisfaction implies an effective relationship of reading to other experiences in the individual's total activity pattern.

Equally important, developmental programs seek the extension of interests. The extent to which teachers utilize, extend, and develop the interests of their pupils is a good criterion of the value of their instruction.

Thus, a sound reading program recognizes the value of systematic instruction, the utilization of pupil interests, the fulfillment of their developmental needs, the articulation of experience in reading with other types of worthwhile activity, and the extension or furthering of their interests. By this approach, steady growth in reading skill and the attainment of emotional satisfaction are made possible.

The Necessity for a Developmental Reading Program in Grades 7, 8, and 9

Developmental reading instruction is necessary in grades 7, 8, and 9 for several reasons:

1. Today the range of reading ability in most classes is large. In a typical seventh-grade class, for example, some pupils will read at the third-, fourth-, or fifth-grade levels. Others will cluster around typical sixth- or seventh-grade attainment. A considerable number will have reading ability which falls at or above the norm for grade 9, or even higher. If we are to provide a curriculum that encourages every pupil to reach his maximum growth, we must help many less able pupils to acquire basic skills in reading, and we must also seek to give stimulating opportunities and encouragement to the more capable pupils.

2. The presence of very poor readers in the typical junior high school jeopardizes effective learning in every area of the curriculum where reading ability is essential to success. Many school administrators cite reading retardation as the greatest block to successful

instruction in the secondary school. Moreover, there are some special reading skills or habits required at the junior and senior high school levels which must be emphasized or developed as they are needed.

During the past few years, the need for instruction in "critical reading" has received increased recognition. Several studies have shown that many pupils in our schools are lacking in the ability to read critically and discriminatingly. For example, one investigator found that groups of elementary school pupils made satisfactory scores on standard tests; yet these pupils were unable to differentiate relevant from irrevelant facts in passages of material which they seemed to comprehend (4). Many children, it appears, can tell what the book says; but they cannot judge either the importance or pertinence of an idea or fact. Significant also are recent studies which show that some high school pupils are unable to distinguish between conflicting conclusions presented in treatments of social issues.

3. Poor reading in junior high school can be greatly improved. Remedial and corrective programs have proved very successful at this level. So, too, have developmental programs.

4. Many rapid-learning pupils also need guidance in their reading and some need to develop more efficient habits. A developmental program may provide this help.

5. A developmental program aims to help students become independent in using various sources for reading. This skill is one of the crucial needs of junior high school students.

6. As noted above, good reading can help pupils to satisfy their developmental needs and to improve their general well-being and personal adjustment.

Developmental Needs and Reading

The Forty-Seventh Yearbook of the National Society for the Study of Education, Part II, points out that a developmental reading program should emphasize:

> (a) the basic skills of reading required of all students, (b) skill in reading and studying different types of subject matter, (c) reading experience to help the student understand himself better and to satisfy with increasing success his personal needs, (d) reading experience to assist him in becoming a more effective citizen in and out of school, and (e) experience that will result in a more enjoyable and profitable pattern of leisure reading (5).

At the Northwestern University Clinic, the professional personnel believe that all children and young people referred as problems to the Psycho-Educational Clinic may be best understood and helped by studying their behavior in relationship to basic human needs. This approach is proving effective regardless of whether the referral is because of reading difficulty, personality maladjustment, or some other problem. After a child has been carefully tested, reading experiences are frequently recommended in accord with "developmental needs" as differentiated from basic human needs. These needs resemble the "developmental tasks" set forth by Robert J. Havighurst and others. According to Havighurst, "a 'developmental task' arises at or about a certain period in the life of an individual, successful attainment of which leads to his happiness and to success with later tasks, while failure leads to unhappiness in the individual, disapproval by society, and difficulty with later tasks . . ." (6).

Given below are illustrations of "developmental needs" which have been used in guiding the reading of pupils referred to the Northwestern University Psycho-Educational Clinic:

1. developing competency in physical skills or recreational pursuits
2. understanding oneself and developing an adequate, satisfying ideal of self
3. understanding one's social environment and adjusting to one's peers
4. understanding one's place in a family group, and achieving independence of adults
5. making desirable adjustments determined by the role of sex
6. achieving an understanding of vocations and their demands
7. understanding the basic premises of our society and recognizing one's responsibility for successful participation in democratic life
8. developing an appreciation of scientific discovery and of life in our present technological world.

Materials to Satisfy Interests and Needs

To direct successfully a developmental program, the teacher must become acquainted with books — old and new — as well as with reliable sources for obtaining additional reading materials. A broad reading program geared to the individual recognizes a wide variety of reading purposes and utilizes many types of reading matter: fiction, biography, drama, essays, poetry, informative prose, and so forth. Moreover, this approach necessitates the use of various kinds of printed matter, including books, magazines, and newspapers. Some books are well known by teachers; however, many excellent books of recent date are not familiar to them. Recent titles may be chosen from selected lists such as *Reading Ladders for Human Relations*, published by the American Council on Education, and *Gateways to Readable Books*, published by H. W.

Wilson Company. "Integrating Books and Reading with Adolescent Tasks" (7) and "Developmental Values through Library Books" (8) are also valuable sources of book titles for the teacher of adolescents. *The Combined Book Exhibit* (9) is an excellent annual list of recent books to satisfy pupils' needs and interests. The most widely used annotated book list for junior high school pupils is *Your Reading*, published by the National Council of Teachers of English. *A Basic Book Collection for Junior High Schools*, compiled by the American Library Association and other education groups is another valuable source. An annotated bibliography of 24 book lists is included in "Aids for Knowing Books for Teen-Agers," Circular No. 450, Office of Education, Department of Health, Education, and Welfare.

Basic Reading Skills

Certain reading habits and skills need particular attention at the junior high school level. By the time the pupil has reached the sixth grade he has often attained a fairly rapid rate of reading and a high degree of comprehension. Also, his ability to read orally may be quite adequate to serve his present needs. The task then becomes one of adjusting his rate for various types of reading and of refining his comprehension skills to meet a variety of new demands. Abilities and skills that often require further refinement or development include:

I. Developing Comprehension
   A. Following directions and finding information
   B. Finding answers to personal and social problems
   C. Reading a story for various purposes
   D. Understanding words and increasing one's personal vocabulary

II. Reading To Remember
   A. Remembering important ideas
   B. Remembering significant details

III. Associating Ideas and Materials
   A. Finding proof
   B. Finding information relevant to particular problems
   C. Examining basic assumptions
   D. Studying the adequacy of presentations

IV. Organizing Ideas and Materials
   A. Arranging events in sequence and making outlines
   B. Summarizing

V. Increasing Speed of Silent Reading

VI. Improving Oral Reading (10)

VII. Reading in the Content Field, With Wide Application of Reading Skills

Some Skills of Importance

Space precludes detailed treatment of all the above-cited reading skills; therefore, we shall consider only a few important skills. For example, reading to obtain material or information relevant to a particular problem is a skill which has wide application at this time. Summarizing, too, is another frequently used technique. Both abilities should be emphasized. Practice in summarizing provides an excellent means of helping some children to improve their general comprehension of reading materials by leading them to grasp and organize meanings.

Noting details is another skill in which some children, poor readers especially, require much practice. The need for development of this skill is often found among high school students. As the child approaches maturity in the development of reading skills, he should be encouraged to read *critically*. He should be led to inquire: Do the materials afford an adequate basis for the conclusions reached? Are the basic assumptions upon which the author has proceeded justified?

Another need that pervades reading programs at all levels is the cultivation of general and specialized vocabularies. The current interest of teachers in the science of semantics has resulted in a renewed emphasis on vocabulary building and has focused attention upon the way *context* affects meaning.

One of the most difficult tasks confronting teachers is the development of a clear understanding of conceptual words — words that have no direct objects to which they may be referred. A soundly conceived reading program makes provision for the mastery of conceptual terms by offering students an opportunity to discover their meaning through investigation, discussion, and critical study.

To improve their silent reading vocabulary, some students should review principles of phonetic and structural analysis which will help them recognize new and difficult words.

Other Ways to Build Vocabulary

There are, of course, various ways in addition to phonetic and structural analysis to build a meaningful vocabulary. Following are some suggestions:

1. We can help pupils to derive the meaning of new or unfamiliar words through attention to context. We can direct them to examine known words around new or unfamiliar words and to attempt to obtain the meaning of the new words from their relationship to words already known. Various exercises can be devised for this purpose. For example, exercises may bring out the way the words

around *case* determine its meaning as in: a *case* of ginger ale, a *case* of illness, a *case* of poor judgment, a *case* in court, and the subject of the sentence is in the nominative *case*.

2. We can extend the first-hand experience of pupils. The term *jet-propelled*, for example, has a definite meaning for a pupil who has seen a jet plane take off. The word *smooth* has meaning also for a child who has felt the texture of silk.

3. We can motivate extensive reading of challenging literature. Wide reading broadens experience and thus provides the basis for meaningful vocabulary development.

4. Pupils should be led to enlarge their special as well as their general vocabularies. They can be encouraged to look for new words in their general reading and to keep a list of them in a section of a notebook entitled *My General Vocabulary*. Another section of the notebook might be labeled *My Special Vocabulary*, and new words might be entered here under headings such as *Science*, *Geography*, *Music*, etc. In similar fashion, vocabularies can be kept for hobbies, sports, and other interests.

5. Pupils should be encouraged to use new words in their conversations, discussions, and writing.

6. Pupils can be taught to derive the meanings of new words by reference to known words. Application of the principles of phonic and structural analysis will aid also. Interesting examples should be given of the way suffixes or prefixes may be added to extend vocabulary.

7. Varied meanings of conceptual terms such as *honesty*, *democracy*, and *cooperation* can be taught in terms of pupils' experience. And we can illustrate how the meanings of these words may be clarified by wide reading, by discussion, and by investigation.

8. We can stress some significant values in wide use of the dictionary. We can illustrate how helpful a dictionary is in finding synonyms or in studying word roots.

Improving Rate of Reading

The good reader cultivates different techniques as they are needed. The poor reader, on the other hand, is often unable to make such adjustments readily. Reading rate does not depend upon a single capacity; instead, it is an aggregate of abilities which one employs selectively in reading different types of material. Consequently, a desirable program of reading improvement must provide opportunities for increased speed in reading various types of material. Important also is the development of the ability to decide upon and to use effectively the most appropriate rates with the different presentations being read. Finally, consideration must be given to the importance of interest, difficulty of material, and familiarity with the concepts presented as factors influencing both rate and comprehension. In fact, rate of reading has little value *per se*.

Improving Oral Reading

Pupils who read as if they were practicing the pronunciation of each word should have opportunities to improve basic skills in oral reading. In addition to practice in pronunciation and enunciation, they will need to learn to read by phrases or thought units. Exercises for these pupils should include practice in phrasing — reading word groups rather than single words; attention to punctuation; and experience in varying tone and pitch to fit the author's meaning. As they improve, they should be encouraged to read and to present stories to their classmates.

In diagnosing the needs of these pupils, the classroom teacher may employ the *Gilmore Oral Reading Test* and then have the pupil turn to the exercises in reading prose, poetry, and other types of materials that are available.

In summary, the chief requirements for effective reading programs are these: clear objectives, careful diagnosis of each student's needs, a variety of books and reading materials, high motivation, and sufficient time to enable the student to develop reading skills in accord with his most pressing needs.

Of course diagnosis, guidance, and appraisal are closely related phases of reading instruction. Only when the teacher knows rather thoroughly each pupil's beginning status can progress be estimated accurately. Such information may be supplemented from time to time by data obtained in the classroom, on the playground, and elsewhere. Periodically — perhaps once a month or bi-monthly — teachers may examine and compare test results and other entries. In this way, evaluation contributes important insights concerning pupils' changing needs. Thus the process continues: diagnosis, guidance, appraisal — and further diagnosis, further guidance, further appraisal.

In these ways the teacher can estimate the extent to which the reading program is actually affecting pupils' lives. When such an approach is widely followed, youth will come to enjoy the act of reading as well as the results. Accordingly, more efficient reading will occur and happier, better-adjusted boys and girls will make up our junior high school population.

References

1. *Television: the New Cyclops*. Business Week, March 10, 1956, p. 91.
2. Simpson, Elizabeth. *Helping High School Students Read Better*. Chicago, Science Research Associates, Inc., 1954.
3. Witty, Paul, Peterson, Miriam E., and Parker, Alfred E. *Teachers Guide for Reading Round-Up*, Book I: p. 2–14. Boston, D. C. Heath Co., 1954.
4. Gans, Roma. *A Study of Critical Reading Comprehension in the Intermediate Grades*. Teachers College Contributions to Education, No. 811. New York, Teachers College, Columbia University, 1940.
5. Witty, Paul. *Current Role and Effectiveness of Reading Among Youth Reading in the High School and College*, The Forty-Seventh Yearbook of the National Society for the Study of Education, Part II, p. 25. Chicago, University of Chicago Press, 1948.
6. Havighurst, Robert J. *Developmental Tasks and Education*. Chicago, University of Chicago Press, 1948, p. 6.
7. Brooks, Alice R. *Integrating Books and Reading with Adolescent Tasks*, The School Review, Vol. LVIII, p. 211–19, April, 1950.
8. LaPlante, Effie, and O'Donnell, Thelma. *Developmental Values Through Library Books*, Chicago Schools Journal, Vol. XXXI; p. 1–21, March–April 1950 Supplement.
9. *Invitation to Believe and Make Believe*. A Book List for Children and Young People; Selected, Classified, Graded, Annotated, Indexed. New York, Combined Book Exhibit. 1957.
10. Witty, Paul. *Reading in Modern Education*. Boston, D. C. Heath and Co., 1949, p. 153.
11. ———, and Ratz Margaret. *A Developmental Reading Program for Grades 6 Through 9*. Chicago, Science Research Associates, 1956.

11. Principles for Selecting Methods and Materials to Promote Growth in Reading

Marvin D. Glock

The principles suggested in the following discussion provide a sound basis for the selection of methods and materials for teaching all pupils. The 1952 *Report and Recommendations on the Education of the Intellectually Gifted in New York City* states that "there are no special methods for teaching gifted children. A capable teacher will employ a variety of techniques, designed to achieve optimum growth."[1] However, "some characteristics of good teaching methods that are of special importance in the education of mentally superior students can be identified."[2]

The Importance of Meeting Pupils' Needs

It is generally accepted that growth in reading cannot be realized unless the pupil practices reading. Yet the old adage that "practice makes perfect" is without factual basis. Sheer repetition does not promote growth in learning as we think of the process today. An author's handwriting is seldom improved as he enters the last chapter of his book. Likewise, there are adults who have read dozens of books but whose reading efficiency is no better than it was when they were graduated from high school. Adult readers may have no reading interests, other than to follow the plots of simple stories. This they can do through a very immature pattern of reading.

A common method of analyzing motivation is by the need theory. An individual presumably behaves the way he does in

[1] *Report and Recommendations on the Education of the Intellectually Gifted in New York City*, p. 9. Brooklyn: Committee of the Division of Elementary Schools, Board of Education of the City of New York, 1952.

[2] Educational Policies Commission, *Education of the Gifted*, p. 71. Washington: Educational Policies Commission of the National Education Association and the American Association of School Administrators, 1950.

order to satisfy a need. Some of the prime motivators of behavior in our culture are the needs for affection, belonging, approval, independence, and adequacy.

Needs of individuals can be satisfied in many different ways. One child can meet his need for social status through his physical prowess. Another gains satisfaction through intellectual achievement. Good teaching suggests structuring the learning environment so that the needs can be satisfied through behavior which assures the growth of an individual's ability to adjust satisfactorily to new situations, to solve problems, and which provides for his fullest development.

By learning to read well the pupil discovers ways of satisfying these important needs. His achievement is approved by his peers and by the adults with whom he is associated. He experiences the thrill of independent research. He is gratified by his feelings of adequacy and the accompanying self-respect. In satisfying his needs through reading, he matures intellectually while he grows in reading skill. He learns to appreciate the importance of this intellectual tool, and he is motivated to become more proficient in its use.

A word of caution is in order, however, because all the needs of able children cannot be satisfied through reading. They demand more than vicarious experience. Then, too, it is important to be aware of personality and adjustment problems which the child finds difficulty in solving. Some of these problems may stem from intellectual maturity, which puts him out of step with his own age group. If he is a good reader, he may withdraw from social contacts and achieve satisfaction through reading. A balance in the child's program is necessary for his all-round development.

Developing the Higher Competencies in Reading

"Easy come, easy go" is a phrase often used to describe the learning of able children. Evidence indicates, to the contrary, that those who learn quickly have better retention. However, some able boys and girls have not achieved in harmony with their abilities. Achievement in the basic skills cannot be taken for granted and the superior pupil left to fend for himself. Neither should he be forced to do all the practice exercises and the drill work required of his less able peers. Since he can master these skills more quickly, he will loathe unnecessary repetition. His time can be better spent doing more constructive assignments.

In general, however, the able student is gifted linguistically. He may possibly be reading when he starts going to school, and he will continue to read widely. Extensive reading is to be commended if it is not divorced from concrete experience. It is important to remember, however, that printed symbols are meaningful only insofar as the reader is able to bring experience to them.

Improvement in reading cannot be divorced from those many experiences which are basic to the formation of meaningful concepts. A child is unable to build his apperceptive mass, to borrow a term from the Herbartians, entirely through verbal and pictorial experiences. If he does, the result will be verbalism — words which are devoid of meaning. Because the able child is often gifted in the use of language, he becomes adept in making statements which sound good; they make sense; they label him as being well informed. However, they may be devoid of meaning because for him the symbols hold no close relationship to the objects or situations they represent.

Horn states that "any symbolization, no matter how abstract, should be connected with experience in a gapless chain, every link of which has had its meaning established by reference to experience."[3] He points out that all too often language plays a dual role of substitution "*for* concrete situations and *for* overt responses."[4] If the pupil is always encouraged to formulate his ideas from language alone, he finds himself in a vicious circle in which new ideas are "fabricated from the vague and inaccurate ideas of the year before."[5] Therefore, new concepts must be constructed out of clear and accurate ideas which are well rooted in direct experience.

There are many kinds of experience which will serve this need. Participation in community activities and involvement in community study are particularly rewarding for the able student. Investigations in which the sources of data are people as well as things provide realistic insight. Excursions and construction activities can be used to advantage. The laboratory offers extensive possibilities for working with the concrete. Reading must be integrated with these activities.

There must be many opportunities for independent reading. Teachers will find that able students like to help plan their assignments. They have ideas and are interested in the why rather than in the how and the what. Their co-operative thinking and sharing of interests will often prevent narrow reading interests. However, emphasis should not be placed on the quantitative aspects of en-

[3] Ernest Horn, "Language and Meaning," *The Psychology of Learning*, p. 386. Forty-first Yearbook of the National Society for the Study of Education, Part II. Chicago: National Society for the Study of Education (5835 Kimbark Avenue), 1942.

[4] *Ibid.*, p. 386.

[5] *Ibid.*, p. 390.

richment alone. Many splendid opportunities for the practice of interpretive skills as well as for the critical evaluation of source material should be provided.

The possibilities for improving reading competencies through projects are unlimited, and, in addition, the able pupil can satisfy his curiosity through independent exploration and study. He has ample opportunity to generalize to principles. He can certainly satisfy a need for creativity. In addition, there can be provision to work in a group to gain experience in human relations.

We should be especially concerned with helping the able learner develop the higher processes of reading. Projects require library research, and the product will be integrative in nature. The pupil must concern himself with the author's purposes and intent for writing the article, chapter, or book. The material itself can often be read for different purposes. A historical novel on early California can be read for the interpretation of the story, or it can be read to develop a better understanding of life at the time of the story. There will also be other clues to broader meaning, such as the tone and mood of the passage. The competent reader needs to know how to "read between the lines" to identify words indicating author bias. He must be concerned with organizational pattern. Time sequence; plan of presentation of ideas; and the relations among sentences, paragraphs, and larger sections of an article, chapter, or book are basic to understanding. Through wide reading, the able student can also be in a better position to achieve searching insight in the light of broader context. Our historical novel can be richly interpreted only if the reader has knowledge of the economic, political, and cultural background of that period, as well as of the present period.

The able pupil needs to evaluate the validity of reading matter. This refers both to the facts presented and to the conclusions drawn from these facts by the author. The able reader will have the problem of reacting critically to the different points of view presented by various writers. He must evaluate the logic of a writer's argument. The ability to criticize, to withhold judgment, to control impulses, to postpone reaction until he has carefully considered the issues requires mental maturity and experience.

Developing Creativity

No characteristic of able learners is of more importance than their ability to create. Yet very little is known about the factors which make up creative ability.

We have ample evidence to show that, before creative thinking can occur in reading, the pupil must master the fundamental skills of reading and the higher processes of comprehension and interpretation. Apparently, however, we need to examine a second factor: spontaneity, which gives evidence of being closely related to creative thinking. Creative thinking demands a flexibility of personality which enables the individual "to manipulate his perceptions and past experiences and to recognize and use his emotional and artistic responses." [6] The contrasting function is conformity. Mental activity of the rigid personality is controlled by all manner of restraints, such as patterns, rules, habits, etc. A person tends to react to different problems with a similarity of behavior patterned by these restraining factors.

The social climate and requirements in the classroom may contribute to a lack of spontaneity among individuals. The able student may lose his independence of thought by accepting uncritically everything he reads. Neither should he merely accumulate information and specific skills, for so doing probably encourages conformity.[7] Rather, as suggested above, there should be opportunities for the student in various assignments and projects to express his ideas and his emotions. The student who writes a play, a story, or a biography of a fictional character has an opportunity to practice a kind of behavior which seems to lend itself to the development of spontaneity. Allowing a pupil to discuss his plans of work and then to pursue independent reading, with guidance when called for, will tend to break the lock step of equal requirements for all — the archenemy of spontaneity. This kind of reading activity may well stimulate creative thinking. The pupil will not necessarily arrive at solutions through set patterns. Although much more research must be initiated to determine effective ways of making reading contribute to creativity, these suggestions may well serve in further explorations.

Developing Effective Study Habits

Although suggested work habits are implied in our discussion of developing creativity, other suggestions are important. The able child may perform as well as the average boy or girl, but it is a serious mistake to compare him with norms on achievement tests or with the average of a heterogeneous class. Norms are merely indications of mediocre performance. The able child's progress should be compared with his past achievement, and he ought to be given the responsibility for evaluating himself. It is important, too, that he be kept working up to capacity. This means that he

[6] W. Edgar Vinacke, *The Psychology of Thinking*, p. 254. New York: McGraw-Hill Book Co., Inc., 1952.

[7] *Ibid.*, p. 256.

needs to work in an effective manner. Inefficiency can follow one of two patterns. Indolence, which manifests itself in superficiality, disorganization, or carelessness, may result from not requiring sufficiently high standards. On the other hand, he may become overmeticulous and spend much more time on a project than the value received from it would warrant.

There is no reason why younger boys and girls should not be taught the basic principles of learning. Why shouldn't they be taught, for example, that the most important factor in forgetting is the interference caused by new learning — that actually this new learning makes them forget the old? Then certainly they need to be aware of how to use recall and review to increase retention. Problems of concentration and systematic use of time should be discussed. Developing an appreciation of the psychology of mental fatigue and the part which change of activity can play in its counteraction is certainly appropriate.

Efficient work-type reading also demands an understanding of, and an ability to use, various reading techniques for different purposes and kinds of materials. There are many specific reading tasks in each of the content fields. Able students can learn to adjust to purpose by skimming, rapid reading, thorough reading, etc. They should be informed of the values of the preface, table of contents, appendix, glossary, and index. Library skills must be mastered. Skill in taking notes and in organizing information is basic to the proper use of reading as an effective tool for learning. The able student must learn how to study effectively. His time is valuable, and he should know how to use it efficiently.

Concluding Statement

In conclusion, let us be mindful that the most important purpose for the selection of methods and materials to promote growth in reading among bright learners is to enable the pupil to proceed at his own rate of growth. He should not be pushed or forced. Neither should he be held back. He should be challenged with materials and methods which will provide for his optimum growth. Some practical suggestions have been given in this paper. It is important to remember that emphasis belongs on the child and not on techniques and reading materials. There is no royal road to teaching, even to teaching the able learner.

PART THREE

The Program and the Student

12. Reading for Therapy

Dorothy Bratton

Miss Creata Reeder numbers among her high school groups a junior class in American literature. Now Miss Reeder herself is a traditionalist, wholly convinced that Emerson, Hawthorne, and Lowell, Sandburg, Frost, and O'Neill have something to say to her. She is not at all convinced, however, that for the present-day sixteen-year-old they are the only writers who speak, or should speak.

She wants her students to read, to pick up a book automatically while waiting for the toaster to pop up or the factory whistle to toot. In spite of being an English teacher, she is to some slight degree a realist, so she has observed that the adults of her acquaintance rarely pick up as companions for idle hours the classic writers of American literature. "Why then," she wonders, "should I expect these young people to? I shall expose them to the great names of the past. I shall attempt to teach them to respect the literary heritage that is theirs. I shall see that they acquire a nodding acquaintance with great minds. All that I shall do, in somewhat piecemeal fashion, perhaps, but I shall do more. I shall attempt as I know these students to know their problems, and I shall try to help them to find the answers, whether those answers are dated

1657 or 1957. I believe sincerely in the therapeutic values of reading, in the ability of a healthy mind to maintain its health."

The journal in which Miss Reeder records random thoughts and observations relating to this thesis of hers she has consented to share with us.

September 10

My junior English class promises to be a challenging one. Thus far we have been feeling each other out, in an effort to see in which direction we shall move. I gave my usual reading questionnaire, in order to start everyone thinking about reading. Although many responses reveal homes in which literate habits exist, and cultural needs are cared for, other answers appall me, though I suppose that by this stage in my career I should be inured to such a casual attitude toward reading.

"*Which magazines come to your home?*" Too often the answer was "None" or "*True Story.*"

"*How many books do you suppose there are in your home?*" elicited such responses as: "We don't have books at home" or "I think there's a box of old school books in the attic."

"*What do your parents like to read?*" was frequently answered vaguely: "Mother is pretty busy and she doesn't read much." "Dad is tired when he comes home. He watches TV and falls asleep. I've never seen him read, except maybe one of my comic books."

The innocent-sounding and apparently irrelevant query, "*How many hours a week do you suppose you spend on TV?*" brought responses varying from ten hours to thirty.

And to the question, "*How many hours do you spend each week on free reading?*" came the answer all too frequently, "Almost none. I don't have time to read."

September 17

While we are dipping into early American literature in our anthologies, we are trying to modernize things a bit by finding out what is being written *today*. Our librarian has stacks of book jackets, vivid in color, and tantalizingly adorned with irresistible blurbs. I think we'd better bring in some for our bulletin board. Melvin has confessed that in ten years of schooling he has never read a book he didn't have to read. I think I'll ask him to select twenty or twenty-five book jackets for our book corner.

September 24

The corner which Melvin decorated is quite colorful. He remarked as he poked in the final thumb tack, "I didn't know there were books about big game hunting." He seemed inordinately pleased when I told him that tomorrow I'd bring him my own copy of *Hunter*. The girls think that bulletin board is a bit too earthy-looking, what with fishing and lumbering and dogs and horses. . . . I've promised them that they may choose next week's display.

Today I listed on the board nine areas of living which present problems to adolescents. For this purpose I used the Illinois Curriculum Publication *Reading for Living*. The areas listed are: Family and Home Relationships; Financial Problems; Personal Development; Physical and Health Handicaps; Racial, Religious, and National Differences; Religious Problems and Conflicts; School and Teacher Relationships; Social Relations; Vocational Problems.

I asked the students in which areas they thought high school students would most enjoy reading. Martha, whose father was killed last month, thinks financial problems should certainly be investigated. Wilma, who was married last summer but hopes to finish high school, thinks that family and home relationships should be considered.

"I see we are scattered all over the list," I said. "Watch closely and I'll show you how to use this index to reading materials. Tomorrow will you each bring me a list of ten books which consider the problems you think would interest high school people. Margie, do you want to practice your typing? Will you take the suggestions and combine them, and type lists for us for our bulletin board? Then if you just happen to know someone who wants a special book, you'll know where to refer him."

October 8

These people are used to my suggestions that they read with open minds ready to find out not just "What does an author have to say?" but "What does he have to say to *me?*" Tim took a very dim view of the prospects when he learned that Benjamin Franklin was on the agenda. "I understand he's a fuddy-duddy" was substantially the way Tim put it. I'm giving the class a week to see whether the boys or the girls can collect the greater number of lines from Franklin that *do* say something to us today. I've suggested that since no one ever seems to have enough money for his desires, we might see what Franklin says about thrift. In this contest, then, there will be two points allowed for a saying about thrift and one point for any other quotable saying.

October 15

The doubter, Tim, led the boys to victory in the Franklin contest. I'm trying to get across the idea that sometimes little quotable lines stored in the memory serve a purpose. Pat is — just maybe — getting the point. "Gotta bank part of this week's earnings," I heard him say.

> For age and want, save while you may:
> No morning sun lasts a whole day.

October 18

The class is beginning to respond good-naturedly if a bit skeptically to my repeated suggestion that they listen to what an author has to say to *them*. "Thanatopsis" started some long, long thoughts. Sixteen-year-olds think about death and fear it. Many of them have never experienced the death of a dear one, and can't possibly imagine themselves as being able to live through such an experience. We became very thoughtful as for several days we worked our way slowly toward acceptance.

I spent a few minutes reading to the class President Lincoln's letter written to Mrs. Bixby. "Read that part again," said Joe, "about the solemn pride." So I repeated, " 'the solemn pride that must be yours to have laid so costly a sacrifice upon the altar of freedom.' " Not until he shyly asked after class, "Could I borrow it to show to Mom?" did I remember that young Marine who hadn't come home.

"Is it possible to come to see death as just as natural a phenomenon as birth?" I asked one day. "Would anyone like to go on living indefinitely? Does the knowledge that we are all mortal bring us a little closer together? Is that why wise men of all ages have tried to make their lives count for good — just the fact that the time is so short?" These were deep questions for sixteen-year-olds, but the sincerity with which they discussed them would do credit to many twice their age.

October 29

Today I listed on the board the following general themes, and asked which ones the class thought high school students would like to investigate further: Patterns of family life; Rural-urban contrasts; Economic differences; Differences between generations; Adjustment to new places and situations; How it feels to grow up; Belonging to groups; Experiences of acceptance and rejection.

After they had expressed their opinions in writing, I showed them how to use the American Council on Education publication, *Reading Ladders for Human Relations*, in order to find book titles on their chosen topics. "How It Feels To Grow Up" proved amazingly popular. Their written requests for books on that theme were revealing. Wrote Jim, whose teachers complain that he demands too much attention: "A lot of kids have found it a little hard to grow up. I have found it hard in many ways. My folks expect more out of me than they used to, and this is a problem to me. I'd like to read books about growing up." I mustn't lose my patience with Jim so easily. At least he recognizes the truth.

And perhaps Marty spoke for several when she wrote: "When we are growing up, it frightens us, and is very strange to us; but at the same time it fascinates us, and leaves us with a good feeling. I want to find some books about growing up."

November 14

Our new method for keeping records of books read for the course is proving successful. We keep a little card file on my desk, and all books are recorded one to a line on a card for each student. The class likes the little short-cut to evaluation I suggested. They mark a book "A" if it is "One of the best books I ever read." "B" means "This was really a good book." "C" means "This was just another book." "D" says "I didn't care for it but I finished it," while "F" means "I didn't care for it enough to finish it. I turned it in and chose another."

Tom, who easily handles any adult reading, delighted the group today by his report on A. J. Cronin's *The citadel*. When he had finished, Brad, who has trouble reading at fourth grade level, exclaimed, "There's a guy Felsen who writes about a fat boy, Bertie. Bertie was a mess, but he came out okay." Several others obligingly pointed out the fact that there were other books by Felsen, even others about Bertie. Brad *feels* his own scholastic limitations very acutely. He tasted success very briefly today, and the success was sweet!

November 27

Yesterday I said, "You're meeting many new people in your reading, learning how they adjust to new situations. Let's imagine! Pick out a character from the books you are reading now. Lift him bodily from the book and drop him down in our high school. . . . Now is he a student, or a teacher, or coach, or a custodian? Don't change his personality. Just show us what happens when he suddenly becomes one of us."

Today's themes were fun to hear, and they revealed some good thinking. We were not surprised to learn that Mr. Chips had a long line of would-be students waiting to have their schedules changed to include his class, or that Thoreau was making a very acceptable biology teacher. We like to feel our own sympathies were broadened as we heard about Louise Baker's artificial limb and her awkwardness in the gym. Brad was able to use Bertie, the fat boy, again, through the simple expedient of letting him work for his meals behind the dessert counter of our high school cafeteria!

How *would* a stranger get along with us? How *does* a new student fare? May I hope that there are plus-values gained from our consideration of the problems of book characters?

December 4

Three weeks until Christmas! There are so many things I'd like to share with these people! There *are* homes in which the deeper meanings of the holiday season are buried beneath a flood of trivia. How can our reading experiences help to made the holiday season more meaningful for those who will never truly experience Christmas unless they experience it at school? Surely we can be forgiven if in the blessed all-inclusive term "Christmas" we find room for cultural experiences not entirely literary.

The Christmas theme has given our world some of its best-loved paintings. Today I asked Barbara and Joan, from two of our very underprivileged homes, to arrange a beautiful collection of Christmas paintings. Raphael's lovely madonnas smiled first of all on those two who most need smiles, and then supplied food for interesting comment on the fact that Christmas in art can be very satisfying indeed!

December 5

Yesterday it was "Christmas in Art." Today it was "Christmas in Music." We talked of different ways of telling a story, eventually getting around to stories in opera. It was then an easy step to the *oratorio*, and next only a few inches to a discussion of *The Messiah* after we had listened to a fine recording of the "Hallelujah Chorus." It now seems natural for us to speak of the various ways in which men have told the Christmas Story, so we turn in our textbooks to Edna Ferber's short story, that matchless tale, "No Room in the Inn," and in discussing this modern variation upon an old theme, we find horizons being pushed back miraculously.

January 17

Whoever said high school students don't worry? Juniors are thinking seriously of their futures. When Jan wrote a few days ago, "I am sure that many students would be grateful for suggestions about summer jobs, as well as for lifetime careers that do not require a college education," I knew the time was ripe for our career study.

Along with all the research we do in our efforts to make a detailed study of one chosen occupation, there is, it seems to me, a definite place for fiction. This is also a fine time to consider financial problems as they are treated in fiction. As one boy wrote, requesting suggestions for readings on financial problems, "We are all growing up very quickly, and before long we'll be earning money for a family. This will present many financial problems." Another boy backs up his request, saying little but revealing much: "Most teen-agers have a lot of trouble saving money for anything. The part-time jobs we have do not pay much. Everyone has financial problems just about every day."

As a class project we've listed a whole array of books dealing with careers and finances. The well-written factual accounts are studied avidly for research purposes, but the fiction titles are the ones that are carried home. If Phyllis finds herself, as she dreams about entering a conservatory of music, in Willa Cather's beautiful *Song of the Lark*, while Jack, by means of Evans' *Bob Vincent, Veterinarian*, is started thinking long, long thoughts, who shall say that such fiction is wholly trivial?

January 24

Any English teacher would be something of an intellectual midget if she failed to recognize the fact that many of our modern writers for young people are quite well trained psychologically. I realize that students think all authors either died before 1900 or else, spared death, settled for long white whiskers! Sometimes we English teachers seem to have that same delusion. Among the most popular writers of teen-age fiction today are Betty Cavanna and Florence Means for the girls, and John R. Tunis and Howard Pease for the boys. All are very perceptive; all apparently were young once. I must type up lists of their books and place them on the bulletin board. Better still, I'll ask Annette to type them. Annette doesn't read widely.

Still Annette did write this a few days ago: "My friends and I have been discussing certain organizations in which a few people are accepted and many are rejected. Some of us feel that the reason they didn't ask us is that we are not as good as they. Rather, I think it is because they can't ask everyone in school." She concluded her bit of philosophizing by asking for titles of books dealing with such experiences as hers. Will hers be reading for therapy? In my book, it will be!

February 13

In spite of the many side-excursions we take, we do travel week by week along a leisurely path through American literature. We have been allowing the nineteenth century poets, beloved of our parents and grandparents, to help us find a philosophy of life.

"Everyone has principles in which he believes," I began, "things for which he stands. Many people have found that sometimes writers know just how to state a thought for us — a thought that gives us something fine and durable that can help us later when we need help. Let us see what these writers have to say to us."

We've spent some pleasant days with Emerson, hoping that a little of his devotion to "plain living and high thinking" would rub off on us; with Poe, giving ourselves up to the magic of rhythm and rhyme; with Thoreau and Lanier, sharpening our awareness of the miraculous world of nature about us; with Longfellow, marveling at "the beauty and faith of a woman's devotion" as we follow Evangeline through the years; with Whittier, seeing the commonplaces of life glorified; with Holmes, wondering how it will really be to leave our outgrown shell behind; and with Lowell, figuratively breaking the ice around us to share of ourselves with the beggar at the door of our hearts.

Shirley writes movingly of her pleasure in such reading, saying: "We are interested, too, in books about racial and national differences. And we are beginning to wonder about religion, no longer just accepting what we are told." Shirley is one of the fortunate ones who all her life will be able to find in books the answers to her deepest personal queries.

And serious little Penny's own problem peers out through her request for books about religious differences: "Mary goes to the Baptist Church and dates Jerry, who is a Catholic. Their parents object to their dating. Mary likes Jerry very much, but she doesn't know how to tell him her parents' point of view without hurting his feelings. This is a problem to many teen-agers." How glad I am that I can show Penny again the lengthy list of books *Reading for Living* includes on that theme!

March 14

In our readings on different problems this year, we have stumbled into a few areas where little was available. Our librarian is understanding. "What do you need?" she asked us. "Books about what? All right — so we *are* a little short on books about prejudice and minority groups. Here are book catalogues. Here are annotated bibliographies. Here are Sunday supplements. Here are lists of forthcoming books. Now get busy and give me your recommendations. You may order twenty-five dollars' worth."

Then followed reading with a purpose if I ever saw it. "Should we buy *Glass House of Prejudice* by Dorothy Baruch, or would it be better to spend a quarter more and get Alice Huggins' *The Red Chair Waits?*" "And would *Clouded Star* by Anne Parrish help us understand the Negro problem as well as would Roi Ottley's *New World A-Coming?*"

April 5

We heard oral reports today, but they were rather a far cry from "Summarize the plot of *A Tale of Two Cities.*" "Do not tell me the story," I begged. "I already know the story, or I *can* quickly know it. What I do not know is your own reaction. Your opinions have dignity and worth, and we are anxious to hear them."

We've had on the board for a week such questions as these:

How did the main character overcome a personality weakness?

Where should the main character have acted differently?

Who used his strong points to very good advantage?

How is someone in the book like someone you know?

Each student chose one question and had two minutes to answer it. The listeners made little private lists of books they thought they'd like to investigate.

April 10

I hope to be able in some small degree to help these people to think through the problem of finding worthwhile recreation. All the rest of their lives there will be hours to be filled as pleasure dictates, and not as the demands of work require. I hope they will turn to books — turn to them naturally and easily and expectantly. Am I, through inertia of my own, allowing them to see reading as something that people do because they must, to satisfy some artificial school requirement — something to be avoided like poison as soon as safety permits? Or am I helping them to find in books a constant source of pleasure, a never-failing supply of nourishment for the mind?

Yesterday I asked, "What do you like to do when there is nothing you *have* to do? Will you each write down five hobbies or sports or pastimes that you enjoy or would like to enjoy? Do you know that, whatever you wish to do, there will always be a book to help you do it better? Tomorrow bring in from the library a book title on each of your pastimes."

Today we listed on the board all the hobbies and pastimes, and we were able to supply book titles for almost all of them. One day next week we'll have a hobby day when all the reports will be on our recreational choices.

April 23

Paperbacks have their place and their value. Let us admit, O heresy of heresies! The supermarkets have been distributing over seventeen million paperbacks annually to persons who formerly were not, in general, purchasers of books. Many of the books are lurid and valueless; others are worthwhile and timeless. Can I help these people to see that there are authors who perennially speak to us; that there are values apart from date and binding; that there are truths for all of us wise enough to recognize them; that there are books, and books, and books!

April 24

It's really spring! We've taken a day to review poems of spring from our anthology. We found special pleasure in Bryant's "Yellow Violet" and "To the Fringed Gentian," and Lanier's "Waving of the Corn" and "Tampa Robins." We paused for a few minutes with Thoreau on Walden Pond. "Do people try experiments like that any more, live like that, really?" wondered Stanley, who chafes insufferably under regimentation.

"Stanley," I answered, "You are an adventurous young man! Get Leland Stowe's new book from the library, *The Amazing Crusoes of Lonesome Lake*, and tell us what you think of it." Stanley will tackle this assignment with gusto, because it is his and his alone, and he likes being singled out. Furthermore, though they do not know it now, Stanley will have several others reading the book before a week passes.

May 6

I feel I've neglected my girls lately. These sixteen-year-olds are beginning to fall in love. The fact that falling out is as effortless as falling in is entirely beside the point. "Let's have a good time with boy-and-girl stories" brought forth squeals of delight from the girls a week ago and tolerant, sheepish smiles from the young gentlemen.

We listed on the board all the appropriate titles we knew, consulting our well-thumbed guide book for others. To keep the matter impersonal, and to allow the few who do not date to "save face," I suggested, "Tell us about a couple who were happy together. Why were they? Or maybe you know a book couple who weren't happy. Why weren't they?"

Dealt with in this objective way, many personal tensions were released, many partially-formed ideals were crystallized. Each could read something at his own level, and each could contribute to the general discussion.

May 15

I made today my little annual spring speech about the public library. Our high school library is *too* good; it is *too* convenient; we cater *too* much to high school tastes and needs. I took time today to remind these students, "After you graduate next year, you aren't going to come back here to find books. You must start going uptown to the public library. You will soon be ready, many of you are ready now, for the adult fare it offers. I know women who drop in at the library every day during their lunch hour to relax and read. I know a man who spends an hour there each afternoon because his ride gets him into town at three, and his factory shift doesn't start until four. I'd like you to be able to find some of the pleasure they find. Shall we start?"

Next week's discussions will be based on a book from the public library, and in utter shame I confess that for some of my students this will be the very first trip there.

This will no doubt be my last entry in this year's journal. For some of these young people, these little excursions we have made into realms of reading are just trips that they would have made anyway, eventually, given no directions at all.

But what of the others, the less imaginative, the slower in intellect, the less mature in emotion. Have I the right to hope that perhaps they, too, may find in books companionship for idle hours, and that in consequence their lives may be made rich and meaningful? Incurable optimist that I am, that hope is mine!

13. Reading for the Gifted in the Secondary School

Bulletin of the National Association of Secondary School Principals

Purposes and Scope

This monograph is intended to be a guide book for instruction of pupils of superior mental ability — a series or compilation of suggestions for those teachers too occupied with the formidable task of leading large heterogeneous classes through scholastic requirements to do the research necessary for adequate differentiation of instructional programs for gifted individuals. Its scope is necessarily limited by interpretation of the words *reading* and *gifted pupils*. Reading is here considered as the all-inclusive use of books and other printed material as tools of learning — not alone the conning of pages assigned by instructors, but the *use* of ideas in critical thinking, in discussion, in sharing the fruits of reading with others, in creative thinking which applies the material read in all its ramifications. Above all, instruction in reading in secondary schools essentially is laying the foundation for adult friendship with good books — with ideas wherever expressed. What is said about instruction in reading will apply to all phases of teaching: literature, the communicative arts, sciences, the social sciences, and human relationships, and mathematics.

The strong admonitions from many sources that we should give special attention to the education of our gifted young people for the benefits that will accrue to the nation does not come to us as a new thought. It was voiced by Plato and others of his time. The voice of the philosophers persisted to reach the ears of practical leaders of the people in other nations and other times. We know that the Romans made adaptations of Plato's ideas and, at government expense, selected and trained mentally gifted youths for leadership in government, in wars, and in oratory.

"In the sixteenth century Sulieman the Magnificent sent emissaries throughout Asia Minor with instructions to examine and select the most intelligent youth of the Christian population for special education. These talent scouts at regular intervals presented the Sultan with the fairest and brightest youths to be found. These individuals were then trained for positions of leadership in the Empire." [1]

The authors of the report tell us also that William T. Harris of St. Louis, Missouri, in 1867 probably made the earliest attempt to provide for gifted children in the public schools of the United States. His plan was to make the school promotional system so flexible that gifted pupils might accelerate their pace and approach the spots in the school program more commensurate with their interest and ability to accomplish. They state that "variations of this procedure followed throughout the United States in the form of multiple-track programs that aimed at saving time for the superior pupils."

The theory of acceleration as a method of providing for the education of superior pupils was superseded by the use of the multiple-track plan to provide curriculum enrichment with a

[1] This is a quotation from a report by Terman and others in the *Forty-ninth Yearbook of the National Society for the Study of Education.*

minimum of acceleration. From the early years of the twentieth century, until World War II brought chaos to much of our educational planning, special curriculum enrichment for gifted children was growing in popularity in the United States. Inevitably the plan had its antagonists, as do all changes or attempted changes in educational procedure. Adverse criticisms hinged upon the question of democracy. That question is so well satisfied in the *Forty-ninth Yearbook* that the answer is here quoted lest some interested persons fail to see a copy of the report. Under the caption of "Philosophical Considerations" the authors say:

> The gifted child is both an asset and a responsibility. He is an asset of incalculable value to society. His potentialities for good are difficult to overestimate. Our socio-economic structure, both national and international, demands leadership of the highest quality and keenest intelligence. Where else may we look for this type of leadership except among those of intellectual superiority?
>
> Democratic education is founded on the ideal of equality of opportunity. Too often equality of opportunity has meant identical opportunity. Opportunity to be equal must be measured in terms of individual abilities and capacities to the end that all will be challenged to utilize their powers to the fullest. Society will reap a rich reward from such a policy. It makes possible the full development of individual capacities so that both the individual and the society which educates him may be mentally benefited. As John Dewey says: "If democracy has a moral and ideal meaning, it is that a social return be demanded from all and that opportunity for development of distinctive capacities be afforded all."
>
> There is nothing undemocratic in utilizing all social resources for the betterment of society. No people can afford to disregard the differences in human materials. Special education aims to prepare the child for the place in society for which he is best fitted. Is it any less important that the child of superior mentality be prepared for leadership?
>
> Society is injudicious in the extreme in neglecting these children who possess the potentialities of high-quality leadership. It is the part of wisdom to prepare these boys and girls for the important social responsibility which will be theirs. Today, as perhaps never before, we face problems of world magnitude which threaten the existence of society itself. Education is challenged to develop leadership for the tremendous tasks which lie ahead. Under such conditions, special education of the gifted is not only justified but is also demanded by the lessons of history.

Very generous applause is due the three people who are responsible for the expression of this philosophy. They are Merle R. Sumption, Professor of Education in the University of Illinois; Mrs. Dorothy Norris, Supervisor of Classes for the Gifted in Cleveland, Ohio; and Lewis M. Terman, authority on gifted children.

Undoubtedly we would want to stress, more than has been done in the section quoted, the personality or character development of gifted individuals. Were it not for our knowledge that the characteristics of a real leader are those of a well-integrated individual free from emotional maladjustments, we would want to stress less preparation for high social responsibility. We would want to emphasize the provision for experience in living the good life as members of a community.

Perhaps there is more of loneliness than of satisfaction in leadership, unless we have that broad view of leadership that takes in the creative thinker, the scientist, the inventor — all that wide group of wonderful people whose leadership consists in making the world better in which to live.

In planning provisions for the education of mentally gifted children, it is necessary to take cognizance of their special characteristics. A gifted child's superior mental ability is indicated by a high intelligence quotient on mental tests. Aside from this he has learning characteristics that make it quite undesirable to use with him the teaching methods applicable to the instruction of normal or slow-learning pupils. Most easily recognizable is his superior reading ability and his rich vocabulary recognition. Lacking some physical deficiency or some emotional disturbance, he has learned to read without formal instruction and he makes reading a tool as well as a pleasure. He learns more rapidly than the average child. He generalizes and makes applications from fewer examples. He sees relationships and thinks logically. The amount of drill and repetition necessary to the learning of the average child is distinctly boring to the mentally superior one. He is impatient with too much routine and is often driven by it to daydreaming.

Dr. Terman says: "His versatility is shown in his wide range of human interests. Because of this, he finds a distinct advantage in the study of many widely differing subjects. These many interests, together with the desire to forge ahead to explore new fields, play a large part in forming his attitudes. His mental traits are usually rounded into an integrated personality, for he is guided by a rather high degree of common sense, breadth of mind, and the power of self-criticism."

This generalized composite picture of the gifted child leaves out some of the brush strokes that show he is a startlingly human being. "He must be taught to suffer fools gladly," said Leta Hollingsworth.

It is often patent that he does not suffer fools gladly. In a junior high school with an average intelligence quotient of a hundred seventeen, an accidental high-grade moron spent half an hour in a bungling attempt to make a report to his class. When he had finished, the usual chance for discussion brought forth the impatience of one of the boys who served to boost the average I.Q. of the school. He said, "It is not a good report because most of it is not true. Besides I do not like to waste my time in listening to such a report."

Frequently the impatience is not so consciously directed at a particular inept person but rather at our lagging methods of instruction in general. The drilling that teachers find necessary in classes of wide ranges in ability brings unconscious revolt from some mentally superior children. One youngster worked his twenty examples in a mathematics assignment correctly when the lesson was assigned during the first week of school, but too many of the class did not comprehend the processes. The lesson was re-assigned and our boy missed three problems. On the third assignment he missed half of the twenty examples. The moral to that is deeper than at first appears. It involves the whole problem of the teacher's understanding the mental hygiene of children and knowing what to do with them when she has the knowledge of how minds operate.

Identification of the Gifted Pupil

Student achievement is not of itself a safe criterion by which to judge intellectual capacity. That achievement is influenced for good or for ill by circumstances. Happily conditioned, the student is interested and inspired to development commensurate with his ability. Unfortunate circumstances and relationships tend to produce emotional maladjustment or mental inertia. The single factor of lack of challenge in learning experiences or methods of instruction may make a mediocre student out of a possible genius. The pages of history are filled with names and deeds of men of great minds whose school records say they were poor or average in their work. Undoubtedly many more failed to accomplish so as to write their names on the rolls of great minds.

There must be a yardstick for measuring mental capacity, lest the schools be thwarted in the hope of finding and training leaders in thinking and planning, creating and inventing. The existing yardstick must be used more judiciously and more effectively. Intelligence tests are the best single measure devised to date. The surest identification of superior intellectual ability is the achievement made on intelligence tests.

Dr. Witty says, "We recommend the use of intelligence tests in identifying gifted children and youth . . . they have been found to provide data from which the subsequent behavior of an individual can be roughly predicted. The accuracy of such predictions is far from perfect, but it is accurate enough to justify use of intelligence test scores, along with other criteria, in such practical operations as identifying gifted students, in making special provisions for their education, and in counseling them. Thus, it cannot be claimed that intelligence tests have 'absolute' validity; but, for practical purposes, they have a useful degree of 'operational' validity."

The best practical procedure in identifying, counseling, and providing adequate learning opportunities for gifted students in high school is the examination of records of intelligence tests administered throughout their school years.

Definition of the Gifted Child

In using the term gifted as applied to school pupils, general acceptance may be given to the definition formulated by the Educational Policies Commission. "In this statement, the term 'highly gifted' is used to designate those who are in the top one per cent of the total population with respect to intellectual capacity (that is, roughly, individuals with an I.Q. above 137). Similarly, the term 'moderately gifted' will apply to individuals who fall within the top ten per cent but below the top one per cent (that is, between 120 and 137 I.Q.)." Thus, in this bulletin, pupils of superior mental ability under discussion will be those with I.Q.'s above 120.

We shall not attempt to force acceptance of a particular term to designate the individual of superior intelligence whose cause we are pleading. Perhaps we shall speak of them (those who, because of exceptional mentality, are able to do more work and much better work than the average student of the same age in the same time) interchangeably as superior, talented, exceptional, *etc*.

We are prone to think of gifted pupils as those in the group with I.Q.'s of 130 and above. However, we acknowledge that many with I.Q.'s of 120 to 130 may belong in the group that needs special educational adaptation. We think often of some statements in a treatise by Hyman Alpern.

> There are in the United States today more than a million individuals who would rate as incipient geniuses by the definition of terms used above. [His one per cent includes those with I.Q. of 130 and above.] There are approximately 2,700 whose intelligence is equal to that of the outstanding leader among the great men of modern times, John Stuart Mill. Some of these people will live and die humble members of the community whose only public praise will be, "He's smart for a garbage collector" or "She remembers more than three hundred recipes and can tell them to you without ever looking in the book."
>
> We do not know how vast a number of individuals of extraordinary intelligence walk the streets of our towns and cities today, their ability unrecognized, their potential usefulness partly or wholly wasted; but,

even if they were a handful, we should consider ourselves guilty of a shameful slaughter. For a civilization based upon democracy must respect the individual and consider each soul precious.

The fault is not wholly that of the school, to be sure, but that does not exonerate us. Why haven't we recognized the brilliant man when he was in our class, and why haven't we helped to mold him properly?

Characteristics of the Gifted Pupil

In all phases of education, in all subjects of instruction, in all methods of teaching, the necessary differentiation for pupils of superior mental ability are plainly indicated by the learning characteristics of the pupils and their need for the opportunity to develop to their full capacity. Delineating the personality traits of intellectually gifted individuals is like describing ideal personal characteristics, yet those of us who have spent years of our lives in intimate contact with large numbers of them realize that the characteristics presented by students of the subject are not exaggerations. We have found, too, that, if high mental capacity is present and the personal characteristics which accompany them are not evident, there is some emotional maladjustment that needs the co-operation of school and home to remove.

If, as is sometimes said, the gifted, the near geniuses, and the geniuses have often been maladjusted people, the chief cause of this is lack of challenge to achieve commensurate with ability — a deep sense of frustration. Some, in fact much, of this frustration may be the fault of schools that fail to realize the guidance function of education is to help develop pupils of exceptional ability and the special ability of each pupil, and to provide for each one, along with intellectual guidance, needed personal and social counsel.

The characteristics of gifted pupils that most affect their learning habits and make necessary differentiated instruction are, as the result of much research, listed in many publications. A summary of the lists would include the following traits of mentality.

Active curiosity — a desire to know
Deep and varied interest in abstract ideas
Ability to recognize relationships and to generalize
Capacity for logical thinking
Ability of rapid learning, requiring little repetitive drill
Long span of attention, commensurate with high degree of intelligence
Original and creative ability
Capacity for self-criticism

In addition to these notable mental traits, gifted pupils are generally above average in desirable character traits.

They are more often leaders than are pupils of average mental ability

They make good social adjustments
They are inclined to prefer association with persons of their own mental level or with those older than they are
They are extremely sensitive to injustice to others and suffer keenly because of social conditions in the world.

Meeting the Needs of the Gifted Pupil

No one can judge more clearly the needs of gifted students and the most adequate methods of meeting the needs than can those students themselves. Two recent studies reveal the judgments of groups of gifted individuals. The studies will be quoted directly. Dr. Irving Lorge conducted a survey of adults who had been gifted children. Their conclusions were as follows:

1. Acceleration by skipping should be avoided in favor of some form of enriched program.
2. Skipping should not bring an intellectually gifted child to senior high school more than two years in advance of his chronological age.
3. Gifted children need instruction in the basic skills and in the development of good habits of study.
4. These children should be encouraged to develop habits of self-discipline for the attainment of goals, regardless of the apparent scope of the interests.
5. Guidance of the gifted child is of great importance — particularly social guidance early in his schooling, and vocational guidance (and placement) later.
6. The teacher of the gifted child must be intellectually, educationally, and socially fitted to teach him.
7. Intellectually gifted children make adequate or superior adjustments as adults.

The second study is an unpublished doctor's thesis based on a survey of gifted high-school pupils. Dr. Marcella Bonsall, who made the survey, considers the needs as indicative of methods necessary in the adequate instruction of gifted students.

Human needs obviously cannot be categorized in any one exclusive, all-embracing statement. Further, the very term human needs implies their universality. It will be apparent to the reader that many of the needs stated below are general adolescent needs. Probably, gifted children feel these needs more acutely than do their less talented contemporaries, and express them more sharply than do lesser analytic children.

They need help in finding and understanding the similarities they possess and share with other children in order to feel comfortable with their social peers.
They need help in adjusting themselves to their differences so as not to develop feelings of inferiority.

They need help in understanding that they do not need to cover up their superior abilities and achievements, so that they will not sink into mediocrity in school endeavors.

They need help in developing a sense of self-adequacy through association with their intellectual peers.

They need help in finding and defining purposes in the satisfaction of curiosity.

They need help in finding weaknesses in their stores of knowledge and in their personality development. But, more, they need assistance in knowing what to do to overcome the weaknesses once they have been identified.

They need help in understanding and in accepting their ability to achieve, both quantitatively and qualitatively.

They need help in understanding the necessity of adjusting their means of communication with those less able than they, so as to be understood by those who do not possess their intellectual abilities.

They need help in becoming well-qualified academically, for this acts as prime mover for further effort in learning.

They need the informal techniques of instruction in which group planning, group execution, and group evaluation are continuous; thus they can gain satisfaction in achievement through lessening boredom and diminishing routine.

They need and demand over-views of subject matter where the pursuit of knowledge starts with the whole, progresses to the parts, and then terminates as a whole.

They need individualization of instruction in order to broaden those interests they already hold and to open new fields of endeavor and new interests.

They demand opportunities for being creative and critical in the realms of expression, of opinion, and of behavior.

They want opportunities to draw generalizations and to apply them in concrete situations.

In our high schools, gifted pupils present a dual problem. First, they need the good general education that "citizens, consumers, and prospective parents" need as equipment for dealing "competently with themselves, their environment and their fellowmen." Beyond this is the need for a deep and understanding acquaintance with people and how they live, familiarity with their language and cultures, with the records of human experience, and with basic training in the concepts of modern science that are necessary for potential leaders in all phases of life in our contracted world at an advanced stage of technological development. To meet this dual problem, schools must provide, not only differentiation in learning experiences, but also the differentiation in instruction that assures that all study shall be purposeful for the pupil.

The purpose of differentiation of the instructional program for better-than-average learners is two-fold. Immediately it is to provide such challenge as to assure for the learner the development of potentialities to their full extent — to enable him to realize achievement and prevent frustration that may leave emotional maladjustment. The end purpose is to conserve and foster for humanity the resource without which all other resources may fail of fruition for want of initial development, discovery, or creation.

Motivation and establishment of differentiated instruction for gifted learners is, of necessity, the duty of school administrators. Its development and maintenance, its inspiration are in the hands of the instructors. The administrator must decide such questions as the degree of separation of this group of learners from the slower learners that is possible or practicable in his unit of administration — his school system or his particular school. He must provide, through their education, for the co-operation of the parent patrons. He must provide for adequate instructors and for adequate instructional materials.

Tireless interest of well-chosen teacher leaders will provide inspiration for gifted learners, but that interest must be fostered by administrative authorization, sufficient time, and enriched teaching facilities.

Meeting the Needs of the Gifted Pupil Through Reading

Though it is possible to identify potential leaders, also to give them the highly technical training which they, as well as less gifted people, will need for competence in their chosen fields, it is extremely difficult, and at the same time, extremely important to help highly gifted children to develop constructive attitudes, insights into individual and group behavior, standards, and ideals. Without such attitudes and insights there is little assurance that the superior child will not become an isolated mind with little contact with humanity, or, what is worse, he may use his powers destructively. *The problem demands solution if humanity is to survive.*

Fortunately, there is available a tool which makes possible the personal development and acquisition of experiences which are so important to all people — leaders and followers alike. This is the tool of books. Only through wide, constant, and increasingly mature reading can the brilliant child gain information, have vicarious experiences, and broaden his mental and emotional horizons. Only through familiarity with the thoughts, the achievements, and the failures of the past can he become truly prepared for leadership in the future.

The superior child should be encouraged consistently to find in books answers to those of his innumerable questions which experimentation and discussion fail to give, and proof of those answers he seems to find. He needs to be guided into reading on subjects in which at first he seems to have no interest. Narrow specialization in his reading must be guarded against. If he learns to read widely, deeply, and sensitively, he cannot but be helped in using his gifts for his own happiness and for the good of mankind.

So long have educators and parents found refuge behind the thought that in the process of being educated the gifted child will take care of himself that it is time to examine the results. In the area of reading, examination points out two deplorable extremes in the group of pupils of superior mental ability. At one end are the caricatured bookworms with noses so buried in their books that no practical application is made of the content read. At the other end, and covering a too great proportion of the scale, are the boys and girls whom neither home nor school exposes to adequate reading materials.

None of the proclaimed learning characteristics of gifted pupils are denied by the acknowledgment that the pupils must be exposed to wide and deep and rich supplies of reading material, that they must be guided in their selections, and that they must be afforded genuine opportunities for discussing the material read. Lovers of literature are not made by the reading of a classic in class and making critical analyses of it. A method or methods must either exist or be created that will enrich the reading experiences of gifted pupils in high schools.

The need for reading enrichment is shown in an informal survey made in a junior high school in a definitely superior district. The pupils with intelligence quotients of 125 and above were asked to report, by listing titles, their free reading for the previous two weeks.

Reports from a statistically significant number of students indicated clearly the need for arousing interest in better free-time reading.

In quality and quantity of reading, there was no appreciable difference between beginning seventh-grade pupils and ninth-grade pupils in their last semester.

Less than one per cent read standard literary magazines, although sixty-two per cent read the *Reader's Digest*.

One hundred per cent of the girls and thirty per cent of the boys read "movie magazines."

One hundred per cent read comic books and magazines.

Forty per cent read no books other than those assigned by teachers.

Twenty-eight per cent read acceptable literature.

Twelve per cent read poetry.

Ten per cent read books and magazines about their hobbies.

Earlier surveys reveal the striking inadequacy of library facilities in the homes of gifted children. These cited facts and further evidences should move to action all educators — not English teachers alone.

Desirable Qualities of Teachers of the Gifted

Ruth G. Strickland states: "Since schooling occupies so little of a lifetime and all the rest of his growth one must achieve under his own power, perhaps the greatest service a teacher can render a child is to build up his self-respect, his sense of obligation to himself, and his sense of inner power to achieve. . . . Children must be taught how to learn and grow, how to stretch on tiptoe to higher achievement, greater satisfaction, more worthy goals."

School administrators — principals and vice principals — and the various members of secondary-school teaching faculties will recognize those among them who are gifted with ability to teach even the most gifted of the school's pupils. The instinctively identified hallmark of high-grade intelligence combined with well-integrated personality characteristics is unmistakable. It so affects the teacher's instruction and his classroom relationships with his students that they are made to feel the pleasures and values of achievement commensurate with their mental ability. In his classes dissatisfied pupils wanting to change classes and courses are rare, and parents adversely critical of their children's educational growth are few.

High-grade intelligence and well-integrated personality are widely inclusive expressions which will be clarified by some elaboration. In general, mental traits of gifted individuals, be they teachers or pupils, are similar. Thus teachers with superior mental ability are understanding of and sympathetic with gifted pupils. (The inquiring mind, ability of rapid learning, versatility of interests, logical thinking, long span of attention, and creative ability of pupils will be met with mature, though not necessarily equal, degrees of the same traits in their adequate teachers.)

Gifted teachers with the same freedom from unreasonable emotional tension held essential for gifted pupils will have developed sensitivity to the individuality of their pupils. They will be marked by keenness of sense of justice, capacity for self-criticism, freedom from excessive sensitivity to criticism, freedom from jealousy even of exceptional ability pupils. They will have, perhaps most important of all, the faculty of imbuing others with a true sense of value of accomplishment commensurate with individual capacity to achieve.

Education, particularly training for teaching, should have developed in instructors of the gifted, a clear and consistent philosophy of education and the knowledge that that philosophy deepens and widens with experience and maturation. Training should have developed a rich fund of general information and the practice of continuous growth, not only in knowledge of "his subject" — which is never so important as are the pupils being instructed — but also in the maintenance of lively and wide interests.

Training should have developed deep understanding of educational psychology as it applies to gifted youth, ability to stimulate and inspire, to create an atmosphere in which each pupil must find incentive for thinking and freedom of expression, a thorough knowledge of the methods and value of creative teaching *versus* lesson assigning and reciting.

Most of the above-mentioned qualities of teachers of the gifted in our high schools are acknowledged as desirable in writings and speeches of educators learned in the subject, but the important quality of creativity in teaching is often overlooked.

The ability to teach creatively is the wonderful ability which, coupled with deep inner security, makes the possessor "original, imaginative, inventive, courageous" in finding and using methods that meet learning exigencies to end them in rich and varied experiences for the pupils — experiences which lead them to respond actively and thoughtfully, not merely to reproduce others' statements parrot-wise.

Creative ability in teaching does not lead to disregard of the "core curriculum" and leave "complete blanks" in the pupils' high-school courses. On the contrary, it enriches courses by providing for application of facts to the solution of problems, thus enhancing the probability of retaining the facts in memory for further use, and making each course a means of further learning.

Not only in the field of original writing is the function of creative teaching exemplified. One young pupil of a group of eleventh- and twelfth-grade mental ability had questions in his mind concerning the subject he was studying. The questions were not answered by reading the pages assigned by the teacher. He had heard much talk and had read in the papers about *world powers*. What is a world power?

That question came to be a live one with the group. The interested boy and a creative teacher discussed the possibilities of finding out why the United States is a world power and why one does not hear other countries of the Western Hemisphere referred to as world powers. Soon all the group were talking about the question and about finding ways of answering it.

The field of interest for the semester became the solving of the problem. It involved study of the countries of the hemisphere in terms of people, industries, politics, history, geography, *etc.* No lesson assignments in any of these related subjects were necessary. Committees were organized to investigate particular aspects and to inform the other members of the group of their findings. These reports were the occasion — the inspiration — of group critical thinking.

So vital was the activity that discussions spread to the homes of the pupils. As the close of the school term neared, an open report and discussion meeting was held for the parents and community. No faculty member or school official worried lest the students were not covering their curriculum subject.

Leadership classes are a proving ground of good teaching. These classes so prevalent in high schools of today either are or are not valuable in developing desirable characteristics of capable pupils. Their value depends upon the understanding and instructional methods of the teacher. There are no possibilities of sterile and stereotyped assignments. Instructors must needs be creative in their guidance of pupils toward the solution of practical problems of the school.

One successful teacher of leadership classes, called a sponsor for obviously appropriate reasons, gives some important information about the character of such classes and the characteristics of good teachers. These classes consist largely of pupils of better-than-average intellectual ability. Such classes are the center of the "Student Activities Program" where are provided actual practical experiences in planning and organizing programs, in obtaining approval from proper faculty authorities, in delegating authority to student co-workers, and in carrying the plans through to completion. Diverse problems of the school, both major and minor, present themselves to the group for discussion and solution. They meet the problems of maintaining a clean school campus, of proper student conduct in halls and on grounds, or suitable student dress, of seemly courtesy to substitute teachers, *etc.*

The leadership class assumes responsibility for developing leadership within groups in the school, and students learn to work democratically with each other, with different racial and religious groups, and to carry through worth-while ideas of fellow students. The experience serves to develop leadership ability, while making the leader realize the importance of intelligent followers. The student learns to accept the authority of others, and yet to work to capacity within his own sphere. Responsibility to local community, state, and nation are fostered. An example of action which the leadership class takes is the following:

One night the high school had an uninvited guest lodged in the girl's gymnasium. In the morning the physical education teachers found that one cot and one blanket were out of place, and that one small window had been broken to admit the intruder. Except for these minor conditions everything was still in order. The general agreement reached was that not more than one person had visited the gymnasium in the night.

The gymnasium teachers dutifully reported the unusual incident to the proper faculty authority. After further investigation a story of the incident was given to the reporters. On the following day two city newspapers carried articles which read somewhat like the following with the caption, "Wild Party in Local High School":

> Gangs of vandals raided the girl's gym at the high school last night. Cots and blankets were strewn all over the floors and windows were broken. Bottles and other evidence pointed to the possibility that a wild party was held in the gym last night. This is another one of the frequent outbreaks of vandalism which have been reported recently in the city.

The leadership class was shocked and angry at the misrepresentation of the truth. The class was determined to see that the truth be told so that their school's reputation would not suffer unjustly. The members composed and sent letters to the two newspapers, explaining the true situation and asking for a retraction. A retraction was printed in one of the papers.

The successful sponsor of a leadership class will be a truly creative teacher. It is his function to provide the atmosphere and guidance for the maximum development of the latent leadership abilities of a new group of student officers each semester. He fosters their growth in the practice of meeting problems and solving them through critical thinking, group discussion, and logical, practicable decisions.

One teacher said, "The sponsor of a leadership class must realize that this is a very different type of class, which indulges in different activities than does any other class. There is continual activity, noise, *etc*. One does not try to keep 'perfect order.' Real business takes time, noise to a degree and patience. The sponsor must take real interest in the group and what it is doing."

Obviously, what the group is doing is not preparing assigned lessons from the pages of a particular textbook. Their "real business" is the solving of a problem or problems in community living. It is practice in learning to lead in the solution of problems in adult community living. The teacher referred to each new class as separate persons each with his own ideas and interests which must grow into an integrated group who think of the school as a whole. "This is a growing process for both sponsor and student leader."

Teaching Method

The intelligent teacher with a sense of professional and social responsibility will have acquired deep understanding of the learning traits of gifted pupils which will lead to the adaptation of methods to the needs of the particular individual or group. The Educational Policies Commission lists and justifies some characteristics of good teaching methods of special importance in the education of mentally superior students. Lest the pamphlet is not readily available the eight important paragraphs are quoted here.

(a) The teacher should share with the learners his reasons for using the methods that he does. Such explaining of purposes is both more important and more rewarding in the case of gifted students than of others. Moreover, they are more likely to demand it.

(b) Learners should have some opportunity to select and plan their own activities. Such opportunities should be afforded gifted students to a greater extent than others. They will have more ideas and their ideas are more likely to have greater educational value.

(c) Assignments should be so phrased that they will invite originality in fulfillment. For the able student assignments can — and *should* — be given in less detail than for others.

(d) The teaching of skills should involve repeated practice until a reasonable degree of mastery has been attained. For fast learners, higher standards of attainment should be required; but less time will be needed. Unnecessary drill beyond the attainment of mastery should be avoided.

(e) Teaching for understanding should focus on explanations of the reasons for things. The understanding achieved by all learners will be increased by the teacher's skillful use of "why" and "how" questions; and such questions are especially suited to guiding the thinking of gifted students.

(f) Learners should have access to a wide variety of books, pictures, realia, and other instructional materials. More materials and a greater variety of such materials are needed for students of superior mental ability than for others. But superior students need less guidance in the selection and use of such materials than do others.

(g) Learners should have direct and guided contact with out-of-school environment. Community study and participation in community activities are particularly desirable means of enriching the education of gifted students. Such activities complement book learning, at which the gifted are specially adept; and they serve as an antidote to excessive verbalization, to which some highly intelligent students are especially prone.

(h) Students should be given a large measure of responsibility for evaluation of their own work. In the case of a gifted student, such evaluation should use his realistic estimate of his capabilities as the norm. It should involve comparison with his own previous achievements and should avoid comparison with the achievements of his classmates — especially if he is in a heterogeneous group.[2]

[2] *Education of the Gifted*, Educational Policies Commission, 1950, pp. 71–73.

Guidance of the Gifted Pupil

The existence of guidance departments and the employment of counselors in most secondary schools is noteworthy. It is an acknowledgment of a general need and of resolution to meet that need. The necessity for competent guidance of pupils of superior mental ability is clearly indicated despite the fact that such individuals tend to be emotionally stable and to possess the stamina of character that enables them to diagnose their own difficulties.

The relationships between counseling, or guidance, and instruction are so close as to make differentiation between one and the other speculative. Certainly there cannot be effective guidance of pupils in a learning vacuum. There can be little pupil growth in stability, in satisfaction, in happiness without growth in scholastic achievement. The value of instruction varies with the teacher's knowledge of intellectual, emotional, and interest factors of pupils. Especially is this true in counseling and instructing pupils of superior mental ability, of whom authorities maintain: "In general these children are superior in mental health as well as in mental ability; they are accelerated in character development as well as in intellectual accomplishment. Contrary to popular opinion, gifted children are not emotionally unstable. If they are disturbed, the area in which gifted persons are most likely to fail are those of social relations and meeting frustrations constructively."

Mental hygiene clinicians say that problems arise from unfavorable home and/or school environment. Home handling inconsistent with superior ability may induce over-selfassertion and over-aggressiveness. Schools may fail to provide learning experiences that gifted pupils need for satisfying development. "So-called behavior problems which arise out of home and school conditions like these often represent the child's efforts to obtain the conditions he needs for his self-fulfillment." It is a struggle for self-preservation which would have been avoided under proper guidance.

Problems of four types were the most frequently mentioned by three hundred gifted high-school students studied by Ruth Strang.[3] They were: (1) feelings of inferiority and inadequacy; (2) unsatisfactory human relations; (3) failure to realize intellectual potentialities; and (4) difficulty in choosing, preparing for, and entering a vocation. Problems that are disturbing and prevent expected development of scholastic growth and personality integration will be brought to light by counselors in personal contact with pupils

[3] A related but more detailed list of specific needs mentioned by high-school students is that on page 13 of an unpublished doctor's dissertation by Marcella Sea.

in response to appeal from observing teachers. Their solution will be fostered by co-operation of instructors and counselors.

It is typical of gifted pupils in high schools that their personality and educational problems are unknown to faculty members. So modest and well-adjusted socially are the mentally superior as to give rise to the often-quoted statement that "they can take care of themselves." Though growth in knowledge is so rapid that the gifted pupil surpasses others of his age by two or three years, little is done to make material of courses mentally or educationally challenging. Little wonder that he loses interest and the impression becomes somewhat general that "The adolescent of a high IQ does not want to be a 'brain.' He wants to be popular with his mates."

The most challenging function and duty of the counselor is to be thoroughly acquainted with the mental ability, interests, and personal problems of students and to confide the knowledge with its implications to their particular instructors. "Although every teacher has a guidance function, many responsibilities in this area can best be handled by specially trained members of the school or college staff. Such specialists should have major responsibility for identification of the gifted members of a total school student body. They should also be asked to evaluate in terms of the 'whole child' the suitability of special provisions proposed for each gifted pupil before such proposals are put into effect."[4]

The Educational Policies Commission make several important statements in their short discussion of guidance of gifted students. They maintain that the ability of college students to make wise decisions concerning advanced study and the choice of careers will rest in large measure on the extent and quality of the guidance they received earlier. Counselors should seek to prevent the making of premature decisions by encouraging exploration of wide varieties of possibilities before choosing a particular field of specialization. Gifted high school seniors should be furnished with much information as to which colleges are best suited to serve interests and needs of each individual student. A somewhat controversial question is touched upon in the following quotation from the Commission's report:

> The central purpose of guidance is, of course, to help the individual to understand himself. Toward this end, counselors of gifted students should help them face the facts of their giftedness with objectivity and modesty. The idea is sometimes advanced that parents and teachers should conceal from the gifted child the true degree of superiority which he has in respect to either intellect or special talents. But to attempt such concealment with intent to foster modesty is no favor either to the gifted or to society,

[4] *Education of the Gifted*, *op. cit.*, p. 70.

for the effort is likely to fail of its purpose while also dulling ambition and generating emotional conflict. Underestimation of their own ability is much more characteristic of the highly gifted than is overestimation. . . .

Certainly gifted children and youth should not be given an exaggerated notion of the importance of their giftedness. Some may need to be reminded that intellectual superiority is not to be equated with moral superiority. If a gifted student does appear to be developing a disagreeable sense of superiority, he needs counsel regarding his responsibility for social well-being. When he fully recognizes this and also realizes the sad plight of society today, the job to be done, and his responsibility for helping to do this job should make him exceedingly modest instead of disagreeably superior.[5]

Multiplicity and variety of organization of secondary schools produce in turn varied types of organizations of guidance departments. One small school may have a part-time counselor who strives to classify pupils by the use of group tests. At the other end of the scale is the school with a guidance office with its staff of psychologists, mental hygienists, *etc.*, who supply the teaching staff with the data concerning each pupil which is necessary for good teaching, counsel with pupils, and confer with parents in need of help.

One school of moderate size — about twenty-four hundred pupils and ninety teachers — which, due to the type of residents of the district, has slightly more than the average proportion of gifted children, is successful in the guidance field with the plan described below. The school recognizes three areas of counseling which they label identification, group guidance, and individual guidance. In identifying pupils of superior mental ability, they first study the cumulative cards and any other records that are gathered as part of pupil entrance routine. Intelligence and achievement tests are then administered and teachers are consulted for results of their observations and judgments of a pupil's general and special abilities, indications of his maturity both intellectual and social, his work habits, *etc.* Accurate records of pupil tests are filed for reference of instructors and guidance officers, and periodic retests serve as checks on mental classification and development from year to year.

Upon completion of identification, a working group of teachers, a faculty committee, consult with other concerned faculty members for recommendations for making provisions for students found to belong in the category of the gifted. Finally-agreed-upon recommendations are submitted to those involved in teaching the students and the co-operative steps of guidance thus continues.

Group guidance for the superior students follows the pattern for

[5] *Education of the Gifted*, *ibid.*, pp. 69–70.

the body as a whole. First-year counseling has to do chiefly with orientation and adjustment to school regime and democratic living with mates. Guidance during this period is in the hands of social living teachers. During the second year, special stress is upon guidance in the value of education *versus* dropping out of school as soon as it is possible to obtain jobs. As juniors, the students are guided through the beginnings of surveys of suitable colleges and possible vocations. As seniors, the consideration of careers and colleges best suited for preparation for particular careers is intensified, with the guidance office lending its aid with its accessibility to up-to-date college catalogues, *etc.*

Because group guidance often leaves something to be desired for fast-learning students, they are given individual counsel by special teachers appointed to that function. If an individual student seems to need it, he is guided into leadership classes where he may work and assume responsibilities in small groups. He is exposed to experiences that take into consideration physical, emotional, and social levels of development as well as intellectual abilities and interests.

In this school in-service-training programs for teachers, administrators, and parents interested in helping gifted children are in process constantly. With such concentrated attention upon instructing and counseling the gifted, teaching methods contribute to the success of guidance. Some samples of immediate guidance teaching in mathematics, life science, and English are described briefly.

MATHEMATICS

During the development of the basic concepts of equations in a first-year algebra class, the teacher's attention was called to the five rapid learners in his class. It is always a challenge to see what brilliant minds will do with a new phase of mathematics and the opportunity to try often brightens the subject for the brilliant minds. Unanimous enthusiasm was the reply from the five when the teacher suggested some special meetings to learn a little calculus.

The procedure evolved intense interest in functional mathematics for the pupils. During the first meeting, they began by taking a simple quadratic equation $y = x^2 + 2x + 1$, and letting y be the symbol for any change y might undergo, and x be the symbol for the change in x which produced the change in y. By the standard procedure in every college math book, teacher and student developed the formula for the exact rate of change of y with respect to x at any point on the curve of the equation.

Though there was no problem of lack of interest in the mathematics, the teacher played on the prevailing interest in science fiction by setting up problems involving the path and speed of a comet, or the acceleration of a space ship in free fall that approaches planets with gravity that is a multiple or a fraction of that of the earth. Later, when the trigonometric ratios — sine, co-sine, tangent, *etc.*, — had been covered in the algebra course, the special students learned how to differentiate trigonometric functions and worked with some simple harmonic motion problems such as those they will encounter in physics. These same students in geometry class the following year look at a proposition and see very quickly the plan by which they will prove it.

LIFE SCIENCE

The teacher began working with two gifted girls on special and standard microscope slide types which involve plant and animal whole mounts, cross-sections, and longitudinal sections. In addition to the science information acquired and curiosity aroused, familiarity with the standard Spencer microscope will be built up. Further enrichment consisted of: vocational guidance in the medical field; aid and guidance in extra reading; trips of biological interest with the science club; development of some type of biological hobbies; and availability of the teacher's own library of biological books.

ENGLISH

Leadership training is encouraged by dividing the class into groups of four to six students with gifted students as leaders, the primary purpose being to give training in planning group procedures, organizing materials, the art of good questioning and of maneuvering conversations and recitations, encouraging discussion, directing debate, and searching for new and more intensive fields of study for the group, thereby, for the leader himself.

CREATIVE WRITING

Gifted students with intense interest in a particular type of creative writing are encouraged to practice in that field instead of to do the daily assignments of compositions and exercises unless some marked deficiency is displayed. The desire for individual writing occurred in the case of a talented girl who writes and illustrates children's stories, a boy who writes poetry, and another girl who writes impressionistic essays. All three have done class exercises well, but much more time has been spent on their individual efforts at creative writing.

It appears this faculty does not hesitate to help pupils in advanced study of a subject or a phase of learning in which genuine interest is evident. If a tenth-grade student comprehends and can profit by using twelfth-grade material in his research, there will be no further heights to climb when he reaches them. The welfare of gifted pupils can but be safe in the hands of teachers and counselors who strive genuinely for the promotion of that welfare under an entire school's spirit of interest.

Reading in the Social Studies

The BULLETIN's title, "Reading for Gifted Students in High School," is not a misnomer although discussion is not confined to instruction in English literature. Much written material of other types contributes to both the cultural and the practical education of gifted individuals. Probably no other subject in the curriculum has so rich a supply of resource material as do the social studies. This is true not only of textbooks, of which there are many for the student to consult and compare for specific data. There are rich supplies of current books, periodicals, newspapers, *etc.*, which give up-to-date information about current socio-economic problems.

The problem for parents and instructors, interested public and curriculum experts, is what should constitute both basic courses and enrichment material for the avid minds of pupils who should be prepared for future leadership. For teachers who are privileged to guide the learning experiences of the gifted, methods of instruction are definite problems. Courses of study may stipulate what shall be taught, and at what time in the school life of pupils any particular phase of a subject shall be presented. Authority decides what textbooks shall be used. Fortunately, methods of enriching instruction and many materials are at the discretion of creative instructors. They know the purposes of teaching the social studies. They know too the futility of teaching content subjects with the expectation that facts in any one text repeated in class recitations will be remembered after the book has been returned to the shelf. Teachers know the importance of training in skill in various kinds and aspects of reading such as the use of reference books, in taking notes and organizing ideas, and in making bibliographies.

Particularly apt to a discussion of enrichment of social studies is a paragraph written by two New York educators active in that city's work with gifted pupils. Helen L. Cohen and Nancy G. Coryell wrote:

> The aims of education for gifted children should include mastery of the techniques of reflective thinking, a sense of responsibility for translating ideas into socially valuable action, a sense of morality in public affairs

expressing itself through disinterested criticism of men and policies and through civic action of a high order, productive industry for the common welfare, and enrichment of life through increased sensitiveness to beauty and through increased diversification and correlation of cultural interests.

One other large American city school system expressed itself concerning its active program in the education of students of high mental ability as follows:

Enrichment programs for superior students are of a more mature nature than is possible or appropriate for average pupils. The reading materials are more advanced and the research and investigation is of a more searching type.

Enrichment programs give the superior students more opportunity to develop analyzing, organizing, and generalizing abilities. They encourage independence of thought and action in the approach to school-wide and school activities.

Enrichment programs seek to utilize and encourage the individual talents of students. Special projects for groups and individuals contribute to interest on the part of the students and the class as a whole. The class where talents are used takes on added life and meaning. Realization is fostered, on the part of the superior student, that he has a responsibility for sharing his understanding and abilities. . . . Exercise of this responsibility brings opportunities for practicing leadership and worth-while group membership.

Ideals for teachers of English-social studies are expressed in a *Progress Report No. II* of the *Co-operative Program for Students with Exceptional Endowment* in the Portland public schools. (This is the program for well-endowed students that is being carried on co-operatively by the Portland schools and Reed College. It is aided financially by the Ford Fund.) The "ideals" are quoted here for the reason that they are expressions of the belief of a school system that is practicing what it preaches.

The philosophy that governs any enrichment program necessitates cognizance of the valuable characteristics of well-endowed students. Programs of enrichment must differ from the regular programs in quantity but more essentially in quality. They must provide for pleasurable practice in the development of those mental gifts so valuable to the world. That is: they must provide the materials and the activities that will promote growth in clear understanding and critical thinking; that will foster initiative and originality in solving problems and in making plans following generalizations and well-drawn conclusions.

It is sometimes maintained that learning experiences for the gifted differ not so much in kind, but in variety, depth, and level of advancement. Without doubt the interests of the gifted are intense and persistent, and there is obvious challenge for the pupil in the attempt to solve problems in which he is interested. The challenge to the teacher lies in seeing that gifted pupils find, in the content subjects they must study, problems to be solved through research, reports, discussions, and application of generalizations.

If the purpose for the pupil in studying the social studies is to acquire knowledge of the subject matter, it must be conceded that facts made use of in the learning are more apt to become tools of acquisition of further knowledge than are those read and recited by rote. If the purpose of social studies courses in the curriculum is the enrichment of reading experiences, the end is accomplished by those creative teachers who see in every course not the limitations, but the wide fields for enrichment. They are the teachers who know their subjects and are interested in them; but they also know gifted pupils and are interested in their development through the course of instruction.

The Portland high schools conduct seminars in social studies by which they hope to "encourage and sharpen intellectual interest." Informality is encouraged within the group in choice of activities. Discussion in the group arises from individual study and reports on related topics or various aspects of a common problem. The method leads to informal exchange and criticism in the whole group or to a summarizing of the problem by a special panel. In general, lecturing, recitation by question and answer, and emphasis upon cut-and-dried answers are not approved.

A seminar course, a project, or a problem to investigate may be selected as a teaching method with rich benefit to the reading of the students. In situations where enrichment for the exceptional pupil must be carried on in regular classes, the pupil may select the field in which he is interested, as do the selected pupils in the "Independent Study" plan at Modesto High School, and he and his teachers may make up his reading list.

The goal is improvement, commensurate with the pupils' ability to learn, in knowledge of subject matter of particular courses and in acquaintance with and critical appreciation of books and periodicals. The most direct and surest way to the double goal is through some type of problem solving or research.

Superior students, in heterogeneous classes, or in more fortunate circumstances will, with the teacher's encouragement, elect to do research and report findings to the group. They will read the books in the room library, the school library, and the public library. If the topic under study is one of present interest, they will come to know periodical literature. If adequate opportunity is afforded for intelligent discussion in school and at home, two things will be accomplished. Critical judgment will be fostered and knowledge of facts will improve.

SOME SUCCESSFUL PROJECTS OF GIFTED GROUPS

The inventory of problems from which to choose is much wider than appears at first thought. The happy selection may grow out of the interest of pupils in some particular phase of the designated course for a particular semester. United States history as told in fiction, biography, and poetry was selected by one group because two intelligent boys questioned whether an historical novel pictured events and conditions truthfully. Of course the question was impossible of a satisfying answer by comparing one history text with one historical novel. The selection of history texts, geographies, biographies, and travel books grew to a small library. Eventually, the pupils and the teacher decided that the study of American history could be motivated through the writing and staging of a pageant of history as pictured in poetry and historical fiction. Not only was the pageant written and produced for the school and interested parents, but also the impact upon the reading habits of the pupils increased the purchase of books in the homes and the neighborhood public library.

Of course the story of the writing of the pictured episodes that made up the pageant belongs to the section on English. However, the creative writing that becomes a part of every well-selected project in social studies is an argument for that method of instruction.

The New York Joint Council on Economic Education recently published a pamphlet description of a unit on *International Trade* which was the basis of the social studies course for a ninth-grade group. The study began in a current events period when the teacher pointed out the prominence of international trade in the news. From that it grew to be a genuine research into the problem: "In the light of contemporary political and economic difficulties, how can we promote world trade and, thereby, increase the standard of living of all people of the world?" In developing their topic the pupils asked such questions as: Why should we import cheese when we can make our own? Why should we spend money developing backward countries? Wouldn't it be better if we were self-sufficient? and How can the dock strike affect me?

Such questions asked of gifted pupils would incite research through reading somewhat beyond the comprehension of the askers. The gifted would get what is desired for individuals of their mental capacity — exposure to and use of books and documents in settling their problems. They would not need a lecturer to explain that different countries must trade with each other because of differences in climate, other national resources, labor efficiency, *etc*. They would go on to answer the "hows" and "whys" of the present limitations, economic and political, on international trade. They would have learned that the source of information is available in print.

The capable teacher who succeeded so well with the "Pilot Project" with an average group in New York would undoubtedly have challenged the gifted in the group to rich reading experiences. These students would have learned the value of current industrial and political literature of their own country and of those with whom exchange of trade was under discussion.

"An Up-to-date Course in American History" is the title given to an experience in teaching gifted tenth-grade students. It is described by the United States Department of Health, Education, and Welfare. There are indications that the same or like courses would be especially helpful and interesting to students of exceptional ability in heterogeneous classes. It happened that the pupils of whom the author is writing had studied some phases of United States history before reaching the tenth grade. There they were faced with their state's requirement for a year of American history. They wanted to study "present problems" instead of chronological history. "The teacher found a cue in the fact that every problem of importance in the field of American history is a recurring one. The mere possibility of such a condition so challenged the pupils that they set to work on listing such problems and classifying them under general headings. Their list of eight problems that recurrently came up for solution from the year 1830 to the present date was:

1. Democracy engages in social reform.
2. Democracy engages in social conflict.
3. Economic revolution overtakes democracy.
4. Democracy establishes a world power.
5. Reforming democracy; the progressive era.
6. Mobilization to make the world safe for democracy.
7. Democracy again engages in social reform.
8. A world-wide struggle for democracy.

"Each of these units is full of present-day issues. The study of the foreign policy of the United States, of imperialistic trends for world domination, of inter-American developments, of social security measures, of labor issues fired the students with enthusiasm for attacking present-day problems on the basis of careful research and consideration of all the elements involved."

An activity such as this inevitably affords valuable opportunities for co-operative work of faculty members. The librarians would concentrate on collecting and displaying material relating to subject under study. English teachers would make lists and book collections of American literature to parallel the events of history. Public speaking teachers could make their assignments from the historical events and encourage the students to rehearse reports in speech classes before making them to their fellows in the history section. Above all, the attention of prospective leaders was focused on some of the problems of democracy and on possible solutions for them. The project necessitated much more reading of a purposeful type than would the traditional course in history.

Teachers desiring to enrich the learning of gifted pupils, even in heterogeneous classes, will see the possibilities for small groups or individual "independent study" in problem solving experiences similar to those sketched. Even the pageant of history through fiction and poetry could be written and ready for production by one highly gifted person. The value of co-operative effort would be lost and the writer would be just another one whose work failed of publication. However, the facts of history would have been learned and acquaintance with books would have been extended and intensified.

Government and civics, as each pertains to community living, are quite interesting to high-school students. Perhaps "Boys Week," with the opportunity for boys to occupy the positions of political officers, is effective in arousing interest. To be mayor for a day is worth the study it requires to be informed about the duties of the office. The government of a city or a state touches the life of secondary-school students at so many points that interest is easily sustained. However, the history or the science of government challenges the understanding of gifted pupils.

Dr. Leta Hollingsworth, noted authority on gifted children, supervised a remarkable learning project with a group of very superior pupils in an experimental school in New York City. The problem was "The Growth of Law and Order." The study began with consideration of such simple thoughts as why rules are necessary in homes and schools, *etc.* It extended to the Constitution of the United States in its historical and political aspects and significance. The study covered an entire year with many visits to see government in operation and many worn out books.

On one of the days I visited the class, three boys who had returned from a visit to Washington were discussing the supreme court. It was a very interesting free discussion with many pointed questions and much note taking. Each pupil had a notebook well worth examination. Notes were classified, for example: Supreme Court.

Visited by — with the names of the reporting students. It was evident that the purpose of a visit was always the study of a single phase of their topic.

The library was distinctly a political science library where people studied. It bore testimony to the amount of reading that was being done. In addition, the library of Columbia University was open to this group of students because the group was under the auspices of the University.

This was ideal teaching under almost ideal conditions. However, it is easy to imagine studies of some question of government that is of somewhat general present interest; for example, a change in the manner of electing the President of the United States. It could be undertaken by one student or a group of students who would report to the class. In all probability the study would make familiar the constitutional provisions about elections and incidentally about constitutional amendments. The consideration of a topic of this sort would introduce a whole field of books and periodicals.

Geography with its many branches, physical, mathematical, biological, political, *etc.*, has fascination for intelligent students, especially when some question arises because of an experience of the students themselves. The experience may be actual or it may be the result of reading. So many news items and so many books about recent troubles in southern Africa could be the incentive for studying the geography of Africa. So, too, the deeply disturbing question of too much or too little water could lead to a study of the nature and value of rivers. That would necessitate a growing knowledge of geography. As a probable result, the pupils might become interested in reading the series of charming books about great rivers.

Sociology, the comparatively new science so prominent in American education, would arouse little interest in the mind of the average high-school pupil. Its deep subject matter involving so many causes and effects would be a direct challenge to the more mature minds of gifted students. They would find many questions and do much research in attempting to answer them.

The purpose of the committee, in compiling this bulletin, is not to present a catalogue of possible projects or problems. It is not to outline a method of instruction. It is rather to erect sign boards along the widening new road to satisfying the acute needs of gifted pupils for adequate education. These sign posts point to more purposeful reading as one of the direct routes.

BIBLIOGRAPHY OF SOCIAL STUDIES MATERIAL FOR TEACHERS

Books

Benns, T. L. *Europe Since 1914: In Its World Setting.* 7th edition. New York: Appleton-Century-Crofts, Inc. 1949. 770 pp. Comprehensive, well-written book. One of the two or three best on the period. Deservedly popular.

Brown, Ralph H. *Historical Geography of the United States.* New York: Harcourt; Brace and Company, Inc. 1958. 596 pp. A very readable book, tracing the history of the growth of the United States, of which a reviewer says, "A grand book, perhaps a must book for teachers of American history."

Christensen, A. M., and Kirkpatrick, E. M. *The People; Politics, and the Politicians*, revised edition. New York: Henry Holt and Company, Inc. 1950. 1,042 pp. Professional political scientists present facts and ideas valuable for the general reader to know. Especially useful for teachers and students.

Coon, Carleton S., editor. *A Reader in General Anthropology.* New York: Henry Holt and Company, Inc. 1948. 624 pp. Systematic, readable. A useful book for teachers of anthropology, sociology, and history.

Curti, M. *The Growth of American Thought.* New York: Harper and Brothers. 1943. 848 pp. Still a valuable book for the teacher's library. It is a valuable tool for the vitalization of high-school history courses with the introduction of the development of American ideals.

Dicken, Samuel Newton. *A Regional Economic Geography.* Boston: D. C. Heath and Company. 1949. 516 pp. Pressing current problems are given particular attention in this well-illustrated textbook that is probably economic geography.

Goodrich, Leland M., and Hambro, Edward. *Charter of the United Nations: Commentary and Documents*, 2nd revised edition. Boston: World Peace Foundation. 1949. 726 pp. The book analyzes the constitution, article by article, and supplies recent significant documents related to the U.N. Very useful in courses in history, world problems, *etc.*

Heaton, Herbert. *Economic History of Europe*, revised edition. New York: Harper and Brothers. 1948. 792 pp. A one-volume treatise, scholarly, richly illustrated, a first choice for the teacher's personal library.

MacIver, R. M. *The Ramparts We Guard.* New York: Macmillan Company. 1950. 152 pp. An interpretation of democracy — a call to defend it from its enemies. For all social studies teachers.

McCune, George M. *Korea Today.* Cambridge, Mass: Harvard University Press. 1950. 372 pp. A leading scholar has written a timely book on the history, economy, and government of Korea. He assesses the policy of America and of the Soviet in Korea since the war. This book is rated as the best on the subject.

Ogburn, William F., and Nimkoff, Meyer F. *Sociology*, 2nd edition. Boston: Houghton Mifflin Company. 1950. 606 pp. A general survey of sociology that is very popular with students. It is usable in sociology, economics, and social problems classes.

Ogg, Frederick A., and Zink, Harold. *Modern Foreign Governments.* New York: Macmillan Company. 1949. 1,004 pp. This is a factional delineation of the historical development of the political systems of the major countries of Europe. Very good background material.

Ranney, John C., and Carter, Gwendolin M. *The Major Foreign Powers: The Governments of Great Britain, France, the Soviet Union, and China.* New York: Harcourt, Brace and Company, Inc. 1949. 865 pp. This is a well-organized treatise on comparative government of the countries whose political policies it is necessary to understand in the struggle for world peace. It is said to be the best single book of its kind.

Van Doren, Carl. *The Great Rehearsal: The Story of the Making and Ratifying of the Constitution of the United States.* New York: Viking Press. 1948. 336 pp. The author points to the similarity of positions between the American colonies and many nations in the world today. Thoroughly readable.

Vaughn, Wayland F. *Social Psychology: The Science and the Art of Living.* New York: Odyssey Press, Inc. 1948. 956 pp. Since the social studies teacher is obligated to know at least one good book on social psychology and the social sciences, this is an excellent one to know. It is readable, practical, general, and particularly valuable to teachers of problems, sociology, and social living courses.

Wesley, Edgar B. *Teaching Social Studies in High Schools,* 3rd edition. Boston: D. C. Heath and Company. 1950. 594 pp. This text, maintaining the high standard of the first two editions, is a constant source of help to teachers, both experienced and inexperienced.

Doob, Leonard W. *Public Opinion and Propaganda.* New York: Henry Holt and Company, Inc. 1948. 600 pp. Inclusive, and a generally readable treatment of a subject of great importance to the social studies teachers. In teaching recent history and modern problems courses, the book will be particularly useful.

Periodicals

American Sociological Review. American Sociological Society, Maurice R. Davie, ed., Hall of Graduate Studies, Yale University, New Haven, Conn. Bi-monthly. Teachers will find this the most satisfactory general magazine in sociology. Book reviews are good. One issue each year publishes a list of research projects in process.

The American Political Science Review, American Political Science Association, Taylor Cole, ed., Duke University, Durham, N. C. Quarterly. An excellent journal publishing articles on a wide range of political science topics. It is the best magazine in its field for the high-school teacher.

Geographical Review, American Geographical Society of New York, Wilma B. Fairchild, ed., Broadway and 156th Street, New York 32. Quarterly. A very attractive scholarly journal. Good book reviews. Useful to all social studies teachers.

The American Historical Review, American Historical Association, Guy Stanton Ford, ed., Study Room 274, Library of Congress, Washington 25, D. C. Quarterly. Each issue contains about three long articles in the field of history, excellent book reviews, *etc.* Excellent publication, the best in the field.

Social Education, National Council for the Social Studies, Lewis Paul Todd, ed., 1201 Sixteenth Street, N. W., Washington 6, D. C. Monthly, October through May. If the social studies teacher reads only one magazine on education, it should be this one. It deals with all fields, in methods, units, content, devices, *etc.* The magazine has sections on books, audio-visual aids, government pamphlets, and news of social studies happenings.

Reading in the Sciences

The teacher of science is able to make use of the rich variety of human and physical resources available in the environment. As a result, the science classroom becomes a learning laboratory. The exhibits, displays, reading materials, and projects found in the well-organized science classroom present a challenge to the gifted to experiment and to investigate. Interest is one of the primary factors in creating and developing a desire to learn. Devices such as the "unexplained demonstration" are useful in stimulating reading for further information. For example, the teacher might prepare a simple demonstration illustrating pressure. This device could then be set up in the room with a card asking, "What happened?" or "Why?". Or, the teacher might read an interesting newspaper article, show a film, or perform some simple experiment to provoke questioning. Having thus aroused interest, the teacher guides the discussion and assists the pupils in exploring the various areas of investigation and in selecting appropriate reading materials for further study. To work effectively pupils should develop efficient reading habits.[6]

I. Locating Specific Information
   A. The Textbook
      1. Locating material in the index
      2. Cross references
      3. Table of contents
      4. Glossary
      5. Interpreting figures, pictures, and diagrams
      6. Reading and interpreting footnotes
      7. Topic headings and running headings
   B. Supplementary or Reference Materials
      1. Handbooks, yearbooks, almanacs
      2. Bibliographies
      3. Government publications and industrial publications
      4. Magazines, pamphlets, and newspapers
      5. Dictionaries and encyclopedias

[6] cf The *45th Yearbook* of the National Society for the Study of Education, 1947, Part I.

II. Interpreting Reference Material
  A. Aids in Understanding Reference Material
    1. Finding main ideas in the paragraph
    2. Following main ideas over several paragraphs
    3. Recognizing words or phrases that in themselves are concepts or processes
    4. Skimming intelligently for main ideas, by words or phrases
    5. Determining the meaning of new words from context
    6. Taking notes while reading
    7. Outlining a topic
    8. Summarizing and showing how it applies to the solution of the problem
    9. Summarizing or interpreting in one's own words material from text
  B. Interpreting Graphic Materials
    1. Obtaining information from various types of graphic material, such as circle graphs, bar graphs, histograms, line graphs, and pictorial graphs
    2. Noting relationships shown between factors
    3. Evaluating conclusions based upon data recorded
  C. Solving Mathematical Problems Necessary in Obtaining Pertinent Data
    1. Understanding metric and English measure
    2. Understanding the mathematical terms used in the problem
    3. Applying essential formulas

III. Problem-Solving Through Observing and Reading
  A. Setting Up a Demonstration
    1. Selecting materials and equipment needed
    2. Working out the demonstration procedure
  B. Observing the Demonstration
    1. Identifying the important facts in the demonstration
  C. Selecting the Important Ideas Presented in Graphic Illustrations, Models, Displays, Pictures, Slides, Motion Pictures
  D. Verifying Results Through Selected Reading
  E. Organizing and Classifying Material
  F. Making Conclusions, Generalizations

The gifted pupil should be encouraged to gather information bearing on the problem from a wide variety of sources. Teachers can help pupils learn to be critical about books as authoritative sources of information by calling their attention to the reliability and recency of information; for example, copyright date, author's background, academic degrees, and position. It will be necessary, in varying degrees, for the science teacher to assume some responsibility for teaching the pupil the skills of reading, such as reading for exact information, comprehension, retention, and differentiating between reading for recreation and analytical reading. The teacher can help develop these skills by provoking questions and eliciting ideas. He might ask the pupil to find what point the author is trying to make and how this bears on the solution of the problem.

Background knowledge acquired through guided reading is the basis for further investigation. The reading table or reference bookshelf becomes an important part of the science room. There should be readily available within the school library sufficient science resource materials to facilitate even wider reading. Scientific magazines, industrial publications, and textbooks of college and adult level are the natural tools for the gifted pupil.

Purposeful or goal-direction reading is essential for the proper intellectual growth of the gifted student, but all work and no play leads to intellectual stagnation. Let us consider provision for what might be called "free reading." If the pupil is to enjoy his educational experience in science, he should be permitted to browse in areas of particular interest to himself, and encouraged to venture off the main topic into regions yet unexplored by him.

The study of science is not limited to the investigation and solution of problems alone. The pupil is able to develop an appreciation for science through the study of the history of science and its broad applications. To stimulate interest in the social implications of science, the teacher may ask broad questions, such as "What contributions has science made to the progress of civilization?" or "What has science done toward the improvement of health?"

Development of these appreciations requires wide reading and discussion in order to arrive at this broad understanding. Some additional areas of general interest might be: (1) examples of problem-solving used by scientists in the past, (2) application of scientific inventions in daily activities, (3) sciences and the conservation of natural resources, (4) science and the consumer, (5) the role of science in human relations, (6) science and mental and emotional health, (7) the role of science in social and economic problems, (8) present developments in science, and (9) the frontiers of science.

SOURCES OF SCIENCE MATERIAL SUITABLE FOR GIFTED PUPILS AT SECONDARY LEVEL

Magazines

Science Newsletter — 9th to 12th grades
Scientific American — 10th to 12th grades; especially for the following departments: the amateur scientist, science and the citizen, and book reviews (suggestions for reading)
Natural History — 8th to 12th grades; book reviews
Things of Science — Science Service — 7th to 9th grades

Free Materials from Industry

(Write for educational materials)

General Electric Co., 212 North Vignes, Los Angeles, California
Adventures Ahead — bi-monthly for teenagers
Motors
Turbines

Westinghouse Electric Corporation, 306 Fourth Ave., Pittsburgh, Pa.

American Iron and Steel Institute, 350 Fifth Ave., New York 1, N. Y.
Steelways — bi-monthly magazine

E. I. DuPont de Nemours and Co., Wilmington, Delaware

Firestone Tire and Rubber Co., Akron 17, Ohio

American Petroleum Institute, 50 West 50th St., New York 20, N. Y.

If we are to gain a wider appreciation for science, then we must take the opportunity to explore the various areas of science from the purely factual to the fanciful. Scarcely a major technological advance exists that was not at one time a projected image in someone's mind. New discoveries and inventions are outgrowths of man's imagination, thinking, and reasoning integrated with his factual knowledge to produce usable ideas and devices. Effective intellectual growth is achieved when individuals can exchange freely their thoughts and ideas, interpreting and modifying the ideas in the process. For this reason, the gifted should be encouraged to read science fiction in its place. It is through the spark of an imaginative idea that man has been able to improve his environment and himself.

Language and Literature for the Gifted

GROUPING BY ABILITY

In the subject field of English, segregated classes of a limited size and with a competent teacher have proved more likely to succeed in challenging the abilities and meeting the needs of the gifted in secondary school. The large range of abilities in the usual English class, together with its enormous size — 40 students or more — allows the teacher little time to give the rapid learners the attention they need. Activities suitable to the average student are too easily or quickly performed by the able. The necessary reteaching and repetition of basic principles of language structure are unstimulating, become boring. While the rest of the class is struggling to understand a story line, to perceive the interweaving of plots in a novel, to look up new words, fathom figurative language, the able student may fail to perform at all because the pace is too slow, or he may never ask the questions which his deeper insight prompts.

If he insists on pursuing a driving interest, two results are likely:

the teacher is obliged to allow him to work on alone, or students of lesser ability are inhibited by his swiftness and comprehension. Neither outcome is best for the bright student, for the class, or for the teacher. The gifted student does not have sufficient competition to challenge his real abilities, the rest of the class comes to rely on him for the "right answers" rather than work up to their best achievement, and the teacher feels he is not effectively meeting the needs of all the students. The able student runs the risk of becoming conceited, frivolous, unpopular, or all three; the class, of becoming lax in its work; the teacher, of becoming "fragmented."

In a smaller class where all the students are of superior ability, a more demanding regime is possible. Especially in a subject like English, this arrangement produces better results. In Portland, Oregon, where this system is being worked out in collaboration with Reed College and supported in part by grants from the Fund for the Advancement of Education of the Ford Foundation,[7] evaluation of the project by parents, teachers, and students indicates improved results and all-round satisfaction. A typical teacher comments: "I can move faster, farther, and deeper into subject matter, demand more student contribution to the course."

IMPORTANCE OF THE TEACHER

Dr. Arthur Gates has written: "In my opinion, no assignment in the entire school curriculum calls for more intelligence and artistry than the teaching of reading and literature." Success or failure of the class rests largely on the teacher's ability. To inspire a genuine interest and to develop a love of literature are her main task. The purpose is not to impart merely a *knowledge* of literature, for it is possible to learn a great many facts about authors, types, periods, "aspects," and "influences," and still have only a nodding acquaintance with literature. Of course, one comes to know a great many of these things while learning to understand literature and to enjoy reading books of worth. But we have ample evidence, as Robert Pooley has said, that it is possible to teach knowledge about literature without developing any love of it; indeed, often to the development of positive dislike.

One of the best equipments for the teaching of English is a well-tempered enthusiasm based on love and solid knowledge of the classics. So equipped, the teacher will have a sound base for appraising contemporary writing, which he also must know in order to guide the reading of his students. It is essential in teaching literature to grasp and pass on the richness and freshness of the

[7] Wilson, Robert C., "The Under-Educated and How We Have Neglected the Bright Child." *Atlantic Monthly*, May, 1955, p. 60 ff.

writer's creative imagination. This involves commentary, which can be lethal if inexpertly or clumsily handled. Too much praise or too much teacher interpretation of a work not read or imperfectly understood by the students may result in a loss of desire to read it. The teacher must have unusual sensitivity in recognizing potentialities — in work being studied and in the various students in the class. She must be adept in asking the kind of questions which will lead them to search eagerly for the truth by personal effort. Again, a question or a remark will stimulate the class to see the symbolic meaning beneath the facts, to find the personal meaning for them which the author has intended. Literature is for delight, but even gifted students do not usually discover this in high school — unless they have a gifted teacher.

APPROACH TO LITERATURE

"It seems to me," Dora V. Smith has said, "that literature has two missions — one is to enrich the human spirit of the individual, and the other is to give social understanding. In our program, I believe the two are equally important." The gifted student, with his intense desire to know, his deep and varied interest in ideas, long span of attention, and ability to recognize relationships and to generalize, is quite capable of winning the enrichment of spirit and understanding of people and society which literature offers.

He should, however, have the opportunity to read literature which will convey these values to him now, in his present state of maturity. Like all other young people, he too has problems of coming to terms with himself, his family, and the world. He does not have to read *all* the masterpieces at an early age. At the secondary-school level, the intensive reading of a small number of selections, carefully chosen for the problems of understanding which they present, suitable to the particular members of the class, and related to the times, is the correct method. At the same time, a planned program of individual reading can be developed.

In working out the objectives of the course, the teacher and students should plan together. Careful testing will indicate whether practice is required in needed areas. After using a standardized test, the teacher should make informal tests to help individual students see what they need to learn. Many bright students are prone to make careless preliminary analyses of a selection, select approximate but inaccurate answers, ignore complexity of structure, substituting their own arrangement of the elements of a sentence or paragraph. Again, they often have difficulty with metaphors and symbolism. They lack a sense of literary form, reading, for example, a poem as if it were a literal statement, or a play or essay as if it were a story. Able as they are, they have something to learn.

In regard to the study skills of reading, these can more economically be practiced where they are most needed — in social studies, science, mathematics, and other classes where reading for information — using many pamphlets, books, and magazines is necessary. When, however, in connection with the study of literature, the students have occasion to use these skills, the teacher of English will give them guidance. These include: (1) the organizational skills, such as note-taking, outlining, finding main ideas; (2) rate skills, such as adjusting rate to purpose; (3) locational skills, like using the index, the card catalog, the *Readers' Guide;* and (4) critical skills, such as reading for inferences, recognizing the author's intent.

The special skills of reading literature require time for their development — and an expert guide. "There are moments in literature which do not yield the secret of their power to any study of language, because the power does not depend on language but on the moral imagination. . . . The moral imagination is not the imagination of violence or of nescience . . . it is not literary depth psychology. It is the imagination that gives us *Anna Karenina*, *Mansfield Park*, the letters of Keats, the dramatic strength of Dickens."[8]

That the student may learn that love of literature increases, not diminishes, love of life, he should have the opportunity for a sympathetic sharing of experience. In class, this means planning together, reading some selections as a class, fruitful discussion, and evaluation together. By developing the habit of responsibility for choosing individual reading that is worth while, and the habit of being critical, students discover many values. The first class experience should be reading a selection not too long, in order to allow expression and to develop discussion powers. After reading a story, they evaluate it in some such terms as these:[9]

1. How well does the selection communicate human experience?
2. How true are the assumptions that are made about human nature?
3. How important is the experience that is being communicated?
4. What is the quality of the language of the selection?

The last question is the most difficult to answer, but all four have implications for the teacher and the class in making their selections of what to read, in organizing the work so that a sense of progress can be felt, and in developing activities to integrate experience.

[8] Trilling, Lionel. *The Opposing Self*. New York 17: Viking Press. 1955. 248 pp.

[9] Carlsen, George Robert, "The Dimensions of Literature," *The English Journal*, Vol. XLI, No. 4, April, 1952.

BUILDING AN ATTITUDE

Although the students may have the capability of learning to read and understand a great poem or novel, bringing them to the task is frequently challenging. In other words, an attitude has to be developed, just as in ordinary classes. Among the most able high-school students are those who prefer reading factual material, science or history, and who have developed a youthful disdain for stories or poetry as being merely escape reading, fanciful stuff, unimportant to the serious business of life. That a work of art creates real persons, and that understanding it makes the same demands upon the reader as those required by a judge of people is something that only extended experience with great literature can teach them.

To lead them to that maturing experience, the teacher educes the realization that the work under consideration is worthy of attention and respect. They will grow to the appreciation that reward is proportionate to effort. Once the teacher has enlisted the pride of the students, their reluctance to be beaten in understanding a selection, their self-esteem, is challenged. With the sense of success with the work, their involuntary interest becomes voluntary. Of course, every teacher knows this. The initial problem is how to make the right reading — that is, the actual meaning of the lines — more satisfying than any other meaning.

One way is to suggest to the class that no writer supplies the full background for the reader. He cannot, for always the major part must be left for the reader to bring in. Assign the reading of a ballad such as "Edward, Edward," or "Old Christmas" as a challenge. Some preliminary questions may be asked to ensure that students know how to read poetry, perhaps some guidance, with examples from other poems, of the question-and-answer type of ballad, some leading questions such as "What happened?" "To whom did it happen?" After the reading, the students ask the questions. Then they re-read to answer their own questions. After that, the teacher asks a few penetrating questions, especially in the case of "Old Christmas," which send them back to the poem again. Finally, the meaning comes out, elicited by the class itself.

That the reader has to bring a great deal of understanding to the writing is next elaborated by means of a short prose selection, which the students are to restate. The first paragraph of Mark Twain's "Our Guides," from *Innocents Abroad*, is an easy one, but affords the opportunity for a number of questions about tone, what to expect on reading further, and the like. Or a paragraph from St.-Exupéry can be used, one which contains action and reflection, suspense and implications. Restating such paragraphs in one's own words forms an introduction to the writer's art, in short, to rhetoric, grammar, and logic — the first three liberal arts. But it is probably not necessary to mention this.

UNDERSTANDING SYMBOLISM

So many modern stories and novels make use of symbolism, that some practice in discernment of this device is perhaps necessary. A story like James Street's "Weep No More, My Lady," (now enlarged into a whole book, *Good-bye, My Lady*) is more than a magnificent dog story. It is even more than a moving evocation of life in the swamps of Mississippi. A small boy reaches, through poignant disappointment, a sudden spurt towards maturity through learning what is due society. But at a deeper level, the entire story suggests the plight of man as he struggles through life trying to know right and wrong and his destiny.

When students have learned to look for the deeper meaning, they will enjoy stories and novels which reward reading with insight. Anthologies like *Short Stories for Our Times*, by Certner and Henry, (Houghton, Mifflin), and *Great Short Stories*, by Schramm, (Harcourt, Brace), are useful, as also the *Atlantic Monthly*, *Harper's*, and the Scholastic magazine, *Literary Cavalcade*.

READING PLAYS

Another beginning is to tackle the reading of a play. Unless they have had experience, and despite their familiarity with the motion pictures and television, even gifted students do not know how to read drama from the printed page. Take one of Shakespeare's that they have not seen, for example. With these students, they might be asked to start reading, say, *Merchant of Venice*, without preliminary help, and silently. After they have read the first scene, ask them some questions: "When the curtain goes up, what does the stage setting look like? What action is taking place? How old are these people in the play? What is their attitude to one another? What mood are they in? When does the mood change? What does the scene accomplish for the audience?" The answers to these questions will indicate what explanations and descriptions are necessary before the re-reading of the scene aloud by the teacher (who reads aloud excellently well). Now come the questions as to Shakespeare's language, the meaning of essential figures of speech, and the like. Not, however, so many as to impede the interest, for the play must go on rapidly.

The characters take on reality as discussion reveals their motivation and truth to life as shown by what they say, what others say about them, and what they, in fact, do. As the problem that each faces leads to the fateful turning-point of the action, suspense increases. The language of the play enchants the ear, then amazes by its variety and depth of meaning, the economy of expression. Acting out of scenes, memorizing famous passages increase enjoyment.

Some acquaintance with literature is desirable before reading Shakespeare in order that the reading be not impeded by too many stops for explanation. That is, students should be able to recognize a figure of speech, even if the explanation of it takes a little time. Before proceeding, the teacher may give a list of unusual words or word-meanings found in the scenes to be read, as *in sooth, fond* for foolish, *ope* for open, *an* for if, *moe* for more, building up a vocabulary for reading Shakespeare. But from the first they must be able to see the characters, the settings, and to image the action from the words. Reading aloud of important scenes is necessary to appreciate the particular power of the dramatic form, the resounding impact of Marlowe's mighty line, and to visualize the action. Only after reading and interpreting the play or part of the play for themselves should they hear recordings or see films. Later, for the great tragedies, like *Macbeth*, *Hamlet*, *Richard II*, they might see the film both before and after reading. The main thing is to keep in mind that there is a text to read, and that the student reader is living in the present. It is reading he must learn, although he must necessarily become acquainted with some of the facts about the historical background, the life and times of the author. The writer must make him *see*, and the selection must be made to speak out to him by itself. The purpose of literature at this level is not, therefore, to explain the author's psychology or the social life of his age, nor is it to be read primarily as a stylistic example characteristic of a period. Until the student has read and appreciated many more works of art, he is not ready to make critical judgments on this scale. He will grow to awareness that even after an intensive and enjoyable study of a Shakespearean play, he is by no means now fully acquainted with Shakespeare.

FILLING IN GAPS

Novelty in the settings of most works of literature is an obstacle to their appreciation. Most students, even the gifted, have little background of knowledge of the Bible, mythology, English or American literature, or even English or European history. They also often show resistance to choice of subject, or even to unusual figures of speech if contacts with them are not tactfully motivated.

They can learn to analyze a new metaphor by the formula:

"What two things are compared? In what ways are these two things alike? Does the comparison make the meaning more vivid, clarify it, separate a single meaning, make us see something in a new way that is also true? Or is it strained, false, inaccurate?" That much of our everyday language is metaphorical, students do not realize. A little study of double metaphors, of mixed metaphors can add interest by demanding more critical reading, careful writing, exact speech.

Filling in the gaps in their literary background can be hastened by guided individual reading. In mythology, a student, probably a girl, after reading the modern novel *Homer's Daughter*, by Robert Graves, may wish to read a translation of the *Odyssey*, and from that, be interested in Edith Hamilton's *Mythology*, or *The Greek Way* and *The Roman Way* by the same author. From there, the student may be able to go on to *Antigone*.

Another method is that of comparative study of two novels, plays, poems, or tales — one modern, one of the past. Stephen Vincent Benét's "The Devil and Daniel Webster" compared with Washington Irving's "The Devil and Tom Walker" come to mind. The themes of each are comparable, but the fact that Benét's story has become a motion picture and also an operetta, gives opportunity for comparison and contrast between the tale and the short story, the motion picture, and the music drama, as well as the artist's method of making a character three-dimensional rather than a stereotype, the complications of plot, style of writing, use of conversation, and the ideals of American society then and now, leading to the discovery of values which remain true for all time.

In Noble and Noble's Comparative Classics, *The Emperor Jones* is set side by side with *Macbeth*, and other examples may be found. However, in a literature class, too eclectic a choice may lead to confusion. By defining objectives clearly and co-operatively with the class, and organizing the work by units, problems, or even by types or chronology, the teacher will help students to integrate their study of literature. Evaluation at intervals as they proceed enables them to perceive growth in understanding and to plan for further work. That there are the well-known and tested methods of causing learning to take place makes them no exception in the case of the gifted. In fact, with the gifted they often work better.

These students are the only ones who will ever make use of what English teachers traditionally like to teach. Matters of literary form and technique, recognition of felicitous phrasing, the exact metaphor, an unusual perception, subtle relationships of ideas can be a joy to them as new doors to delight are opened. Although other students may also learn to understand and enjoy literary technique, it is the gifted who will make use of it. But they must be led, not driven; for the real purpose is to make appreciative readers through understanding and enrichment.

TEACHING TYPES OF LITERATURE

In order properly to understand a selection, the student must acquire a knowledge of literary form. A study of types of writing is indicated, however it may be organized. Before beginning a course in English literature, for example, the students should know the difference in purpose which determines the form of essay or short story, poetry or prose, novel or journalistic account, history or fiction. If, in preliminary courses, they have had experience with a number of examples of each general type, they may then be able more rapidly to read and appreciate specific varieties of each as they appear in their chronological settings.

As these students come to the ninth grade, their reading has usually, and not unnaturally, been of two kinds — narration and matter-of-fact explanation. That is, they are accustomed to reading fiction to "find out what happened," and history, science, the newspaper, or magazines for the same purpose. Narrative verse or musical ballads may not frighten them, but lyric poetry is outside the experience of most in this scientific age. The business of the teacher is to find out what each reads and what next step he should take.

SHORT STORIES, ESSAYS, NOVELS

If the class is used to the surprise-ending story, begin there. Increase the enjoyment by noting how the author secured his effects, discovering the deeper theme, perceiving the structure. Follow with one of the classic short stories, perhaps one by Hawthorne or De Maupassant, to drive home the economy required of the author in this genre. Every sentence, every word, counts towards the main effect — and there can be only one main character, one scene, one climax, one mood, or tone. Contrasting this little lesson in the classic with novels they have read, and again with good motion pictures, television dramas, one-act plays, gives them a basis for further understanding.

To increase perception of technique, the next experience may be with a story which has a hidden meaning for the reader, one like Hemingway's "The Killers," for instance. The main point of the story, as in his other "The Snows of Kilimanjaro," was not revealed in the two motion pictures. Could it have been? After the class has found out what the stories are really about, they can answer this question.

Most anthologies have a good selection of stories of the various types. What used to be called the stream-of-consciousness story has become quite familiar even to the young. Applying the structural formula to one of these is an interesting exercise. The class might also read one of the more modern stories which seem to be merely narrative sketches. In these, they find that the ending has to be completed by the reader, from his depth of understanding and background of experience. Again applying the structural formula, the class can perceive why the author did not need to write it himself. It is all *there*, but a great deal of art was necessary to provide the implications.

Shifting to a reading of essays may at first seem dull. Essays are usually not dramatic, have no plots, leading characters, or excitement. Perhaps one should study essays first, unless it seemed best to the teacher to start off with an absorbing interest already present. If, however, a beginning is made with the informal essay — and there are many which are short, timely, incisive, witty, and stimulating — the students discover in the essayist a good conversationalist, a person of ideas. Moreover, he is writing what they have been trying to write in themes — only much better. The purpose of the essay evolves. As they themselves attempt to write brief essays, the value of words, the structure of sentences, the necessity for thinking becomes evident. They read and try their hand at writing various types, making use of illustrative example, description, explanation, comparison and contrast, and various other means of expanding an idea, whichever is most suitable. Trying to write increases appreciation of good writing. They may also study editorials, if they and the teacher can find enough good examples, noting how the writer makes his points by reasoning, clarification, or interpretation of the facts.

The reading of a novel by the class as a whole, while a procedure of long practice in schools, has been objected to, and rightly, because it usually takes all the joy out of reading that particular book. Yet students, particularly fast readers, will miss many of the finer, even the most important, values of a great novel unless they are required to find them. The problem of the teacher is to get the whole book read rapidly, say in about two weeks, and yet, by skillful questioning or discussion, promote enough study and rereading, if necessary, to make sure that no essential value is missed. The reading of the book may thus take no longer than two weeks. Those who are more rapid, able, or experienced may be also reading other novels of their own choice for comparison — to add to the interest of class discussion — or for individual projects.

Reading a nineteenth century novel together is useful to the gifted in leading them to appreciate and read for themselves, now and later, the great novels of that period. Twentieth century writing has become so streamlined that sometimes the first quality modern young readers need to acquire in order to enjoy Dickens or George Eliot or Thackeray is patience. The long sentences, no less than the long descriptions, and the philosophical or social commentary are perennial stumbling-blocks. If the teacher has a sincere liking for these books, knows the interests and background experience of the class, he will know how to initiate his students into the enjoyment of this rich heritage. One thing they must learn is how to listen. The *sound* of the language of Dickens, as a passage is read aloud, helps the student to *see* those unique personalities, or those vivid scenes of Victorian life. Oral reading is necessary to bring out humor. Students should hear Mark Twain, too, but reading him is no problem; communication is instantaneous.

Unlike a short story, which can be read at a single sitting, a novel is a world in which the reader lives for a good many days. He comes to know its skies and its climate, and its people, of course, better than he knows those around him. When the student realizes that this is what the author is doing for him, he will, perhaps, give him a chance, and do his own part. The reader's part is to cooperate by bringing all his knowledge of life and people to the effort of understanding. In the older type of novel, unlike the modern journalistic type, the author sometimes talks directly to the reader. Sometimes various characters take up the story. At any rate, there is a point of view to be perceived. It may be not the author's at all, it may be quite foreign to the reader's experiences, perhaps repulsive. Young readers need to learn to become aware of what effect is intended. Of course there are many more aspects of the novel good teachers know how to teach. They all have their place, but probably they all do not have to be taught in relation to one single novel, taking ten weeks to do it.

For individual reading, students need guidance in order to develop discrimination. So many novels of the present day, especially best-sellers, are of the naturalistic school, that inexperienced readers may receive a lop-sided view of life if their leisure reading includes many of this type.

READING BIOGRAPHY

Students usually read a great deal of biography, for today's best-sellers are chiefly in this field. They need, however, to learn, first what makes a biography good, not merely good reading. To judge a biography, they will have to ask some questions, and do a little research. First, the obvious ones about the author, his access to sources, and his use of those sources. Compare two biographies such as Lytton Strachey's *Elizabeth and Essex* and Neale's *Queen Elizabeth*. Which has the more objective point of view? For all the wit and charm of Strachey, is his account reliable? Can it be depended upon? There have been so many biographies, plays, and motion pictures of Queen Elizabeth the First that a project of hunting for the truth about Good Queen Bess would not be hard to carry out. Another subject for such a project is Abraham Lincoln.

After studying the qualifications of a good biography, through reading and research, the students may generalize from their experience: given that a certain biography is true and reliable, is it literature? To answer this question they may have to read one of the biographies which have taken their place among the classics: Lockhart's *Life of Sir Walter Scott*, Boswell's *Samuel Johnson*, Sandburg's *Abraham Lincoln*, Freeman's *George Washington*. Then, cooperatively, they may develop a workable definition of what constitutes literary merit.

AND POETRY

The trouble with poetry is that it is not what students think it is. In this unpoetic age, almost all of them think it is (1) rhyme, (2) pretty, (3) unnecessary. Teachers like it and we have to study it, but it has no relation to our own lives, to the world of ideas, or to growth in understanding anything. To overcome these misconceptions, the teacher needs to move warily.

It may be well to start where the students are in their experience of poetry, with narrative verse. They enjoy the sound, the rhythm, and the story. Bright students, in the relaxed atmosphere and enjoyment of the class, may ask, or be led to ask, questions about versification, figures of speech. To introduce them to the fact that poetry can state succinctly and dramatically some home truth about ordinary people, they might read "The Death of the Hired Man." After they have understood the story, they might develop their perception of what poetry is: this poem is not "pretty" and it does not rhyme — why is it poetry? Why did Robert Frost not tell this as a story? How would it have to be changed if it were a short story, or an essay? What does poetry *do?* These points are not to undergo such intensive explication that all interest dies. Perhaps just asking the questions is enough before going on to another poem.

The next one is a contrast, like Walter de la Mare's "The Listeners," which suggests more than it says. This one they should apprehend just by listening as it is read. Their comment will determine the discussion. Sometimes, at this beginning stage, not much comment is necessary. When the magic strikes, it is better to let it take hold before going into intellectual analysis. At this point, it is time to let individual students choose a poem they would like to read or hear. There are a number in the textbook, of course, and more in the library, but there should be several books of poetry in the room library. The teacher has a right to choose one, too. During this reading they learn the connotative quality of words.

After they have become familiar with imagery and have learned that the sense of a line usually carries over to the next, they may be introduced to the lyric. Now they have to get down to fundamental thinking. They must elucidate the meaning and test it and prove it. Images produce ideas and are produced by ideas. They produce emotions and are produced by emotions. Students learn that the more consistent the imagery, the more clear the meaning, the more moving the poem is. Paraphrasing a poem is a method most revealing of the power of language. A poet of ideas who conveys his meaning chiefly in images suffers dismally from logical paraphrase. Yet one cannot read just anything into a poem. Students learn that the words alone do not make the meaning come clear. The reader's thought, imagination, and emotion together operate to bring out the meaning.

Poetry should be part of every English course. As students study the various types — the epic, the ode, the elegy, the sonnet — they learn the patterns of verse and the traditional imaginative conceptions. As they read, they define emotional attitudes, and are prepared to discover changes. Much of modern poetry is obscure to many because traditional connections between image and idea, attitude and emotion are upset. Unless such poetry defines an attitude the young people can appreciate, its reading should be postponed.

TESTING AND EVALUATION OF EXPERIENCE

Frequent evaluations, or tests, are part of the teaching method. Most of the tests should be short, so that answers can be read while the interest is high. The questions should challenge the ability of the class to identify clues, to realize comparisons, to perceive interrelationships of character, scene, and action, to reflect upon values. Some questions test the vocabulary — not only the literal meaning, but the connotations, the emotional impact. All the questions should be interesting. Because the class wants to know the reaction to what they have written, and because the ensuing discussion is necessary to promote further understanding of the selection being studied or the undertaking of the next — the papers must be read and handed back the next day.

The teacher has selected various answers to be read aloud — often several answers to one question for comparison and discussion. Both ideas and method of expression are to be featured. This discussion of the test answers is planned like a radio program. Pupils learn that real thinking is asked for as well as terse expression. Correctness of spelling and structure are of course necessary. The first tests are easier until the students learn what is required. With the growth of their power of interpretation and command of the language of literary discussion, the tests become more difficult, making use of their experience background.

Various types of tests are used. Some are open-book tests, some are one-word answers, some are made by the students themselves. But they all meet the main objective of the course — to increase enjoyment in reading. They also help the students to note their progress as maturing readers.

As they develop a specific skill, they are tested on it; for example, after learning the various patterns for following a line of thought, they are given a selection to analyze. After studying various types of humor, they may be asked to contrast two selections, and tell how the author secures his effects. Or from memory they can cite examples of different types. These are run-of-the-mill assignments, but sometimes necessary. If they are brief and conducted briskly, they are often more enjoyable. The gifted are more interested in purpose than mere lesson-getting. The appreciation of humor, or satire, irony, understatement, and all the more subtle types of wit requires not only intelligence but also a background of historical, political, and literary experience not often possessed by young readers. Even if the humor is beyond them, the gifted will need to know what they are missing, with an eye to future reading.

John Gehlmann [11] has cited an interesting assignment for developing an appreciation of the need for background in understanding allusions. He asks each student to bring to class a joke or a cartoon to which he does not see any point. He says, "Such an activity is very revealing. Recently in one of my classes a cartoon was submitted, in which a mother mouse was saying to several of her children, 'And never, never go near a house that has a beaten track to the door.' No one in the class could see why anyone would think this funny." Perhaps, if all the class were gifted, someone might recognize the allusion. Perhaps not.

[11] "Competence in Interpretation of Literature," *Improving Reading in All Curriculum Areas.* William S. Gray, editor, Univ. of Chicago Press, Supplementary Educational Monographs No. 76, November, 1952, p. 209.

In a time of such rapid change as our own, a time when children have been a target for mass communication media, a teacher may expect many lacunae in the literary backgrounds of secondary-school students. At the same time, of course, the teacher makes use of the potentialities of radio, television, and motion pictures for helping students to appreciate the older medium of interpreting the world in which they live — books.

CONCLUSION

The ways of teaching literature mentioned in this section are intended to suggest methods to be used. They are not complete, nor do they exhaust the possibilities. The resourceful teacher can vary and intensify the assignments. Real success in developing love of literature and ability to interpret the more adult types of writing depends upon the teacher. His own enjoyment and appreciation of literature may be communicated by contagion, if he also knows and understands each individual student. Then he may be able to achieve his purpose of teaching them to distinguish between the lasting and the ephemeral, to recognize truth to human experience as contrasted with the stereotyped, the glamorous, the false, and to make them aware of the many areas of life to which a balanced program of reading may contribute.

Although we have stressed the desirability of separate classes for gifted students, providing them is not always feasible. While waiting for better provision for these students, teachers can begin by helping them as much as possible even in an undifferentiated group. As Margaret Neuber of Penn State University suggests, "Simply be on the lookout for children with breadth of interest, creative ideas, ease of expression, insight, and ability for abstract thinking." [12]

THE ROLE OF PAPER-BOUND BOOKS

There is disagreement among educators about many aspects of education for the intellectually gifted students. To segregate or not to segregate; to begin specialization early or to emphasize broad acquaintance with human knowledge; to concentrate on academic studies or to include vocational, recreational, and creative subjects in the curricula of mentally superior adolescents — these are some of the hotly debated areas of uncertainty and dispute. Despite these differences, however, there is one aspect of education for the gifted on which all schools of thought agree: superior students *must* be led to and given opportunities for wide, varied, and mature reading. Only through such reading can the potential

[12] *Teacher's Letter*, February 7, 1953.

leaders of the future receive the information, the background of ideas, and the stimulation which will enable them to use their powers fully and constructively. The need is recognized, but the means for meeting it are often difficult to obtain.

Few teachers and librarians feel wholly satisfied with the amount of reading material which they are able to provide even for their "average" students. Libraries are rarely adequate. Books, magazines, and newspapers are increasingly expensive. At budget-making time no pressure groups appear to plead the cause of books before boards of education. The desperate need for buildings and equipment and teachers forces school trustees to economize wherever possible. It is not surprising that lay board members, untrained in educational matters, often think of library and textbooks as being less vital to education than are cafeterias and shop equipment. Books are bought for average students; the gifted suffer.

A possible answer to the problem of providing superior students with a wide variety of reading matter has appeared in the new phenomenon of the paper-bound book. This technological miracle gives promise of becoming as valuable an adjunct to teaching as the motion picture has already become, without the cost and complexity which the latter medium involves. The paper-covered book deserves examination.

At first, paper-covered books made no claim either to quality or to permanence; their only advantages were low cost and easy accessibility. Educators and publishers of conventional books tried to pretend that these newcomers to the world of print did not exist; if their presence was recognized, it was usually in the form of a pronouncement to the effect that the whole enterprise would be as ephemeral as was the reputation of some of the authors whose works appeared in paper bindings.

But, surprisingly, the new book form survived and flourished. Quality began to improve. Publishers experimented with reprints of standard works (usually of fiction) on which copyrights had expired. Dressed in lurid covers, these reprints were first offered to readers as blood brothers of the spicy potboilers with which the paper-book business had begun. To the amazement of cynics, these reprints sold, and sold well. Emboldened, some publishers put good non-fiction on drugstore display racks. People bought these books, too. "How-to" books and works on science were followed by poetry, philosophy, drama, and literary criticism. Established contemporary writers accepted commissions to write specifically for paper-book publishers.

There is now available, in paper covers, at prices ranging from twenty-five cents to a dollar a volume, a large segment of the great thought and literature of the world. This is a fact which educators cannot afford to ignore if they are to be faithful to their educational responsibilities. The fact is of particular importance to the teachers of students whose intellectual capacities and needs are great.

How can paper-covered books be made to serve gifted pupils? Several ways have already been tried. Others will of course suggest themselves to alert teachers. *First*, the outstanding student can be encouraged and helped to build for himself a personal library in his particular field of interest, even though he is alone among his classmates in having that interest. Personal ownership of great books, in any field, can lead to the thoughtful rereading, comparison, study, and reflection which help the intelligent student to increase his knowledge and develop his viewpoint. True, such a library is not permanent. But is not "permanent" a relative term? Will the gifted youth who meets Plato in the impermanent paper binding learn less from the Athenian than if he first met him clothed in tooled leather? Will John Dewey's *Reconstruction in Philosophy* be either less valuable or less difficult to read in soft covers than in hard? And surely Shakespeare's sonnets. . . . The permanent collection of books can come later.

Second, each classroom can have a classroom library of paper-bound books. This will neither replace nor compete with the central library of the school; it will not, in most cases, be a substitute for a textbook. Rather, it can be a means of introducing the intellectually curious members of a class to a wide range of written matter of high quality. Browsing is easy in the relative intimacy of a classroom; a helpful teacher is readily available. The superior student, who finishes assignments far ahead of the rest of his class, can put to valuable use the time which might otherwise be dissipated in idleness or mischief.

Third, the paper-covered book can serve a valuable social purpose by helping to combat one of the characteristics of our cultural climate. That characteristic is anti-intellectualism. Mistrust, fear, and even antagonism toward ideas and the media which purvey them are, unfortunately, widespread in contemporary society. Perhaps this attitude is more prevalent among adults than it is among adolescents; if so, the latter need help in escaping the infection. Quite possibly some administrators and some teachers reflect this feeling. Whatever the adult situation may be, the paper-bound book offers to the gifted high-school student the opportunity to read widely and deeply without exposing himself to the stigma which the frequenting of libraries often brings. The book which can be bought in a drugstore is less apt to cause its reader to become known as a "brain" than is the conventional tome. In many communities it is unhappily true that, in order to remain in good adolescent standing, the gifted student must avoid at least the appearance of being interested in things of the intellect. This the paper-bound book can help him to do.

Fourth, the paper-bound book can be used to provide a general enrichment of curricular materials at a very low cost. Some school districts actually offer selected paper-book titles for sale to students at student-body stores. Others include paper-covered books on reading lists issued in specific courses. All students, but especially gifted ones, are thus given opportunity to read very widely in the preparation of special reports and projects. The great advantage here, it must be repeated, lies in the fact that purchases need not be restricted, as of necessity they are with expensive books, to those titles which will benefit the *majority* of students. Instead, there can be a catering to the needs of a minority — the minority which will probably lead the world in the next generation. Budgetary limitations need not deprive the gifted boy and girl of the best of what man has set down on paper.

Perhaps the best way to show the wealth which is now available in paper covers is to group some of the titles which have appeared recently. This is a very small sampling, covering a short period of time. The following list is merely a slight indication of what can be bought at the same price as that commanded by comics and "fan" magazines.

SCIENCE

The Sea Around Us — Rachel Carson
The Life of the Bee — Maurice Maeterlinck
The World of Copernicus (Sun, Stand Thou Still) — Angus Armitage
Viruses and Man — F. M. Burnet
Microbe Hunters — Paul De Kruif

GOVERNMENT AND POLITICS

Thomas Jefferson on Democracy — Saul Padover, Ed.
America in Perspective — Henry Steele Commager
The Prince — Niccolo Machiavelli
Russia — Bernard Pares
Theory of the Leisure Class — Thorstein Veblen

PHILOSOPHY AND RELIGION

Philosophy in a New Key — S. K. Langer
The Meaning of the Glorious Koran — Marmaduke Pickthall, trans.
Song of God — Mahabharata-Bhagavad-Gita
Out of My Life and Thought — Albert Schweitzer
Meaning of Evolution — G. G. Simpson

LITERATURE

New World Writing (four volumes)
Introducing Shakespeare — G. B. Harrison
Leaves of Grass — Walt Whitman
The Inferno by Dante — John Ciardi, trans.
The Golden Treasury — F. T. Palgrave

THE ARTS

Ballet in America — George Amberg
Beethoven — J. W. N. Sullivan
What to Listen for in Music — Aaron Copland
Woodcuts of Durer — Barlow
Russian Icons — Rice

Here is a challenge to the schools. This is a new tool; educators must learn to use it, especially to help their gifted students. It is not *the* answer, but it surely is *an* answer, to one of the great problems of education.

PERMABOOKS SUITABLE FOR SALE TO STUDENTS IN THE BOOK PROJECT IN HIGH SCHOOLS IN THE CITY OF NEW YORK

Beau Geste — P. C. Wren
Beau Sabreur — P. C. Wren
Bennett's Welcome — Inglis Fletcher
Best Loved Poems — Edited by Richard Charlton MacKenzie
Beyond the End of Time — Edited by Frederick Pohl
Bright to the Wanderer — Bruce Lancaster
Bugles Blow No More — Clifford Dowdey
Chad Hanna — Walter D. Edmonds
A Concise Treasury of Great Poems — Louis Untermeyer
Crossroads in Time — Edited by Groff Conklin
Crusade in Europe — Dwight D. Eisenhower
Famous Scenes from Shakespeare — Compiled by Van H. Cartmell
Gentleman's Agreement — Laura Z. Hobson
Gone With the Wind — Margaret Mitchell
The Greatest Book Ever Written — Fulton Oursler
The Greatest Story Ever Told — Fulton Oursler
Green Dolphin Street — Elizabeth Goudge
Guard of Honor — James Gould Cozzens
Immortal Wife — Irving Stone
Killers in Africa — Alexander Lake
Kon-Tiki — Thor Heyerdahl
The Lost World — Sir Arthur Conan Doyle
Lusty Wind for Carolina — Inglis Fletcher
Lydia Bailey — Kenneth Roberts
Men of Albermarle — Inglis Fletcher
My Lord America — Alec Rackowe

New Standard Book of Model Letters for All Occasions — Leo J. Henkin
Perma Cross-Word Puzzle Dictionary — Compiled by Frank E. Newman
Perma Rhyming Dictionary — Langford Reed
The Plymouth Adventure — Ernest Gebler
Queen's Gift — Inglis Fletcher
Rainbow in the Royals — Garland Roark
Raleigh's Eden — Inglis Fletcher
River to the West — John Jennings
Roanoke Hundred — Inglis Fletcher
Rogue's Honor — Anne Powers
Scarlet Cockerel — Garald Lagard
The Scarlet Patch — Bruce Lancaster
The Shadow and the Glory — John Jennings
Shadow of Tomorrow — Fred Phol
The Shorter Bartlett's Familiar Quotations
The Silver Chalice — Thomas B. Costain
The Story of the Bible — Hendrik van Loon
Thunder in the Wilderness — Harry Hamilton
Toil of the Brave — Inglis Fletcher
Trumpet to Arms — Bruce Lancaster
Venture in the East — Bruce Lancaster
Word Power Made Easy — Norman Lewis

Selected Bibliography

Brandwein, Paul F. *The Gifted Student as Future Scientist.* New York: Harcourt, Brace and Company. 1955. 108 pp. Discusses identification and characteristics of gifted and tells of types of teachers who have been successful working with gifted. Also includes hypothesis and proposals.

Cornog, William H. *College Admission with Advanced Standing.* New York: Advancement for Education Fund. January, 1954. 91 pp. Describes the program; also gives detailed curriculum offerings for gifted students in the academic fields.

Cunningham, Harry A. "Some Challenging Problems in Teaching High-School Science to Gifted Students," *School Science and Mathematics*, 52:373–384. May, 1952. Gives detailed specifics in the area of science teaching.

Denver University. *Some Enrichment Techniques.* Denver: Denver University Press. 1952. 22 pp. Compilation of materials from a workshop. Includes reasons for enrichment, techniques used to challenge the gifted learners, and procedures.

Department of Instruction. *Enrichment Projects.* Denver: Public Schools. February, 1954. 33 pp. Presents reasons, aims, role of staff in an enrichment program. Also projects in reading, social studies, math, woodwork, music, *etc.*

Edwards, Newton. "Education of the Able Student, Social Significance and Goals," *The School Review*, 62:328–332. September, 1954. States why American education needs a new orientation. Pleads the gifted be educated in order to be trained to participate in high-level policy making.

Flynn, Ella L. "For the Superior Reader," *Library Journal*, 79:492–495. March, 1954. Discusses several ways to enrich reading of gifted students and list appropriate leisure reading books for them.

Fox, Mildred, "Providing for the Gifted," *The Education Digest*, 19:10–12. February, 1954. Describes educational programs for the gifted high-school pupil in Evanston Township High School.

Fund for the Advancement of Education, *School and College Study of Admission with Advanced Standing*. August, 1953. Takes stand that best teachers of seventeen-year-olds are often found in secondary schools, and that the increased need of manpower for the professions puts increasing emphasis on the efficient use of the student's time.

Gregory, Margaret, and William McLaughlin. "Advanced Reading for the Bright Child," *The Clearing House*, 26:203–309, December, 1951. No. 4. Considers the reading problems for outstanding students.

Gross, Richard E. "Challenge of Social Education for the Gifted," *The Social Studies*, 45:199–204. October, 1954. Discusses the various educational programs offered in the U. S. A. for gifted. Tells specifically the enrichment projects that may be used for the gifted in a regular high-school class in social studies. Also gives good suggestions for evaluating the work of these students.

Hamman, Olga. "Whom Should We Educate?" *California Teacher Association Journal*. November, 1953. pp. 19–20. Describes the Scholarship Awards Committee of California.

Hollingworth, Leta. *Gifted Children, Their Nature and Nurture*. New York: Macmillan Company. 1926. 374 pp. Presents the history of the study of gifted children, their characteristics and development, the organization and curriculum of special education programs, and the social economic implications.

Justman, Joseph. "Academic Achievement of Intellectually Gifted Accelerants and Non-Accelerants in Senior High School," *The School Review*, 62:469–473. November, 1954. Found that saving of one year without loss in achievement constitutes one good reason for special progress classes in a junior high-school framework.

Kent State University. *The Role of the Parent in the Education and Training of the Mentally Superior Child*. Ohio: Kent State University Press. 1951. 44 pp. Prepared by parents and teachers for the conference on this subject. Covers emotional adjustment, human relations, health, physical education, art, music, travel, creative expression, guidance, *etc.*

Lehman, Harvey C. *Age and Achievement*, Princeton: American Philosophical Society. 1953. 358 pp. This is a summation of 20 years of research. Tells of the quality and the quantity of achievement in relation to age in various professional fields and artistic fields. Includes athletics and politics, too.

Los Angeles County Schools. *The More Capable Learner in the Secondary Schools*. Los Angeles: Office of County Superintendent of Schools, Division of Secondary Education. January, 1951. 69 pp. An account of the progress made in the Los Angeles County schools in providing enrichment and other adaptations for superior learners.

Mead, Margaret. "The Gifted Child in the American Culture of Today," *The Journal of Teacher Education*, 5:211–214. September, 1954. Describes the present cultural patterns in the U. S. A. which negatively affect the education of gifted students and suggests ways for educators to help overcome these patterns.

Modesto City Schools. *Instructional Programs for Gifted Students.* Modesto, California: Curriculum Department, Secondary Schools Division. 1953. 110 pp. States the framework of the Modesto Plan and gives detailed program profile of the independent study program.

Newland, T. Ernest. "The Gifted," *Review of Educational Research*, Vol. X 23, No. 5, December, 1953. pp. 417–431. Summarizes 80 research studies which have been published in the various journals on the gifted covering the period from 1944 to 1953. Indicates there is a greater interest now in social contributions of gifted people and more curiosity on the nature of ability. Extensive bibliography.

Passow, A. Harry, and Abraham Tannenbaum. "What of the Talented in Today's High Schools?", *Educational Leadership*, 12:148–155. December, 1954. Offers some guides for thinking and planning programs for talented and gifted students.

Portland Public Schools. *Progress Report No. II of the Co-operative Program for Students with Exceptional Endowment.* Oregon: Portland School Administration, Gifted Child Project. April, 1954. 52 pp. Describes the program, the progress and evaluation of the two-year project. Also includes some curriculum offerings.

Pressey, Sidney L. *Educational Acceleration, Appraisal, and Basic Problems.* Columbus: Ohio State University Press, Bureau of Education. Research Monograph, No. 31, 1949. 153 pp. States the basic reasons for acceleration and notes some of the problems related to it.

Roberts, Helen Erskine. *Current Trends in the Education of the Gifted.* Sacramento: California State Department of Education. October, 1954. 59 pp. Report on programs in operation throughout the U. S. A. including elementary through college-level programs, emphasis on secondary schools.

Robinson, Helen M. *Promoting Maximal Reading Growth Among Able Learners.* Chicago: University of Chicago Press. Supplementary Educational Monographs, No. 81. December, 1954. 191 pp. Comprehensive coverage of characteristics and identification of gifted at all educational levels. Also specific patterns of organizing enrichment offerings, special classes, materials, and techniques, and methods for gifted from kindergarten through senior high school.

San Diego City Schools. *The Gifted Child Program and Teacher Consultant Service.* San Diego, California: San Diego City Schools, Secondary Division. September, 1953. 26 pp. Describes the program, some of the school offering, and the responsibilities of the teacher consultant.

School of Education. *Guiding Your Gifted.* Philadelphia: University of Pennsylvania Press. 1954. 89 pp. Answers many questions which arise on this subject. Gives answers on what can be done for the gifted in regular as well as special classes. Gives many specifics on the high-school academic subject fields.

Stoughton, Robert W. *Provisions for the Gifted, Current Practices in Connecticut Secondary Schools.* Hartford: State Department of Education. September, 1954. 18 pp. Gives organizations and tells of class offerings.

Strang, Ruth. "Guidance of the Gifted," *The Personnel and Guidance Journal*, 21:26–30. October, 1952. Describes counselors' special responsibilities to the gifted. Lists the counseling and guidance areas.

Symposium on "The Gifted or More Capable Learner in the Secondary Schools," *California Journal of Secondary Education*, Vol. 29, No. 8. December, 1954. pp. 470–485. States there is an increased understanding of the needs of gifted; presents a portrait of a gifted high-school pupil; states some of the problems gifted children have and a program to lessen these problems; three theories are offered as to why gifted are not accomplishing what can be expected of them.

Terman, Lewis M. "Are Scientists Different?", *Scientific American*, Vol. 192, No. 1. January, 1955. pp. 25–29. The question stated above has been raised by the current friction between scientists and government officials. Terman answers it by reporting data collected from his study.

Terman, Lewis M. "The Discovery of Exceptional Talent," *American Psychologist*, Vol. 9, No. 6. June, 1954. pp. 221–230. Reviews his origin of interest in this field, talks of methods of identification and special problems in the education of gifted as they affect those who possess outstanding abilities.

Terman, Lewis M., and Melita H. Oden. *The Gifted Child Grows Up.* Stanford: Stanford University Press, Vol. IV, 1947. 448 pp. Twenty-five-year follow-up study of a superior group started in 1930. Findings corroborate conclusions presented earlier.

Terman, Lewis M., and Melita Oden. "Major Issues in the Education of Gifted Children," *Education Digest*, Vol. 20, No. 4, December, 1954. Gives good answers to the arguments so frequently met when discussing the education of gifted children.

Terman, Lewis M. *Scientists and Non-Scientists in a Group of 800 Gifted Men*, Psychological Monographs, General and Applied, No. 378, Vol. 68, No. 7, 1954. 44 pp. Discusses pertinent differences between these two groups of gifted.

Wedemeyer, Charles A. "Gifted Achievers and Non-Achievers," *Journal of Higher Education,* Vol. 24, No. 1. January, 1953. Reports on a study done at college level. Out of 102 students, 79 per cent were achievers, 22 per cent non-achievers, 29 per cent of non-achievers were above the 90th percentile. Between one fourth and one third of most intelligent students not achieving. Serious problems for counselor and those responsible for planning college offerings.

Witty, Paul, editor. *The Gifted Child.* New York: American Association for Gifted Children, D. C. Heath and Company. 1951. 338 pp. A compilation of articles written on all phases of gifted children by people who are authorities in this field.

Wolfe, Dael L., *et. al. Human Resources, The Needs and the Supply.* Pittsburgh: University of Pittsburgh Press. 1951. 64 pp. Five lectures delivered at a conference on Human Resources and Higher Education at the University of Pittsburgh. Discusses future needs for scientific and specialized personnel along with identification, encouragement, and development of talented youth.

Some Suggestions on the Teaching of Creative Writing

The normal young child is a creative human being, and a communicative one, if we define creativity as building new forms from already existing materials. The child who calls hail "thunder stones" is being creatively communicative.

However, adults, in their eagerness to guide children to conform in ways considered essential in our society, tend to discourage original or non-conformist behavior. Consequently, by the time a child is able to write, his creativity has either remained undeveloped for lack of encouragement or has been crushed. As Albert Einstein has said, "It is nothing short of a miracle that the modern methods of instruction have not yet entirely strangled the holy curiosity of inquiry; for this delicate little plant stands mainly in need of freedom." The same seems to be true of creativity.

It is the teacher's opportunity and responsibility to provide specific stimuli, incentive, guidance, and training-in-skills so that meaningful writing may result. Creative writing can help the teacher in every required and elective English class for it helps the pupil to grow not only in skills like capitalization, spelling, and punctuation, but also in the recognition of the "meaningfulness" of these mechanics. It helps in his observation and analysis of the world around him; in the understanding of his own inner world — its needs, its motivations, its mechanisms — and in the elation and deep satisfaction that come from sharing creative expression with others.

When it comes to a discussion of the basic objectives of education, creative writing holds its own important place. Whether the objectives be as simple as, "The well-rounded growth of an individual is a basic aim of education," [13] or more extended, as are the Ten Imperative Needs of Youth,[14] creative writing makes a definite contribution. In the above-mentioned Ten, for instance, creative writing meets the four following needs:

All youth need opportunities to develop their capacities to appreciate beauty in literature, art, music, and nature.

[13] Barr, A. S.; Burton, W. H.; and Brueckner, L. J. *Supervision.* New York: D. Appleton-Century Company, Inc., 1938, p. 187.

[14] *Planning for American Youth.* Washington 6, D. C.: National Association of Secondary-School Principals. 1951, p. 9.

All youth need to be able to use their leisure time well.

All youth need to develop respect for other persons, to grow in their insight into ethical values and principles.

All youth need to grow in their ability to think rationally, to express their thoughts clearly, and to listen and read with understanding.

Or again, from the Report of the President's Commission on Higher Education,[15] three objectives apply to the creative writing field:

To understand the ideas of others and to express one's own effectively.

To understand and enjoy literature, arts, music, and other cultural activities as expressions of personal and social experience, and to participate to some extent in some form of creative activity.

To attain a satisfactory emotional and social adjustment.

In attempting to meet whatever objectives we set for ourselves, it will be helpful to compare the present-day approach to the teaching of writing with the traditional approach.

Traditionally	*Today*
1. Teaching was by uniform assignment.	1. Teaching is based on the experience of the pupil as he is made aware of that experience.
2. Teaching was based primarily on literary form.	2. Teaching is based primarily on the needs of pupils.
3. The main source of material was the external world.	3. The main source of material is the pupil's internal world and its relationship to the external world.
4. Subject matter was limited.	4. Subject matter is unlimited.
5. Emphasis was on the development of the *product* and the discipline of achieving technical perfection in form and mechanics.	5. Emphasis is on the development of the *pupil* and the discipline of deciding what one wants to say and of finding the specific words which will most effectively communicate the author's thoughts and feelings.

This present-day point of view is suggested in the following quotations:

Growth, rather than art, then, is the aim of creative expressional activities. Any growth, it must be remembered, is from within. It is personal. It can be stimulated from without, but it cannot be imposed.[16]

[15] W. L. Werner, "College English for American Democracy." *College English*, 10:210.

[16] Parker, Roscoe Edward. *Principles and Practices of Teaching English.* New York: Prentice-Hall, Inc. 1937, p. 189.

The real objective of teaching creative writing is the development of the pupil's capacity for creative experience.[17]

Creative writing occurs when the pupil recognizes the dignity and value of his own experience, and when he imposes on that experience the discipline necessary to an attempt to transfer it to others.[18]

Any writing which forces the writer to discover new words for old thoughts, or to the discovery for himself of new thoughts, however trite the phrases in which they are couched, is creative writing.[19]

In what we here distinguish as creative writing, the source of the material is within the student's real or imaginative experience, and the writing is "free" in the sense that the student has chosen his own material and is seeking his own most adequate form of expression.[20]

No amount of playing about with words or phrases will ever make anyone a good writer. Words are nothing in themselves; it is what goes on in the writer's mind that matters.[21]

So we find that creative writing attempts to stimulate first the awareness, then the expression, and later the analysis of each student's individual responses to his internal and external experiences. This expression is viewed in relation to the contribution it makes to the writer himself through

the interest and value in reliving past experiences

the fascination in discovering meanings, motives, ideas, correlations, impressions through the process of writing. "Thoughts summon words, and words bring thoughts in turn."

the growing consciousness of one's capacities, one's characteristics, one's patterns, paralleling the growing consciousness of similar components in others.

growth in the ability to be accurately verbal

growth in the ability to free the meanings entrapped in the words of others

the deep and lasting satisfaction resulting from exercise of one's creativity.

Perhaps the greatest single contribution that the teacher of writing can make toward the development of the "whole child" is to create a conviction on the part of students that all material for creative expression comes from the artist's own experiences, conscious and unconscious, real and imagined; and that, in order to write, one must be able to recognize every moment of his own living as "material" for writing.

Gradually, written expression comes to be viewed in relation to its communicability, and the world of form, precision of word choice, emotional effect of sound, word connotation brings unity to substance and structure. The pupil comes to

[17] John T. Frederick, "The Place of Creative Writing in American Schools," *English Journal.*

[18] *Ibid.*, p. 11. [19] Parker, Roscoe Edward. *Op. cit.*, p. 186.

[20] Conrad, Lawrence H. *Teaching Creative Writing.* New York: D. Appleton-Century Company, Inc. 1937, p. 17.

[21] Anonymous.

realize the function of writing skills and to perfect their use through personally motivated learning

gain respect for himself, his ideas, his feelings

look with more analytical eyes upon himself and his relationships and so to grow in self-understanding

begin to analyze the actions and feelings of others, and so to grow in understanding his world

sense the "greatness" of creativity, and so to grow in appreciation of all creative arts.

Although some examples of classroom techniques are sketched briefly elsewhere in this discussion, these are merely suggestions. Each teacher will find his own ways of stimulating awareness and creativity and writing production in whatever courses he may be teaching. Basic guideposts to all sound teaching are the needs of the pupils being taught. An example of a "set" of needs worked out by a senior high-school class and worded by the teacher follows:

Each person needs to learn to recall with clarity, to identify, and to communicate effectively a personal emotionalized experience.

Each person needs to learn to become observant and analytical of an emotionalized experience in another and be able to communicate that experience effectively.

Each person needs to learn to see himself in relation to members of his own family and to see those members as individuals with feelings and needs and problems.

Each person needs to learn to sense how others might feel in an experience he himself has not had or witnessed.

Each person needs to be able to face problems and make constructive decisions about them.

Each person needs to learn to think through, gather information about, and analyze things that frighten, puzzle, or disturb him.

Each person needs to be able to sense and accept varied individual reactions to the same experience.

Each person needs to learn to convince his parents of his trustworthiness and maturity.

Each person needs to prepare himself for some of the unpredictable experiences confronting individuals in a complex society.

Each person needs to come to realize that each moment holds a stimulus for the writer who can *see.*

Each person needs to be able to accept some of the inconsistencies, faults, disappointments in life with growing objectivity and humor, and to differentiate between those about which he can do something and those about which he can do nothing.

Each person needs to control the tendency to generalize about individuals on the basis of obvious characteristics or group belonging and to accept persons on the basis of individual worth.

Each person needs to explore the latitudes of language and to be provoked into thinking about the wonder of words.

As one can sense, the basic motive behind the teaching of creative writing is the development of greater sensitivity, understanding, and maturity through the expression of experienced, observed, and imagined life situations, and skill in the communication of these in words on paper.

SUGGESTED PATTERN OF WORK

The pattern of work in creative writing will depend to a certain extent on the teacher, on the nature of the class, on the maturity of the students, and on the extent to which time is devoted to writing. This simple schedule worked well on the secondary level:

Motivation (planned and prepared by the teacher)
Writing of rough draft (always done in class)
Author's evaluation and, where necessary, re-writing
Class evaluation and, where necessary, re-writing
Teacher's evaluation, and, where necessary, re-writing

With some students there is, of necessity, much teacher evaluation and re-writing going on during the creation of the rough draft. However, when the teacher's analysis and the student's polishing are too thoroughly done before the manuscript is read to the class, much of the opportunity for the recognition and identification of weaknesses is taken from the students, as is the satisfaction of observed improvement from hearing two drafts of the same story.

The classroom teacher will come to recognize stimuli to creative writing in all of her daily experiences as well as in the experiences of her students. Recording daily observations in a notebook may help teacher and pupils at times when someone says, "I have nothing to write about." An example of a manuscript based on a "daily observation" is to be found at the end of the section dealing with poetry.

EVALUATION OF MANUSCRIPTS

One of the major strengths of a course in writing can be its method of manuscript evaluation. Evaluation should come from the writer himself, from the class, and from the teacher. If off-campus help is available, a stimulating procedure is to have students hear a tape recording of a professional writer's (or literary critic's) evaluation of student manuscripts. Also of value is the commentary of students in a comparable class in the same or another high school. Preparation of manuscripts for contribution to magazines, contests, and newspapers also stimulates critical evaluation and gives impetus to further writing and polishing. There are many methods for organizing the "criticism" of manuscripts. One procedure follows:

Each pupil chooses a pseudonym, known only to the teacher and the pupil, which he uses on all his manuscripts.

Each submitted manuscript carries a note indicating whether it is to be read aloud by the author, by a specified student, by a volunteer student, or by the teacher.

On evaluation day the teacher appoints a "strengths-critic" and a "weaknesses-critic," each of whom takes notes and, at the end of the evaluation period, summarizes the class-mentioned strengths and weaknesses for each manuscript read.

Each pupil hands in, at the conclusion of each evaluation period, at least one strength and one weakness for each manuscript read during that period. These unsigned comments are collected, screened by the teacher, and later handed to the authors concerned.

Autographed copies of *Best Poetry of the Week* and *Best Prose of the Week* as chosen by the class, and *Teacher's Poetry and Prose* as chosen by the instructor appear on display either in the room or hall.

Kept in each pupil's notebook is a record of the characteristics of good writing, items being listed one at a time as they are studied and understood. The last few minutes of each evaluation period are spent in discussing these in the light of the day's manuscripts if they have not been discussed during the reading period.

Evaluation day can be the most eagerly anticipated part of the creative writing program, and the avenue of great progress for individual authors.

LITERARY FORM

Literary form, too often the main objective in writing courses, should, on the secondary level, be a means rather than an end. The study of fixed forms in poetry, of types of essays, of styles of writing all broaden the understanding of the endlessness of modes of expression, give practice in versatility for the young writer, and help make convincing the principle of unity between form and substance. The continuous emphasis, however, should be on the development of the student's individual style, allowing form to be an outgrowth of the subject matter and emotional tone the writer wishes to communicate.

POETRY

An approach, other than through form, for stimulating the reading and writing of poetry, is suggested below.

A. Create an atmosphere of freedom from fear about poetry.
   1. Quote and discuss from Archibald MacLeish's "Ars Poetica" the last line, "A poem must not mean, but be." *Because* children should have the security of knowing
      a. they will not be required to "explain" the poetry they read,

b. young people and adults can enjoy poetry without fully understanding its meaning. (Coleridge said, "Poetry gives most pleasure when only generally and not perfectly understood.")
c. depth of understanding grows with experience in life and experience with poetry.

2. Discuss Robert Frost's comment that there are only two types of rhythm in the English language: regular and irregular iambic. *Because* students need to be taught that even though there may be highly technical aspects to poetic structure, poetry can be enjoyed without technical knowledge, just as a car can be driven without a knowledge of mechanics.
3. Quote and discuss Maxwell Anderson's comment from an address given before the Carnegie Institute: "The supreme artist is only the apex of the pyramid; the pyramid itself must be built of artists and art lovers, apprentices and craftsmen so deeply imbued with the love for the art they follow or practice that it has become for them a means of communion with whatever has become highest and most admirable in the human spirit. To the young people of this country I wish to say, if you now hesitate on the threshold of your maturity, wondering what rewards you should seek, wondering perhaps whether there are any rewards beyond the opportunity to feed and sleep and breed, turn to the art which has moved you most readily, take what part in it you can, as participant, spectator, secret practitioner, or hanger-on and waiter-at-the-door. Make your living any way you can, but neglect no sacrifice at your chosen altar.

   "It may break your heart, it may drive you half mad, it may betray you into unrealizable ambitions, or blind you to mercantile opportunities with its wandering fires. But it will fill your heart before it breaks it; it will make you a person in your own right; it will open the temple doors to you, and enable you to walk with those who have come nearest among men to what men may sometime be." [22] *Because* young people need to know that through participation in a creative art, no matter how minor that participation, one associates with the great minds and hearts and spirits of all ages and so enriches his own being.
4. Read and discuss "To Yourself" by Witter Bynner. *Be-*

[22] *New York Times*, An address given before Carnegie Institute, October 17, 1937.

cause young people need to know that the simple experiences of daily life are the materials of which poems are made, and that fragments which may seem insignificant at one time may become motivation for writing another time.

5. Read and discuss the quotation by Albert Schweitzer, "Just as a tree bears year after year the same fruit and yet fruit which is each year new, so must all permanently valuable ideas be continually born again in thought." [23] *Because* young people need to know that
   a. whatever ideas they express, no matter how many times "someone has written about that before," or how distant from a pre-conceived idea of poetic subject matter they may be, they are acceptable,
   b. the multiplicity of ways in which similar ideas have been expressed is one of the wonders of creativity. Just as no two persons are identical, so are no two ways of saying "the same thing" identical,
   c. the process of putting ideas into words on paper helps us assimilate ideas more than do thinking, talking, or reading. At a convention of the Southern California Association of Teachers of English at Riverside, California, on March 12, 1955, Robert Pooley said, "There is no single skill in language arts that has more significance for the totality of education than writing."
6. Show that *you* have overcome your fears about poetry by admitting that there is poetry you do not understand, and poetry that you do not enjoy. Be able to accept, even though you may not class them as poetry, such contributions as

   "Roses are red,
   Daisies are yella,
   What's a puer
   Without a puella." — Anonymous

   And be able to join in the fun sincerely when your pupils produce such gems as

   "Roses are yellow
   So is this daisy;
   They think I'm stupid:
   I know I'm just lazy."

   "Daylight is bright
   Night light is dim.
   I'd rather die
   Than dress for gym."

[23] *Albert Schweitzer: Out of My Life and Thought.* New York: Henry Holt and Company. 1949, p. 223.

"I like Jim,
I like Jack,
But after dancing with them
Oh, my aching back!"

"Roses are red
And so was my pater
When I said, 'Twelve o'clock,'
But got in much later."

7. Discuss Max Eastman's comment, "The surest path to the experience of poetry lies through making it." [24] *Because* young people need to experience, recognize, and articulate the "good" feelings they have within themselves when they have *done* something creative, and differentiate, as philosophers and psychologists differentiate, between the spectator and the participant, between real experience and vicarious experience.
8. Discuss Saroyan's comment to young writers: "Look at the world: look at people. Listen to the world: listen to people. The most magnificent things are found in the most ordinary people and events." *Because* young people need to be helped not only to *look at* the world, but to *see* the world, and to recognize the fact that each moment of each individual's life bears the substance from which literature is made.
9. Read and discuss John Donne's famous quotation, "No man is an iland, entire of it selfe; every man is a peece of the continent, a part of the maine: if a clod bee washed away by the sea, Europe is the lesse, as well as if a promontorie were, as well as if a mannor of thine friends or of thine owne were; any man's death diminishes me, because I am involved in mankinde: and therefore never send to know for whom the bell tolls; it tolls for thee." *Because* each individual needs to be aware of his bond with all humanity.
10. Read and discuss from Edna St. Vincent Millay's "Renascence" the lines beginning with "For my omniscience paid I toll . . ." *Because* young people need to be helped to understand and develop the ability to empathize which is so essential to effective adult living.
11. Read widely to them from poetry that is easily acceptable on the basis of emotional appeal, subject interest, age-level

[24] Eastman, Max. *Enjoyment of Poetry.* New York: Scribner's. 1951.

appeal, or provocative thought. *Because* making friends with poetry, like making friends with people, is easiest where a readily observable common bond exists. (Much of the poetry a teacher may wish to read to her classes may not appear in anthologies available in classroom sets. Since there is much to be gained when pupils can see poetry as the teacher reads it, the projection of poems from slides proves a valuable device.)

12. Provide simple incentives for pupils to read widely and purposefully from a rich classroom library. Building such a library may tax a teacher's ingenuity, but books may be brought by pupils, given on permanent loan by friends, picked up at second-hand bookshops, donated by bookshop owners known to the teacher, borrowed from the school and local libraries. Scrapbooks of favorite poems contributed by semester after semester of pupils should be included. *Suggested incentives*: While browsing during a class reading period, look for one poem which
    a. you think the class might enjoy hearing. (Reading aloud by pupils should not be forced. A teacher might say, "You may read it aloud, I'll read it aloud, or you may ask someone else to read it aloud.")
    b. has some humor you'd like to share with the class
    c. has a very unusual title
    d. has a title you would like to change
    e. has an unusual or vivid figure of speech
    f. presents an idea you'd never thought of before
    g. talks about something you've always felt or thought but never really put into words
    h. characterizes a person (Have you ever known anyone like this person? What were the differences between them? What were their similarities? Can you put this into words? You might start by saying: John was ———— while Jim was ————.)
    i. has a rhyme scheme you like (Put the rhyme scheme on the board.)
    j. has a rhythm you like (Write one or two lines on the board.)
    k. deals with three somethings ("Jane found a poem dealing with three people. Can anyone else find a poem dealing with three anything? How many different significances can you think of relating to three? What common sayings can you think of? Like, 'Three's a crowd,' 'Three on a match,' 'The third

time's the charm,' 'If at first you don't succeed, try, try again.' ")

13. Read as many definitions of poetry as you can find. *Because* students need to know that there is no simple, universally accepted definition of poetry. Houseman said, "I can no more define poetry than a terrier can define a rat, but I think we both recognize the object by the symptoms which it provokes in us." ("What do you suppose those symptoms are?")

B. Create situations in which success in creativity is achieved fairly easily and quickly. *Because* success is a welcoming hand.

1. Write two-word couplets as captions to pictures displayed around the room. *Examples:* Shy Guy — Quiet Riot — Regal Eagle — You Too? — Proud Cloud — Spring Fling
2. Write last lines to limericks.
3. Write original versions of "Roses are Red," "I Never Saw a Purple Cow," "On Top of Old Smokey," nursery rhymes, and other well-known songs and verses suggested by the class.
4. Write parodies of popular songs in which much of the wording of the original may remain the same, slanting them to specific use: class songs, school songs, Valentine songs, *etc.*
5. Change singing commercials to advertise new products. (Having read of the tons of rubber particles given off by tires and absorbed by smog and breathed, one pupil suggested a slogan for the Los Angeles Chamber of Commerce: More bounce to the ounce!)
6. Write acrostics based on your name or the names of others.
7. In other words, use any device to bring pupils to exclaim, "Gee, I've written a poem!"

C. Read and discuss references to poetry found in commonly read periodicals. *Because* students need to know that poetry is not just something out of the past; that since it has continued through all the ages of man as a major form of communication, it must be worth getting acquainted with, and that it has a place in the daily lives of many people in *today's* world. *Examples:*

1. *Time Magazine*, September 13, 1954: "What is the most perfect line of poetry in the English language?"
2. Los Angeles *Mirror-News:* the column "Let's Explore Your Mind" by Albert Wiggam carried the question, "Which is nearer the 'truth': 'facts' of science or 'romance' of poetry?" The answer: The late William Lyon

Phelps "proved" poetry contains the most "truth." He pointed out that when scientists buy a book of poetry, they pay large sums for first editions, but when they buy a book of science, they take only the latest editions, because they have proved that previous editions are wrong.

3. After reading excerpts from Ogden Nash, discuss the relationship between Palgrave's *Golden Treasury of English Verse* and Nash's *Golden Trashery of Ogden Nashery.* Compare: Nash, page 99, with Palgrave, page 4; Nash, page 58, with Palgrave, page 319; Nash, page 242, with Palgrave, page 149.
4. *Time Magazine*, January 10, 1955: "Of Time and the River," by Thomas Wolfe, quoted in Rand McNally advertisement.

D. Plan stimuli for writing that appeal to a variety of moods, emotions, needs, and interests.

1. Discuss and write about "What-Would-You-Have-Done?" situations from their own lives. *Example:* "You are a teen-ager with a driver's license. Your father has lent you the family car for a date on condition that you let no one else drive it. Someone in the crowd insists on driving. What would you do?"
2. Present the class with a title and see how many ideas for poems, or actual poems, can be produced.
3. Have each pupil list the things he likes most as perceived by each of five senses. Encourage expression in poetic form. Read Elinor Wylie's sonnet, "Down to the Puritan Marrow," Richard le Gallienne's "Catalog of Lovely Things," and Dorothy Parker's "Inventory." Lines from "The Great Homer" by Rupert Brooke.
4. Discuss the implications of inanimate objects. Have each pupil choose one object to think and write about. Read "Walls" by John Russell McCarthy, "City Roofs" by Charles H. Towne, and "Mending Wall" by Robert Frost.
5. Write serious and humorous epitaphs. (The epitaph is an excellent outlet for aggression as one can tell from John Dryden's

   "Here lies my wife: here let her lie!
   Now she's at rest — and so am I!"

   Read "Epitaphs" by Countee Cullen, "Epitaph" by Dorothy Parker.
6. Experiment with combining, amplifying, or changing proverbs. *Example:*

"Now I'm in a quandary,
I'm really losing sleep.
If he who hesitates is lost
Why look before you leap?" — Ricky Dunn

7. Compare words of popular songs and poems with similar themes, rhyme schemes, *etc*. *Example:* Song "Joey" by Weiner, Kriegsmann, Salmirs — Bernstein, and "The Look" by Sara Teasdale.
8. Discuss ideas for which we have no single words in the English language. Try to create new words. *Examples:*
   a. Find a synonym for "teen-ager."
   b. Originate a word meaning "former wife."
   c. Create combined words like "smog."
9. Clarify definitions of similar items. *Example:* Answer the question, "What's the difference between a burro, a donkey, a mule, and an ass?"
10. Write a title to a picture and include one figure of speech.
11. Using one of the figures of speech written by the class, extend the image by listing supporting evidence for the original statement. *Examples:*

"The wind is a rustler:
It sweeps swiftly over the plains
creeps stealthily around houses
herds cattle into dark canyons
frightens the fearful
is here today and gone tomorrow
The wind is a rustler."

* * *

"My love is as varied as the ocean.
It is uncontrollable and treacherous when the wind of jealousy blows
But when the sun of happiness shines
It is deeply contented and serene and lets its tide carry it in and out at will."

12. Describe anything (person, place, thing, experience) using details apparent to only one of the senses.
13. Build a poem based on ideas which come to you as you think about the line, "The clock cuts time into little bricks and walls up the past with them."
14. Write about the ideas which come to you as you think about Shaw's comment, "If you must hold yourself up to your children as an object lesson, hold yourself up as a warning and not as an example."
15. Do you agree or disagree with William Faulkner's state-

ment, "Man is man's most dangerous enemy"? Write about anything that comes to mind that would support your point of view. Try to *show* by someone's action that you agree or disagree.

16. Use "daily observations" which each pupil compiles in his notebook as motivation for writing. *Example:* I saw a girl enter the auditorium late, in the dark, and creep up to a pillar and stand there.
    a. From the point of view of the observer:
       She was short and it was tall.
       She was dark and it was light.
       She was soft and it was hard.
       Yet each with each was silent.
    b. From the point of view of the girl:
       I move silently into the still, filled dark,
       grope awkwardly for sure support,
       tentatively finger the air for textures recognizable,
       scrape painfully against grit-grains of wall,
       caress electrically rough wool, sleek satin,
       then find you, my pillar, my anchor in the lessening light.
       I can be silent with you.

PROSE

Whatever the motivation used, the products may be prose *or* poetry. The wise teacher will react welcomingly to both, giving no indication that she considers one "superior" to the other, and gradually most of the members of her class will make efforts at expressing themselves in both forms. A few suggestions which have proven successful in motivating the writing of prose follow:

A. Projects based on "needs" worked out by class and teacher
   1. *Need:* to learn to sense, interpret, identify, and put into words the emotional tone of human relationships.

      Needed is a "situation" picture, never before seen by any members of the class, depicting three or four individuals in what is not an immediately clear relationship or incident.

      After silent observation of the picture, each pupil writes down *one* word naming, as accurately as he can identify it, the emotion expressed by each individual in the picture, numbering words to correspond to the numbered figures in the picture. After all suggestions are written on the board, much discussion about shades of meaning follows (with dictionary and thesaurus help) and each person encircles the word he finally feels best describes each person pictured.

Pretending that this is an illustration for a short story, each pupil writes a caption for the picture, a title for the story, and names for the characters. Next, first sentences are written, and the writing period is on its way.

As always, the pupil may write anything he wishes: any length, form, subject. Whether the word "story," "composition," or "manuscript" is used in discussing writings depends on which word is most likely to allow freedom of expression. With some groups, the word "story" would mean any written prose. With others the word might imply definite literary form. It is up to the teacher to establish a conviction on the part of her students that any work is acceptable.

2. *Need:* To learn to recall with clarity, to identify, and to communicate effectively a personal, emotionalized experience.

   For a few minutes at the beginning of the period, each pupil rapidly lists names of specific feelings or emotions, reads his list to himself, and checks one word which recalls an incident in which he felt the named emotion.

   With dictionary and thesaurus, words which do not name emotions are eliminated; synonyms, antonyms, and various forms of the same word are discussed.

   The remainder of the period is spent in telling, on paper, the story of the experience in which he felt the emotion he checked.

   For the individual pupil who says, "I can't get started," suggestions like, "Just tell it the way it happened," or "Pretend you're telling your best friend about it," or "At first don't worry about how you say it, just get the ideas down on paper," may help.

   To the pupil who is still unable to get started, the teacher may say, "Tell me about it," writing down the first sentence or two the pupil relates. Then, "Well, here's the beginning for your story! Now tell the rest on paper just the way you were going to tell it to me."

3. *Need:* To learn to sense how others might feel in an experience the writer himself has not had.

   A real-life incident (the daily papers are full of suggestions!) is related by the teacher. In discussion, students list the various persons who might have anything to do with such an incident, each pupil choosing to "be" one of the characters. On paper, each relates in any form he wishes any aspect of the incident he wishes, changing or supplying any "facts" to meet his needs.

This type of "role-playing" often brings attitudes, actions, responsibilities in relation to basic life values to mind for the first time. Such activity can perform a major function in suggesting modes of behavior for emergency situations and in clarifying ethical concepts. Some suggested incidents are:

How would you feel and what would you do if you found something of real value on the school grounds and knew no one had seen you?

How would you feel and what would you do if you were driving a car and hit a pedestrian?

How would you feel and what would you do if you had promised folks you'd be home at a certain hour and your friends called you "chicken" for not staying out later?

How would you feel and what would you do if a friend asked to copy something from a test you were taking and you knew it was wrong?

How would you feel and what would you do if the child you were caring for hurt himself because of your negligence while you were on the phone?

B. Writing based on conversation:
1. Monologue
2. Dialogue
3. Soliloquy
4. Parallel soliloquy (two entirely different reactions to the same situation)
5. Three-way conversation (teenager on phone with younger sibling or parent at elbow)
6. Radio script
7. One-act play

BOOK REPORTS

Since formal book reports tend to limit the reporter's opportunity for creativity, varied ways in which students may be stimulated to share their reactions to reading are suggested below. As a springboard to the stimulation of variety and individuality in the expression of reactions to reading, certain premises should be considered:

There is no virtue in having the class conform to one pattern for all book reports.

There is definite educational value in having each pupil present several different types of reports.

Allowing only for the written book report continuously rewards those who write fluently and penalizes those who can draw, speak, act, or do other types of presentations, as well as those who work better with a group than alone.

One grows in his ability to communicate by seeing, hearing, and sensing the reactions of others to what he has to say.

Book reports may become a varied, stimulating, creative experience for both individual and group rather than a paper-checking chore for the teacher and a monotonous ordeal for the class.

Since one of the purposes of sharing reading experiences is the stimulation of reading interests in others, teachers need to plan for this sharing process.

Since one of the bases of sound education is meeting the needs of the many, teachers need to devise ways in which the non-academic students, comprising half of our national secondary student body, can gain confidence in their ability to take an equal part in class presentations and ways in which the gifted student can learn to accept and understand the limitations and contributions of others.

Since the sharing of reading experiences among adults is usually in the form of the friendly letter, informal dialogue, or informal group conversation, it is the responsibility of the teacher to provide practice opportunities and direction for such reading reactions.

The following list of suggestions for book reports was compiled over a period of three years by one teacher who allowed her pupils freedom of expression in sharing reading experiences.

A. Written reports

A friendly letter involving reactions to a recently read book

Two letters: one from the author submitting his manuscript for publication, one from the publisher accepting or rejecting the manuscript; both telling *why*

A series of letters (a correspondence) between any two characters in a book, between one character and the author, between the author and his literary agent or a literary critic, between two authors, between the author and director of the book in play, radio, or movie form, *etc.*, *etc.*, *etc.*

A monologue, dialogue, playlet, poem, expressing or interpreting the major conflict, the major mood, the major action, or the major character

A column of literary criticism

Reporter's interview with author or any one of the characters, with the director or star who is making the picture, TV or radio play, stage play

Diary of one of the characters

Analysis of a major character through things said (direct quotations) by him, about him, and to him

Comparison of book and movie, book and play, book and comic book version, abridged and unabridged versions

Student interviews with several recent readers of a book (Local and school librarians can be of help here.)

Letter to the author (really mailed) and possible answer

Writing new ending, justifying change and showing it to be consistent with characterizations, mood, theme, *etc.*

New title, justifying change by analysis of weakness of original and strength of new one

Actual interview with literary critic of local paper

B. Oral reports

Informal talk in form of scene at noon depicting two students eating lunch and discussing a book

Imagined talk by author and readers

Reading of part or parts, justifying choice and indicating relationship to the whole

Scene showing director instructing cast, assuming story is to be filmed

Radio interview with author

Panel about theme, characterizations, *etc.*

Debate: Resolved that the ending was true to the character of the hero

Pantomime with class guessing characters (in situations where entire class has read story or novel)

Reading from a movie or radio play, or TV script based on novel, indicating difference in preparation of various scripts

Comparison of several professional reviews

Telephone conversation, usually monologue, with class members writing down questions they think other party has asked

Improvisations growing out of character, conflict, plot

Sales talk during book hour by local librarian, bookstore owner, *etc.*

C. Visual or graphic book reports

Newspaper of at least one page (particularly adaptable to historical fiction or non-fiction; excellent project for two or more students)

Original dust jackets (including student-written summary sentence of story, introduction of characters, and one-sentence comments by "literary critics")

Playing cards illustrating characters, setting, and action, with captions. (One girl who said she just *could not write*, agreed to find pictures illustrating the major aspects of her novel and to write a one-sentence caption for each. She chose playing card backs for illustration, wrote a paragraph (!) about each, ending with a 400-word book report judged one of the five most interesting that month!)

Slides as guide to talk

Chalk talk

Maps

Costume sketches

Stage settings

Cartoons

Models — houses, theaters, *etc.*

Diagram of plot organization

Photographs of actual or similar scenes to illustrate another student's talk or written report

Visits to related places — exhibits, lectures, restaurants, international house lectures, plays, *etc.*

Obviously the above categorization is artificial. Almost any of the above suggestions can be carried out orally, graphically, or in writing, by individuals or groups, by combining methods and media.

Once students feel the freedom to express individuality and creativity, they will suggest and devise and enrich to their hearts' content, to the teacher's amazement, and to the class' enthusiastic anticipation of book reports. As a result the teacher will find real satisfaction in fulfilling her obligation to encourage young people to read about, talk about, and think about the books they have read.

CONCLUSION

Teaching is its own reward where the adult allows himself the freedom to allow his pupils freedom from entrapment within rigid forms of traditional correctness. Consideration of the following points may lead the way to the successful teaching of creative writing.

Creative expression cannot be forced, but it can be stimulated. The most important part of getting pupils to write is getting them to feel they *can* write.

In reacting to a pupil's early efforts, a teacher needs to spare the red pencil, noting at least one strength for every weakness. Often the one strength is as minute (yet as definite) as one fairly well-chosen word.

The major emphasis in the beginning must be on thought and feeling, not on mechanics or form. Pupils should be in-structured *first*, to *write*, not letting doubts about spelling, punctuation, *etc.*, hamper the flow of idea; and *second*, to re-write and polish, making a manuscript "look as good as it really is."

Situations should be created whereby evaluation of manuscripts and checking of errors in mechanics can be done by classmates to facilitate the individual and group growth towards higher standards of writing. A helpful technique is to use but one mark for all types of errors, forcing the student to discover the type of error checked.

A teacher will find much richer and more meaningful production where no limitations are placed on subject matter, style, length, or form. The teacher should be the first to see all manuscripts (except where authors themselves have shown their manuscripts to others) and should be the sole judge in deciding what may or may not be appropriate for classroom reading. It is the teacher's responsibility to practice understanding acceptance of each pupil, his views, and his writings, even though his material may not be usable for group sharing. It will take real skill on the part of the teacher at times to guide criticism from discussion of a political or religious *point of view* expressed in a manuscript to the *writing aspects* of that manuscript.

The teacher, too, should write, carrying through on whatever projects he has planned for his classes, for there is no end to the development of insight and skill through writing, and "elation and deep satisfaction" come to pupil and teacher alike.

CREATIVE WRITING BIBLIOGRAPHY

For Teacher's Use

Allen, Walter. *The Writer on His Art*. New York: McGraw Hill. 1949.

Armour, Richard. *Writing Light Verse*. Boston: The Writer, Inc. 1947.

Campbell, Walter S. *Writing: Advice and Devices*. New York: Doubleday and Company, Inc. 1950.

Hogrefe, Pearl. *The Process of Creative Writing*. New York: Harper and Brothers. 1947.

McCleary, Dorothy. *Creative Fiction Writing*. Boston: The Writer, Inc. 1947.

Mearns, Hughes. *Creative Youth*. New York: Doubleday and Company, Inc. 1925.

———. *Creative Power*. New York: Doubleday and Company, Inc. 1929.

Osborn, Alex F. *Applied Imagination*. New York: Charles Scribner's Sons. 1953.

Raphaelson, Samson. *The Human Nature of Playwriting*. New York: The Macmillan Company. 1949.

14. Setting College-Bound Students into Orbit

Phillip Shaw

Until recently, pupils received formal reading instruction only until the sixth grade. Above this grade, as they went up the educational ladder, students were expected to take increasingly difficult textbooks in their stride. It was presumed that at each rung of the ladder students would fill their mental storehouses with book learning. Then came the shock that was heard 'round the educational world: the development of aptitude and achievement tests. These disclosed that many students' heads contained miserably little knowledge compared with their storage capacity. Teachers began to examine themselves critically. Were students really learning from their readings? Were they doing their homework conscientiously? Were they getting the most out of what they read?

Soon teachers were conducting classroom studies of many kinds. Significant discoveries were made. Students together in a class were found to differ in reading achievement by four or five grades. Students also varied potentially, yet potentiality and achievement were not always matched. Nor were their reading preferences matched with what they were required to read. Even methods of teaching individuals and groups differed significantly as instruments of education. This outburst of research was widespread, relating, according to William S. Gray, "to practically every aspect of reading instruction at all school levels."

The impetus of the new research created increased concern over retarded readers. School and private reading clinics sprang up everywhere. Providing special help to the poorest students would, it was hoped, give American education a much-needed tonic. Instead of being a tonic, however, remedial instruction proved to be a sedative. As expressed recently by the President of Bowdoin College: "In unsuccessfully trying to raise the slow learners to the level of the average, the gifted have been retarded, and the average itself has been depressed." In secondary schools, "the efforts of teachers — and, more important, the efforts of students — fell off."

The mass atrophy of effort in American education is especially noticeable among the college-bound students. Commenting on observations of fifty-five high schools, James B. Conant reported: "In no school which I visited did the teachers or students feel that the majority of the academically talented boys or girls were working to full capacity." The atrophy of effort among our college-bound students becomes alarming when we remember two particular statistics concerning our high-school population. First, a staggering number of able American high school students fail to go to college — 150,000 such were reported by the Educational Testing Service in 1957. Second, in only a few years, the high school population will begin to swell as a result of the baby boom of the late 1940's. With an average of 7,600 babies being born daily since 1950, this swell will be no passing tidal wave but a lasting rise of level.

How can we help our college-bound to get into orbit? How can we stimulate talented secondary-school students to develop their power to the full in preparation for orbiting around college? How can we orbit the large number of able students who lack the motivation to soar off into higher education?

These questions are currently being met by drastic re-definitions of the roles of two different kinds of educators concerned with secondary education: the high-school reading specialist and the high-school classroom teacher.

Several recent studies of the job-characteristics of reading specialists have brought out a tale that might have been told by an idiot. First of all, if you were visiting a high school and you wanted to ask for the reading specialist, you would not know what title to use. A recent study by Ruth Strang revealed the absence of professional standards about the designation of "the reading person." It also brought out that particular duties of reading specialists likewise lack professional standardization. Now, to return to your supposed visit to a school, when you finally identify "the reading person," you could not guess where in the building you are likely to find him. He may be sitting behind a desk in the principal's office, shelving books in the library, or teaching in an English classroom. This picture of a jack-of-all-trades we can deduce from a report by H. Alan Robinson that disclosed that about half of the secondary-school reading specialists studied are expected to be specialists also in another subject. An added fact brought out by this report is that, almost to a man, each reading specialist who commented on his training to teach reading found it wanting. In this regard, Albert J. Harris has asserted that "so far as I have been able to find out, at least half of the people being appointed to positions of this type [i.e. as reading specialists] have had minimal training for it, or no training at all. They are given a job and then told, 'Go out and find how to do it.' "

Such a loose definition of the role of the reading specialist has come about because the demand for reading teachers has constantly exceeded the supply of trained personnel. Drafting of classroom teachers to do specialized work for which they lack professional training has been inevitable. This improvised recruitment has especially hurt the college-bound student. He in particular should be prepared so as to get the most out of learning from books. It is chiefly for him that Conant recommended a developmental reading course in high school. The college-bound student will suffer if the new reading programs are not staffed with professional reading teachers.

In proposing a developmental reading program for each high school, Conant made clear that such a program is not designed for slow learners. Now, remedial programs generally preserve their character because better readers are excluded. Developmental courses, however, tend to swell into "catch-all" programs. In particular, untrained reading teachers generally lean toward an "open-door" policy of admission to a reading program. Trained reading specialists, on the other hand, know that both corrective and developmental cannot effectively be taught together. Yet, being members of a special group without a clearly defined role and without exact professional status in the educational world, the trained specialist often cannot resist pressures for a supposed democratic reading program open to all comers. His alternative is to give up the developmental aspect entirely. Either action works to the detriment of college-bound students.

If only to provide college-bound students with the most professional program in reading, more college and graduate students must be attracted to study in the field of reading. On the other hand, the role of the reading specialist should be re-defined in terms of standards of preparation. The Board of Directors of the IRA is presently acting on such re-definition.

The role of a second kind of educator in the school career of a college-bound student is being re-defined today. This is the classroom teacher. Both the Conant Report and the Rockefeller Report on Education envisage the classroom teacher not only as a teacher but also as a counselor. In the following quotation from the Rockefeller Report, note the stress on the teacher's role in providing educational guidance to his students: "It cannot be emphasized too strongly that such guidance is essential to the success of our system. As many teachers as possible should be trained to take part in it. As many high schools as possible should have special guidance officers to supplement the teachers where greater technical knowledge is required." The suggested key to our present need for greater direction of able high-school students thus is the very key to the whole educational system: the teacher.

In their guidance role, teachers would be expected to do more than counsel their students concerning their future education. The Rockefeller Report refers to the kind of guidance expected of a teacher as follows: "The objective of all educational guidance is to stimulate the individual to make the most of his potentialities." The re-definition of the classroom teacher thus represents him as a comprehensive educator with three particular functions. He teaches the "content" of his subject, he helps his students with educational decisions, and he guides his students to do their best work in his subject.

The conception of the classroom teacher as a comprehensive educator certainly is not new for certain high school teachers. Some teachers are remembered forever by their students not for the facts that they learned from them but for the increased mental effectiveness they developed through being stimulated by them. In particular, they remember gratefully the teachers who helped them develop their ability to learn from and appreciate books.

Unfortunately some teachers regard reading instruction as a rival of "content" instruction. They acknowledge the value of reading instruction but declare that they would have to give up "content" in order to include it. This is a limited view of "content" and a passive view of the role of the teacher as an educator. In our system of education, books are important sources from which the student learns a subject. The teacher should guard against the possibility that his students substitute him for the course textbook. He should offer his students guidance in effective reading lest they rely too heavily on learning the subject from him. How to learn a subject from books is as valid and vital an aspect of "content" as is learning the matter itself.

Actually, many teachers are teaching reading without fully realizing it. When a mathematics instructor suggests to his students that they read the whole of an assignment before working out any of the problems and that they attack a verbal problem by looking for the key instructional word; when a biology teacher helps his class read a chart in a textbook and when he draws attention to the headings within a chapter of the textbook; when a history teacher advises his students to read the textbook "like a story" and to note, especially, cause-effect relationships and sequence of events; when a language teacher insists that students sift main ideas out of a mass of translated details and that students use context clues to deduce the meaning of unfamiliar foreign words — these teachers actually are offering guidance in effective reading.

Often a classroom teacher does not realize that he actually has been teaching reading, until he participates in a formal reading program. Such programs have been flourishing on the elementary level for years. More are needed on the secondary level. A recent report concerning high school instructors in Michigan is an example of the magnitude of this need. Of 570 teachers studied, 90 per cent received no college instruction on how to teach reading, and the majority were not even taught how to adjust reading materials to the wide range of ability expected in their classes. What is required for classroom teachers is more high-school in-service reading courses, more class demonstrations by reading consultants, and more attendance of workshops at college reading centers, and of professional reading conferences.

It is altogether possible that a classroom teacher with no training in or even inclination for scientific research could gain satisfaction out of what is called "action research." Action research concerns informal classroom experiments with teaching methods and materials. A number of journals publish reports on action research in reading. Teachers with modest professional ambitions can thus participate on a national arena. A good beginning for the avocation of being a writer on classroom practices in reading is examining reports of action research by other classroom teachers in such publications as *The Reading Teacher* and *The Journal of Educational Research.*

As we proceed from the proposed guidance function of the classroom teacher to further definition of his role in instructing college-bound students, we reach some unpleasant facts. One is that people in the profession of educating others are not notable for being well educated themselves. In 1956, more than 21 per cent of all public school teachers had less than four years of college. As for those with a B.A. degree, in the field of English — the presumed bulwark of literacy — a third of our states consider people eligible to teach high school English if they have only fifteen college credits in the subject. Massachusetts demands but nine credits! This year the National Council of Teachers of English is bringing the matter of certification of English teachers before accrediting associations.

About one third of our teachers seem not to spend their leisure time reading. While reporting this statistic, Dr. Alvina Burrows, director of a research project concerning teachers' reading, wrote rather charitably, as follows: "Teachers as a group are not outstandingly active in the wider reaches of literate pursuits." In another article, Mable F. Altsteller is more frank: "In general, teachers are not readers and have never known the delight and fullness that books can give." (On the other side of the ledger we have the Brooklyn high school teacher who was recently sentenced in court for the "unlawful detention" of twenty library books for periods ranging from two to five years.)

A second unpleasant fact is that, as a profession, secondary school teaching lacks community respect. Merle A. Tuve, of the Carnegie Institution, in making the point that we need more "high-quality teachers" in our secondary schools, described the following doleful state of affairs: "We have allowed the teachers of our high schools to drop from their old position of relatively high esteem in our communities to the workingman's level of grocery clerks or filling-station attendants or countless other service people in our present social fabric."

A third unpleasant fact is that teachers below the college level are, as expressed by the Rockefeller Report, "handled as interchangeable units in an educational assembly line. The best teacher and the poorest in a school may teach the same grade and subject, use the same textbook, handle the same number of students, get paid the same salaries, and rise in salary at the same speed to the same ceiling."

What these three unpleasant facts add up to is that high school teachers vary greatly in quality. The conclusion seems inescapable that the better teachers should teach the better students.

In defining the role of the better teachers as instructors of the college-bound students, no implication is intended that better teachers should be an elite circle into which neither the students who are not college-bound, nor the less gifted teachers ever move. Part of the abler teacher's school time should be devoted to lecturing through television and preparing sound-motion pictures and tape recordings of their lessons. This Arthur I. Gates urged in an article concerning future means of improving reading. He wrote further: "The subtle arts of the master teachers should be made widely available on television and in sound-motion pictures for other teachers to observe. Television offers opportunities for master teachers to teach pupils and less gifted teachers at the same time. Instructors thus engaged in teaching both college-bound students in classes of regular size and also other students and teachers in large groups would, of course, receive extra pay. Good compensation for this work would attract a greater number of gifted teachers into the high schools. Our college-bound students would benefit most from an improvement in the quality of people who become high school teachers.

15. Improving the Reading of Academically Untalented Students

Edwin Mingoia

The characteristic most prominently associated with the student having a history of poor grades in the academic subjects is deficiency in reading skills. He often complains that he cannot understand the texts he reads; consequently, he is referred to as a "reading problem." In many cases the student is a case of arrested development in reading. He does not have the skills, attitudes, and habits necessary for adequate performance in the academic subjects as ordinarily taught.

If his problem is one of negative self-concept which says, "I am a person hating reading and am no good in it," a remedial reading class will do little good. By the time the poor academic student has arrived in high school, he is thoroughly convinced he is dumb. The "D's" and "F's" have too thoroughly done their job in reinforcing this picture of himself. Counseling may be the only means to help this student overcome his conviction that he is stupid.

If the poor academic student can read the newspaper, he no longer needs basic phonics as much as he needs a reading program which will develop further the skills he already possesses. Also, he needs the opportunity to explore the world of books. In so doing, his taste for book learning will increase, and so will his vocabulary. A student cannot be expected to read his English, science, and social studies texts with adequate understanding unless he has a wide background of information gleaned from incidental reading.

The remainder of this article will be devoted to suggestions on teaching procedures, materials, and plans to be used with these students.

Some Teaching Procedures

1. MAKE POSSIBLE INDIVIDUALIZED, SELF-SELECTION IN READING.

The individualized, self-selection program is one that inspires the student to become acquainted with the world of books. This program, offering the student the opportunity to assume responsibility for his own learning, is not to be confused with free reading or the "book reports" routine. It is a program that has a unique, definite structure. The teacher should have many weeks of orientation and planning to launch such a program. Self-selection incorporates the ideas of a good literature program, individualized reading, recreational reading, and bibliotherapy.

Self-selection is based on the principle that the student, under proper guidance in a rich literary environment, will choose reading experiences best suited for his own particular development. In addition to the idea in the motto, "There is a right book, short story, article, or poem for the right student at the right time," there is also the idea of a right assignment sheet or project.

It is important that a "lush" reading environment be established — shelves of books and periodicals, vertical files of assignments, and work centers affording the student the opportunity to use phonetic games, crossword puzzles, filmstrips, reading accelerators, and earphones plugged to recordings of plays and poems.

Although the student is encouraged to read material on his level which is suitable in the school situation, he is under no commitment but his own. The program operates entirely on a self-commitment and self-service basis. He may choose to spend a half-hour superficially skimming through a novel or he may even re-read one. It is the teacher's role, however, to help the student reconstruct the reading experience through appropriate projects of reporting that challenge the best kind of thinking.

The self-selection differs from most reading programs in that record keeping and flexible, small-group instruction become the two basic, indispensable processes that keep the program alive and growing.

Both teacher and student keep a variety of records. The teacher's anecdotal recordings continuously appraise the student's reading development — attitudes, interests, skills, and difficulties; the student keeps records of materials read, new vocabulary, and ways he reconstructed the reading experience.

The class as a whole employs projects (i.e., a central file of book commentaries, a growing mural of storybook characters, the expanding class project chart) to serve as record of movement toward commonly established goals.

In addition to individual counseling, the teacher uses small group instruction, a method that saves literally hours of teaching because of its high degree of interaction among students and teacher. Groupings are flexible depending on the purpose, i.e., skill building, discussion of common reading, planning projects, stimulating interest.

2. TEACH READING BEFORE ASSIGNING A CHAPTER IN THE TEXTBOOK.

a. Stimulate interest in the chapter. Build a background. Engage students in a discussion on the subject the chapter will cover.
b. Raise questions, problems, and purposes which will serve as a guide for reading independently.
c. Pave the way for smooth, independent reading by listing the anticipated new vocabulary to be encountered in the chapter. Discuss the pertinent abstract concepts.
d. Instruct the students on how they should read the chapter (skim, reread, study, outline).

Caution: The textbook may be so much above the "D" and "F" students that this procedure will do them little good. Average and fringe students benefit greatly.

3. TEACH PHONICS.

Poor academic students have difficulty with the main unit in syllables — the phonogram. To attack words phonetically, the student should start with the phonogram, then apply the initial consonant or blend to it, and then add the suffix. For example, how would one help him to recognize the word *brightly?* Start with the *ight* phonogram. Add before it the *br*, and then add the *ly*.

The phonograms presenting a certain amount of difficulty are: *ue, eet, ive, com, cot, ight, ich, ore, ent, ass, uy, ilk, ead, ease, om, east, ith, orse, out, arm, ird, ern, our, eak, ink, alk, arm, ove, ora, ick, ile, old, aid, int, cod, ought, tion, atch, itch, eel, orn, oast, ound, ough, age, oil, aight, uice.*

Anagrams consisting of initial consonants and blends (i.e., *b, c, d, g, dr, br, th, sm, fl, sw, sp*), and phonograms (listed above) can be used for several interesting games. For example, matching initial consonants to phonograms to make real or nonsense words can be fun as well as educational. Students could go to a phonics center to work out these anagram games, or even construct them.

Many poor academic students do not have a clear understanding about the syllable. For instance, they may not realize that:

a. Every syllable, as a rule, has a vowel.
b. Some syllables are stressed more than others.
c. A syllable can be represented by one or more letters, although most syllables are represented by one to three letters.

Most poor academic students are ready to understand the difference between short and long vowels and the reasons underlying these differences. They know most of the suffixes, although they are still troubled with *tion*, *ous*, *ious*, *iest*.

Caution again: Often the student is acquainted with principles of phonics, and recognizes them in the abstract in order to do artificial assignments. Nevertheless, he has never developed the habit of applying what he knows to his own reading. This is the next step. It is very important. The teacher must teach the student to apply knowledge about phonics in his daily reading and writing.

4. TEACH RESEARCH SKILLS.

Often teachers assume that their students know how to do research, but the poor academic student is staggered by an assignment requiring research skills. He may resort to behavior such as forgetting pencils, books, papers, and homework. On days when a book report or an important assignment is due, he may be tardy or absent.

A sensitive teacher should be able to interpret whether or not the inappropriate behavior is in reality a cry for help. In many cases, inappropriate behavior can be a sign that the student is unable to cope with an assignment without extra direction and guidance. The teacher should be aware that the poor academic students are extremely dependent on the teacher for help in the execution of assignments requiring research and composition skills. They do not know how to use the encyclopedia, *Reader's Guide*, the library card catalog, and other sources to find information. Even after a student has located the material, he may not know how to utilize the information. Since he does not know how to interpret or decide what is pertinent, he may resort to copying pages verbatim. A teacher who can guide the student to raise specific questions outlining the nature of the written report will help him to compose a purposeful report having an original, unique organization and style.

Materials for Teaching

1. *Science Research Associates' Reading Laboratory*. Through its definite, well-spelled-out procedures, it gives both teacher and students the security of a progressive routine. The security given the teacher should release him to experiment with a more creative approach, i.e., self-selection or book-making. The SRA *Reading Laboratory* is a valuable instrument in teaching content reading, dictionary skills, comprehension, phonics, and vocabulary. It inculcates the ideas of self-motivation, self-correction, correct study techniques. It is individualized.

The *Laboratory* places less stress on the importance of the practical uses of reading, and tends to bypass the stage of extended, voluntary reading. Nevertheless, most students profit greatly from it. It has been used successfully in most reading improvement courses. Unfortunately, some poor academic students cannot profit from packaged courses because of certain problems that require counseling or a tutoring program utilizing a more creative approach to the teaching of reading.

2. *American Adventure Series.* The Wheeler Publishing Company has published a series of corrective readers of high interest level. The success of these books is predicated on the teacher's following the manual (*Handbook on Corrective Reading* by Emmett A. Betts) faithfully and devoting time to small-group instruction. The teacher is the focal point who guides the student page by page to do reading at a level where he recognizes 100% of the words. This program is mainly slanted for the most reluctant, and therefore, most dependent-on-the-teacher readers.

3. *Reader's Digest Skill Builders.* The lowest level approximates a third-grade reader. The content is of high interest value.

4. *Be a Better Reader Books, Prentice-Hall.* A few poor academic students can profit greatly from Nila B. Smith's workbooks on reading in literature, mathematics, social studies, and science. A student reading on a seventh-grade level or better can profit from this instruction emphasizing vocabulary, phonics, structural analysis of words, diacritical markings, pacing, and eye movements. Caution: Most poor academic students, especially those reading below a sixth-grade level, would profit little. These workbooks are especially good for the average and above average student.

5. *The daily newspaper.* Students might report on news that is appropriate to the school situation.

6. *Life magazine.* Teacher-composed questions can guide the reading.

7. *Science fiction, sports, and automobile stories.* These stories have been known to be the match that set the fire of reading interest among reluctant readers.

8. *Driver's examination handbook.* A terrific motivation to read for those preparing for a license examination.

9. *Western novels.* Clay Fisher, Jack Schaefer, and others have written some very good western stories. It is difficult to challenge with works of Keats or Dickens the student whose cultural background consists wholly of western TV plays and "cowboy and Indian" movies. Start with the best of the cultural background of the students, and move them only gradually and at the opportune time.

10. *Classic Comics and Dell Comics.* The Classic Comics and Dell

Comics have done much to give a superficial survey of our cultural heritage. Everybody likes them. They do much to build a positive attitude towards literature, which otherwise would remain forever foreign to some students. Not all the Classic Comics are abridged. "The Lady of the Lake," for example, is presented in its entire text with explanatory notes and worthy illustrations.

11. *Landmark Books, Random House.* A whole social studies program can revolve around the easy-to-read Landmark books. The best children's authors have worked to make certain historical events read like novels. Many students have confessed that a Landmark book had been the first book that they ever had read from cover to cover on their own.

12. *Big Little Books TV Series, Whitman Publishing Company.* This series includes *Gunsmoke, Sir Lancelot, The Buccaneers, Jim Bowie, Andy Burnett, and Wyatt Earp.* The Whitman Publishing Company has published much material which, because of its popular, current interest, can appeal to the most reluctant reader in the class.

13. *Tachistoscope and Controlled Readers.* For students reading below a fifth-grade level, drill on the Dolch List words is helpful. Because the student can recognize them, the drill should be on the speed of recognition. Similar drill should aid in speeding the slow reader.

Mechanical aids with programs for their use are: (a) Controlled Readers with filmstrips, and Tach-x. (Coast Visual Education, 5620 Hollywood Blvd., Hollywood 28), (b) Rateometer (Audio-Visual Research, 523 S. Plymouth Ct., Chicago 5), (c) Tachistoscope and Reading Accelerator (Keystone Viewing Co., Meadville, Pa.), (d) Accelerator (Science Research Associates, 57 West Grand, Chicago 10).

Mechanical aids stress speed of reading and purport to encourage visual accuracy and retention; the rationale is that better readers organize their eye movements more efficiently by better attention, focus, and directional attack. Moreover, good readers can correlate the reading with past experiences.

Caution: Although mechanical aids are an excellent means to arouse interest, their use alone cannot help all students. They have a place, however, in the reading improvement classes organized around either the SRA *Reading Laboratory* or an individualized, self-selection program. In speed reading classes usually reserved for learners approaching maturity in reading, they are an indispensable part of the program.

14. *Reading for Understanding, Science Research Associates.* This program offers material that carries the process of reading beyond the elementary mechanics — word recognition, word attack, speed —

to the real end of reading — understanding the ideas and meanings words convey. This self-administering, learning-thinking program contains materials indexed from a third-grade level through twelfth. The program purports to teach the student to do careful and critical reading. During the process of completing paragraphs, students make use of the tools of logic-inference, analogy, syllogistic reasoning — and improve ability to work with verbal aspects of problem solving.

Administrative Plans for Helping Poor Readers

1. READING IMPROVEMENT TEACHERS

The services of reading improvement teachers with a background in counseling and corrective reading are essential. In addition to teaching reading improvement classes, they may offer intensive reading therapy on an individual or small-group (four to six) basis for students unable to profit from reading classes.

Through the use of SRA materials, it is possible to accommodate thirty to forty students reading from a third- to ninth-grade level. The heterogeneity of the reading improvement class is encouraged to the extent that one-fifth of its members should be superior students. This heterogeneity is one of the advantages of the reading improvement class over the remedial reading class which too often becomes a dumping ground for reluctant learners.

The selection of the students should be based on common sense rather than on an elaborate formula based on test results. First, the student should be willing to participate, and should be accepted fully by the teacher; second, he must be able to read a third reader or better if the *Laboratory* is to be used; third, his regular English teacher should feel that the reading improvement would provide a more valuable learning experience than the one being provided.

Materials making heterogeneous reading improvement classes possible are the SRA *Secondary Reading Laboratory* and *Reading for Understanding*. The use of mechanical aids is optional, but is recommended as a valuable supplement. The Coast Visual Education's controlled reader has a place in the reading improvement classes as well as in speed reading classes.

The individualized, self-selection program can adequately be the basis of a reading improvement class instead of one organized exclusively around SRA materials and mechanical aids, since it makes use of all materials, mechanical aids, and workbooks.

Caution: Students poor in academic subjects cannot tolerate a heavy load of academic subjects in their school program. The reading improvement class should be an alternative to one required, and should be given credit accordingly. An added elective in reading improvement may overbalance his program.

In every high school there will be students unable to profit from reading improvement classes because of language problems, study and "motivation" difficulties, or simply because of inability to read a third reader or better. The reading improvement teacher should tutor these students three or four periods a day. Unlike the reading improvement class with its well spelled out procedures, these tutoring periods should be extremely flexible. The services provided by the teacher working with individuals or small groups are: (a) find suitable materials; (b) plan projects or assignments that can be executed under the direction of the English or social studies teacher; (c) provide directive or nondirective counseling; (d) counsel parents and teachers; (e) help with research and written reports; (f) give instruction in phonics, structural analysis, and vocabulary; (g) provide bookmaking for the nearly nonreader and kinesthetic training for those reading from first to second grade level; (h) provide instruction in study habits.

Caution: All students having reading or study difficulties should be given a Keystone visual survey through the use of the Keystone Telebinocular in order to discover those to be referred for professional eye care or to be benefited by adjustments in their school work as related to visual requirements.

2. ALTERNATIVE COURSES

Alternative courses have been organized in some schools for both poor students and those of average or better ability. These courses would be based on the needs, abilities, and interests of the student. Some of the courses might be organized as:

a. Reading improvement classes (described above).
b. Remedial reading class for students unable to read a third reader.
c. Speed reading class. These classes devoted to developing maturity in reading have a definite place in the comprehensive modern high school. It is doubtful whether the poorer academic student could profit from them. Such students need a more comprehensive approach. Good students would profit from speed reading classes making use of:
   (1) Controlled reader with film-strips
   (2) SRA *Reading for Understanding*
   (3) *How to Become a Better Reader* by Paul Witty can be used to develop reading rate, comprehension, vocabulary.

3. SELF-CONTAINED CLASSROOMS IN ACADEMIC SUBJECTS

For some students, this may be the solution. A classroom under the direction of one teacher teaching English, social studies, science, and perhaps mathematics could be considered. Difficult psychological problems accompany so-called homogeneous groupings. A certain amount of self-hate is perpetuated or even magnified by such an organization that prevents the class from being welded into a group. A *crowd* of reluctant readers resisting instruction will not learn much. In certain situations, a skillful teacher may be able to maneuver around this pitfall.

4. RESEARCH TEACHER

The librarian, research teacher, or reading improvement teacher can assume responsibility for teaching proper research skills.

5. COUNSELING SERVICE

Counseling has an important function. Through less than twenty hours of individualized counseling, many poor academic students have been transformed into students who liked study. Both directive and nondirective counseling should be used. Good counseling, although expensive from a short-range viewpoint, offers the best avenue of hope for the poor academic students, especially those who do not achieve commensurate with their potential. It is an advantage of the reading improvement teacher plan that a part of the school day can be scheduled for working with individuals or small groups (four to six).

Literacy development goes hand in hand with discipline and school morale. It is a true but sad fact that most of our students who are crippled by inadequate literacy development are the ones most likely to resort to aggressiveness, inattention, and truancy. When schools help the poor reader to become more literate, they go a long way in eliminating other related problems. A combination of reading improvement classes and tutoring services under the guidance of a reading improvement teacher can contribute not only to the development of the reading program but also to the betterment of discipline among students and morale among teachers.

16. Reading Ability and High School Drop-Outs

Ruth C. Penty

As director of counseling in the Battle Creek High School, I had opportunity to talk with boys and girls about both their scholastic difficulties and personal problems. I also had opportunity to talk with teachers and parents about the problems of young people. In addition, I had access to the mental maturity and reading scores as well as to the cumulative records of the boys and girls enrolled in our high school.

All of these contacts seemed to point to trouble with reading as one of the basic difficulties in connection with academic problems. Trouble with reading also appeared to be related to some personal problems. Therefore, while I was continuing my work in the guidance area, I also took some courses in secondary school reading so that I could better assist these young people who were having difficulties with reading and so that I could better assist teachers in helping them.

Reading test scores showed that many of our incoming sophomore students were reading far below grade level, and corresponding mental maturity scores pointed to the fact that these students had potential for growth in reading. At the other end of the scale, our Principal-Freshman Conferences were informing us that some of our freshmen college students were not doing well in their content areas or were staying up until one or two o'clock in the morning in an attempt to prepare their assignments, as they read so slowly, did not comprehend or know how to comprehend what they read.

In 1951, we therefore started a reading improvement program in our high school, concentrating our help on our sophomore and senior students. We encouraged all teachers to assume responsibility for the development of vocabulary in their respective subject areas, to help students enrolled in their classes to read and study the content involved, and to organize that material through note-taking, outlining, answering of questions, or some other method appropriate to the subject. We also encouraged all classroom teachers to adjust textbooks and other reading materials to the reading level of students. The tenth- and twelfth-grade English teachers assumed responsibility for many aspects of the reading program: (1) the diagnosing of individual difficulties, (2) helping with techniques of finding main thought and important detail, (3) improving speed of comprehension and several other skills needed by the boys and girls in their classes. Special reading groups were also organized to assist those students who were very retarded in reading and who needed help with basic vocabulary and the development of word attack skills. For these students, very easy reading material had to be provided.

As you who work in public schools would predict, not all teachers became enthusiastic participants in this reading improvement effort, either because they felt that the high school was assuming an elementary school task, because they actually believed that high school students should be able to read and study their assignments if they applied themselves, or because they felt insecure about giving help because of lack of training.

At this time, our high school administration became very interested, as did administrators across the nation, in the number of boys and girls who were dropping out of school before high school graduation. We therefore increased our extracurricular program, set up a Basic Living Course requirement for all sophomore students, and prepared an Exit Interview Sheet for the use of all counselors so that we could gather together some data based on reasons why young people leave school. We had a hunch that reading ability might be an important factor connected with the school leaving of boys and girls. However, we did not have valid evidence. The reasons most frequently given on our Exit Sheets were (1) work too difficult, (2) lack of interest, (3) work not suited to the abilities of students, (4) desire to get a full-time job.

Here was a doctoral research problem in which I was really interested — a study of reading ability and high school drop-out. I felt that it might give impetus to our reading program and that the findings might add to the literature on early school leaving. In searching the literature, I found only four very brief studies of reading ability as a factor in school drop-out. None of these was a concentrated study of the specific problem.

In addition to the reading and mental maturity testing data on sophomore students for a four-year period, for those who left school and for those graduated, and Exit Interview Sheets for drop-outs, we decided to interview the poor readers enrolled in the current senior class in the high school, the poor readers who had graduated in the three-year period, and all of the poor readers who had dropped out of school. Interviewing was done after school, evenings, week ends, and during the summer in the homes of former students or in a private office in the local YWCA.

The order of presentation of data was then prepared. It was planned to study (1) reading achievement of the group studied, (2) proportion of drop-outs and graduates among poor readers and good readers; then to make (3) a more intensive study of the poor readers with the questions in mind: (a) What percentage dropped out of school? (b) What percentage remained to graduate? (c) At what time did students drop out of school? (d) How did the drop-outs and graduates among poor readers compare in intelligence test scores? (e) What was the reading growth potential of the poor readers who dropped out and those who graduated? (f) How did a sampling of these two groups feel about themselves and their school subjects? (g) What was their attitude toward reading and toward teachers? (h) What were their relations with other students? and (i) What reasons did they give for leaving school or for graduating?

The interviews held with both drop-outs and graduates were very interesting in themselves and they also yielded highly significant data. The free response questions asked of the school leavers were these:

1. Please think back to the time you left school. What reasons did you give for leaving school?

2. As you think back now, what would you say were your *real* reasons for leaving school?

The free response question asked of the graduates was: What do you think are the main reasons why you remained in school until graduation?

The structured questions included:

1. Those related to subjects liked and disliked
2. Types of reading troubles encountered when reading was mentioned as a source of difficulty
3. The amount of time spent in preparation of subjects
4. Frequency of participation in class discussions
5. Feelings of students toward themselves, toward other students, and toward teachers
6. Participation in extraclass activities
7. Help obtained in the reading area

In very few cases were reasons given on the Exit Sheet by students at time of school leaving like the reasons given by these young people from one to six years afterwards. Only 5 per cent of the students who dropped out of school gave the same reason at the time of school leaving that they gave later in their interview. The type of answer given at exit was in most cases one which was acceptable and which permitted easy escape. In the later conference, reasons given seemed more nearly like basic reasons. The following are selected from reasons given by drop-outs who were far below grade in reading:

I was discouraged. I was not getting any place in school. I thought the Marines was a better place to be. I had difficulty in reading. I couldn't remember what I read. I was often embarrassed in class.

I didn't like school too well. I wanted to get married. I couldn't remember what I read. I didn't like to go to classes and be around other kids who seemed to learn more easily than I did.

I left school because I had to help support my mother and I was under the impression that I was inferior to the rest of the kids. I had trouble with reading, too. I couldn't keep my mind on it. I was afraid of being laughed at if I didn't know the answers. I would like to read better and still would.

I was nervous at school. I felt all right when I started to work outside. I had trouble in getting the ideas from my reading. The words bothered me, too. I didn't like to recite in class. I would rather write my answers than give them before the class.

We were always quarreling at home. I wasn't getting along in some subjects at school either. I wanted to get married. I think now that marriage isn't always rosy. It is better for kids to finish school first. I understand what I read if I am interested. English and history were hard for me. I didn't know some of the words so I couldn't understand them.

These statements made by poor readers during the interviews emphasize the multiplicity of reasons why boys and girls leave school before graduation. They also point to the influence which reading difficulty has in causing young people to make a decision to leave school when that difficulty causes them to fail subjects, to receive low grades, and to feel that they are inadequate and not able to learn through reading.

In response to the interview question, "What do you think are the main reasons why you continued in school until graduation even though you had some difficulty with reading?" these were some of the answers given:

Because I realized that you couldn't get much of a job if you did not graduate.

My parents encouraged me.

It was taken for granted that I would. My parents finished high school.

My dad and my counselor encouraged me.

I liked the classes, especially the discussions. I also liked band and physical education.

I had a deep desire to graduate. I am the only one in my family who did.

My mother and dad wanted me to. I liked the kids.

Strong personal desire to graduate, encouragement of family, family expectation, interest in specific subjects, interest in sports and other extracurricular subjects, desire for a better job, help from counselors and teachers, and liking to be with other young people were among the reasons why these students who had trouble in reading continued through school until graduation.

The following is a summary of findings,[1] followed by conclusions and implications for education.

More than three times as many poor readers as good readers dropped out of school before graduation; the peak of the school leaving among the drop-outs was during the tenth grade.

There was no significant difference in average reading scores at the tenth-grade level of the poor readers who dropped out of school before graduation and of the poor readers who remained in school until graduation.

The interview data emphasized that difficulty in reading played a very important role in the school leaving of boys and girls, especially when certain other problems and pressures were present.

It was evident from the data that the poor readers who remained in school also had difficulty in reading. However, the better emotional and social adjustment of the graduates, probably the result of home security, interest, and economic status superior to that of the boys and girls who dropped out of school, and also of more fortunate school experiences, permitted them to be less burdened by a multiplicity of problems among which the reading problem was one. Among the poor readers who graduated were some who felt that people expected them to graduate: they had always expected to graduate from high school; their parents encouraged them; their teachers and counselors helped them; they had "made up their minds" to graduate and had set this as their goal. A few thought a high school education would help them get a better job. Last, but not least, they were getting some real satisfactions from school: they enjoyed the school dances, athletics, and other extraclass activities, were interested in doing well in one or more subjects, and "liked the kids" in their school. These seemed to be some of the reasons why pupils of low reading ability persisted in school until they graduated. To prevent a high percentage of drop-outs, more attention should be given to these favorable conditions.

A study of the disparity between reading ages and mental ages of the poor readers who dropped out of school and of the poor readers who remained in school but who experienced difficulty in reading, revealed that a very large percentage of the young people in both groups had potential in reading ability. With proper help, these students could have shown marked improvement in reading ability, which would probably have contributed to better scholastic achievement and personality adjustment.

[1] For more detail see Ruth Penty, *Reading Ability and High School Drop-Outs*, N. Y.: Bureau of Publications, Teachers College, Columbia University, 1956.

PART FOUR

Student Motivation

17. Campaigning to Get Students to Read

Dwight L. Burton

The title of this article reflects our assumption that it is important to develop in students an interest in personal reading. The challenge to do this more successfully sharpens as accumulating research reveals a disconcerting picture of poverty-stricken reading lives among high school, and in only slightly lesser degree, college students. Secondary-school faculties interested in campaigning to lead their students to a habit of reading for personal pleasure and profit might ask themselves four major questions.

Are All Teachers on the Reading Team?

"Every teacher a teacher of reading," a popular slogan for some time, needs translation into actual classroom practice if many students are to realize the value of personal reading. English teachers have important, but by no means total, responsibilities in the broad reading program which contributes toward some of the most important personal and social objectives of general education in which every teacher has a stake. Too often, extensive or "outside" reading, as it is called erroneously sometimes, has been considered only a frill on the solid fabric of the curriculum. Teachers need to realize that the extensive reading program makes important contributions in many content areas.

In the social studies class, for example, time and place concepts remain perennial learning problems as anyone can discover by asking a group of adolescents to tell what was going on in the "late 1870's," to indicate when "the Middle Ages" were, or to describe the meaning of "postwar austerity" in Great Britain. Reading of imaginative literature as a supplement to history and other kinds of factual material can do much to build clear and enriched concepts of time and place. For many students, despite a liberal exposure to American history, the American Revolution remains a hazy melange of tea in the Boston harbor, a midnight ride by Paul Revere, and frozen feet at Valley Forge. The momentous issues and actions of that day become real as they are pondered and experienced by specific young people in such books as Emma Patterson's *The World Turned Upside Down* and Esther Forbes' *Johnny Tremain.*

The whole story of America's past has been dramatized in imaginative literature which social studies teachers can draw upon as a way of furthering learning in their subject as well as building enduring reading interests. Bacon's Rebellion, a remote occurrence covered perhaps in Chapter 7 of the history textbook, is something to be lived through for a young indentured servant in Gertrude Finney's *Muskets Along the Chickahominy.* The Lewis and Clark Expedition can be a thrilling personal adventure in James Daugherty's *Of Courage Undaunted.* People and events in our country's westward movement are brought out of the pages of history for moving close-ups in such books as *Caddie Woodlawn*, a story of pioneer life in Wisconsin, Shannon Garst's *Sitting Bull*, and *Chanticleer of Wilderness Road*, Meridel LeSueur's vigorous and humorous story of Davy Crockett. Extensive reading in social studies need not be restricted to imaginative literature of only America's past but might include the ancient and medieval world by use of such titles as Malvern's *Behold Your Queen*, the story of Esther, young queen of Persia, Price's *The Dragon and the Book* which is set in England in the Middle Ages, or modern Europe through the reading of Nina Baker's biographies of Garibaldi, and Lenin.

Social studies teachers have an opportunity to draw upon a wealth of American regional writing which can provide understanding through vicarious living in the various sections of the nation which no amount of textbook material can supply. Again, this can be extended to the world scene. In Hahn's *Francie*, for example, British postwar austerity is reduced to day-by-day specifics in the life of a high-school girl, and events in Korea take on added meaning from a reading of Crockett's *Pong Choolie, You Rascal.*

Extensive, individual reading is important, too, in the study of social problems, a major concern of the social studies class. American literature, from *Uncle Tom's Cabin* to *The Grapes of Wrath*, has had important things to say about our group problems. Study of topics such as minority problems, housing, crime and delinquency, labor unions, and World War II gives an opportunity to guide wide reading in fiction, poetry, biography, and other non-fiction and to instill the idea that literature treats not only of "hearts and flowers" but also of the whole gamut of man's experience.

Perhaps no teacher is in better position today to build reading interests while at the same time enriching his own program than the science teacher. Events, in particular the dropping of the atomic bomb and the popularization of television, have lifted science from the esoteric and abstruse to the vital and everyday. Since 1945 when "the bomb" was dropped, public reading of science materials has doubled. The phenomenal mushrooming of interest in science fiction has been due in large part to the amazing and terrifying vista opened by the atomic era. Science fiction, particularly by authors of the caliber of Ray Bradbury, Isaac Asimov, and Robert Heinlein, is a legitimate part of the materials for the high-school science class. So, too, is related non-fiction like *Your Trip Into Space* by Lynn Poole and *Guided Missiles: Rockets and Torpedoes* by Frank Ross, Jr. Books on television like Floherty's *Television Story* and Tolley's *The Television Workshop* also belong in the science teacher's repertoire.

But atomic energy, science fiction, and television are not the only possibilities the science teacher has for tapping reading interests. The American public has been enthralled with Rachel Carson's *The Sea Around Us*, a unique book of ocean lore, and *Annapurna* which is not only a story of mountain climbing but also an authentic source of information on the science of high altitudes. And for students who really want to talk about the weather, the teacher could recommend *Wind, Storm, and Rain* by Miller. The keen junior high-school interest in animals could lead, for some students, to *Burglar in the Tree Tops*, a book of animal life, and the science library would not be complete without some of the excellent biographies of men of science, such as *William Crawford Gorgas: Tropic Fever Fighter*.

For many boys, the physical education teacher or coach would have more influence in recommending reading than any other teacher and for some girls, the home economics teacher. It should not be too far-fetched to expect the physical education teachers or coaches to recommend reading from the world of sports, hobbies, and recreation. Many home economics teachers who have gone beyond the skills of cooking and sewing in their courses have an opportunity to guide reading in the areas of etiquette, grooming and dress, home decoration, and the very important field of home and family life.

Extensive reading has a place even in such classes as industrial arts and agriculture, often thought of as remote from the realm of literature. For in these classes, some students may become acquainted with materials such as special interest magazines which they will read for the rest of their lives, reading to which they would not be introduced otherwise. Henry Lent's *O-K for Drive-Away*, a book on automobiles and automobile makers, might be an absorbing reading experience for some boys. The agriculture teacher's library might be the source of Billings' *All Down the Valley*, the story of T. V. A., or Bailey's *Tim's Fight for the Valley*, an exciting novel involving old and new methods in farming.

The teachers in each area of the curriculum will be able to "reach" certain types of students. Our best hope of capitalizing on interests which may lead to enduring reading tastes and habits among most students is a broad program of guidance in reading which permeates the entire school curriculum.

Is the Literature Program a 1955 Model?

So far nothing has been said of the English teacher's role in the program of extensive reading. Naturally, the English teacher retains a key responsibility in developing appreciation and taste in literature. School faculties need to examine the principles undergirding the program in literature which the English teachers spearhead. This examination will be watchful of over-emphasis on two moss-grown traditions in the teaching of literature which have tended to stymie rather than kindle real enthusiasm among students. We might label these traditions as the academic and the feminine.

The academic tradition establishes the selection of literature as the point of departure. The assumption is that all or most students can be brought to an appreciation of the selection through dint of ingenious and unremitting labor on the part of the teacher. Certain "classics" such as *Evangeline*, *The Vision of Sir Launfal*, *The Merchant of Venice*, *The Idylls of the King*, *Ivanhoe*, *The Lady of the Lake*, *Silas Marner*, and *Macbeth* are allocated to the several grade levels, and the task of the teacher is to make students aware of the beauty and inspiration which she, supposedly, finds in the selection. Another touchstone of the academic tradition is a pre-occupation with literary history, especially at the eleventh and twelfth grade levels where the literature study is likely to be organized chronologically, and with literary technique. Students are likely to spend a good bit of time finding the climax of the short story and learning what iambic pentameter is.

It is certain that high-school students should develop some basic understanding of the technique of literature and *some* students should read some of the great literature of our culture. Yet an over-emphasis on this academic approach to literature has been deadly to the development of real interest in reading. After a grueling four-week bout with *The Idylls of the King*, the disgusted tenth-grade pupil is likely to decide, "If this is what it's like to read good literature, I'll take Budweiser."

Closely allied to the academic tradition in teaching literature is the feminine which refers to an approach to the subject rather than to the fact that the large majority of secondary English teachers are women. From this tradition, in which literature is presented as something rarified, students get the idea that it deals with a precious world of love, the beauties of nature, lofty philosophy, and "all that stuff." Eighth-grade boys and many girls are disgusted, for example, by having to read *Evangeline* which has a theme of adult, passionate love. They tend to think it perfectly stupid that a woman spends her life chasing a man around the North American continent. Or the twelfth-grade boy finds no rhapsody in tripping through the daffodils with Wordsworth despite the starry eyes of his teacher.

In the area of poetry particularly, the approach of the teacher is important if interests are to be engendered rather than extinguished. Somehow, children who delight in rhymes and the music of words in the early elementary school come to a very negative attitude, generally, about poetry by the time they reach high school. To many students, especially the boys, poetry is something feminine, sissy. Teachers need to acquaint them with poetry about the virile, mundane experiences of life. Reading a class the poem "From This the Strength" by Fred Lape, a beautifully written poem about dumping garbage over a cliff, might be a good way to introduce a unit of poetry. Use of selections from such an anthology as *Poems for a Machine Age* [1] would help.

If we are to reject over-emphasis on the academic and feminine traditions in our literature programs, what guiding principles can we identify which will give promise of help in our campaign to get students to develop a habit of reading? Certainly a major one is that students — their problems and concerns and interests — should become the point of departure in the literature program rather than the selection. When boys and girls become soundly convinced that literature has to do with them, with their lives, their sorrows and hopes and joys and worries, a sturdy basis for enduring enthusiasm for reading will have been built.

[1] McGraw-Hill Book Company, 1941.

Does this mean that students merely will be turned out to the literary pasture to graze and ruminate as they will? It does not. Real reading interests and tastes are seldom developed that way. Guidance is all-important. But it does mean that we can first get our foot in the door by analyzing the natural interests, in general and in reading, which boys and girls have. We know, for example, that the seventh-grade pupils entering our secondary schools are devouring comic magazines voraciously. It will pay us to consider this a positive factor and go on to discover what we can learn from this interest in comics that will help us in developing more lasting tastes. The appeal of the comic magazines probably lies in the following factors:

1. *They are easy to read* — Although the vocabulary of the comic magazine is not always easy, the text does not have to be read in order for the reader to get the story. Superior readers read as many comics as inferior, but the poor reader may be attracted especially to the comics if the required reading in school is continually beyond him.
2. *They appeal immediately to more senses than does "straight" reading* — It takes less imaginative effort to read the comics. The reader need not conjure up his own images in his mind's eye. The situations and characters, complete with golden tresses and bulging biceps, are already there in bright colors. The comics are a haven for the sluggish or lazy imagination.
3. *The content of the comic magazines fits the nature of early adolescence* — The magic ingredients of action, suspense, mystery, adventure add up to real "punch" in the mind of the young reader. The frequent stress on the unusual or bizarre is in line with the fantastic flights the imagination is likely to take in early adolescence.
4. *The comics magazine's picture of life and the assumptions underlying it are naturally acceptable to the immature mind* — Life is an exciting adventure. People are good or bad. Authority in the form of policemen, parents, and teachers is often stupid and ridiculous. The main problems of life involve love and money. The end justifies the means.

The value of this analysis is that we can steer pupils to selections of literature which contain these same basic appeals and yet represent a step upward toward a more mature and wholesome reading experience. What qualities will these transition selections have?

1. *They must be easy to read* — Reading difficulty will be appropriate to the reader. Recognition difficulties with more than one in one-hundred words quickly will kill off pleasure. Although the reading difficulty is low, the selection still may be aesthetically satisfying in the use of language. Barrenness of vocabulary is a mark of the comics.
2. *They must reflect experience close to that of the reader* — Literal identification with characters and situations, vital to the immature reader, must be possible. Preferably characters will be about the age of the reader. Their experiences will be the exciting kind with which adolescents wish to identify.

3. *They should lack the gross distortion of experience characteristic of the comics* — Experience will be simplified since life for the young adolescent is still relatively uncomplicated, but the plots should avoid the wild coincidence and improbability of many of the comics. Action still will be mostly on a physical plane. Traumatic experiences involving excessive violence and the sordid should be avoided.
4. *They must have the magic ingredient of "punch"* — action, suspense, peril are the watchwords. Students should not get the idea that the book the teacher recommends is likely to be dull.
5. *They must be made as available as possible* — Classroom libraries will help.

There are a number of books available which have these transition qualities. Contemporary authors like Jim Kjelgaard, Stephen Meader, Doris Gates, Montgomery Atwater, Kenneth Gilbert, who have written books which fit this category, are important in the junior high-school literature program along with traditionally established favorites like Mark Twain, Robert Louis Stevenson, and Jack London. In her *Substitutes for the Comics*,[2] Constance Carr lists a number of titles which can be used to lead students to more rewarding reading fare.

In planning the reading program, teachers may capitalize upon certain predominant interests which students exhibit at various age levels. The all-consuming interest in sports which many boys have by the time they reach the seventh grade can lead from novels like *Keystone Kids* by John Tunis and *Southpaw from San Francisco* by Philip Harkins to a broad field of fiction, biography, and non-fiction in the whole world of sports and recreation. Similarly, the prevalent interest of seventh- and eighth-grade pupils in animals can lead in ladder fashion from the dog stories of Jim Kjelgaard and the horse stories of Walter Farley and Dorothy Lyons into *Lassie Come Home*, *My Friend Flicka*, and, for some students, eventually to *Moby Dick*.

Ninth- and tenth-grade students, caught in the bewildering no-man's land between childhood and adulthood, are pre-occupied with problems of relations with parents and other adolescents, particularly of the opposite sex. For many students in these grades, Maureen Daly's *Seventeenth Summer*, Betty Cavanna's *Going on Sixteen*, Mary Stolz' *To Tell Your Love*, Paul Annixter's *Swiftwater*, and James Summers' *Girl Trouble* are more appropriate than *Ivanhoe* or *Silas Marner*, although some students may have moving experiences with these. This period of middle adolescence presents a superb opportunity to develop in boys and girls the realization that literature deals with the stuff of their lives.

In the eleventh and twelfth grades, students retain their interests

[2] National Council of Teachers of English.

in sports, adventure, and a whole range of personal problems. Interest in love deepens as engagement rings appear on the fingers of some of the girls. A deep, albeit vague and often uneasy concern appears in group ethics, the problem of what to believe in a confusing adult world. The draft-bound and draft-preoccupied boys find real significance in the world's war literature. And to all these concerns, literature has a close affinity, although a chronological study of English or American writing may not make it clear even while Shakespeare and Tennyson, Emerson and Whitman may speak meaningfully to some students.

How, within the group process of the classroom situation, is the beleaguered teacher to carry on this program of literature and individual reading guidance without a vast and buzzing confusion as the result? Many teachers have found a successful solution in the topical or thematic unit. The broad topic or theme provides the unity or centering ground, but there is still much opportunity for individualized reading and activity within the unit. For example, a frequently taught unit at the University of Minnesota High School is "Heroes, Past and Present" in which seventh- or eighth-grade pupils read widely about people, real and fictitious, who have been heroes in different ways at different times. Although the students read different selections, class discussion centers around such questions as "How did the characters in your books or stories become heroes?" and "Judging from what you have read, how would you define a 'hero'?" Excellent examples of topical units in literature are outlined in recent publications by the teachers of Denver [3] and the University of Minnesota High School.[4] Literature study organized around topics of concern to students at various levels will provide needed class unity, the vital opportunity for individual guidance, and the significant context which will link reading to the students' world.

Does the Library Really Have Something to Offer?

The success of the kind of reading program outlined here will vary directly with the adequacy of the school's library materials. Obviously, a campaign to get students to read is absurd if the school has only the campaign without the materials to read. In attacking its individual budget problems, each school must keep in mind the importance of a well-stocked, well-balanced, and

[3] *A Guide for Teaching the Language Arts.* Denver, Colo.: Denver Public Schools. 1953.

[4] *Illustrative Learning Experiences.* Minneapolis: University of Minnesota Press. 1952.

attractive library. There is no escape from the fact that a good library costs money, but it is depressing to find lavish equipment for the athletic program or the band in schools with barren libraries. Certain approaches, often overlooked, offer rays of hope in the perennially acute matter of lack of funds for library materials. One is that less expenditure for expensive sets of identical anthologies and textbooks and more for diversified materials may benefit the all-school reading program. Another possibility lies in greater use of paperbound books and inexpensive editions such as *Cadmus Books* published by the E. M. Hale Company, *Landmark Books* published by Random House, and the *Permabooks* and *Anchor Books* of Doubleday and Company.

Mere quantity in library materials is not the only requirement, of course. Balance and appropriateness are essential. Many schools have a ponderous backlog of out-of-date, never-read books gathering dust on the shelves. In addition to general guides such as the *Standard Catalog for High School Libraries* published by the H. W. Wilson Company, schools may find it helpful to use some of the following current sources of information about books:

1. *Books for You.* National Council of Teachers of English. 1951 edition with supplement — An annotated list of materials for grades nine through twelve organized around such topics as "Personal Growth," "Other Lands and Other Peoples," "Values and Beliefs."
2. *Reading Ladders for Human Relations.* American Council on Education. 1949 — Titles are arranged under headings such as "Differences Between Generations," "Rural-Urban Contacts," "Adjustments to New Places and Situations."
3. *We Build Together.* National Council of Teachers of English. 1948 — An annotated guide to literature of Negro life.
4. *Gateways to Readable Books: An Annotated Graded List of Books in many Fields for Adolescents who find Reading Difficult.* Compiled by Ruth Strang, *et al.* H. W. Wilson Co. 1952 — Features such themes as "Personality and How To Be Popular," "Careers," "Adventure."

The following periodicals contain reviews of current books for high-school readers:

The English Journal. 8110 South Halsted Street, Chicago 21. Published monthly from September through May.

The Horn Book. 250 Boylston Street, Boston 16. Published six times a year.

The Booklist. American Library Association, Chicago. Published semimonthly September through July and monthly in August.

Library Journal. R. R. Bowker Company, New York. Published semimonthly from September through June and monthly in July and August.

Bulletin of the Children's Book Center. University of Chicago Library. Published monthly except August.

Making books accessible to students and providing a physically attractive library setting are important parts of the program to promote interest in reading. Frequently, schools actually provide very little time for students to use the library. The five minutes between classes or an abbreviated lunch period may offer the only possibility, especially for bus students, for a hurried dash to the library. Class periods spent in the library can be productive particularly if the librarian takes seriously her role as a teacher and guide of reading as well as her responsibilities as keeper of the books. In many schools, classroom libraries, established temporarily in connection with certain units or topics of study, help much to make books more accessible and build greater interest. Talking about a book in the teacher's hands is more effective than talking about one that is "up in the library."

The physical setting of the library has a good deal to do with appetite for voluntary reading. The more the library looks like a comfortable and well-kept lounge and the less like a dreary storage vault, the better for the reading program. Attractive displays, exhibits, and posters and comfortable places to sit will help achieve the right affect. Some modern school libraries have "book corners" with easy chairs. The combination library-study hall with its formidable rows of bolted down desks fortunately is becoming *passé*. The appearance of the books is important. Librarians have found that a bright, appealing book jacket greatly helps the circulation of a book. Making of book jackets for drab-looking volumes might be an excellent project for some of the classes or school service clubs.

An important incentive to interest in the library and in reading is furnished by student participation in book buying. Some schools allot a certain amount of money to each grade, and book buying projects are carried on in English or other classes. As well as stimulating interest, this activity provides some excellent teaching opportunities.

Are Book Reports Helping?

Class activities carried on after or in connection with reading have much to do with students' approach to reading and the attitudes they develop toward it. The venerable tradition of book reporting is still very much with us though the book reports may take forms different from the name the book — name the author — what is the setting — list the main characters — briefly summarize the plot — how I liked the book routine which usually wastes the time of both students and teachers. Often students tend to view book reports and activities following reading with distaste rather than anticipation. Teachers might profitably evaluate these activities to decide whether they are igniting or short-circuiting interest in reading.

Individual book reports may not be necessary invariably. One valuable type of activity following reading is group discussion, a kind of book reporting especially suited to the topical unit where students may have read different selections. For instance, after a period of reading around the theme "Sports and Sportsmanship," a group of eighth-grade pupils might discuss such questions as: (1) How much actual game action is in your books? (2) Do the players and coaches seem real in your books? Do they talk as players and coaches actually do? (3) How do the heroes in your books gain success? What kinds of problems do they meet and how do they solve them? (4) Does the author of your book have any other point to put across, any idea in mind other than just to write an exciting story? Such a discussion revolves around ideas important to the topic or theme and to discrimination in reading, and it does not matter that the students have not all read the same thing.

Sometimes groups of three or four students who have read the same selection might present a discussion to the class on the order of the radio program "Invitation To Learning" in which three people discuss a certain book. Or the small group might present a dramatization or oral reading of a key scene. Doing this as a "radio broadcast" and using public address equipment sometimes adds interest. The small group report may take other forms such as a puppet show. In one senior class, the students were entranced by a puppet show presented by four students on scenes from *Romeo and Juliet*.

Occasionally, the "buzz session" is a useful device for book reporting. Students discuss their books in groups of five or six, choosing one of their group to make an oral report to the whole class. Students interested in or talented in oral reading might make their report sometimes by reading a scene orally to the class. Or the class can make brief oral talks about their books, centering on a common, specific topic. During a unit on war literature, one senior class gave talks on what their books revealed about patriotism and its effect upon people in time of war.

Making a book jacket is an excellent kind of book report especially for younger students. The teacher can tell a great deal about the pupil's reaction to and understanding of the book from the way he chooses to illustrate it and the kind of "blurb" he writes. The finished jackets make attractive displays, and the best ones might actually be put on books in the library. For some students interested in art, this could be extended to interpretative painting based on selections read.

Naturally, too, the regular written book review has a place with older students. Taking a number of forms, the time-honored book report can bring added zest and motivation to the reading program.

A desire and habit to read for personal pleasure and profit: a worthy and feasible objective for the secondary-school program.

18. Some Start With Comics

George E. Murphy

Any high school English teacher can teach his pupils to read — if he wants to. I know. I did.

After I was convinced that my main job was to teach young people to listen, to speak, to read, and to write more effectively — and more in line with modern communication needs — all it took was courage. It did take courage. Peer-group evaluations, tradition — pretty strong forces!

I didn't need an analyst to convince me that something was wrong. My pupils hated English. They dropped out of school. Neither Tressler, Woolley and Scott, nor I had any noticeable effect on the student's "Jack, he" or his "I ain't got no book neither." I never found anyone reading except as an assignment.

I switched to a more functional approach to language.

I began with a once-a-week "free reading" period. "Bring in what you would read if I weren't here — whatever you read at home," I told one of the classes. (I had read somewhere, "Take the pupil from where he is.")

I'll never forget that first session! The books those pupils had! Twain, Dickens, Scott — all held up so I would be sure to note the titles and authors.

"Now look here," I said, "who's fooling whom? Why are you bringing in those books?" Stripped to its core, the reply was, "This is what you're supposed to read in English. These books get you grades."

By the end of the period we had an understanding. Next week

the readers would bring in what they *really* read at home. And they did! Almost every ninth grader had a comic. But what concentration! What a change of attitude toward books. I could have dropped a dozen eggs and no one would have noticed. Interest was there all right. I'd heard someone say, "Work through pupil interests to pupil needs." Maybe this was what it meant.

During the last ten minutes of the class we had an evaluation. Those pupils opened my eyes to the values of comics. They had enjoyed the reading. They had picked up surprisingly accurate information about science and history. Their moral values had been strengthened.

I felt good about my start when I was alone with the class. But I felt guilty when one of my peers would say, "We're reading *Lady of the Lake*, and my pupils love it!" I felt an utter failure. Very few of my pupils even tolerated the *Lady*. I wondered when my administrators would "lower the boom." My conscience hurt. At home I'd resolve to go back to the anthology. In class, the groans were too calamitous. I continued with the "free reading."

Comics were read for about six weeks. They went around the class in dizzy circles. Gradually I came to recommend books, magazines, and newspaper articles and gradually my pupils' readings became more individual. Boys read mystery, sports, and adventure stories. Girls read stories of romance.

At one point we wanted to know how we were doing as readers, so we entered a "testing phase." We used any test we could get our hands on. By this time we were spending two days a week on reading.

A professor of mine had once demonstrated the value of having pupils record their achievement and set up "levels of aspiration." I tried it. It worked. Each pupil accordingly kept a chart of his growth in comprehension and speed. A committee and I, once a month, made a composite class chart. We also kept a record of our reading by listing titles under headings like Novels, Essays, Poems, Dramas, etc., on the inside of a manila folder for each pupil. His chart and any comment he wanted to make about books were kept there.

About this time we learned our most important lesson: you can be a good reader in English and a failure in science. We began to analyze our needs in the subject-matter areas. Within our class, we had pupils from history, science, mathematics, Latin, and German working in groups on the skills needed for the particular subject mastery.

Soon, the pupils discovered that reading was not the same as study. They suggested that reading was a preface to study. "What you do with what you read is study," was their conclusion. This observation led to trying out various techniques.

The most popular was to ask yourself after any unit of reading, "So what?" This question was then split into four: "So what for me now?" "So what for me later?" "So what for the United States?" "So what for the world?" Such questions led to good thinking, and we agreed that good thinking constituted study. Another technique was to ask yourself, "Who? Did what? Where? When? Why? How?" Later I learned Robinson's formula, SQ3R — Survey, Question, Read, Recite, Review. I could have used that to advantage had I known it back there in the Ice Age.

We tried experiments. One day we might have half the class just "read" the history lesson, while the other half "studied" it. The next day we would give a test in comprehension, including the "So what?" We learned that if one read very carefully he could sometimes accomplish as much in one session as he might in studying the material. But in general, particularly in the class quizzes, you gained through study.

Oh, we had headaches. The assistant principal came into the classroom one day during the time we were in our "Comics Phase." He invited me to his office where, without a single question, he forbade comics. Fortunately an assistant superintendent backed me. We went on reading comics, but I learned that I should have had *all* my administrators in on the operation from the beginning.

By April, I could leave my classes alone, and they would proceed as though I were there. We had student chairmen and secretaries. But the ribbing I took from my fellow teachers!

Miss X, for instance, was a very severe critic. She ridiculed everything we did — everything I believed or thought I had learned. But that day in April did it. I had left my classroom, and she sneaked down to record the bedlam she expected to find — the bedlam she *knew* she would have had in her classes had she been absent. Instead, she found work going on. She was treated in the same fashion as were any of our guests when I was there. She asked pointed questions. She listened to intelligent answers. She was generous enough to express her surprised admiration to me and to my supervisor. She never ridiculed our practices again.

I learned a great deal about teaching, learning, adolescents, language, and reading that year — mainly, I believe, because *I wanted to do a better job*. For so many years I had "covered" books and "gone through" courses of study without thinking. *Why*. For so many years, teaching had just been something I suffered through. The year I started teaching young people to use language more effectively in helping them solve developmental tasks — that was my first "growing" year. It was a year of "blood, sweat and tears," but it was also one of satisfaction.

It has been many years since I met with those ninth graders — some are probably grandparents. They taught me more than I ever learned from books, courses, or conferences. The latter have their places, but the basics are found in a particular adolescent in a particular group, in a particular culture, at a particular time. When I learned from my ninth graders that I couldn't do much with reading unless I knew the individual's problems and interests, I learned something I've used to advantage ever since.

Bob, for instance. He began to read after I praised his achievement in swimming. Bill got nowhere until he realized that the class cared for him as a person. Elsa, our diabetic, "joined" us when she became convinced that diabetes was just another problem to us. Everyone, we agreed, had problems as long as he was alive. And who would trade problems for death?

Earlier I would have jumped all over Beth for not studying, for day-dreaming, for being lazy. But I learned that "behavior is caused." I looked for the cause and found it. Beth's mother was dying of cancer. Who feels like reading when he has such a worry? When Beth felt free to share her worry with us, the "subjective became more objective" and the "tension on the subject" was lessened. Beth read everything she could find about cancer. "Maybe I can find something to help mother," she explained.

Much has been discovered about reading in recent years. I wish I could go back and atone for all the "sins" I committed in those early days of English teaching. If any of my old pupils now reads, it's a miracle! I actually taught hatred of reading. I loved to shred that much-hated *As You Like It.* Everyone shredded the same passage in the same way at the same time, and we shredded each classic for at least half a semester. That's an awfully long time to do nothing but shred!

Now I would define reading in a different light. It is the process of releasing ideas, feelings, and experiences from the symbols in which they have been stored, so that they can be taken away, improved upon, and put to work. I would hope that through reading, such attitudes toward living would develop that prejudice never would become behavior which could hurt people.

My objective would be to have pupils learn to read for recreation and for learning. I would try to realize my objective by helping my pupils realize theirs. This very important consideration was driven home to me in Mexico. The objective of the teachers at Patzcuaro was literacy. The objective was not fulfilled until the

Indians needed and wanted to be literate. When the teachers showed the Indians how literacy would help them achieve their own objectives, the Indians wanted to be literate. They learned.

I would still "take the pupils from where they are." I wouldn't want segregated groups, since I have now learned that slower pupils learn from those who are brighter than they. I have discovered that some people learn well by reading, some by listening, some by doing. When I put these different types of students together, the "egg heads" learn that their function is to serve as leaders. They learn that minds in isolation are like the "acorns falling in the forest when no one hears." The members of the class learn to evaluate leadership and to follow it.

People who are labeled "woodpeckers" and "dummies" don't have much incentive to learn. Their objective is to get status, even if they have to use revolvers to get it. Even they can learn — maybe not what we stereotypers think they should learn, but they can learn. Furthermore, they *will* learn if we grant that each of them is as important as any other person.

Many people are living very happily right now without knowing *Ivanhoe* from iodine. Then why should everyone read Shakespeare, who wrote plays for adults in another time, in almost another language, to be seen and heard, not shredded silently? Some students can read Shakespeare. Let them. Encourage them and help them. But feel the same way about the kid who is reading *Sports Illustrated*.

Starting with the pupil, I'd make use of every aid I could get my hands on. I'd test. I'd use. I'd evaluate. ALWAYS with my pupils. I wouldn't eat arsenic if every one of my pupils didn't read. There are some young people who, because of attendance laws, must stay in school today, but they just do not appear to have what it takes to grow in reading. Usually they can grow through listening — and always through doing.

We need doers. My job would be to teach the doers the communication skills they need to be economically self-supporting and culturally in tune with positive moral and ethical values.

Age has made me less impatient to get things done NOW. I remember Joe in the Army. It took him three days to learn to print J-O-E. I had never realized how tricky J and E could be! But his expression of satisfaction when he said, "Now I don't have to put a X no more!" was worth it.

I've learned that it takes patience and time to develop a writer or a reader. And it is always my hope that among my students will be those who will continuously draw upon their reading to solve problems, to widen horizons, to live more richly.

19. Relationship of Mass Media to Reading Interests

Paul A. Wagner

The phrase "mass media" is so awe-inspiring in its connotations that only those who delight in being known as mass-media specialists ever attempt to discuss such a subject. I would like to drop any pretense of being a specialist in either the field of mass communication or the field of reading, and to approach the subject of the relationship of the two from a very simple and direct point of view. As a teacher, I am interested in all media of communication, from reading to lecturing, from field trips to television. As one who is interested in the sociological aspects of education, I am concerned with the communication of ideas, no matter the size of the audience or the medium employed.

It is from the vantage point of the classroom that one can understand the dilemma facing the average teacher in the performance of his duties. It is a dilemma that can be stated best in four terms: (1) Society expects the school to educate young Americans in the abstract values of American society. (2) Reading is the medium best suited for carrying the individual to the ultimate abstractions embodied in the concepts of American liberty and justice. (3) Reading of serious and significant writing is an activity engaged in by a pitifully small percentage of our population, at any age level. (4) Democracy, to be successful and creative, must be based on intercommunication among *all* citizens. (I dislike the phrase, but "mass" in intercommunication is an important American concept.)

Reading and "Other Languages"

What does society demand of a teacher? "Prepare our children for life." Prepare them for fatherhood, motherhood, brotherhood; for statesmanship and ethical dealings in business, labor, and politics. Prepare them to vote intelligently on the problems of segregation, atomic-energy control, use of public lands, the admission of Red China to the United Nations. In almost every case the unit objectives would have to be stated in abstractions of a high order.

In communicating the abstract ideals of our society during the past several centuries, the teacher has relied mainly, in fact almost completely, on books. This is quite natural, for the book still remains the finest tool for the absorption of ideas and ideals by the individual. Democracy is an individual phenomenon, and reading is a medium allowing for the widest variety of individual differences of mind and heart.

But the sharp horn of the dilemma is first felt in the fact that the language of books has always been the province of the elite. In past eras, only the most wealthy or the most dedicated had access to books. Later, only those who could afford college were allowed the luxury of thoughtful reading. And now, as Lester Asheim reminds us (chapter iv), fewer than 10 per cent of our adult population are reading books of any stature or profundity.

At the same time that the language of books is largely ignored by the "masses" (strike that word and use "90 per cent of the American voters"), other languages are being called into play for the communication of attitudes and opinions on the Bricker Amendment, the government control of network telecasting, or the sending of arms to Israel. Each of these issues requires the most careful study, often the delicate balancing of other abstract ideas. And each of these issues is determined by the vote of every adult American — not just those who can or will read — but *every* American.

The "other languages" used by the 90 per cent of Americans who are not interested in books include the language of radio; the language of the cartoon; the language of the bold, black, condensed Gothic headline; the language of the motion picture; and the language of television.

The word "language" is repeated for one reason only. It has more validity in an educational discussion than the term "mass medium." For one can read a book, listen to the radio, see a film, or watch television, all in the privacy of his own den. The old distinction of mass media requiring the auditor to be part of a large crowd no longer holds. Unless you wish to give a numerical definition to "mass," the book is as much a medium for communicating with the masses as is a kinescope. Those who understand the language of books are called "readers." But those who cannot read books often are very adept at "reading" these other languages. Indeed, we can teach our students to read these other languages. Just as we teach them to read between the lines and beyond them, so too can we teach them to read behind and beyond the scenes. When we teach these other languages, we will succeed in winning converts, among a majority of the American population, for the most important language of all, that of books.

Films and Recordings to Develop Interest

Making the shift in thinking from "mass media" to "languages" is not easy. Since we teach as we were taught, and since I was taught for eighteen years almost entirely by textbooks, I did not realize the true significance of these other languages until after two, for me, rather dramatic teaching experiences.

During the depression of the thirties, I became an apprentice teacher in a metropolitan high school. Most of the students were still in school only because they could find no employment elsewhere. Although they exhibited none of the viciousness of the class in the *Blackboard Jungle*, they did share with that group a complete antipathy for anything intellectual, especially in English class — and most particularly in American poetry.

With this group my first assignment was to teach the beauties and philosophic serenities of "Thanatopsis." To say I failed is to put it mildly. And each succeeding assignment found the class gaining the upper hand in its battle against reading books. I decided to catch their interest with a novel that no literary critic would put very high on the list of American classics, but certainly one that had all the elements that might appeal to such a group of nonreaders: the opening of a new territory in the Southwest, a slam-bang story of oilmen fighting with the earth and with each other, and a rip-snorting finale in which the main male figure dies in an act of heroism. Edna Ferber's *Cimarron* had all of this, but I could not sell even that.

And then a friend of mine suggested I obtain a short film entitled *Men and Oil*. Perhaps it would tie in with the lessons of the moment. The next day I showed it to the class. For the first time, these antagonistic nonreaders sat on the edges of their seats and attended to something at the front of the room. They asked questions; they argued; they wanted to see the film again. They were even ready to listen to passages from *Cimarron*, and, most important of all, they began to read, *really read*, a book whose covers they had previously refused to crack. For the first time, I was able to communicate with the class, because the language of the film was a language they understood, a language they could read. Once I contacted them in *their* language, I could begin the transition to communication in *my* language.

Lest you think that I have taken an extreme case and attempted a

Pgymalion-like moral, let me remind you that these other languages are read by many students who are, by our standards, excellent readers of the printed page also.

The most literate students I ever had the pleasure of teaching were in a Sophomore English class in a Wisconsin secondary school. The principal had invited me to give a demonstration class, "to show how to use movies." I had agreed, provided he allowed me to visit the class every day for a week and then take the regular teacher's place on the fifth day, carrying on the normal work of the week. The class was studying Shakespeare. The teacher was an attractive woman, physically, mentally, emotionally. And the class was devoted to her. They were studying *Julius Caesar* that week and were enjoying it. In short, this was an ideal teaching situation. I would like to stress this point since it is so important to an understanding of the relations of all the languages used by modern youth.

On the fifth day I became the substitute teacher. The class was about to discuss Act III, Scene 2, the immortal Forum scene. By way of introduction, I asked them to characterize each of the principal figures. Cassius was dismissed as a "bad man," and Brutus as one who was just a cut above. Caesar — there was a man they admired. He had refused the crown; he was a man of the people. And Antony — there was a man who could talk to people, talk from the heart. Having established their beliefs in general terms, I then asked them to record the scene by means of a tape recorder. The student who played Brutus made him sound like a cheap, regional politician, while Mark came out a younger version of Clark Gable.

It was appropriate to remark that Shakespeare lent himself to various interpretations down through the ages and that it might be interesting to hear other versions. Did they know of Orson Welles's production of *Julius Caesar?* None of them had (this was a decade later). They guessed what part Orson Welles had elected to play. Most of them voted for Antony; some, for Caesar; none, for Brutus. And then we played the recording. The sonorous lines forged by a master-actor: "Not that I loved Caesar less. . . ." (Their teacher had attempted a reading of some of the great lines, but no soprano, even a beloved one, can do justice to the rolling, biting, cruel male lines of this greatest of tragedies.) The class was no longer so certain of its original interpretation.

Then we showed a ten-minute excerpt from a British film, *The Forum Scene.* Here we had not only the voices but the costumes, the background, the swaying mob against which the rhetoric pounded.

Then, and only then, could we discuss such things as dictatorship, and the courage it takes to stand up against the mob, to be an individual in a conforming society. Then, and only then, could I teach the abstractions these students needed for an understanding of an individual in modern society. Only then could they begin to *read* the greatest play ever penned.

This anecdote is not so immodest as it might seem on the surface. The regular teacher was a master-teacher; I was not. But I had tools with which to teach, and she had only a textbook and her voice. She could reach the students with only one language; I could employ three or four.

I wonder what would happen to the status of Shakespeare in American high schools if all English teachers were equipped with the proper tools? (Not long ago a school superintendent took a poll of students in his school system and reported that 87 per cent of them voted Shakespeare "the subject they hated most to study.")

From these experiences I learned that what we educators condescendingly call "audio-visual aids" or "the mass media in the classroom" are not mere *aids* in the teaching of reading, but tools that are as integral a part of the teaching process as books themselves. Unless I as a teacher learn to use the idiom of my students, I will continue to be a teacher to the elite.

Perhaps a tired analogy may be forgiven if it serves to spotlight this concept of the inevitable interrelationship of reading and the other language arts. Communication may be likened to a loom, the warp of which is the child's experiential background. The reality of his life is joined by the near-reality created by vivid electronic and mechanical screens, and on this combined "reality" he builds all future understandings. The term "near-reality" is added because it is the peculiar power of the radio, the film, or the televised image to draw the student into situations that make him feel as if he were *really* involved. Rightly or wrongly, he sees this warp of personal experience as LIFE, real life.

Coupled with the warp is the woof of reading. You and I know it as the best method of weaving life-experiences into a meaningful pattern, an ordering of the parts, a maturing. But to the hard-headed youngster, bred of pragmatic parents, the woof seems gossamer, and he will have none of it. It is true that this young American who will not accept reading is settling for a life in which experience remains a series of disjointed threads, providing no covering from the elements, no beauty for the wearer. But let us not castigate him too severely. What have we, as teachers of reading, done to show him the relation of the warp and the woof? Have we worked in his idiom, or have we ignored it? Have we taken the best of radio and Hollywood and television and captured "reality" for him, before leading him on to the higher and more abstract planes of that reality?

The answer is a resounding "No." Less than 10 per cent of the school systems of America have professional audio-visual co-ordinators; less than 10 per cent of our teachers use audio-visual aids with any regularity at all; and less than 30 per cent of our teacher-training institutions are willing to acknowledge the fact that teachers need to learn about languages other than the language of books. We teach as we were taught.

So is it any wonder that, when the subject is discussed at general educational conferences, the consensus seems to be, "Nice, but not necessary"? Occasionally, someone will even ask the rhetorical question, "Are the mass media conflicting with reading?"

A professor for whom I have always had the profoundest respect once described literature as "a window to the world." That happens to be the slogan of a Chicago television station, WTTW. It is an apt phrase for both windows, located as they are in a tower — ivory, granite, flame, whatever stuff we build into our individual towers. The view from the window is essentially the same. He who raises the shade at WTTW has the same landscape in mind as you who raise it in the classroom — the same abstract understandings and appreciations. It is a prejudice of mine that the book represents a window higher up in the tower. It affords a wider view; both the immediate scenery and the distant hills are in better perspective.

But (and this is an important but) the window at WTTW, or the window in Ed Murrow's studio, has far more interested viewers than has your window. It is fulfilling the task of mass intercommunication better than you and I. We can continue to ignore it and teach reading by books alone to one, two, or a few. Or we can harness that energy and that interest, and take a majority of our classes to higher planes of learning.

Future Relationships

The teaching profession may be forced to recognize these other languages sooner than we think, for within a score of years the world will see international television, and it will see tape-recorded television programs, playable on any set in the land. These records will be book-size, book-weight, book-cost. They will be sold in bookstores and carried by libraries and be as available as any book is today. Whatever the subject, a video recording will be available.

Is this a threat? No, I don't think so. It is, rather, a thrilling opportunity. Once a man becomes engrossed in the history of his country through vivid video, he will be led inevitably to the vivid volumes that extend his horizon even more. Imagine, if by 1980, you and I could give good books a status they have never before enjoyed in recorded history: the status of being *wanted* and *used* by a majority of the citizens of a great democracy.

With this challenge in mind, and as you discuss the topic in your sectional meetings, refer to the following questions:

1. Do I have an adequate understanding of the function and power of these other languages?
2. Do I have a professional audio-visual coordinator to help me obtain the best material?
3. Do I, an administrator, understand the grave need for an integration of these various language skills?

20. Mass Media and the Interests of High School Youth

Charles G. Spiegler

The birth of any new medium for communicating to the mass audience is often accompanied by fears on how it will affect that mass — psychologically, intellectually, culturally.

This was true of the newspaper; it was true of radio. Today the hue and cry is against TV, which, it is predicted, will yet make reading as unimportant in our lives as the vermiform appendix.

The prognosticators of doom have been wrong about newsprint and wrong about earphones. They will be proved just as wrong about the TV screen which will become, not the roadblock to reading which its critics accuse it of, but a new thruway to the printed word for those who would travel it.

To see what I mean, join me in my office one Monday morning dreary as I'm sitting wan and weary composing my weekly bulletin. Suddenly we hear a tapping at the door and greet two students, one preparing to become a butcher, the other a baker. They ask me —

"Got sumpn' by Ogden Nash?"

"Who?" I ask, startled.

"Ogden Nash! You know," they exclaim, "the guy wid dose crazy rhymes —."

My ears perk up. Surprised, indeed delighted, that my boys are interested in reading one of America's most literate creators of verse, I probe a little.

"You boys doing a book report on Mr. Nash?"

"Naaa!" they parry, "no book reports — we just wanna read sumpn' by him. We went up to the library but the udder guys beat us to it. *You* got sumpn'?"

Happily I had. And happily, Tommy Gorman, a 15-year-old butcher-to-be, and Peter de Stefano, a 16-year-old baker-to-be, walked off with the two copies I owned of *The Golden Trashery of Ogden Nashery*. When you realize that before this day the Popular Song Sheet was the closest Tom and Peter had come to voluntarily exposing themselves to rhythms and rhymes, you realize what a move forward they had made toward broadening cultural horizons through reading.

This did not come full grown from the head of Zeus. It happened at a time when Herman Saunders, their English teacher, found the going rough as he started a unit on poetry. So he looked for help. Since television is not a dirty word in our school, he looked to see how that week's TV programming *could* help. That Sunday Ed Sullivan *could*. For Sullivan had invited Noel Coward to read from the works of Ogden Nash to the background music of Saint-Saëns, as it would be played by André Kostelanetz. Thus the homework assignment for that Sunday was "Watch Sullivan" — not just the song, not just the dance — but *all* of it! The results we have seen.

At first blush these results seem hardly remarkable. You point to students in your classes who *need* no assist from an Ed Sullivan show before they'll pick up a book of poetry. These are the children whose earliest memories are of the delightful bedtime stories spun for them at twilight; children who have grown up in homes where books and magazines have always been welcome friends; children who now read with an interest that has never been blocked by physical, emotional or cultural barriers.

There are, however, American teachers not quite that fortunate. These are the teachers who daily face that vast army of slow and reluctant readers with whom compulsory education laws in every state have flooded their classrooms.

As a chairman of an Academic Subjects Department in a New York City vocational high school I meet hundreds of such youngsters daily. Here are 750 boys who want to be butchers, bakers, cooks, cafeteria workers. Their median IQ is 85; their reading score approximates 6. Practically all of these boys come from homes which have fallen under a cultural blight. They sit in the classroom bored sometimes to the point of hostility. The body is here but the mind and heart are often miles away. You may talk to them of *Silas Marner*, but they don't hear you. Their ears are tuned to the change-of-period bell. You may appeal to them with a lovely print of Stratford, but they don't see it. Their eyes are on the clock.

But TV surveys tell us those very same ears and eyes will stay glued to a TV set for anywhere from one to four hours. In this phenomenon lies a second chance for us to motivate an interest in reading. My faith is based on this syllogism:

1. TV is a new window to the world; for many boys the only link to the human story, with all its color, variety and glory. It opens for many a full, rich array of new interests.
2. Interest is the key to reading.
3. TV, by creating interest, becomes a road to wider reading.

To see how valid this syllogism is, look at the survey I conduct in my school, where I ask boys to list their ten top TV programs and then tell me what new reading, if any, these have suggested. I would be utterly disingenuous if I did not report to you that *Your Hit Parade*, *Abbot and Costello* and the *Gunsmoke* type of programs lead all the rest. Yet, when TV did *A Night to Remember*, dozens of boys remembered it vividly enough to read the Walter Lord original. When I asked one boy, "Why? After all, you *got* the story on TV," he answered, "Sure, but I wanted to get my own feeling of how it was to be on a sinking ship — on a cold ocean — on a pitch-black night. You didn't feel that on TV. There were too many lights."

There are many youngsters who want to probe more deeply into those people, places and things about which TV has merely whetted an appetite. Many dozens of boys, for example, saw the *Jim Piersall Story* on TV and went to the library for *Fear Strikes Out*, the book about the player's fight against mental illness. Scores love *The Adventures of Jim Bowie* on Friday nights and have, as a result, read the Bobbs-Merrill version of Bowie's early life. Thanks to *Flash Gordon* and *Science Fiction Theatre*, there are boys in my school who are walking mines of information on jets and space travel. Thanks to *Mr. Wizard* and *Zoo Parade* some are walking encyclopedias on science and animals. Thanks to the quiz shows some have moved toward a public library entrance for the first time in their lives to see what makes a Charlie Van Doren, a Teddy Nadler, or a Robbie Strom tick!

This is not to say that TV's influence for good is exclusively on the non-academic mind. A look at the record reveals its powerful effect on the reading of others too. In March of 1956, for instance, *Publishers' Weekly* asked 15 of the nation's biggest stores, "What effect has TV on the sale of books for young people?" Of the 15 polled, 11 agreed substantially with Charles Reed of Reed's in New Jersey: "In spite of the crepe hangers, TV has stimulated book sales all across the board."

Librarians and book club directors I have talked to support this position. So does Frank Santori, Reading Co-ordinator of the South High School in Valley Stream, New York — a school, incidentally, that accepts TV as a fact of life, that gives TV for homework, that turns out a "TV Tips for Teachers" regularly, that encourages teachers to read TV *Guide*, *Teleguides* and *Teacher Guides* the minute these come off the press. Reports Mr. Santori: "I surveyed 1000 of our students recently and asked, 'Did a TV show ever inspire you to read?' Fully 600 students said 'Yes,' listed 36 different programs that did it, and suggested many new book titles that had come within their ken because of TV. These run the gamut from *Annapurna* to *The Barretts of Wimpole Street* to *Joan of Arc* to *The Silent World* — 187 titles in all!"

You demur at what seems to be an apology for commercial TV and you remind us of the hordes of American youngsters who sit glued to their TV screens watching the shoddy and meretricious — addicts to a new type of drug.

Agreed! But what are we doing to cure the addict drugged by heavy hours of meaningless viewing? Do we teach him what *TV Guide* has called "dialmanship" so he can learn to divide the chaff from the wheat? Do we encourage librarians to prepare a weekly bibliography that will say to a child, "After you flip a dial to this program, why not turn a page to this book?" Do we think of TV as a civilized friend who can help a youngster cross a bridge from an interest to a printed word and then move him along from this bridge to the speediest, smoothest thruway man has ever known to the land of books, brochures, magazines and newspapers?

Given teachers, parents, librarians who say "Yes" to these questions, given more men like Edward Stanley of NBC who has said, "Nobody ever went broke overestimating the IQ of the American people. We must program up, not down," we shall yet live to see that exciting new classroom in America where TV and Shakespeare can live together in peace — and, what is more, in a state of deep mutual affection.

21. Using Radio and Television in Grades Seven Through Nine

David V. Curtis

This paper deals with the use of radio and television in the classroom of a Chicago public school. It will tell first about the over-all city program and then about an experiment in an eighth-grade classroom of a crowded area where the teacher is making a definite contribution to inciting reading interest through the use of these media.

The Radio Council of Chicago

The Radio Council, Division of Radio and Television of the Chicago public schools, offers many interesting series of programs which can be used as springboards for preparation and follow-up activities in reading. The radio station is on the air seven hours each day. It presents series of programs from the kindergarten through the college level. Some of the major networks in the Chicago area permit some of these programs to be broadcast over their stations. These programs are carefully rehearsed in the radio and television workshops. The Division of Radio maintains two student workshops for training young people who are interested in radio acting, writing, or engineering.

Each week a bulletin listing the programs for the following week is sent to the schools. The programs include "Skyways of Science," prepared by the staff of the Adler Planetarium, which is a series of science programs designed for upper-elementary and high-school study. A social-science series called "The Plains to the Pacific" tells of the trail that Lewis and Clark took to the Pacific Ocean. The "Elizabethan Theater" presents Elizabethan and Shakespearean tragedies. "Exploring Music" is designed to help young people develop an ear for classics, as well as for good modern music. The series "Background in Government" acquaints the student with the working structure of government agencies. "How It

Began" is a series on "first" things, such as baseball, electric lights, moving pictures, etc., that make our American life enjoyable today. "Books in Review" is designed to encourage better reading. Many more programs are prepared for every grade level, including material related to art, history, geography, literature, social studies, music, and reading.

These programs are used in the classroom to help meet a specific educational need. The teacher must prepare the children for listening. The teacher must also initiate the children's interest in the program to be heard. On the other hand, the program must relate to the content of what is being studied in the classroom. The students should engage in discussion before the program starts and after it is finished. The teacher should use any method that he can to encourage the children to give their undivided attention to what is being said over the air.

Using Programs to Increase Reading

It is apparent that follow-up activity is an essential part of classroom listening or viewing. For example, a class may be studying a unit on electricity and may see a television program which demonstrates the usefulness of carbon. In order to understand the carbon rod in the dry cell, several boys read about it in one of the supplementary books on electricity. As a result of this extra reading they are able to understand that carbon is needed in order to start the flow of electricity in the dry cell. These boys also perform many other experiments with the carbon rod. This is one example in which the television broadcast is used as a stimulus for reading activity.

Many of the bulletins suggest supplementary reading materials which are related to the radio or television programs. Through observation of the children during free-reading periods in the classroom, the teacher can evaluate the effectiveness of his preparation and follow-up program. The radio and television programs chosen for classroom use should be those that fit into the basic course of study and not those which help to relieve boredom.

Many of the children in my classroom have read books in the public library because they saw television programs which were beyond their comprehension and they wanted to increase their understanding. They have recommended these books to me. I in turn have recommended the books to the school librarian for possible purchase for our school. As a result of this interest our school librarian has met with me on many occasions and has sent books for the entire class to examine. We have a room library, from which students take books to read for the unit they are engaged in or the recreational reading that they are doing. We also keep a shelf of magazines.

Radio and television have been accepted by many educators today as media for stimulating children to do serious thinking, to increase understanding, and to stimulate children to read. For example, children who have seen pictures on television or heard stories about guided missiles, atom bombs, and the like are motivated to read scientific literature on these subjects because they become interested in this material. We cannot measure the extent of this reading accurately because it is not a part of the course of study but is done on a voluntary basis. If, however, the children express themselves in classroom discussions, we can measure, to a certain degree, their knowledge on these subjects.

An Eighth-Grade Experiment

The neighborhood in which our school is located is crowded, and the people are in a low-income bracket. A recent survey of the homes of our students revealed that most of them have a radio or a television. But most of the homes have no books and do not subscribe to magazines, except a few who subscribe to a Polish magazine. Hence the school must provide these children with reading materials to satisfy their interests.

As part of the current-events assignments, the upper-grade children are required to listen every morning to the news broadcasts presented by the Chicago Board of Education. We have discovered that those who listen read the newspaper more than they did before they became avid listeners to the newscasts. Some children say that they have talked about the programs with their parents. There are some who bring the newspaper to class every morning and lead in the daily classroom discussions. As part of the homework assignment, they have a choice of listening to the radio or looking at television news broadcasts. These aids seem to increase their understanding of the world about them and help to promote critical thought and participation in classroom discussions. Some students who are not interested in reading may listen to the radio or watch a television broadcast. It is much better that they get this limited amount of information than none at all. Those children who are interested in further details will be stimulated by the radio and television to read the newspaper.

Thirty eighth-grade students wrote compositions on the effect of radio and television on their reading. Some said that the radio did not make them want to read because the announcers talked too fast. Others, however, were stimulated to read. One student wrote: "I think television makes me want to read more because

I can see what is happening and if I do not understand I can read for details." This girl has an interest in the stars. As a result of a trip to the Adler Planetarium, she read *When the Stars Come Out* (Viking, 1942). Another student claimed that he did not get much stimulation for reading from viewing programs. He wrote: "As a matter of fact, I haven't read a really good book in almost a year. I do watch a lot of TV. The reason I got a high reading average is from reading comic books. They are very interesting to me. Radio and TV are helpful in my education, for I remember most of what I see, but they do not make me want to read more." Asked if he had read *Tom Sawyer*, he said, "I have seen it on television." A few passages from the book were read to him, and he was asked to take it home and examine it. He finished the book in a week and gave a report on it to the class, in which he said that he had missed a lot of action in the television program. Comments from other students follow:

Television helps me to read. When I am watching "Science Fiction Theater," I always get interested in their experiments. One picture that interested me a lot was about the moon. A photographer developed a camera that could photograph the stars and moon very close. He decided to try it on the moon. When he developed the film, he saw big streaks on the print. When he studied it closely, he saw a rocket ship doing something on the other side of the moon. After the picture was finished, I took my encyclopedia and looked up the moon and learned a lot about it. Sunday I watched "You Are There." They had a program on the Chicago fire, how it started and how much destruction it did. After that I looked up the Chicago fire, the date it happened and why they could not put the fire out. The "Quiz Kids" is a good show because I try to answer the questions they ask and, if I'm wrong, I find out the right answer and look up more information about it. When I listen to the news and I want to find more information about something, I take the newspaper and read about it.

I do think radio and television help in encouraging you to read. I think television more so than the radio. The radio does a little, but I think the television does more, because it gives you the whole picture. It shows you pictures of where the things are happening and pictures of the people. If you see a science show in which they do an experiment and you want to know why the experiment turned out that way, you find books and read about it and some of these books give you an interest to read more books.

Some people think that radio and television are just for pleasure, but in a sense they are educational too. To get anything out of a program, you have to listen or watch carefully to see what is happening. Radio has many fine programs that make you want to read. The news broadcasts tell of interesting things, but I think the broadcasters talk too fast, so the people who try to catch up with what they are saying read the newspaper to get more details. Television also makes people want to read more.

Some programs are about history which you have already read, so when you watch the program it makes you want to read that particular part of history over again.

There are two programs which I like. They are "Medic" and "Dr. Hudson's Secret Journal." I chose these two programs because I am interested in what goes on in a hospital. About a year ago I turned on our TV, and I saw "Medic." I thought it was very interesting. A few days later my friend suggested a book for me to read, and I did. The name of the book was *Sue Barton, Neighborhood Nurse*. Then I discovered "Dr. Hudson's Secret Journal," and I began watching it regularly. I went back to our library and found some more books about Sue Barton. Then I found that I had read all her books about nursing. Gradually I began to read more books as a result of watching television.

One student stated that he enjoyed reading but could not find books that he could read: "They are all baby books." This particular student had a low reading-achievement score. He was introduced to the "Landmark" series of books, and the good readers in the class helped him with difficult vocabulary. On the last reading test his achievement had increased from Grade 5.0 to Grade 5.8 in six months.

Concluding Statement

In utilizing any radio or television program related to art, music, geography, science, social studies, and history for study in the classroom, the techniques must vary with each broadcast. They should be related to the children's thought, reactions, and personal experiences. Any spark of interest in reading that children get from listening or viewing television helps to meet some of the educational needs.

PART FIVE

Developing Reading Skills

22. Comprehension in the Reading Program

E. Elona Sochor

I. *Reading and language*
   A. In thinking of comprehension in reading, we cannot think of reading alone. We must think of language in the larger sense, for reading is one aspect of language communication.
   B. Reading involves the use of symbols that are seen. Symbols are also basic to all other language abilities.
   C. As a result, understanding in reading cannot be discussed in isolation. We must consider the ability to understand language.

II. *Scope of comprehension abilities*
   A. Basic interrelated factors in comprehension
      1. Experiences, the materials for comprehending
         a. Experience gives meaning to language, since language has no meaning of its own. Language has meaning insofar as the speaker or writer is using it to express *his* experiences and ideas, and as the listener or reader can bring similar experiences to what is heard or seen.
         b. Therefore, experiences must be appropriate to the

task at hand. Experiences must also be organized, i.e., related and classified, and generalized. The process of acquiring experiences, organizing and using them involves another basic factor — thinking.

2. Thinking, the process for comprehending
   a. Experiences provide the materials for thinking.
   b. Thinking involves, however, more than just experiences, organized though they may be. It includes the manipulation of these experiences, evaluating them, applying them, etc.
   c. We think while acquiring facts, whether it is by doing or through the use of language.
   d. We must think if we are to understand.
   e. The development of understanding or comprehension necessitates the development of thinking.
3. Language, the product of the need to communicate
   a. Of the four ways we have for communication, two are basic to understanding visual symbols — listening and speaking.
   b. Before we can proceed to develop comprehension in reading situations, we need to make certain that listening and speaking abilities have been sufficiently developed.
   c. In general, we can say the school has the final responsibility for developing understanding in reading and writing situations.
   d. In so doing, we must keep in mind that the different ways of language communication are not mutually exclusive. Moreover, the same thinking abilities basic to one way of communicating through language are basic to all other methods of language communication.
4. Thinking in a reading situation, then, is like thinking in any situation involving language and like thinking in practical situations which are basic to language-type situations. It necessitates the use of appropriate experiences adequately organized and associated with printed symbols. It makes possible the reconstruction of what experiences and ideas the author had in mind when he wrote the selection.

B. Thinking abilities basic to understanding language
   1. The scope of a program designed to develop understanding must be as broad as living intelligently and effectively in a democracy.

2. Grasping the facts, though relatively simple, may still involve complex thinking abilities.
   a. For example, the facts may be very abstract. The understanding of antecedents, interpretation of punctuation, shifts of meaning in word usage — all these may produce difficulties even when facts alone are involved.
   b. Understanding the facts involved is basic to all higher level thinking abilities.
3. Other thinking abilities by their nature tend to be more complex than getting the facts. Seeing relationships among ideas in sentences and paragraphs, synthesizing ideas, grasping the topic, organizing, evaluating, verifying new ideas, drawing inferences — all of these abilities plus many more are necessary for understanding language — regardless of the form, oral or printed.
4. There is a danger in concentrating on one kind of thinking, such as acquiring facts.
5. There is also a danger in limiting the development of understanding to one kind of situation — reading. Or even more narrow, limiting this development to reading basic readers.

C. The place of word perception in the development of reading comprehension
   1. The ability to think as needed comes first.
   2. However, word forms or other visual symbols are necessary if the writer is to convey his ideas.
   3. It is equally necessary that the reader be able to associate meaning with the visual symbols and that the meaning must be appropriate.
   4. Thus accurate word perception including recognition, word-attack, or the use of some outside source, is a necessity — but its purpose is to make possible the understanding of what is being read.
   5. We must also keep in mind that meaning aids in word perception and that the context in which a word is used gives us a check on the accuracy of our associations.

D. Our goal, educationally: to provide for a comprehensive and adequate development of as many thinking abilities as possible.
   1. The program should be as broad in the beginning as the child's development allows.
   2. The development of thinking should increase in depth and breadth as soon and as rapidly as a learner's

capacity and maturation permit. It is further limited at any one point by such factors as background of experiences and information; the nature, number and organization of concepts; the level of abstraction of the ideas, etc.

3. The task is not completed in the first grade, the twelfth grade, or at any other level.
4. The development of thinking cannot be limited to a basal reader, arithmetic problems, or a science text. It includes all situations.

III. *Sequences for developing the thinking abilities needed in the use of language*

A. Basic factors

1. Acquisition of experiences
   - a. Direct experience provides the basis for the acquisition of vicarious experiences; "concrete" ideas are easier to understand than abstract ideas.
   - b. Experiential background is used to form concepts. The further removed from the real and the concrete, the more abstract and difficult becomes meaning. *Farm* is more abstract than *dog*, *temperature* than *heat:* the first in each case is broader and includes more.
   - c. The more abstract the concept, the more experiences are needed to understand it and more organization is needed. If a child has no concept of *dog*, he can't understand a *farm* which uses *dogs*.
   - d. Guidance is needed in what should be observed when we supply the opportunities for experiences. Different people will "see" different things when they walk into a room. Some notice light or color; some, furniture arrangement; others might notice a vase of flowers on a table. It is possible to miss completely the obvious or anything else present.
   - e. Regardless of age, if experiences and background are lacking at a concrete level, this must be the beginning point.
   - f. Experiences must be organized. *Dogs* and *cats* may be known as pets. A *cow* may have been seen in a dairy. A *goat* may have been in a zoo. A *horse* may have been seen on a bridle path in a park. All of these together help to understand the concept of *animal*.
   - g. The organization of experiences results in seeing the

whole and the relationship(s) of the parts to the whole.

(1) A *dog* is not a tail and a body and ears, etc.; it's a whole.

(2) A child may have noticed that snow melts outdoors, ice melts when the refrigerator is defrosted, and ice cubes melt in a glass of Coca Cola. He may relate none of these to the influences of *temperature* when he reads about the latter.

h. The acquisition of experiences, relating them, organizing them, demands thinking.

2. Thinking abilities: developed in a sequence
   a. The ability to manipulate a few simple facts precedes the ability to manipulate many complex facts.
   b. Learning how to draw conclusions that are quite obvious precedes those that are less obvious, and this level precedes the least obvious.
   c. A learner must be able to think first in concrete, practical situations. If a child cannot solve a real problem of how to open a door when he needs to get through with his hands full, he'll not be able to get the implications of a story character solving a similar problem.
3. Language: developed sequentially
   a. Basic to language are experiences, the ability to think using these experiences, and a need to communicate.
   b. The child listens first; then he speaks in words, simple sentences, etc. These are basic to reading, and writing depends on reading abilities. All are interrelated as and after they are acquired.

B. Point of initiation for developing understanding abilities
   1. This depends first on the needs a learner has that are basic to understanding.
      a. The number of experiences needed
      b. The nature of these experiences
      c. The organization of these experiences
      d. The ability to think (capacity and learning)
   2. It depends on the physical, social and emotional development of the learner.
   3. In reading it depends on familiarity with word forms, structure of the language and all the other factors basic to dealing with printed symbols.
   4. Wherever the child may be in his development — that

is where we begin. When he comes to school, we already have something to work with: experiences, thinking and language. We must keep in mind, however, that individuals differ in their development.

C. Guidance in developing understanding abilities
  1. Basic thinking abilities begin to be developed by the teacher as soon as the child enters a classroom, regardless of the grade level, from kindergarten on.
  2. All basic thinking abilities are necessary at each reader level. This is also true at the level of "readiness for beginning reading."
     a. The differentiation between the same word used in different speaking situations must take place in readiness for beginning reading or the pupil cannot listen intelligently. He must do the same with words at the preprimer level and eventually in using the dictionary.
     b. Children in kindergarten can discuss a problem of mud on the playground and work out a solution to the problem.
     c. Comprehension, or thinking abilities, basic to and a part of any level, are basic to the next level.
        (1) If a reader cannot synthesize ideas on the first basal reader level, he will not be able to do so on the second or third basal reader levels. He must be guided into developing this ability on the first reader level before he can move on.
        (2) If a reader does not understand the function of a story title, he will not be ready or able to relate paragraph topics to the title.
        (3) In dealing with relevancy, if the learner does not recognize the obviously relevant or irrelevant, he will not be able to recognize the remotely relevant or irrelevant. He must begin with the former.
        (4) A child begins by drawing inferences from pictures, moves to short stories and simple content materials, and finally draws inferences from any kind of material he is ready to handle.
     d. Any thinking ability developed on an easier level needs guidance to be utilized appropriately and efficiently at a more difficult level. The need for such guidance never ceases.
  3. The development of thinking abilities must be syste-

matic. Whenever a need for development is apparent, guidance must be supplied. Moreover, these abilities must be developed and applied until the learner can think and communicate independent of the teacher's guidance.

4. The development of broader and higher level thinking abilities never stops.

IV. *The need for developing better thinking abilities is reflected in research on communication and may be observed in everyday experiences with people.*

A. High school and college students with reading difficulties have far more and greater comprehension problems than they have word recognition problems. They can pronounce the words but they don't "get enough from their reading."

B. There are far too many adults who can manipulate words, but who lack understanding and the ability to think critically.

C. There must be more development of thinking, or we will never solve these problems.

D. Good readers are good comprehenders.

23. Semantics in the Secondary School

Richard Corbin

Though a few administrators still live in the gramaphone age and some others seem not to have gotten beyond the headphones-and-crystal-tickler era in their thinking about English, most school administrators today seem fully aware of the problem of Mass Communication and its impact upon our society and, consequently, upon our school programs, especially in the social studies and in the teaching of English.

The progress in developing communication devices that we have witnessed in our lifetime has been rivaled only by the speed with which men have developed techniques for making language either their weapon or their tool. Unfortunately, too much of this progress in communication research has been as specialized and as misdirected as that in the concurrent race for atomic superiority. But where men have yet to prove their morality, or lack of it, in the handling of the atom's destructive power, they are already hip-deep in the calculated misuse of language. Whether engaged in peddling cigarettes or alien philosophies, the amoral hucksters of the world have been more appreciative students of semantics than the great majority of their customers.

If we are to continue to regard the "gift of tongues" as God-given, it behooves us to reverse this trend. The schools alone cannot accomplish this, yet they are patently the most powerful single agency upon which we can rely at present to bring speech and writing back to a respect for Truth. In a single generation we have seen language in the hands of the fascists and communists, both home-grown and foreign, used to destroy ideals, morale, and the political, spiritual, and economic security of millions of men. We have seen and heard the record of a Hitler debauching with words the German spirit in the Wilhelmstrasse. We have received firsthand accounts of the "brain-washing" of our friends, even our fellow-citizens, by the men of Stalin and Mao. Some of us have personally witnessed our communities circularized and our neighbors perplexed by the Zolls and the Harts. All of us are watching now with growing apprehension the weaving of verbal nets about some of our respected officials and fellow-citizens by the Machiavellian tactics of the big and little McCarthy's in our midst. These are matters of public record. Is it possible to know these things and still, as conscientious administrators and teachers, to consider *Silas Marner*, the nominative absolute, and trochaic trimeter the proper approach to a mastery of our language?

To imply that semantics has a pressing claim for space in our curriculum today is not to derogate the importance of grammar and rhetoric. It does seem evident, however, that the language program, like the motion picture, has reached a point where forces beyond our control make necessary a three-dimensional treatment. There is not much value in a well-constructed sentence, gracefully styled, if the thought is expressed in symbols that have little relationship with reality.

Once upon a time perhaps, life was simple enough for Goldilocks to have little trouble in finally determining the ownership of the beds in which she had briefly rested. Life today is a somewhat more complex matter, and it isn't as easy as some would have us believe to discover whether or not we have been inadvertently lying in the old Bear's bed. Mr. Hitler simplified life to the single choice between two words, *YAH* and *nein;* Mr. McCarthy would reduce us to almost as simple a design. In neither case is grammar or rhetoric a factor; in both cases, it is essential to understand the meanings, and the meanings of the meanings, of the words upon which our lives and liberties depend. As no generation ever has before, our young people need to be taught not only about the mechanics and style of language, but also about the process by which meaning is produced.

Semantics is new in name, but not in concept. For centuries the great minds in every culture have groped, often with some success, for an understanding of the nature of words and meaning. But not until our own century when we began to apply the scientific method to the study of language, has there been available an organized body of knowledge about language that could be given to everyone for use in their everyday affairs. Unhappily, we are losing the benefits of much of this knowledge by default; it has had its most effective use in the hands of our enemies. It is no exaggeration to say that language has ranked in importance above all the other weapons in their arsenals. It is time, and past time, for us to acknowledge the decisive power of language and to devote at least as much energy to understanding it as we are devoting to the search for atomic knowledge. Most schools today include units on the atom in their programs. How many schools give space to even an elementary study of semantics?

Linguistic Insights Needed

What are some of the important linguistic insights that our students (and all of us) need, and that can best be revealed through the study of semantics? Briefly, they are these:

1. *An understanding of the symbolic nature of language* — The realization that words are not the things they stand for — that words like *fascist*, *Christian*, *warmonger*, *subversive*, *gentleman* used to symbolize a person do not make him any one of these. Not even a fool would try to appease his hunger by eating the word *food*, yet every day supposedly knowing people accept without question millions of products on the basis of imprinted symbols like "100 *per cent pure*," *superior*, *super-safe*, "*they satisfy*." In other words, we habitually treat words as if the words themselves are identical with the things for which they stand. So long as these words stand only for the trivia of life, no great harm may result. But confusing symbols for reality at the more complex levels of thought and communication may have consequences disastrous both to ourselves and others.

In wartime, as history shows, sea-raiders have often found it most effective to fly flags other than their own.

Too many of the so-called "educated" live largely in a world of symbols that have no reference to reality; their actions and attitudes growing out of this symbol-world are often valueless and sometimes irresponsible. Nor does the fact that they associate with morally responsible groups decrease the danger to our culture that lies in the distorted meanings of their pleasant sounding words.

2. *An understanding of the nature of differences* — The recognition that words used to classify the endless variations in our universe often overlook the common characteristics of the things classified. Because we name one group of men *White*, and another *Negro*, or one type of school *public* and another *private*, we are likely to disregard the characteristics common to both unless we understand exactly how words function in the classification process.

3. *An understanding of the process of abstraction* — The appreciation of the relativeness of meaning of many words. Almost anyone can see that the word *cold* might signify something different to a northern Canadian than to a Floridian. But in more complex areas of life we cannot make intelligent or just decisions unless we can also discern degrees of difference in our more abstract symbols. We are not likely to get effective action from people in whose minds the terms *crime* and *juvenile delinquency* are equated. Many of our citizens might have avoided present embarrassment if they had related *communism* with the facts of Russian life in the '20s and '30s rather than with the abstractions of Marx and Lenin. We do not grow apprehensive about a man's *wealth* if we know that it is a *cow* and not *half the State of Texas.*

4. *An understanding of the nature of judgments and inferences* — Accurate reports have always been essential to human progress, and one of the commonest obstacles to progress has been men's inability to distinguish between reports and judgments or between reports and inferences. There is no intelligent reading of the daily newspaper without going behind the reporter's words to determine how much is verifiable fact. One paper reports a slain labor leader's cortege "accompanied by many members of his union." A second paper reports that it was "guarded by a mob of hired goons." The semantically trained reader is surely in a more favorable position to appraise accurately either or both of these sets of symbols than the reader who is unaware of "loading," "slanting," and other devices common in mis-reporting.

An administrator, facing his normal daily harvest of teacher reports on pupils, can well appreciate the problem of discriminating between judgments and reports.

5. *An understanding of the nature of metaphor* — The old game of stalking figures of speech in the Iliad, chalking them on the blackboard, then standing back to regard them with esthetic awe seems hardly the way to make students conscious of the elemental importance of metaphor in their daily speech and writing. Conversely, the reader who has not learned to recognize the structure of metaphor and to discriminate between functional and merely decorative metaphor is likely to be easy prey for the unscrupulous advertiser and the political rhetorician.

These brief sketches do not pretend to do more than suggest some of the major general areas of semantic interest. These are, perhaps, the areas in which the largest proportion of errors and distortions in communication by language symbols are apt to occur.

In fairness, it should be pointed out, of course, that there are certain moral and intellectual dangers to be faced in the teaching of semantics. But these dangers are different only in kind from the risks we chance each time we admit a class into a gymnasium with its variety of bone-breaking games and machines. In spite of the occasional broken arms, concussions, and chipped teeth, physical training is still considered a "must" in the school program. Certainly the strengthening of the thinking and language habits of our pupils is worth a comparable risk. In the opinion of many, it is worth more.

How Much Semantics?

Assuming that an administrator, having heard frequent mention of semantics by some of his fellow service-club members or having noted articles referring to it in his professional journals, decides that some attention should be paid it in his school's program, certain questions of procedure arise. How much semantics shall be taught? And by whom? At what level or levels shall it be introduced? And just how shall it be taught? Since there is little experience to draw on, the general answer has to be that a school must approach the problem with a frankly experimental attitude.

Under these conditions, the English or social studies classes provide the most natural setting for the study of words, their meanings, and their effect upon human behavior and institutions. There are few schools that do not have in these departments at least one or two venturesome teachers of sound judgment to whom the project can be entrusted. If these teachers also have a lively or creative interest in language and life, so much the better.

But before there can be actual planning and teaching, both administrator and teachers will want to "orient" themselves by reading widely in the literature of semantics (which fortunately is not extensive and, even more fortunately, is exceptionably readable). Most well-trained teachers will find a great deal of this material familiar — in fact, may find that they have been using certain semantic principles in their teaching unaware that they were doing so. But however familiar some of the material, its organization will be new, and not until a teacher has formed a philosophical point of view on the subject of semantics is she ready to select the matters to be taught. This selection is made in the usual manner, in terms of maturity level of students, their attitudes, previous language training, and the like.

Because of its recency, few high-school teachers have had formal training in semantics. However, formal courses in semantics are multiplying in the colleges, and many other departments are concerning themselves with it. Two books widely used as texts are S. I. Hayakawa's *Language in Thought and Action* and Irving Lee's *Language Habits in Human Affairs*, both of which are indebted to the work of the late Alfred Korzybski of Yale. That more and more secondary schools are turning attention to semantics is evidenced by the increasing space and emphasis given the subject (without actually labeling it) in the more recent textbooks. A number of high schools have reported success in adapting Hayakawa's book for use with their more mature pupils. A newly published book that is concerned specifically with the teaching of semantics at the junior and senior high-school level is *Words and What They Do To You* by Catherine Minteer.

Once underway, an alert teacher will find that the best "textbooks" for semantic studies are the daily newspaper, radio, television, the school community and, of course, the gossip and public affairs of the larger community of which the school is a part. No one can say how much of semantics should be taught in a given course anymore than one can prescribe how much grammar or spelling should be taught — that is a matter for the teacher's judgment. However, it might be suggested, that, in general, lessons in semantics are likely to be more effective if woven into the pattern of the course or, better yet, presented when some incident or statement in the classroom or on the local or national scene presents a timely point for the lesson. In a history class, a semantic analysis of the Declaration of Independence or the Bill of Rights will likely make a far deeper and more lasting impression on the students' minds than the dull techniques traditionally employed to perpetuate the knowledge of these sacred documents. But if a school is fortunate enough to have within one class a fairly homogeneous group of mentally alert pupils, there is no reason why a more formal approach to semantics cannot profitably be tried. Care should be taken, however, that such a class does not deteriorate into a mere concern with formal labels, as happened so often with the exciting study of English grammar.

Evaluation of results is of course an important step in any educative process. Here again, the newness — not to say the nature — of the material makes reliable objective testing difficult and, as most humble teachers will admit, the results of subjective testing of thought and attitudes of any kind are hard to assess with any degree of certainty. As with any subject, familiarity with the vocabulary of semantics can be tested, but whether or not a pupil has also attained a deeper, personal insight into the processes of language and a lasting desire to use it honestly can probably best be judged by the teacher on the spot. If we may believe those teachers who are pioneering, the results are easily observable and eminently worth-while. The impartial testimony of pupils who have experienced semantic study is equally favorable.

Apart from the normal responsibility of familiarizing himself with materials taught in his school (especially in a relatively new area like semantics), the administrator is likely to realize some unexpected bonuses from his own study. For from the material of semantics he may well obtain many ideas for improving individual and group relations in his schools, and, perhaps of even more practical value, between his school and the community.

Many a bond issue has been voted down not because a community opposed the idea of adequate education, but because boards of education and administrators often present their cases in ill-chosen words. Many a flourishing program has been thrown out of school, not because the parents objected, but because shrewd opponents were able to focus the voter's attention on the label rather than on the program. In fact, it does not seem dangerous to generalize that the school administrator who is not well-grounded in the semantics of language in most cases is not a very effective leader of or spokesman for the schools of his community or education at large.

In a world confused by sudden and vast movements in the field of communication, in a world made dramatically aware of its differences by these changes and by equally revolutionary and related changes in the field of transportation, what valid argument can be advanced against the claim that we need a deeper, surer understanding of the role of language in our lives? What small understanding we now have must be disseminated to all our people including the young, not preserved as a secret weapon for the sole use of the unprincipled hucksters and politicians who would dominate our world.

Suggested Readings

For those who are not already familiar with the literature of semantics, the following books are suggested. They are recommended for their reliability, their general readableness, and their special value to the teacher or administrator interested in introducing semantics into the school program.

Chase, Stuart. *The Tyranny of Words.* Harcourt Brace. 1938.

Hayakawa, S. I. *Language in Thought and Action.* Harcourt Brace. 1949.

Lee, Irving. *Language Habits in Human Affairs.* Harper. 1941.

Minteer, Catherine. *Words and What They Do To You.* Row, Peterson. 1953.

National Educational Association, Department of Classroom Teachers. "It Starts in the Classroom" (Handbook).

Ogden, C. K., and Richards, I. A. *The Meaning of Meaning.* Harcourt Brace. 1930.

Thomas, Cleveland A. "Exploring Language in Senior English," *English Journal.* May, 1953.

Walpole, Hugh. *Semantics.* W. W. Norton. 1941.

24. Problems Met When Reading Critically in Grades Seven to Ten

Charles B. Huelsman, Jr.

The methods used in promoting growth in interpretation, when the aim is to react critically to what is read, may be evaluated in the light of three questions: Do the methods used promote skill in critical reading? Do they aid the reader in avoiding common pitfalls in critical thinking? Do they insure the use of critical reading skills in functional situations?

Three Basic Questions

In any effort to promote growth in critical reading ability, it is necessary to know, first of all, what important skills are involved.

As a means of identifying these skills, a careful study was made of fifteen recent articles and reports relating to critical reading ability. The following abilities and skills were emphasized by one or more of the writers:

To define and delimit a problem
To formulate hypotheses
To locate information bearing on specific problems
To determine that a statement is important for a given purpose
To distinguish the difference between facts and opinions
To evaluate the dependability of data
To recognize the limitations of given data even when the items are assumed to be dependable
To see elements common to several items of data
To make comparisons
To organize evidence that suggests relationships
To recognize prevailing tendencies or trends in the data
To judge the competency of a given author to make a valid statement on a given topic
To criticize data on the basis of its completeness and accuracy
To criticize a presentation on the basis of the completeness and logic of its reasoning
To suspend judgment until all evidence is assembled and evaluated

The second needed type of information relates to the pitfalls met in critical thinking. According to one or more of six different writers, such pitfalls may be characterized as follows:

Failure to detect errors in inductive and deductive reasoning
Failure to examine all the alternatives
Failure to detect false analogies
Failure to detect overgeneralization
Failure to identify oversimplification
Failure to distinguish between observations and inferences
Failure to detect the shift in meaning of a term
Failure to detect distortion or suppression of the truth
Permitting emotions to anaesthetize critical powers

The third question relates to the provision made for the effective use of critical reading ability in functional situations. The evidence available indicates that it is not sufficient merely to teach children about critical reading but that training is also essential in the use of these abilities in functional situations. Osborn,[1] for example, found that providing knowledge about propagandistic methods was insufficient to develop resistance to propaganda. This challenges the validity of the usual patterns of instruction given in critical reading and suggests doubt about their relative sufficiency.

[1] Wayland W. Osborn, "An Experiment in Teaching Resistance to Propaganda," *Journal of Experimental Education*, VIII (September, 1939), 1–17.

The study of recent literature, supplemented by classroom observations, shows that at least three approaches to the development of critical reading ability are in current use: the direct approach, the incidental approach, and the functional approach. The remainder of this paper describes each of these approaches and attempts to point out their strengths and weaknesses.

The Direct Approach

In certain instances, teachers plan their work so as to cultivate directly certain critical reading skills. They attempt, for example, to teach methods of logical reasoning and to acquaint readers with the errors that may easily be made in reasoning or the devices used by writers and speakers to influence the reader or the listener. Kottmeyer [2] has described the efforts made by the St. Louis schools to do the latter. Through an in-service training program, teachers were stimulated to try several activities with junior high school pupils. During the training program, they were aided in creating materials to use with their classes, utilizing advertisements, editorials, and cartoons as aids. At all times the teachers aimed to stimulate independent thinking and to train pupils to read critically as distinguished from assimilative reading, recreational reading, and fact-finding reading.

Advertising material that appeared in current magazines was utilized as a means of instruction in the analysis of propaganda. A set of guide sheets was created to aid in the identification of the seven common types of propaganda. These were classified as "Bad Names," "Glad Names," "Transfer," "Testimonial," "Plain Folks," "Stacking the Cards," and "Band Wagon." A brief description of each was included, written with a vocabulary readily understood by junior high school pupils. Seven bulletin boards were prepared, one to illustrate each kind of propaganda. In addition, a series of advertisements was collected and placed individually in numbered envelopes. These served as materials for independent reading of advertisements, since the reader had to identify the propaganda technique, utilizing his newly formed knowledge of the various methods.

Another source of materials for teaching critical reading skills was located in the editorial pages of newspapers and news magazines. However, since many of the editorial writers employ difficult styles and vocabularies for junior high school pupils, it was necessary to provide background information and translations of some

[2] William Kottmeyer, "Classroom Activities in Critical Reading," *School Review*, LII (November, 1944), 557–64.

of the more difficult terms and concepts. The editorials selected were pasted on the lefthand inside page of a folder with the additional information required to make it more meaningful to the reader. This technique enabled the teacher to adjust the task of reading to the achievement level of the group and, to some degree, to take individual differences into account. On the righthand side of the folder was placed a typewritten silent-reading exercise designed to stimulate critical reading skill and, to a lesser degree, to stimulate assimilative reading. A similar technique was utilized with cartoons.

The methods described by Kottmeyer were doubtless effective in stimulating pupils to react critically to advertisements, editorials, and cartoons. In all probability, the methods gave teachers excellent opportunity to teach the various skills that aid the reader in reacting critically and provided the teachers with a chance to help the reader identify pitfalls in critical thinking. However, Kottmeyer presented no evidence of growth in critical reading skill nor of transfer of the skill to the reading of history, science, or literature.

The Incidental Approach

In talking with teachers, the present writer found that many were promoting growth in critical reading without being fully aware of it. In other words, they used an incidental approach.

In one school the social-studies instruction in Grades VII and VIII was organized in units, utilizing pupil-teacher planning, committees to solve special problems, oral reports, and questioning by both teacher and pupils of the reports and of the reading which is done. One such unit in Grade VII, based on industrial changes following the Civil War, involved the work of six such committees, each unit with a chairman and a co-chairman. The committees, formed after a week of general reading and orientation, defined their own problems, instituted search for sources that would provide answers to these problems, and prepared to discuss their findings with the class and make their reports. In connection with this procedure, the children passed through four stages: acquiring general background information; formulating problems; locating, comprehending, and evaluating needed information; and organizing and reporting the information and conclusions. At all stages teacher guidance was provided in the amount necessary to foster relative independence on the part of the students in this kind of reading. At specified hours during the week, the children were free to visit the library, where the librarian helped them to find reference material as needed. A teacher was frequently present at committee meetings to help with the planning, to make suggestions on the formulation of the problems, and to guide the kind and amount of reading being done.

Growth in several kinds of critical reading skill may result from this sort of instruction. Skill in formulating problems and in defining hypotheses can be developed in early stages of the units. Skills in the co-ordinate reading of several sources on a given topic, in locating the information required for specific problems, and in determining the relevancy of the material read can be taught in the intermediate stages of the unit, when the pupils are preparing to discuss their topics and to make their reports. Librarians assist the teacher at this stage. During the final stages of the units, the pupils become more cognizant of the necessity of determining the relevancy of the material read, of differentiating facts from opinions, and of determining the logical reasoning that supports opinions. The comments of the teachers and pupils, however, reveal that the development of critical reading skill was secondary in importance to the development of social concepts and attitudes and to the acquisition of information.

Growth on critical reading skills at this school appears to be an outcome of the way the teachers have approached the unit method of instruction. The faculty has made no special effort to organize or identify the various critical reading skills so that all the skills will be taught or reviewed or given repeated practice at this level.

The Functional Approach

Ferrell [3] reported an experience in teaching history and critical reading simultaneously. She emphasized the evaluation of historical source material instead of the acquisition of information from secondary works. At the beginning of the year, the teacher and the class spent several days looking through newspapers and listening to radio speeches, noting essential features of good thinking and common pitfalls in logic. Once a definite understanding of the objectives had been attained, class work was begun. Primary sources were approached with several questions in mind, among which were the following:

1. Are the statements of fact that are offered as evidence reports of observation, inferences, or hearsay?
2. Why should (or should not) the statements of fact be considered reliable? Who made them? What was his purpose? What were the conditions of observation? Was memory relied upon?
3. Is the evidence relevant to the question?
4. Are relevant facts, both for and against, presented?

[3] Frances Ferrell, "Critical Thinking," *Chicago Schools Journal*, XXX (October, 1948), 42–45.

5. Do the facts mean what the author thinks they do?
6. What is the proposal? Should we believe it? Why?
7. What are the consequences of acting on the conclusions drawn?
8. What are the possible alternative conclusions?

During the first semester, each group of five students was responsible for organizing and presenting one or more topics and leading class discussions. During the second semester, the groups were less formal, and extemporaneous round-table discussions were used more frequently.

The functional approach, as reported by Ferrell, was limited to one subject and one year. It would appear, however, to offer promise as an effective method of instruction if it were extended and widened to incorporate more subjects over a greater number of years. Instruction in all critical reading skills could be incorporated into the plan, attention directed to all errors in logic, and the critical reading skills taught and practiced in real situations. It would involve all-school, all-faculty participation. It would have continuity and sequence. It could be made flexible in terms of the needs of individuals and of groups. It would provide a stimulating setting for growth in these reading skills.

Summary

Three approaches to the teaching of critical reading skills have been described: direct, incidental, and functional.

The direct approach provides instruction in the specific skills to be utilized and is organized, for example, around the reading of editorials and cartoons or the analysis of propaganda. It places less emphasis upon critical reading of history, geography, science, etc. The incidental method places emphasis upon critical reading in the content fields but does not provide guaranties that all the critical reading skills will be taught in sequence and with continuity.

The functional approach appears to offer the most promise if the various members of the faculty co-operate in implementing the program throughout the school. Such a plan involves decisions regarding the sequential order in which the skills should be taught, plans for the continuity of practice after instruction, provision of increasing opportunity for pupils to use critical reading skills more and more independently, and constant appraisal of the effectiveness of the procedures.

The teachers who are looking for methods of teaching pupils to read critically are convinced, as Russell is, that mere literacy is not enough to save a democracy. All its citizens must learn to comprehend the ideas and problems about which they read. They must be able to react critically to whatever they read.

25. Developing Critical Reading as a Basic Skill

Roma Gans

The first quality of mature readers, I would say, is that they draw upon their reading and relate it to topics in their conversation, to problems and to studies. In other words, reading *feeds* their thinking, broadens their thinking. It gives a kind of credence to their ideas. A critical reader sees relevance in what he reads. He uses reading in relation to other ideas and to his needs. It becomes a part of an integrated outlook or an integrated insight. It adds to him.

The second quality that marks a mature critical reader is the ability and the awareness of the need to evaluate the sources of material read. Evaluation of authors is one part of this. In a discussion the good reader refers to the newspaper in which he saw an article. This is evaluation of sources. A critical reader doesn't assume that if it's in the book or if it's in the newspaper, it's so. A critical reader wants to evaluate the idea presented in terms of the author who presents it. We have presses that have one slant and presses that have another slant. But the person who is unaware of that may not have developed a kind of critical reading which in certain strategic points in life is essential. The second quality, therefore, is the ability to evaluate authorship, authenticity, even if necessary to seek the date of copyright or date of publication.

Certainly the third quality in critical reading is the ability to assess the ways in which words influence ideas. It has taken us so long to come to understand the influence and the power of words. This becomes very important in the assessment of ideas that are often colored, or slanted. How is this coloring and slanting done? The critical reader becomes aware; he knows and he is not influenced emotionally by words that are there to color his thinking.

The fourth quality of a critical reader is ability to select wisely what he reads. A critical reader has acquired values and outlooks and has a basis for selecting. He does not need to wait until the lists are published in the Book Section of the Sunday *New York Times* or the *Herald Tribune*. He doesn't wait for some authority to say what is all right or good. He has developed the ba is for selecting in the process of growing up.

The selective reader bases his selection upon his own intellectualizing processes — not upon authority. There may be times when he goes into an area which is not of his own background. Then he says to one who knows, "Can you recommend a good book on this topic?" He does that, however, not because he is a dependent reader or a dependent chooser. He does it fully aware that in that area he does not have the competence and is, therefore, getting assistance. But he is selective in the person whom he asks. He finds somebody who does know and asks for help.

So much for these four qualities.

The fifth characteristic tends to be an effect as well as a cause and is noticed when a reader is able to stand up and be counted in his opinion upon what he has read. I shall always remember going into a social evening right after reading Pearl Buck's *The Good Earth*. Knowing nothing about Pearl Buck, I read it and was tremendously held by this gripping story with a feeling of the background of China. That evening people said, "What have you been reading of late?" (A wonderful kind of conversation opening!)

I said, "I've just finished a book by someone I know nothing about. She's been in China and she is a missionary's daughter. The book is called *The Good Earth*."

"Oh," said one of the group, "tell me what you think of it. I read it too."

I said, "Well, if you read it, I'd like to know what you think."

She said, "Well, I'd rather hear from you first."

I sensed that she was a person afraid of her own ideas. It wasn't *not* being sure. It *was* being afraid. This is the ability to stand up and say — as a third grade child told me, "I don't care if the whole world likes this book, I don't like it."

It seems to me this quality is related to the integrity of the reader. Either this person has the kind of makeup that helps him to say "I don't like it" or "I like it" or "I don't care if none of you likes it, I still enjoy it." Whether or not it may start with one who takes such strength and integrity to his reading or whether, in the process of becoming a reader, he develops it — it is part of the process of critical reading. Thus, it can be both cause and effect.

We test the readers among us on their ability to stand up and be counted. The person who has this quality of integrity is a marked person. We seek his judgment because we know he's not going to avoid taking a stand. Those who write reviews, who dare to take a position, will also give you their reasons. Thus, the critical reader is not only selective, and not only courageous, but also he is a person who has reasons for his choices. And he has convictions that he can describe.

Developing Skills in Critical Reading

Now how do we develop these general qualities for developing critical reading as a basic skill? I've listed five, and there are others.

First, children are going to grow into readers who are able to relate what they read to what they do if they have opportunities to do just that. It is interesting to go into a first grade and have children show you books, pictures, and diagrams that they have made. They are already getting ideas from printed pages in the form of instructions and recipes and relating these ideas to the job at hand. Much experience in varied opportunities all through the school years will be necessary to develop a reader who just doesn't apply reading to his life in a patchwork fashion. Therefore, he needs very much to find ideas through materials that relate to his interests or to the job at hand.

I listened to a thrilling report of a youngster who had recently completed a study of Iceland. He had read everything on Iceland that was in his school library, and he said, "I will say we need a lot more material about Iceland. Iceland is not very well known. I also read a lot of stuff that was old and no longer is true." That youngster was applying wonderful, adult, mature ability to read critically.

The second set of opportunities or experiences that are needed relate to discussion. Children should be able to discuss ideas in material read and then look up authorship, authenticity, and date of copyright on sources of ideas. I wish that every book (and I would like to say every textbook) included a story of how it was written, by whom, how revised, how edited. Then a youngster is helped to understand books, and gains an added tool for building this kind of skill.

Yet a reader needs many experiences to alert him. A youngster said to me, "Why can't you stay a little longer? We're getting a big box of books today and one of them is going to be a new book by the D'Aulaires." Here was a youngster who knew authors. How did that happen? They were in a program where that was being done. It wasn't a patch on life and it wasn't in that peculiar Friday-afternoon 30 minutes known as "recreational reading."

Third, children need guidance in reading so that they acquire some of these skills that have to do with understanding why they like what they like. A program that develops taste will find topics that they like and styles of writing that they like. The respect for the integrity of children and their right to test their own individual taste is important. I'm worried when I hear tremendous emphasis on balanced reading. We are told we have to go round the wheel. But which one of us does? I haven't read a historical novel in years, but I love historical novels. I don't know how I would have developed this taste if somebody had said to me: "Now, how many historical novels? How many biographies have you read? And how much poetry?" But some people seem to like this nice mechanical process.

So children need to become readers of taste who choose wisely. They also need to understand the techniques of writing. I saw a third grade where youngsters were looking at the advertisements for different breakfast foods which all made the same claims. They noticed that if you ate this food — but not any others of course — you'd be a champion. The children told me, "They say that because they want you to buy it." This is a tremendous insight which we need to recapture.

Children must have an opportunity to choose if they are going to be selective. To see this happen is a thrill. I watched a book-mobile come up to a school and a third-grade group of youngsters come out to choose their books. The person in charge of the book-mobile was standing by. The books were all there. It was one of those trucks that could be walked into. Children could stand around, look and put back, and talk over with somebody. No one was saying, "Oh, this is the book for you." There wasn't anybody there little enough or insulting enough to say, "Peter, here is a good book for you." The development of selection comes through opportunities to select. These same third graders went back into their room just in time for recess. They said to the teacher, "We just got our books, must we go out to play?" It was thrilling to hear the way they shared "What did you take?" or "I read that once before" or "Isn't that a wonderful book?" or "You'll love it." One said, "I haven't read a fairy story in years. My mother will drop dead."

I saw a wonderful group in Harlem where the teacher was giving her children opportunity for selective reading. All she did was to bring the books in and say, "New books, wonderful books, and books from the library. Put them on the shelves in the back of the room. Whenever you have time, your work is finished or you're stuck on something and I can't come to help you (notice *that* wonderful point), don't *sit* there, go back and take a book (and notice this next) and *browse* through it, look at it."

She didn't say read it. The nonreading group began to look and browse. Youngsters who sat with hands folded or who rapped pencils were told "Take a look at some books." For the first time in this teacher's career (and she had been teaching 16 years) she said, "The conversation in my room was about books. It would hearten anyone. These youngsters love to talk about books. They love to handle books. The amazing thing is, without my ever suggesting it, they are reading books. And they are finding books which they want to read." What an opportunity to develop the kind of reader who becomes selective, who learns how to reach out and how to feed his appetite.

The last point related to this development of integrity and honesty in reading means that we must discuss materials.

Youngsters in a Westchester County school talked about a geography book that made a very poor statement about the kinds of western ranches. One youngster said, "They talk about only one kind of ranch. They don't say anything about dude ranches. And the ranch they talk about is not true any more." These youngsters were evaluating that book when they said, "Maybe this book tried to tell us too much" or "That wasn't right." And the teacher listened and she said, "You know, I never thought about some of these points." She never thought that a geography book as a book might give you just a meager concept. That teacher honored the thinking of children, each one with a God-given right to be an honest person. No child of such teaching says "yes" because it is in the book, "yes" because the teacher likes it, "yes" because somebody says he should like it. In other words, we are developing basic skills in honest, forthright, critical assessment and evaluation.

I would say there are three things we'd better do in a hurry, at least much more frequently than we do:

1. Have a program in which children have experiences that challenge and motivate reading that is not a patchwork, but that becomes an integral part of the program for all ages.

2. Have a program that encourages personal choice and the development of taste, that does not try to make children all alike — the standard brand.

3. Schools must encourage these ideas by a different concept of selecting reading materials and a different concept of budgeting to buy these materials that are needed in this kind of program.

26. Reading Skills and Methods of Teaching Them

Kansas Studies in Education

Reading Skills and Habits Needed in the Language Arts

I. A good reader in a language arts class should be able to:

A. Utilize sources to locate materials.

1. Indexes.
2. Tables of contents.
3. Glossaries.
4. Card catalogues.
5. *Readers' Guide to Periodical Literature.*
6. General references.
7. Newspapers, magazines, pamphlets.
8. Tables, maps, graphs, charts.
9. Dictionaries and word guides.

B. Adjust reading speed to the type and difficulty of the materials and to the reading purpose.

1. Gaining a general appraisal of the material.
2. Skimming the contents of the material.
3. Reading for memorization of general concepts and/or details.
4. Reading carefully and critically.

C. Comprehend written material.

1. Understanding word meanings.
2. Determining general significance of the context of sentences, paragraphs, chapters, books, lines of poetry, scenes and acts from plays, and complete dramas.
3. Recognizing important details:
   a. Isolated facts.
   b. Evidence to buttress main ideas.
   c. Answers to specific questions.
4. Noting and understanding use of transitional words, phrases, and clauses as bridges to join ideas.
5. Realizing the author's purpose in writing.

D. Evaluate the material intelligently.
   1. Determining the competency of the author and reliability and relevancy of the content.
   2. Comparing new concepts gained in reading with previously held concepts.
   3. Analyzing the significance of the date of publication.
   4. Adopting the mood which the author wants to create.
   5. Judging the validity of character portrayal.

E. Apply concepts gained from the reading material to confronting situations.
   1. Solving problems.
   2. Taking part in a discussion.
   3. Doing additional reading to get more adequate information.
   4. Observing and analyzing life situations and comparing them to material read.
   5. Stimulating imagination and thought.

F. Present written material orally.

G. Understand the importance of reading and ways to satisfy intellectual curiosity through reading.

H. Make accurate self-evaluations of progress in reading in the language arts.
   1. Realizing the importance of self-evaluation.
   2. Using a self-evaluation check list periodically.

Illustrative Methods and Devices a High School Language Arts Teacher May Use to Improve Reading of Materials in His Classes [1]

I. Methods that might be used in teaching language arts pupils:

A. To utilize sources to locate materials such as:
   1. Indexes, tables of contents, glossaries, the card catalogue, and the *Readers' Guide to Periodical Literature*
      a. Discuss where to find each of these sources and the material that each contains.
      b. Conduct "treasure hunts" for information requiring the use of these sources.
      c. Assign each student a different item to report on.

[1] The illustrative methods and devices suggested follow the same plan of organization used for listing reading skills and habits in each of the five fields. For example, the methods and devices listed for the Language Arts under A illustrate the reading skill or habit listed under A in the preceding section. The same organizational pattern is used for B and all succeeding sections.

2. General references, newspapers, magazines, and pamphlets
   a. Discuss the general references, newspapers, magazines, and pamphlets that are most likely to be used, where they can be found, and the information that they contain.
   b. Assign speaking and writing problems requiring the use of these sources.

B. To vary reading speed:
   1. Set up time limit appraisals to determine the value of a quick look at table of contents, titles, subtitles, and pictures to gain an overall idea of the contents.
   2. Set up time limit tests to see how much general content and/or details can be learned from looking at each paragraph quickly and noting italics, dates, and figures.
   3. Compare the time necessary to read a section of a seventh grade book with the time necessary to read a section of the same length in a book written for high school juniors.
   4. Compare the time necessary to read a section of a book when the reader wants to generalize with the time necessary to read the same section when he wants to find specific details.
   5. List purposes for which pupils might read and determine the possible speed of reading for each purpose.
   6. Compare the time necessary to read sections of the same length in different types of literature: essay, novel, poetry, play news story, problems in mathematics, a law report or directions on a commercial product or a game.
   7. Determine speed of reading and repetitions necessary for memorization of general concepts and of details by trial and tests with parallel paragraphs.
   8. Compare reflective reading with story reading of the same novel by different persons when both are reading for pleasure.

C. To comprehend written material in such skills as:
   1. Understanding word meanings
      a. Use the dictionary for specific word study.
      b. Discuss etymology.
      c. Explain "New Word" sections of the dictionary.
      d. Give opportunities to use new words in oral and written reports.
      e. Discuss the meaning of new words that will be appearing in reading assignments.
      f. Show pupils how to keep a notebook of new words.

g. Discuss usage of slang, euphemisms, metaphors, "colored" words, and figures of speech.
h. Show pupils how to keep a personal dictionary of new words.
i. Make word lists or drill cards for individual and class use.
j. Develop crossword puzzles for individual and small group use.
k. Give opportunities for "guessing" the meaning of words used in context.
l. Provide visual experiences for vocabulary building through field trips, film strips and motion pictures.
m. Teach pupils how to get word meanings from context aided by a knowledge of grammar.
n. Teach roots, prefixes, suffixes and how they may be used in a variety of combinations.
o. Place a new word in a conspicuous place on the board each day.
p. Explain and assign pupil exercises to teach the different ways in which an individual word may be used as different parts of speech and with different meanings.

2. Determining general significance of the context through assigned pupil activities such as:
a. Restate sentences and lines of poetry in pupil's words.
b. Find basal parts of difficult sentences in poetry and rearrange in normal word order to discover meaning.
c. Read poetry and difficult material aloud to get meaning through proper observance of punctuation.
d. Write newspaper headlines that summarize paragraph content.
e. Discuss the relationship of the content of one paragraph to that of another paragraph.
f. Discuss the relationship of the content of one paragraph to that of an entire section or chapter.
g. Outline a chapter after hearing a one-sentence summary of each paragraph in sequence.
h. Write a summary of information gathered from various sources.
i. Write a good sentence with modifiers and understand that the subject, verb, and complement express the main ideas and that the modifiers supply the details; expand the sentence into a paragraph or theme using the main ideas and details.

j. Practice précis writing.
k. Summarize a chapter of a book or act of a play.
l. Outline a chapter of a book or act of a play.
m. Discuss the relationship of one chapter or act to that of another chapter or act.
n. Discuss the relationship of one chapter or act to the entire book or play.
o. Select one character and describe his action and reasons for action from the beginning to the end of the story or play.
p. Prepare oral and written reports of a single book or play.
q. Prepare oral and written reports comparing two or more books or plays.
r. Suggest other titles for books and plays.
s. Illustrate books or plays with appropriate cut lines from context.

3. Recognizing important details
   a. Give specific questions on some types of literature that pupils can answer as they read.
   b. Give specific questions that pupils can answer after reading.
   c. Have the pupils determine the topic sentence of a paragraph and then find evidence to support the idea expressed.
   d. Secure class agreement on the main idea of a paragraph or a whole selection and have pupils find evidence to support this idea.
   e. Have pupils jot down important details as they read and then rank them in importance according to criteria agreed upon by the class.
   f. Ask pupils to compose questions about details of the selection that they consider important.
   g. Assign pupils to write topic sentences with supporting details and then construct paragraphs.

D. To evaluate reading materials:
   1. Develop with the class criteria such as author's background, position, experience with the subject, prejudices, style of writing, and date of publication for determining competency of the author.
   2. Develop an idea and have pupils find relevant and irrelevant information and valid and invalid information concerning the idea.
   3. List authorities in specific areas and discuss whether

their writing should be accepted or not. Determine why or why not.
4. Find differing views on a subject and discuss which are most valid and why.
5. Compare the style of writing of various authors and determine strengths and weaknesses.
6. Hold panel discussions with students presenting various views on the validity of various opinions.

E. To applv concepts gained from reading materials:
1. Use problems in which the pupils must follow exacting written directions.
2. Teach pupils to predict how various authors would solve certain problems.
3. Have pupils observe the behavior of fellow pupils and determine how reading might have influenced this behavior.
4. Assign pupils to rewrite what has been read in a different form such as a play as an essay, a book as a play, or an article in the style of different authors.
5. Teach how cartoons or pictures may be used to show comprehension of material read.
6. Have pupils rewrite endings of selections and explain reasons for changes.
7. Assign the pupils to write a theme on "Reading Problems" or "What is Effective Reading?" which may be read to the class or given as a speech while the listeners criticize the organization and effectiveness of the theme.
8. Select some concepts or themes and assign pupils to cite pieces of literature which substantiate each.

F. To present written materials orally:
1. Play records of a "good" and a "poor" oral reading.
2. Tape record and play back student oral reading attempts.
3. Have pupils note and analyze characteristics of news reporters and other readers on TV.
4. Provide opportunities for pupils to read orally to many different audiences.
5. Assign pupils to tell the story they liked best as a child.
6. Provide situations in which books may be shared in small group discussions to answer questions such as: How are our books alike? How are they different? Which book reported on would I like most to read?
7. Teach basic principles of speech giving.
8. Provide opportunities for choral reading.

9. Develop a class set of directions for preparation of oral presentation or written material.

G. To understand the importance of reading and ways to satisfy intellectual curiosity through reading:
1. Maintain a room library and stimulate pupils to participate in selection of materials.
2. Inform pupils of new materials and new authors.
3. Suggest materials to pupils according to their individual reading interests.
4. Have pupils prepare bibliographies that are divided into specific areas of interest.
5. Provide free reading periods during the school year.
6. Provide opportunities for pupils to discuss reading through sharing opinions about books in small groups as well as class discussions.
7. Help pupils make use of the city library and other available libraries.
8. Review books and read parts of them to the students.
9. Arrange for "resource persons" who can stimulate readings.
10. Encourage pupils to note public speakers', especially ministers', frequent reference to materials read.
11. Assign interviews with successful people who have deep and lasting reading habits.
12. Assign a definite article to each pupil which he will read and report orally.
13. Encourage pupils to build personal libraries.
14. Introduce Pocket Books or other inexpensive editions to stimulate pride in ownership of books.
15. Introduce pupils to and encourage them to use the book section of newspapers and magazines.
16. Conduct lessons which discuss such questions as, What have you previously read by or about this author? Does this selection relate to anything occurring in the world now? What mental pictures did you get from this selection? Did these mental pictures remind you of anything? Would you have acted the way the characters did in this story? Why or Why not?

H. To make accurate self-evaluations of progress in reading:
1. Point out to pupils individually the relationship of success and failures in preparing class assignments to competence in reading.
2. Prepare a self-evaluation check list appropriate for read-

ing in the language arts and encourage pupils to use it periodically.

3. Provide opportunities for students to take speed and comprehension tests to determine growth in both speed and accuracy of reading.
4. Study evaluation of competence in reading by use of class evaluation of oral and written reports as to their comprehensiveness and accuracy.
5. Organize "interrogation periods" in which a pupil leader asks questions about material read and evaluates responses.
6. Help pupils analyze their responses to tests or other written assignments to determine how wider or more accurate reading would have produced a more adequate response.
7. Teach pupils to check habitually the adequacy of their outlines or summaries of materials read.

Reading Skills and Habits Needed in the Social Studies

I. A good reader in the social studies class should be able to:

A. Acquire the vocabulary of the social studies.

1. Having an interest in words as tools of communication and of thought.
2. Using thought processes as well as memory to develop an adequate social studies vocabulary.
3. Having a systematic, continuing method of word study for social studies vocabulary building.

B. Find intrinsic motivation for reading social studies material.

1. Having an interest in the content that can be acquired through social studies reading.
2. Recognizing that social studies reading may be pleasurable.
3. Desiring to discover the truth about social situations by wide, well-selected reading.

C. Comprehend the material of social studies.

1. Using graphs, charts, tables, pictorial presentations including maps and globes, and other social studies materials to gain social studies concepts.
2. Using methods for organizing materials, locating specific facts, and interpreting abstract ideas.
3. Understanding the basic concepts of time and space.
4. Understanding chronological order and the relationships between past and present.

   5. Comprehending sequences of events, groups of simultaneous events, cause-to-effect and effect-to-cause relationships.

D. Adjust speed of reading to purpose and type of content.
   1. Determining purpose for the reading of particular items and appropriate speeds for reading them.
   2. Recognizing types of content, the relative difficulty of comprehension, and appropriate speeds for reading each type.

E. Use library methods to locate materials.
   1. Knowing sources of social studies materials.
   2. Knowing how to locate and use sources to find specific kinds of social studies material.

F. Read social studies material to achieve specific purposes.
   1. Solving problems of social significance.
   2. Understanding general significance of a selection.
   3. Discovering specific details.
   4. Answering specific questions.
   5. Evaluating statements.

G. Make accurate self-evaluations of progress in reading in the social studies.
   1. Realizing the importance of self-evaluation.
   2. Using a self-evaluation check-list periodically.

Illustrative Methods and Devices a High School Social Studies Teacher May Use to Improve Reading of Materials in His Classes

I. Methods that might be used to help pupils in the social studies:

A. To build vocabulary:
   1. Help pupils to correlate the new words or terms with a current event to show their importance to the particular age group.
   2. Send pupils directly to the dictionary for brief periods of study of a word, have them use the different meanings in meaningful sentences, determine which of these sentences best expressed the intended meaning of the word in the context being studied.
   3. In building background, call attention to new words in class discussion. Place new words on the board, or duplicate on discussion sheets, in sentences which give meaning, and illustrate how these discussions can be

applied to later uses of the word as the pupil needs them. (New words are either individual, as they stem from personal activities, or of class significance in connection with units or projects.)

4. Give pupils experiences such as the following to help them recognize the various meanings of words: The word "mandate" is first encountered as "mandamus" in the Marbury vs. Madison case. Later in the Tyler administration, the students read that Polk's election was considered a "mandate" from the people. Discuss the new meaning or the variation of the word. Later, when in discussing the League of Nations "mandates," it is not difficult to refer to the earlier meanings and point out the differences.
5. Hold daily discussion of words and terms giving special attention to word roots and to shades of meanings. After such study, relate the words or terms to the assignment.
6. Use Latin derivatives and prefixes to increase vocabulary. For example, make clear such a word as "monotheism" by referring to such familiar words as "monotone" and "monoplane."
7. Have pupils underline new words in the text and write the meanings at the bottom of the page.
8. Help pupils to work on the pronunciation of difficult words.
9. Have pupils tell what they think a word means from the context.
10. Encourage pupils to use difficult words in sentences of their own.
11. Teach pupils how to make and use a personal card-file dictionary of words of interest and of value to them. Include on each card the word, its pronunciation, its meaning, and its use in a sentence.
12. Help pupils understand how words are tools of communication rather than problems to be solved.
13. Teach pupils thought methods, rather than memorization alone, for gaining word power in pronunciation, recognition, meaning, and spelling.
14. Encourage pupils to add the words in the glossary at the back of the book to their vocabularies.
15. Teach pupils to relate new words to various language sources and to their acquaintance with roots, prefixes, and suffixes in order to gain meanings readily.

B. To find intrinsic motivation for reading social studies material:
   1. Project questions or problems by taking the critical viewpoint of the principles presented or by taking a contrary opinion so the class will need to justify their opinion.
   2. Pose some questions that the material should answer.
   3. Assign a project that requires reading of description or directions such as the making of a globe.
   4. Encourage statement of opinions; then challenge pupils to bolster their opinions by reading.
   5. Employ the "mystery" element or the "build-up" to catch interest; then ask pupils to read to satisfy their curiosity.
   6. Tell pupils a story up to a crucial point; then assign reading to find out the conclusion of the story.
   7. Tell pupils a story, but leave out the names of those involved; then assign reading in order for them to identify the characters.

C. To comprehend the materials of social studies:
   1. Recall the experiences of former pupils in their initial contact with the material and plan ways to help present pupils to avoid anticipated difficulties.
   2. Develop a list of resource materials that are readily available for use and adapt it to individual needs.
   3. Ask pupils to relate vacation and other experiences and to bring available types of illustrative material from their experiences to make social studies readings more meaningful.
   4. Use films, pictures, stories told by members of the class, displays, and maps to illustrate readings in the social studies.
   5. Stress current news in government classes to show that the text material is in action at all times with such activities as: take trips to court during a study of the judiciary; assign one or two pupils to accompany the city manager at his work during an entire day and report to the class; use mock sessions of Congress, debates, panel discussions, and oral reports to clarify meanings.
   6. Use films, recordings, drawings, opaque projections, dramatizations, cartoons, models, pantomiming, storytelling, and exhibits to add meaning to materials read.
   7. Ask pupils to bring clippings or pictures relating to something they have studied such as picture of Mayflower II when or after studying about the Pilgrims.

D. To adjust the speed of reading to the purpose and to the type of content:
 1. Point out that different material, different subjects, and different paragraphs within the same story have great variance in the degree of readability and comprehension.
 2. Develop the idea that it would be impossible for all pupils to cover the same material in the same time and that each must try to adjust his reading speed to his comprehension level.
 3. Adjust the length of the daily assignments to the estimated average speed of reading of the group.
 4. Teach the place and the value of skimming in preparation of assignments.
 5. Instruct in the methods of reading for the varied purposes of reading the same, similar, or different materials.
 6. Early in the school year, spend one week or more on informal teaching and testing the pupils' rate and comprehension. Encourage pupils to experiment with different rates for different types of material and different purposes for reading.
 7. Stress intensive reading by suggesting periodically the proper way to read a textbook: (a) reflect on chapter topic, (b) read preface material and unit titles, (c) read questions and study vocabulary at end of chapter, (d) read chapter material, and (e) check questions again seeing how well material was read.
 8. Advise those who have difficulty understanding or retaining the information to take notes or outline the material.
 9. Have students first read chapter titles and section headings and from them formulate questions to be answered by reading.

E. To use library methods to locate materials for social studies assignments:
 1. Early in the year, take pupils to the library and help them in observing and practicing library procedures.
 2. After a visit to the library, have pupils ask and discuss questions about library usage.
 3. Teach library skills in special projects such as research reports and predictions. Give assignment sheets to pupils with suggestions in outline form, and have them use original sources and confirmed eye-witness accounts.
 4. Teach the use of Readers' Guide, Card Catalog, and other aids in locating material.

5. Give each pupil two or three cards with the names of people, places, or events listed on them. Instruct the pupil to use any textbook (except his own) or any reference book available to find data on his topics. Throughout this exercise, help pupils who need help with the use of sources.

F. To achieve specific purposes:
1. Motivate pupils to read for specific purposes such as: locating a certain fact, answering a certain question, determining a general concept, verifying information or opinion, and comparing different points of view.
2. Discuss in class the steps to follow in problem solving.
3. Point out the need for understanding why there are conflicting points of view on many social problems and how, by wide reading and critical thinking, an individual can develop his own point of view.
4. Make active use of projects which aid in clarifying meanings, aid in retention, stimulate critical thinking, and aid in developing initiative and planning, such as, reading related materials, outlining material for retelling, publishing a newspaper, and exhibiting displays of pictures or other materials.
5. Use the discussion method which encourages each pupil to give his own opinions and to explain why he arrived at his conclusions.
6. Use tests which include reading excerpts from actual historical documents and involve the use of critical, analytical thinking to answer the questions.
7. Develop a pattern of logical thought and a pattern of analysis by class discussions of the part emotions and vested interest play in history.
8. Use analysis of current news to estimate truth or falsity.
9. Ask examination questions that involve reflective thinking rather than memory of facts.
10. Use debate-type presentation of beliefs and supporting factual evidence to teach pupils how to collect and evaluate facts and how to relate facts to points in an outline.
11. Hold class discussions in which pupils express their own viewpoints and listen to those of others and then attempt to select the viewpoint which seems to be tenable in the light of the evidence.
12. Teach pupils to locate the facts about an area of con-

cern; then determine the truth or falsity of statements about it.

13. Draw a pupil into expressing an opinion based on material read; then ask him to defend his opinion by showing how the material read is related to it.
14. Develop in pupils a habit of determining the implications of historical events for present day situations.
15. Teach pupils to read critically, that is, to look for fact rather than opinion, to consider the qualifications of the author in the area on which he writes, and to test whether the idea presented is consistent with known facts.

G. To make accurate self-evaluations of their progress in reading:

1. Point out to pupils individually the relationship of successes and failures in preparing class assignments to competence in reading.
2. Prepare a self-evaluation check list appropriate for reading in the social studies and encourage pupils to use it periodically.
3. Study evaluation of competence in reading by use of class evaluation of oral and written reports as to their comprehensiveness and accuracy.
4. Organize "interrogation periods" in which a pupil leader asks questions about material read and evaluates responses.
5. Help pupils analyze their responses to tests or other written assignments to determine how wider or more accurate reading would have produced a more adequate response.
6. Teach pupils to check habitually the adequacy of their outlines or summaries of materials read.

Reading Skills and Habits Needed in Science

I. A good reader in a science class must be able to:

A. Utilize sources to locate materials.

1. Indexes of books.
2. Tables of contents.
3. Glossaries.
4. Card catalogues in libraries.
5. *Readers' Guide to Periodical Literature.*
6. General references.
7. Newspapers.
8. Specialized books, manuals, pamphlets and abstracts.
9. Footnotes.
10. Literature from manufacturing companies, catalogs.

B. Adjust reading speed to the type and difficulty of the material and the purpose for reading.
   1. Having a conscious or subconscious realization of a purpose for reading the material.
   2. Having a conscious or subconscious realization of the reading difficulty of the material.

C. Comprehend written material.
   1. Determining what the pupil should get from the passage.
   2. Determining the author's interpretation of controversial items.
   3. Understanding meanings of specialized presentations as:
      a. Technical symbols in science and mathematics.
      b. Technical words.
      c. Graphs.
      d. Charts.
      e. Diagrams.
      f. Scales.
      g. Formulas.
      h. Equations.
      i. Cross section and longitudinal models.
      j. Maps, pictures, and flow charts.
   4. Understanding the meanings of non-technical words and phrases used in science context.
   5. Determining the general significance of content of: sentences, paragraphs, sections, chapters, books, illustrations, charts, graphs, and pictures.
   6. Recognizing important details such as:
      a. Isolated facts.
      b. Evidence or the lack of evidence to buttress main ideas.
      c. Answers to specific questions.
   7. Recognizing familiar portions of new words.
   8. Using roots, prefixes, and suffixes.

D. Evaluate the material intelligently.
   1. Understanding its relevance to the problem.
   2. Developing standards for establishing the competency of the source.
   3. Estimating reliability of the content.
   4. Comparing or contrasting concepts gained with previously held concepts.
   5. Correlating written textbook content with everyday experience.
   6. Determining author's purpose.
   7. Recognizing relevance of empirical results to author's purpose.
   8. Recognizing style of presentation of facts (objective or subjective).

9. Understanding the difference between results and opinions or facts and opinions.
10. Noting the significance of date of publication.

E. Use the content of written material in situations requiring scientific method.
   1. Formulating hypotheses.
   2. Collecting evidence.
   3. Evaluating evidence.
   4. Organizing pertinent evidence.
   5. Drawing conclusions.
   6. Testing conclusions.

F. Apply concepts gained from the reading material to confronting situations such as:
   1. Experiments.
   2. Problems.
   3. Discussion.
   4. Further reading.
   5. Observation.
   6. Everyday living.

G. Develop the habit of extensive reading in the science field to stimulate and to satisfy intellectual curiosity and to participate more effectively in a physical world.

H. Follow directions.
   1. Recognizing the sequence of steps.
   2. Recognizing the relevance of steps in sequence to the purpose of the directions.

I. Make accurate self-evaluations of progress in reading scientific materials.
   1. Realizing the importance of self-evaluation.
   2. Using a self-evaluation check-list periodically.

Illustrative Methods and Devices a High School Science Teacher May Use to Improve Reading of Materials in His Classes

I. Methods that might be used in teaching science pupils:

A. To utilize sources to locate materials such as:
   1. Indexes, tables of contents, glossaries, the card catalogue, and the *Readers' Guide to Periodical Literature*, dictionaries, bibliographies, and reference cited sections.
      a. Conduct "treasure hunts" for information requiring the use of these sources.
   2. General references, newspapers, specialized books, manuals, and pamphlets.
      a. Discuss where these sources are found in the library and the information that can be found in them.
      b. Discuss the reliability of references such as newspapers.

c. Assign reports, experiments, and research problems requiring the use of these sources.

B. To vary reading speed:

1. Compare the time necessary to read a section in a science book on the seventh grade level with one the same length that is written for high school juniors.
2. Compare time necessary to read a section of a science book when the reader wants to generalize with the time necessary to read the same section when he wants to find specific details.
3. List purposes for which pupils might read science materials and estimate the possible changes in speed of reading.

C. To comprehend written material:

1. Understanding technical symbols:
   a. Discuss the meaning of new symbols that will be appearing in the reading assignments.
   b. Write the meaning of the technical symbols in sentence form.
   c. From experimentation, derive symbols that are new to the pupil.
2. Understanding technical words:
   a. Discuss etymology of important scientific terms.
   b. Give opportunities to spell and use technical words in oral and written reports.
   c. Discuss the meaning of new words that will be appearing in reading assignments.
   d. As a class exercise compile a science dictionary of new, technical words.
   e. Teach pupils how to develop a word-card-file of science words and symbols.
   f. Develop crossword puzzles with science words.
   g. Explain how to use context clues to get meaning and provide practice opportunities in using them.
   h. Encourage the writing of poetry and jokes with a science motif.
   i. Require pupils to pronounce and spell words correctly.
   j. Emphasize the use of the dictionary while pupils are reading science material and preparing reports.
   k. Use new words in class discussion, explain, and discuss them.

3. Understanding graphs and charts:
   a. Bring in illustrations of various types of graphs and explain them.
   b. Discuss the purpose of specific graphs.
   c. Define the meaning of the scales on the horizontal and vertical lines.
   d. Show pupils how to compare two quantities at different times in a single line graph.
   e. Show pupils how to compare the quantity of different items at one period of time in a multiple line graph.
   f. Give practice problems for pupils to graph, using various types of graphs.
   g. Propose conclusions that might be drawn from a specific graph and have pupils decide on their validity.
   h. Have each pupil bring a graph to class and explain it.
   i. Show how graphs are derived.
   j. Discuss the purpose of specific charts.
   k. Give practice problems for pupils to chart.
   l. Discuss the relationship of specific charts to a specimen or model.
4. Understanding diagrams:
   a. Discuss the purpose of specific diagrams.
   b. Discuss orientation of diagrams.
   c. Give practice problems for pupils to diagram.
   d. List and illustrate as many conclusions as possible that may be drawn from a specific diagram.
   e. Make drawings of items described in science readings such as amoeba and crayfish.
5. Understanding scales:
   a. Assign pupils to become acquainted with differing scales and to compare and discuss the measurements found on each.
   b. Give an opportunity for pupils to make individual readings of all scales available.
   c. Conduct experiments requiring the plotting of scale readings.
6. Understanding formulas and equations:
   a. Hold class discussion on the meaning of new formulas and equations that appear in the reading assignments.
   b. Assign pupils to write the meaning of formulas and equations used in class in sentence form.
   c. From class experiments, have pupils derive formulas and equations that are new to them.

d. Emphasize general rules (such as the balance of electrical charges) that affect all equations and formulas.
e. Show pupils how to identify factors or facts that the formula implies.

7. Understanding models:
   a. Discuss the purpose of specific models with the class.
   b. Have students make models.
   c. Use models for student demonstration.
   d. Teach the making of models of various items of interest in the class.

8. Understanding and summarizing sentences and paragraphs:
   a. Show pupils how to restate sentences using their own words.
   b. Assign the writing of newspaper headlines that summarize paragraph content.
   c. Discuss the relationship of the content of one paragraph to that of another.
   d. Show students how to look for different sources and presentations of one concept.
   e. Discuss the relationship of the content of one paragraph to an entire section or chapter.
   f. Outline a chapter on the chalkboard after hearing a one-sentence summary by the pupils of each paragraph.
   g. Explain to the pupils how to write or give orally a summary of paragraph content and provide practice in using this skill.
   h. Help pupils to determine the author's style of paragraph organization in text and reference books and to make use of this organization in understanding the paragraph.

9. Understanding sections and chapters and entire books:
   a. Direct the pupils in the writing of chapter summaries.
   b. Discuss the relationship of the content of one chapter to that of another.
   c. Discuss the relationship of one chapter to the entire book.
   d. Outline a book with a single sentence summary of each chapter and use as unit or semester review.
   e. Write statements that may be concluded from experimental evidence and discuss them with the class.

f. Assign the preparing of oral and written book reports, after the class has developed its own outline of content for such a report.

10. Recognizing important details:
    a. Give specific questions for pupils to answer as they read.
    b. Give specific questions that pupils can answer after reading.
    c. Have the pupils determine the topic sentence of a paragraph and then find evidence to support this idea.
    d. Agree on the main idea of a paragraph or section and have pupils find evidence to support this idea.
    e. Require pupils to jot down important details as they read and then rank them in importance according to established criteria.
    f. Teach pupils how to get meaning of a paragraph taken from text with key words and details removed.
    g. Assign pupils to prepare a short test over the section.

D. To evaluate reading material intelligently:
  1. With the pupils develop criteria to determine the validity of material such as author background, position, experience with the subject, possible prejudices, and the date of the writing.
  2. Develop a scientific hypothesis and have students find information concerning it from competent and incompetent sources and distinguish between them.
  3. List "authorities" in specific scientific areas and discuss whether their testimony should be accepted or not and, if so, on what topics.
  4. Find differing views on a controversial subject and discuss which one represents the most likely "truth" and why.
  5. Compare actual specimens and/or models with pictures, diagrams, and written material and show pupils how to determine the validity of the pictures, diagrams, and written material.

E. To use the content of written material in situations requiring scientific method:
  1. Provide projects in which pupils use information read about weather in understanding and anticipating weather changes.
  2. Provide opportunities for pupils to predict weather changes and compare their predictions with those of the

weather bureau as well as with the actual weather change that occurs.

3. Teach pupils the application of principles read in the textbook to laboratory situations and make them conscious of the six steps used in the scientific method. (See Section E, page 252.)
4. Develop projects in which pupils have an opportunity to evaluate advertising by applying the steps used in the scientific method.

F. To apply concepts gained from the reading materials to experiments and problem solving:
   1. Use experiments and problems in which the pupils must follow exacting written instructions.
   2. Use experiments and problems in which the pupils must apply generalized principles that they have read.
   3. Teach pupils to derive their own generalizations or principles from a set of examples or illustrations collected from their reading.
   4. Show pupils how to derive their own experiments and problems that are a result of their reading.
   5. Use accurate reading and interpretation of test questions as part of the basis for grading examinations.
   6. Have pupils keep accurate records of experiments carried on in the classroom.

G. To develop the habit of extensive reading in the science field:
   1. Maintain a room library containing science books, magazine articles, and photographs.
   2. Use bulletin board to advertise available materials including materials and literature from industries and businesses.
   3. Inform pupils of new books and magazine articles that have been written on science.
   4. Suggest books to individual pupils according to their interests in science.
   5. Prepare bibliographies that are divided into specific topics in science.
   6. Provide for "free reading" periods during the school year.
   7. Help pupils make use of the science section of the city library and other available libraries.
   8. Take advantage of school discounts and group buying to enable pupils to buy selected books for their own science library.

9. Briefly discuss interesting science material that you have read.
10. Encourage pupils to write short plays based on scientific facts and events, tape record, and play back to the class to stimulate interest in reading.
11. Assign pupils to prepare one-page summaries of their favorite science literature reading, to exchange these summaries, and then, in turn, tell each other about what they have read.
12. Assign articles from magazines for student reports in class.
13. Give short unfinished reports on books and articles and challenge pupils to finish them.
14. Post lists of available books and periodicals with brief evaluation of each item and change these lists frequently.
15. Require pupils to read and report on one article each week.
16. Use a point system for outside reading and give recognition — grade, credit — for extensive reading.

H. To follow directions:
1. Require the pupils to number the consecutive steps when reading directions.
2. Discuss the reasons for the particular sequence indicated.
3. Point out to pupils the value of reading the entire set of directions first to obtain a general understanding of purpose and method.
4. Require the pupils in the second, more deliberate reading of the directions to determine how the steps in sequence, if followed, will achieve the purpose.
5. Show, by demonstration, the value of rereading directions during the process of completing a long series of directions to be sure that they are followed exactly and in sequence.
6. After the completion of a project, when the purpose has not been achieved, restudy directions to see where the error has occurred.

I. To make accurate self-evaluations of progress in reading:
1. Point out to pupils individually the relationship of success and failures in preparing class assignments to competence in reading.
2. Prepare a self-evaluation check list appropriate for reading in science and encourage pupils to use it periodically.
3. Study evaluation of competence in reading by use of

class evaluation of oral and written reports as to their comprehensiveness and accuracy.

4. Organize "interrogation periods" in which a pupil leader asks questions about material read and evaluates responses.
5. Help pupils analyze their responses to tests or other written assignments to determine how wider or more accurate reading would have produced a more adequate response.
6. Teach pupils to check habitually the adequacy of their outlines and summaries of materials read.

Reading Skills and Habits Needed in Mathematics

I. A good reader in the mathematics class should be able to:

A. Use efficiently the vocabulary of the subject.

1. Technical mathematical terms.
2. Terms, and their abbreviations, that are frequently used in mathematics.
3. Roots, prefixes, and suffixes that aid in understanding mathematical terms.
4. Literal numbers.
5. Alphabetical, operational, grouping and relationship symbols.

B. Read and interpret verbal problems.

C. Read and interpret materials used for showing functional relationships.

1. Rules, principles, and formulas.
2. Tables.
3. Charts.
4. Graphs.
5. Figures and diagrams.

D. Proofread to verify solutions and/or to locate errors.

E. Through extensive reading, recognize and make use of the quantitative data in newspapers, magazine articles, and books.

F. Acquire meaning from the statements of rules and definitions so they may be used with understanding.

G. Make accurate self-evaluation of progress in reading in mathematics.

1. Realizing the importance of self-evaluation.
2. Using a self-evaluation check list periodically.

Illustrative Methods and Devices a High School Mathematics Teacher May Use to Improve Reading of Materials in His Classes

I. Methods that might be used to help pupils in mathematics:

A. To develop vocabulary:

1. Teach pupils to recognize the contrast between the mathematical meaning of words and terms and their meanings in other areas of study.
2. Provide opportunities for the study of the meanings of new terms and for use in mathematical situations.
3. Accustom the pupils to the importance of using the glossary for pronunciation, spelling, and meaning of mathematical terms.
4. Teach pupils to recognize the relationship between new words and their parts to known words, prefixes, suffixes, and roots: mononomial-monoplane, binomial-bicycle, trinomial-tricycle.
5. Group mathematical words and terms in lists that are similar or dissimilar, such as synonyms, antonyms, and homonyms, and develop their specific mathematical meanings by compariso ı or contrast.
6. Explain the derivation of mathematical terms; for example, the word decimal comes from the Latin word *decem* which means "ten."
7. Stress the preciseness of mathematical vocabulary and show how this is applied in verbal problems and theorems.
8. Require the pupils to use the specific vocabulary of mathematics; for example, a rectangle is a parallelogram but a parallelogram is not always a rectangle.
9. List new words pertaining to the topic being studied and have the pupils learn to spell and define them.
10. Make copies of both general and mathematics dictionaries available and encourage pupils to make use of them.
11. Encourage the pupils to keep a personal card file of new words including spelling, pronunciation, definition, and use in a mathematical expression.
12. Use a committee of pupils to keep up bulletin board displays of important words in mathematics showing their origin together with families of words containing the same root but different prefixes and suffixes as well as appropriate synonyms, antonyms, and homonyms.

13. Teach the pupils how to obtain word meanings from the context of the sentence.
14. Teach the pupils to remember mathematical symbols through likeness to or abbreviation of the figure or term they represent.
15. Insist upon accurate usage of names of symbols; for example, do not allow references such as "that thing there" or "that doohicky."
16. Encourage pupils to bring to class mathematical symbols which they find in newspapers, advertisements, trademarks, and cartoons and discuss them as to origin, significance, and meaning.
17. Provide opportunities in which the pupils change sentences or phrases into symbolic expressions, such as, "three times a number" is "3n."
18. Place emphasis upon the proper symbols for labeling and the correct use of units, such as, mi./hr., ft./sec., lb./cu. ft.

B. To read and interpret verbal problems:
   1. Teach the understanding and proper use of cues in verbal problems, such as "is" may mean "equals" and "of" may mean "multiply" in specific situations.
   2. Explain to the pupil that in solving problems he must determine (1) what facts are given, (2) what he is trying to find out, (3) what operations should be used, and (4) in what order. For pupils having difficulty ask them to write out the following: (1) facts given, (2) what is to be found, (3) process or processes to use, (4) steps in proper order for solving the problem; and, if the pupil still has difficulty, help him to solve the problem using small numbers first.
   3. Teach the pupil who has difficulty in interpreting mathematical terms to substitute synonyms that he can understand.
   4. Show the pupil how the verb in a verbal problem often acts as the equal sign between two parts of an equation, as, "Mary's age two years ago was 10 years less than twice her age now." $X - 2 = 2X - 10$.
   5. Emphasize the value of slow reading and rereading of verbal problems observing details including basic parts of sentences such as subjects and verbs, parts of speech, and punctuation.
   6. Set up a learning situation in which pupils individually, or in committees, examine a number of supplementary

texts and list the steps in the plan of attack for solving verbal problems suggested by various authors; and from these lists develop a master plan.

7. Provide supplementary verbal problems for the class by listing problems of varying levels of difficulty on separate sheets.
8. Work sample verbal problems with the class and list the steps used in the plan of attacking the problem.
9. Use different types of diagrams to illustrate the steps in the solution of a verbal problem. For example: How many nickels, dimes, and quarters are there in $5.75 if there are twice as many dimes as nickels and two more quarters than dimes?

Kind	*Number*	*Value*
nickel	X	5X
dime	2X	10(2X)
quarter	2X + 2	25(2X + 2)

$5X + 10(2X) + 25(2X + 2) = \$5.75 \qquad X = 7$

10. Give pupils practice in reading directions in constructing figures, reading micrometers, and using the slide rule, and test their ability to follow directions.

C. To read and interpret materials showing functional relationships:

1. Provide classroom experiences in understanding what the horizontal and vertical scale each represent and the relationships between them in a chart or graph.
2. Assign the pupils to draw logical conclusions from the data represented on a graph or chart and to determine conclusions implied but not justified by the data.
3. Provide exercises in which the pupils portray the relationships among sets of data by preparing tables, graphs, charts, figures, and diagrams.
4. Instruct the pupils to select graphic and tabular representations from newspapers and magazines in such areas as sports and finance, and explain the relationships represented to the rest of the class.
5. Collect pictures and drawings relating to mathematics, post them on the bulletin board, and encourage pupils to interpret the relationships represented and to suggest possible theorems and generalizations which might apply.
6. Show pupils how verbal explanations may often be made clearer by accompanying graphic representations.

7. Help the pupil to understand the meanings and relationships of figures and diagrams in geometry by giving him the opportunity to see and handle the figures produced from cardboard, thin wood, plastics, or other material.

D. To proofread to verify solutions and/or to locate errors:
1. Encourage pupils to read a problem orally when they have difficulty with any of the terms used or details mentioned when they read the problem silently.
2. Instruct the pupils to read the total problem for a general understanding and then to read it analytically by parts to determine the steps necessary for solution.
3. Make notations in the teacher's desk copy of "trouble spots" in the reading of problems and prepare devices to cope with them as they occur.
4. Prepare exercises in which pupils rewrite incorrect statements of problems for drill in proofreading.
5. Encourage the development of the ability to recognize a reasonable answer and the practice of rereading a problem if the first solution to the problem seems to be unreasonable.

E. To read extensively and thus recognize and make use of the quantitative data in newspapers, magazine articles, and books:
1. Encourage pupils to read books and articles on such subjects as astronomy, navigation, history of mathematics, and the development of the calendar, and make reports on the mathematical implication of the content.
2. Prepare a reading list of biographies of famous mathematicians and encourage pupils to read and report on these biographies.
3. Make the pupils aware of the importance of mathematics by frequently referring to the use of quantitative data in current magazines and daily newspapers.
4. Use mathematical fun books, puzzles, and games to stimulate interest in reading mathematical material.
5. Keep a class mathematics scrapbook of clippings, including pictures, drawings, trick problems, magic squares, and new developments in mathematics, that are contributed by class members.
6. Cooperate with the school librarian in preparing lists of books and library exhibits of material on mathematics.
7. Keep a classroom library of mathematics books and magazines for supplementary reading.

8. Make available to pupils such magazines as *Popular Mechanics*, *Popular Science*, *Mechanics Illustrated*, and *Kansas State Engineer* which contain interesting articles, pictures, and problems pertaining to gear ratios, lumber dimensions, chemical mixtures, scale drawings, and many other aspects of mathematics.
9. Encourage pupils to read books about mathematics as a career or about other careers requiring mathematics.

F. To acquire meaning from the statements of rules and definitions so they may be used with understanding:

1. Use the inductive method of arriving at rules and definitions by asking pupils to develop their own rules or definitions after many illustrations are given; then compare this rule or definition with that of the author.
2. When applying a rule or definition to a specific situation, ask the pupil to state the generalization in his own words and then show the relationship to the specific situation.
3. Ask pupils to state the converse of a rule or definition and test its validity.
4. Make application of rules to real-life situations, such as, comparing the number of steps required to walk around two sides of a park with the number of steps to walk through it diagonally to illustrate that the shortest distance between two points is a straight line; also, show how this is related to the Pythagorean Theorem.

G. To make accurate self-evaluation of progress in reading in mathematics:

1. Point out to pupils individually the relationship of success and failure in preparing class assignments to competence in reading.
2. Prepare a self-evaluation check list appropriate for reading in mathematics and encourage pupils to use it periodically.
3. Organize "interrogation periods" in which a pupil leader asks questions about material read and evaluates responses.
4. Help pupils analyze their responses to tests or other written assignments to determine how wider or more accurate reading would have produced a more adequate response.
5. Ask pupils to bring to class actual or fictional stories of loss and inconvenience caused by inaccurate reading of mathematical statements.

Reading Skills and Habits Needed in the Industrial Arts

I. A good reader in the industrial arts class should be able to:

A. Use the vocabulary of the subject.
1. Names of tools, equipment, and materials.
2. Brand names.
3. Common abbreviations used (including symbols as ° ′ ″).
4. Technical and special terms.

B. Follow written direction for shop procedures.
1. Assembling materials.
2. Organizing the work area.
3. Proceeding by steps or units in sequence.
4. Checking process and products periodically.
5. Making the final assembly.
6. Finishing the product.

C. Read illustrations and diagrams.
1. Visualizing the whole finished product.
2. Identifying parts.
3. Recognizing symbols.
4. Applying the legend or scale.
5. Interpreting correctly the illustration or diagram.

D. Read the catalogs, journals, and advertisements pertaining to the industrial arts.
1. Index — table of contents.
2. Quantity-quality clues.
3. Approval and/or ratings by appropriate agencies or users.
4. Discount or wholesale symbols.
5. Critical analysis of description of specifications and prices.
6. Order forms.

E. Develop skill in reading other special materials.
1. Color charts.
2. Design (balance, size, and weight).
3. Markings on dials or scales on equipment.
4. Warranties and instructions for use and care of equipment.
5. Service procedures and parts lists.
6. Details on illustrations or diagrams.
7. Maintenance and lubrication charts.

F. Do extensive reading in the field.
1. Trade publications and professional magazines such as *School Shops*.

2. Information about careers.
3. Avocational possibilities.
4. Reference reading, as publications by Hardwood Associations.
5. Books relating to individual interests.

G. Develop differentiated reading speeds.
1. Skimming.
2. Reading for details.
3. Reading for general significance.

H. Make accurate self-evaluations of progress in reading in the industrial arts.
1. Realizing the importance of self-evaluation.
2. Using a self-evaluation check list periodically.

Illustrative Methods and Devices a High School Industrial Arts Teacher May Use to Improve Reading of Materials in His Classes

I. Methods that might be used to help students in the industrial arts:

A. To develop vocabulary:
1. Require the pupil to identify all tools and equipment specifically — not just "that thing-a-ma-jig" or "that thing you use to ——."
2. Use strip and sound film provided by equipment manufacturers and other sources.
3. Penalize the pupil for asking for or bringing the wrong tool.
4. Teach significant words used in textbooks, references, and charts.
5. Teach symbols directly — especially in drafting.
6. Require that all plans and diagrams have proper names, legends, and symbols and be drawn according to American standards.
7. Keep special word lists for technical terms — give periodic tests.
8. Direct pupils to keep a card file of terms to study for memorization.
9. Require pupils to identify all wood grades by their names: F.A.S., common, select, construction, etc.

B. To follow written directions:
1. Require, after working drawings are made, step-by-step plans and a materials list along with tools to accomplish the task.

2. Have pupils draw up plans, exchange plans, and see if they are clear enough for another pupil to follow.
3. Test comprehension by requiring the pupil to explain his step-by-step plans to the instructor.
4. Have pupils assemble and disassemble simple machinery according to the manufacturer's assembly directions or charts.
5. Draw up plans lacking one or more steps and have pupils identify and supply omitted steps.
6. Use simple games that require accurate following of written directions.
7. Require pupils to read and explain directions furnished with machinery before they use it.
8. Give both written and manipulative safety tests before a pupil begins work on a machine.

C. To read illustrations:
1. Use direct teaching of illustrations in drafting.
2. Have pupils draw working plans from pictures in catalogs, magazines, or actual objects.
3. Show pupils how to expand scale drawings to actual size and the reverse.

D. To read catalogs, journals, and advertisements pertaining to the industrial arts:
1. Provide a readily accessible shop library.
2. Have pupils locate advertisements of needed materials and write critical descriptions and compare prices and specifications.
3. Have pupils find in a catalog at least two of each piece needed for each job and compare them as to specifications, availability and price.
4. Help pupils to make up orders from catalogs for the hardware needed for a job.
5. Require pupils to secure from literature materials list and prices and to make cost estimates for every job.
6. Have on display similar looking tools and materials that vary in quality and require pupils to determine advantages and disadvantages of each from reading.
7. Have pupils make reports on different tools or equipment from *Consumer's Guide* or similar sources.
8. After hardwaremen or tool salesmen have discussed the quality characteristics and have demonstrated their products to the class assign pupils to read to verify claims made.

E. To develop skills in reading other special materials:
   1. Use charts to teach dial markings.
   2. Assign pupils the responsibility of servicing machines according to manufacturers' instructions.
   3. Have pupils keep notebooks including drawings, specifications, and service policies.

F. To do extensive reading in the field:
   1. Keep a shop library.
   2. Use the *Kuder Book List*.
   3. Take pupils to the library.
   4. Have librarian feature industrial arts books at least once during the year.
   5. Have counselor suggest vocational reading.
   6. Subscribe to trade journals for the class.
   7. Designate certain days as "reading days."
   8. Follow up the showing of commercial films and talks by representatives from local industry and trade unions with assigned readings on vocational possibilities.
   9. Have pupils read extensively and give reports with demonstrations on wood used in furniture.
   10. Provide opportunity for class discussions which require that the pupils do some reading on the subject.
   11. Call attention to interesting articles and books about industrial arts subjects.

G. To develop differentiated reading speeds:
   1. Encourage pupils to use skimming to locate specific information in books and magazines.
   2. Have pupils read a set of directions and list the steps in order.
   3. Assign pupils to read magazine articles on a specific topic and report the main points to the class.

H. To make accurate self-evaluations of their progress in reading:
   1. Point out to pupils individually the relationship of successes and failures in preparing class assignments to competence in reading.
   2. Prepare a self-evaluation check list appropriate for reading in the industrial arts and encourage pupils to use it.
   3. Help pupils analyze their responses to tests or other written assignments to determine how wider or more accurate reading would have produced a more adequate response.
   4. Teach pupils to check habitually the adequacy of their outlines or summaries of materials read.

27. Teaching Essential Reading Skills

Bulletin of the National Association of Secondary School Principals

Introduction

The aim [of this chapter] is to supply a variety of drill exercises and suggest others for use in developing various reading skills. The teacher must not lose sight of those essential processes of comprehension and discriminating reaction which invest drill with significance. Emphasis has been laid on word study and on the means of enlarging and enriching the pupil's vocabulary. In order to think clearly and accurately, he must have an adequate vocabulary, for his thinking is carried on in concepts or symbols, usually words. Also, in order to draw correct inferences, form logical conclusions, and react intelligently to ideas, the pupil must be able to extract the meaning of the material he is reading. In order to understand world events, he must be familiar with the techniques of reading maps and interpreting graphs and charts. In order to open the storehouse of information in the library, he must know how to use reference books, encyclopedias, and the card catalog. In order to appropriate and utilize these resources which he has discovered, he must have skill in summarizing, analyzing, and organizing the material he wishes to use.

These outcomes and this self-direction are dependent upon repeated experiences and upon training. Drill, therefore, though never an end in itself, is essential for the development of creative thinking and discriminating evaluation; and the pupil who is successfully motivated will realize its relationship to ultimate achievement.

To study effectively, a pupil must develop efficient techniques of study in many different content fields. Since improving the study-reading habits of every pupil is the responsibility of every teacher, one objective of every classroom teacher should be to provide continuous guidance in using the textbooks and references that pupils use in his classes.

Teachers should analyze carefully the attitudes, abilities, habits, and other characteristics of pupils that may affect their study-reading habits and then plan a program of activities and experiences that will meet their specific needs. Such a program should provide the type of instruction and guidance that will enable each pupil to use textbooks and reference materials effectively to an extent that is commensurate with his level of maturity, his purpose, and the type of material.

The question of whether instruction in the use of books should be given as an integral part of the semester's work or by the use of isolated drill materials is one that must be answered by the teacher in terms of the particular situation.

There is much to be said in favor of having pupils use the study helps in textbooks and references as the need arises, for the necessity to learn to use books effectively is then more readily apparent, and, therefore, the pupil's interest is stronger. This awareness of specific needs will increase learning efficiency. Another advantage of this type of functional approach is that it saves time. It assists in familiarizing pupils with the books available for the study of a particular problem, it acquaints pupils with terms and background information for the study of a unit, and it enables pupils to compile lists of page references for use in gaining information about problems of topics to be studied.

Practice materials, when carefully selected and prepared in terms of the specific needs of pupils, are definitely useful. The use of such materials probably insures that none of the important techniques for using study helps will be neglected. Such materials may either provide additional practice or serve as informal tests to assist pupils in analyzing their own needs and in setting up their own objectives for the semester.

Teachers should provide instruction in using different types of materials and should plan activities that will give pupils practice in the use of study helps in their textbooks and references. Teachers, who effectively combine study helps in textbooks and references, duplicated lesson sheets based on the problems that the pupils are studying, and lessons not related to what is being studied, are using a functional approach which provides instruction in the use of books as an essential part of the semester's work.

Guidance in the Use of Study Helps

A semester's study or the study of a unit of work, of a major problem, or of one lesson may be divided into four parts: the overview, the study period, the presentation of the findings, and the review and evaluation. In each one of these phases of study, pupils may be given instruction and practice in the use of study helps.

In the introductory period, pupils may be given an overview of the semester's work. During this time, pupils acquire background information and set up problems for study. In this way, the pupils' efforts will be so directed that they will understand the purpose of the study. This is the period in which readiness for study-reading is developed. Secondary-school teachers should remember that the reading readiness approach is just as essential on the secondary level as it is in the first grade. Study helps in books provide one means for building background information and creating readiness for study-reading. Thus, while pupils are gaining a preview of the various problems that they may study during the semester, they are becoming acquainted with the study helps in the books they will use and are having practice in using them.

When the pupils begin the study of the major problems of the unit or lesson, effective work will require the use of the study helps found in textbooks and references. During this part of the lesson or unit, teachers should give individual guidance and, whenever necessary, should provide instruction for small groups of pupils or for the entire class.

During the period or periods when pupils are discussing the results of their study, questions may arise concerning accuracy of certain facts. At such times, reference to authorities will probably require the use of the table of contents, index, summaries, tables, maps, or graphs. During such discussion periods pupils should be given practice and guidance in using study helps in books.

Chapter and topic headings, summaries, questions, tables, graphs, and the index in a book are all useful to the pupil who is reviewing a problem or problems in order to participate in an oral evaluation of a study, to summarize the value of a study, or to master materials in preparation for a test.

By utilizing all the opportunities which arise during all stages in the study of a unit, a problem, or a lesson, teachers can provide continuous guidance and effective practice in the use of study helps. During any of the steps outlined here, pupils may be given instruction in the use of the study helps in the books in the regular classroom and, also, in the reference books, such as encyclopedias, which are to be found in the library.

In the introductory or overview period and in the study periods, carefully selected or prepared practice lessons may be used to supplement the experiences the pupils are having in using books. These additional lessons may be used to aid individual pupils, a small group, or the entire class to develop facility in using study helps.

Instructional materials prepared by the teacher or selected from special reading books may be used in the review and evaluation period to insure progress of pupils. The best test of a pupil's ability to use study helps effectively, however, is through critical observation of the way in which he uses books when he is working alone. The use a pupil makes of the table of contents, the index, topic headings, and other study helps when he is attacking a new problem is indicative of the effectiveness of his training in this area.

Advance preparation made to anticipate the study-reading problems that pupils may find in the semester's work or to deal with the results of informal teacher-made tests given during the first week of school may reveal a need to review quickly the purpose and use of all study helps. Such survey may show that definite and detailed instruction in using one or more of the study helps will be required to establish study habits.

The exercises throughout Part II are such that any teacher can adapt them for use in his class. Interested teachers will provide many learning experiences and a variety of practice materials to enable each one of their pupils to develop proficiency in using all the study helps in accordance with his needs and level of maturity.

A. GENERAL FEATURES OF BOOKS

To assist pupils in becoming familiar with the books which they will use during the semester, teachers should plan both informal and written lessons. A quick survey of all the study helps in a textbook may well be made first.

EXERCISE 1

1. What is the title of your book?
2. When was it published?
3. Why should you notice the date of publication?
4. What study helps do you find in your book?
5. Where is the table of contents?
6. Where is the index?
7. Where is the word list or glossary?
   a. Why is it a good study habit to use the word list in a book?
   b. If a book does not have a glossary, what reference do you need to use?
8. Does your book have a preface or introduction?
   a. What does the preface usually tell you?
   b. When do you need to read the preface?
9. Does your book have an appendix?
   a. Can you find another book that has an appendix?
   b. In what part of the book is it found?
   c. What type of material is in the appendix?
   d. How does the appendix help you?
10. Does your book have a bibliography?
    a. If not, name a book that does have a bibliography.
    b. How does the bibliography help you?

1. Does your book have section headings?
   a. If so, of what value are they?
   b. What types of books usually have section headings?
2. Find a book that contains a type of heading different from a section heading.
   a. How does this heading help you?
   b. What is a side heading?
   c. Find two examples of a side heading and note the references.
   d. How does a side heading help you in your study of a topic?

EXERCISE 2

1. List two books in the classroom library which contain each of the following:
   a. Index
   b. Table of contents
   c. Bibliography
   d. Glossary
   e. Appendix
   f. Preface
   g. Section headings
   h. Table of illustrations
2. Tell in what part of the book each study-help was found and explain how each study-help will aid you in your work.

EXERCISE 3

Below are two columns of words or phrases. One phrase or group of words in the right-hand column means the same, or almost the same, as one in the left-hand column. In the space before each item of the left-hand column, place the number of the expression in the right-hand column which most nearly defines or describes its meaning.

......Index	1. Name of book
......Table of Contents	2. Part of a book giving additional information, as notes and tables
......Bibliography	3. Introduction
......Appendix	4. List of books for further reading
......Glossary	5. Alphabetical list of topics with the page on which each is found
......Preface	6. Year when book was published
......Title	7. List in front of book with chapter headings or topics in sequence and page on which each begins
......Date of publication	8. List of words with their meanings

The sections that follow contain discussions of various kinds of study helps together with exercises for developing facility in their use.

B. TABLE OF CONTENTS

To provide practice in using the table of contents, teachers may well plan exercises similar to those in the following examples. To develop background for problems to be studied during the semester, the pupils may write on or discuss orally questions based on the textbooks or references available for use in their study.

EXERCISE 4

1. About what topics can information be obtained in this book (selected text or reference)?
2. List questions which are discussed in this book.

To assist pupils to develop greater skill in finding information about units to be studied, have them examine selected books and answer questions concerning them.

EXERCISE 5

1. Which parts of this book (selected text or reference) contain information about the unit we have planned to study?
2. What questions about the unit are discussed? What other topics are discussed?
3. On what pages would we probably find information about the unit?

To provide additional practice in using the table of contents, prepare a lesson on a book available for use, prepare a sample table of contents with questions based upon it, or select a lesson from a special reading book. Where possible these lessons should be mimeographed.

C. INDEX

In preparing lessons on the use of the index, such points as the following should be considered: alphabetical arrangement, main topics, subtopics, punctuation, listing of maps, abbreviations like "illus." and "ff.," cross references. To develop the skill needed to use an index effectively, exercises similar to the following are suggested.

EXERCISE 6

Head your paper and list the topic to be studied. Beneath the topic, list references and give pages upon which information may be found. Use the following pattern:

Subject ....Name......................
Period ....Date.........................

COAL

Casner and Peattie, *Exploring Geography*

1. In industry, 113, 137, 267
2. Kinds of, 226–227
3. Methods of using, 229–230

To assist pupils to know under what word or words to look for information in an index, exercises of this type are useful.

EXERCISE 7

1. If you were looking for information about the topics listed below, for which word would you look first? Copy each topic or question. Then draw *one* line under the first key word (the word which you would look for first) and *two* lines under a second key word (the word you would look for if you did not find the first key word).
   a. history of highway transportation
   b. night flying in an airplane
2. Now list the pages in your book on which information is given about these topics. Be sure to look up the *first key word first*. Were the topics always listed under the word you have underlined with one line?

To measure pupil growth in skill in using an index, comparable forms of a test-study lesson on topics unrelated to the problems which the pupils are studying may be used to advantage.

D. GRAPHS, TABLES, AND CHARTS

There is a real need for systematic instruction to develop greater skill in reading graphs, charts, and tables because this type of presentation is found not only in certain special fields but also in the reading materials of general education. Graphic or tabular presentation of information is frequently found in newspapers and magazines. Textbooks in the social sciences, in mathematics, and in science contain much information in graphic form; and success in many high-school courses depends on skill in interpreting facts presented in charts, graphs, or tables.

Instruction should be provided in reading various types of graphs, such as the bar graph, circle graph, line graph, and picture graph. Leary and Gray describe the different levels of complexity involved in interpreting a graph as follows:

In its simplest form it involves the ability to recognize what the graph is about — to understand the title, the meaning of the horizontal and vertical axes, and the meaning of the different lines or bars. The next step requires the ability to note the rate and direction of change in one variable made by corresponding change in the other and to realize that the data are only approximate. The third step involves the ability to read the major facts which the graph shows — the value of exports from the United States in a given year, the relative heights of mountain peaks, *etc.* The fourth involves the ability to "read into" the graph what may account for the facts represented. As these steps are followed in the study of bar graphs, circle graphs, broken-line and curved-line graphs, pupils should gradually grow in power to read and interpret graphs and see the advantage of the graphic method of presentation over a series of related statistics. Then by degrees they come to the graphical interpretation of the verbal problem, of the formula, and, ultimately, of the linear system.[1]

Guidance in reading and interpreting graphs, charts, or tables should be given as the need arises in mathematics, social studies, science, or other classes where this type of material occurs. Whenever advisable, special exercises or lessons which can be mimeographed should be prepared in order to provide additional practice. Exercises based on the text or on special practice material should be graded so that pupils can be assigned tasks commensurate with their ability.

To develop ability to interpret graphs, charts, or tables, the following suggestions for exercises are offered:

1. Have pupils prepare graphs, tables, or charts to present facts to be given in a report to the class. The practice of preparing such materials from verbal explanations of facts aids pupils in understanding graphic or tabular material which they are asked to interpret.
2. Prepare and have pupils use a general guide for interpreting graphs, charts, or tables encountered in their reading.
3. To measure pupil growth, prepare comparable forms of an informal test. Types of exercises used in standardized tests which test work-study skills may be used as guides by teachers who wish to prepare such tests for their pupils.

E. MAPS

The ability to read maps accurately is necessary today in order to understand many articles in newspapers, magazines, and books. Maps are also used in many lines of work such as agriculture, manufacturing, and commerce. Map making in itself is an important occupation in meteorology, military and commercial aviation, and navigation. To help pupils develop greater skill in interpreting maps correctly, systematic instruction in the different levels of complexity in reading maps is essential. Such a series of lessons should be carefully prepared so that pupils will receive training in using the different skills required in reading maps.

The reading problems that pupils of a particular class may encounter in map reading during the semester should be anticipated, and materials should be selected and procedures outlined to assist the pupils in improving their skill in interpreting maps. The needs of pupils may be discovered by listing the types of map reading to

[1] Bernice E. Leary and William S. Gray, "Reading Problems in the Content Field," *Reading in General Education*, A Report of the Committee on Reading in General Education, edited by William S. Gray, chairman. Washington: American Council on Education, 1940, p. 150.

be done during the semester and then preparing an informal test or using a standardized test to determine the strength and weakness of the pupils. The results of the test should be analyzed and instruction planned to meet the needs of the individual pupils in a particular class.

In preparing exercises in map reading, teachers should remember that it is easier to get descriptive ideas from maps than it is to understand relationships and to interpret facts.

To assist pupils to locate maps which may be helpful to them, teachers should provide practice (1) in finding maps listed in textbooks and references under the heading, "Maps and Illustrations," and (2) in using the book index.

Sets of small atlases and a globe should be available for classes in the social studies. Teachers should be sure that pupils not only are familiar with the types of material to be found in an atlas, but also that they know how to find the information quickly.

In order to read and interpret maps correctly, pupils must understand the common language of maps. There are various terms common to all, or nearly all, maps. Some of these are direction, distance, scale, latitude, and longitude. To help pupils understand this common language of maps, teachers should list for their own guidance the terms that the pupils in their classes must be able to interpret in reading the types of maps to be used. A pretest on these terms will aid the teacher in preparing the pupils to read the maps as they are encountered in the reading materials of the course.

The terms or concepts found necessary for the interpretation of all maps should be studied first. If pupils are unfamiliar with the terms used in reading a particular map, specific help should be given at that time. A background for understanding the new terms should be built up by the teacher and pupils working together before pupils are asked to interpret the map independently. Following are some exercises which will be helpful in developing understanding of the common terms in the language of maps.

Direction. Exercises giving experience in indicating the four cardinal points of the compass should be given first.

EXERCISE 8

1. The Mississippi River flows in what general direction?
   North........; South........; East........; West........
2. Name one continent which lies entirely north of the equator.
3. In what part of North America is the Continental Divide?
   North........; South........; East........; West........

Distance. Distances between points can usually be determined with approximate accuracy on a "large-scale" map (one which shows a small area in considerable detail) by use of a scale. Distances may also be computed by reference to latitude and longitude, although this method requires mastery of more difficult concepts and can well be made the subject of a separate discussion.

Scale measurements cannot be used with accuracy on a flat map which represents a large portion of the earth's surface (a "small-scale" map), for in this case the measurements are rendered inaccurate owing to the distortion inherent in all projections of a spherical surface onto a flat one. Measurements of distance should be made on a globe whenever possible. The following exercises are examples of questions relating to the use of scales on maps.

EXERCISE 9

1. Which of the following cities is farthest from Cairo?
   Tunis......; Moscow......; Athens......; Stalingrad......
2. If you were a pilot flying from London to Berlin, how many miles in flying distance would you travel?
3. How much closer to Chungking would an air base at Fairbanks, Alaska, be than a base at New York?

Location. Places may be located on maps in terms of their relationship to other places and by their latitude and longitude. Again, it seems advisable to teach the latter method separately. Here are a few exercises typical of problems of location in relationship to known places.

EXERCISE 10

1. The Kiel Canal connects what two bodies of water?
2. In what continents are the following mountain ranges located:
   Andes......; Apennines......; Himalayas......; Atlas.......
3. Brazil is bounded by what countries?

Names of Water and Land Areas. It is necessary for pupils to know the names of types of bodies of water and land masses in order that they may express themselves clearly in locating and describing places. It is also necessary for them to understand these terms thoroughly so that they may grasp the significance of historical events caused or affected by geographical characteristics. In using exercises to develop understanding of these terms, the teacher should begin by developing simple definitions, and then, when these are learned, he may use various types of thought questions.

EXERCISE 11

1. On what are the Caucasus Mountains located?
   An island......; An isthmus......; A peninsula......;
   A sound......

2. Name two straits or channels that were important in World War II.
3. Name an archipelago which was taken from the United States by Japan and then retaken by our armed forces.
4. Explain why a peninsula may be difficult to defend by military forces.
5. What cities lie on or near the parallel 50° north of the equator?
6. Draw a map showing a few city streets running at right angles to each other. Show the position of three or four buildings and then explain in words how to find them; for example, the post office is three blocks east of Main Street and two blocks north of First Street. Show that to locate a place on a Mercator projection we must know not only how far north or south it is, but also how far east or west.
7. Mark meridians of longitude on an orange. By checking with a globe, draw the continents on the orange, being careful to place them correctly as to longitude.
8. If you were a pilot and were given orders to locate a city which is at approximately 8° east longitude and 53° north latitude, what city would it be?
9. Degrees of latitude are shown by lines called ....

Time. If pupils are to understand various problems of transportation and communication, news reports from foreign countries and the setting back or ahead of watches on transcontinental journeys, the concept of global time must be taught. The following exercise is an example:

EXERCISE 12

1. Name the time zones in the United States.
2. When it is noon in Santa Barbara on Monday, what time on what day is it in New Orleans, 60° east of Santa Barbara?

Longitude and Latitude. Longitude and latitude are among the most important concepts for pupils to grasp. Basic to an understanding of longitude and latitude is awareness of the significance of direction. The term equator also should be understood. Latitude should be explained to pupils before longitude. A discussion of the history of the two concepts and the reasons for their formulation as an aid to navigation may prove interesting and helpful. Some suggestions for studying the ideas of latitude and longitude are given in the following exercise:

EXERCISE 13

1. Using a Mercator projection of the world, locate the equator. Then locate or draw the parallels of latitude.
2. Through what continents or large islands do the following parallels of latitude pass? 20° South..........; 20° North.........

To understand the common language of maps, pupils must be able to understand the various symbols used on maps. The symbols used for rivers, railroads, cities, capital cities, *etc.*, should be taught through practice in reading maps to find specific information. After pupils have had sufficient practice in reading the common symbols, matching exercises may be used to measure pupils' skills in reading the legends on maps. Their knowledge may also be checked by giving them maps with names of cities, rivers, *etc.*, written on them. Then have the pupils place correct symbols on the maps and fill in the spaces provided for the legend.

It is certain that the formation of the habits of reading the legend on a map, noting the meaning of the symbols used and applying the facts given in the legend when reading a map, will help pupils to develop the ability to read correctly various types of maps. Emphasis should be placed on the understanding and interpretation of symbols rather than on how to read particular maps.

In order to be sure that pupils know how to interpret symbols correctly, practice should be given in reading various types of maps, such as physical, political, rainfall, product, *etc.* In this way pupils are given practice in reading and interpreting a variety of symbols. The following exercises may be helpful:

EXERCISE 14

1. Physical Maps
   a. Draw a map of an imaginary island and add mountains, a river, a harbor, and a railroad.
   b. Draw an island and a lake, showing their difference by the way the shoreline is drawn.
2. Population Maps
   a. On an outline map of the United States, indicate the most densely populated areas.
   b. Using a population map of England, write the names of five cities which have populations of over 100,000.
3. Political Maps
   a. What countries can you name which have natural boundaries?
   b. What countries can you name whose boundaries have been changed several times during the last century? To the advantage of which countries were these changes made?

F. DICTIONARIES

Proficient skill in using the dictionary helps pupils to develop a useful and meaningful vocabulary. Because the efficient use of the dictionary requires many different skills, systematic instruction is necessary. The following steps should be included in lessons used in teaching pupils how to use the dictionary effectively.

1. Discuss the reasons for alphabetical arrangement of words
2. Provide practice in finding the letters of the alphabet in the dictionary. Teaching the following approximate divisions of

a dictionary may help to train pupils to find the different letters quickly:
a. First fourth: A, B, C, D
b. Second fourth: E, F, G, H, I, J, K, L
c. Third fourth: M, N, O, P, Q, R
d. Fourth fourth: S, T, U, V, W, X, Y, Z

3. Train pupils to arrange words and lists of names alphabetically
4. Provide practice in finding words in the dictionary
   a. Discuss the use of guide words
   b. Provide adequate practice in using guide words
5. Teach pupils how to pronounce words by using the dictionary
   a. Discuss syllabication and accent
   b. Discuss the re-spelling which shows how the word is pronounced and provide practice in pronunciation of words
   c. Develop the habit of looking for synonyms
   d. Provide practice in using the key to the pronunciation of vowel sounds
6. Train pupils to find the correct meaning of a word
   a. Be sure that pupils form the habit of asking the question: "Does the meaning fit the sentence?"
   b. Teach pupils to look for the meaning of common stems, prefixes, and suffixes
   c. Develop the habit of looking for synonyms

G. ENCYCLOPEDIAS

An encyclopedia is a comprehensive summary of knowledge or of a branch of knowledge, a work in which the various branches or fields of learning are treated in separate paragraphs or articles, usually arranged in alphabetical order. To get a general background before writing a paper or preparing a talk as well as to obtain factual information, pupils should form the habit of referring to encyclopedias. The following information should be given to all pupils:

1. Aids for Using Encyclopedias
   a. Volume guides — labels on backs of volumes to aid the user to determine in which volume a subject will be found
   b. Guide words — indicating in upper corner of each page the first and last subject to be found on that page
   c. Arrangement — giving subject heading with many subject divisions, alphabetically
   d. Cross references ("See" and "See also") — mentioning other articles containing different additional information
   e. Index volume — giving smaller topics included in larger groups

Name of Encyclopedia	*No. of Vols.*	*Lengths of Articles*	*Bibliographies*	*How Kept Up-to-Date*	*Index*
The Encyclopedia Americana	30	Short specific articles	Occasional short lists at end of articles	Annual supplement	Classified, in Vol. 30
The Encyclopaedia Britannica	24	Articles in 14th edition more popular in style than previous editions. Vary in length.	Bibliographies at end of articles	Annual supplement	Index and atlas in Vol. 24
Compton's Pictured Encyclopedia	15	Articles vary in length according to subject. Planned for juvenile and school use	Bibliographies and study outlines at end of large topics. Occasional bibliographies at end of articles	Partial revision each year	"Fact-Index" in back of each volume
The New International Encyclopaedia	27	Articles vary in length according to subject	Bibliographies at end of articles	Annual supplement since 1907: NEW INTERNATIONAL YEAR BOOK	No index. One alphabet with cross references. "Courses of Reading and Study," Vol. 24
The World Book Encyclopedia	19	Articles vary in length according to subject. Juvenile encyclopedia approximating form and treatment of standard works for adults	Lists of related subjects at end of articles. Occasional bibliography at end of articles. General bibliography by subject and grade at end of Vol. 18	"Continuous revision"	Cross references with topics in main alphabet. "Reading and Study Guide" in Vol. 19

2. Special Rules for Use of Encyclopedias
   a. Abbreviations are arranged alphabetically as if they were words spelled in full, *e.g.*, *St.* as if it were *Saint*
   b. One of two forms of alphabetizing may be used
      (1) "Letter by letter" alphabetization considers all the letters in a subject heading, *to the first comma*, as if they were one long word; *e.g.*, *Newark* will be found before *New York*, and *Man, Isle of* before *Manhattan*.
      (2) "Word by word" alphabetization places expressions in order first *according to the first word* of the expression. Expressions having exactly the same first word are then arranged in order according to the second word, and so on, thus:

New Albion	Newark
New Deal	Newspaper
New York	Newton

   c. "The," "An," and "And" are disregarded in alphabetizing if they are initial words in expressions.
   d. Entries should be sought first under the distinctive word of the phrase, *e.g.*, chambered *nautilus*, Treaty of *Ghent*, *Pan* American Union.
3. General Information Concerning Commonly Used Encyclopedias (latest editions) (See page 282.)

EXERCISE 15

1. Find a biography of Franklin D. Roosevelt.
2. Find an article on treatment for mushroom poisoning.
3. Find a description of an octopus.
4. Learn what you can of the homing pigeon.
5. What is the climate of Hawaii?
6. What is the chemical formula for common salt?
7. What is meant by "reparations"?
8. What is the population of New Orleans? The height of Mt. Blanc? The greatest depth of Lake Superior? The chief export of Mexico?

H. FACILITIES OF THE LIBRARY

The high-school librarian is concerned with two fields of endeavor; namely, aid to pupils and aid to faculty members. High-school librarians of today seem united in their belief that the real purpose of the high-school library is to stimulate in the pupil a desire to read, to create good taste in reading, and to help him achieve an enjoyment of reading which will stay with him through later life, whether in advanced education or in a work-a-day world.

The actual, factual information which he unearths or which is unearthed for him may be of little importance; but it is of the greatest importance that the spirit of inquiry, the respect of truth, the excitement of learning should be kept alive. It is important that the young person retain or acquire confidence in his world and his associates, a sense of hope and self-reliance, and an appreciation of his responsibilities. It is important that his horizons be widened and, if possible, clarified.

The librarian should strive to provide those facilities and materials which will guide in this direction. Some of the services which the library can render to pupils are listed below:

1. The creation of a friendly, attractive library, where the student will really like to go
2. Easy accessibility to many types of library materials — magazines, pamphlet files, maps, pictures, as well as references and regular book collections
3. Aid in using the card catalogue, the *Readers' Guide to Periodical Literature*, and other indexes to sources
4. Aid in using reference works such as encyclopedias, *The World Almanac*, *Who's Who in America*
5. Individual attention and interest, sympathetic encouragement, attention to individual projects, and as much personal guidance in reading as possible
6. Opportunity for browsing to see exhibits, bulletin boards, special book collections, book lists, and other materials which will stimulate interest in reading.

Obvious types of library service for faculty members are listed below.

1. Availability of all library facilities and materials
2. Circulation of books and magazines to faculty members
3. Individual or departmental notices calling attention to books newly added to the library collection
4. Compilation of bibliographies and reading lists upon request of any faculty member
5. Temporary loans of books as special classroom collections
6. The placement on reserve of reference materials most in demand or especially needed during periods of special units of instruction. (Faculty members should give advance notice to the librarian of their plans for the use of specific library materials.)

The constant use of standard book selection aids, such as *Book Review Digest*, *The Booklist*, Wilson's *Standard Catalogue for High School Libraries*, evaluated lists of books for high-school libraries issued by the California School Library Association and other similar state lists, and innumerable announcements from publishers and book jobbers enable the librarian to keep in touch with new titles in all fields. This information should be gladly shared with interested faculty members. The librarian should welcome suggestions from the faculty for book purchases.

Knowing how to use their high-school library will enable pupils to prepare class work more efficiently and to find interesting reading for leisure hours. Pupils should be familiar with the general outline of the Dewey Decimal Classification:

000–099 General Works — for example, encyclopedias
100–199 Philosophy, psychology, conduct
200–299 Religion: the Bible and mythology
300–399 Sociology: education, economics, government, legends, folklore, army, navy
400–499 Language: dictionaries, grammars
500–599 Natural science: mathematics, astronomy, chemistry, birds, insects, animals, physics, electricity
600–699 Useful arts: invention, vocational guidance, hygiene, engineering, agriculture, gardening, handicraft, cooking, sewing, aeronautics, industries
700–799 Fine arts: drawing, painting, music, the theater, photography, games and sports
800–899 Literature: poetry, essays, plays
900–999 History, travel, geography, collected biography

Books of fiction are arranged alphabetically according to author.

Practice exercises should be given to stimulate pupils to use the library facilities. Simple exercises are given below.

EXERCISE 16

1. Find 100 on the shelves and then walk around the library, locating the sections you will use most frequently this year.
2. Give the number of the class to which each of the following books belongs:
   a. *Animal Heroes*
   b. *Myths of Greece and Rome*
   c. *Music Through the Ages*
   d. *Argonauts of '49*

Instruction should be given in the use of the card catalogue. All cards are filed alphabetically. Below are listed the primary types of catalogue cards:

1. The author card, showing the surname first
2. The title card, beginning with the first word of the title, but omitting *a*, *an*, and *the*
3. The subject card

Most pupils will need considerable practice in using the catalogue before they become really familiar with it. Exercises similar to the following are:

EXERCISE 17

1. Under what letter or in which trays in the card catalogue will you look for cards for the following:
   a. *The Call of the Wild* (a title)
   b. Charles Dickens (an author)
   c. Hawaii (a subject)
2. Locate two books in your library by each of the following authors:
   a. Booth Tarkington
   b. Hamlin Garland
   c. Mark Twain
3. Find the most recent book in your library on aviation
4. Give the classification in the Dewey Decimal Classification System for the following books:
   a. *Boots and Saddles*
   b. *Bambi*
   c. *Short Plays About Famous Authors*
5. Find the cross reference card for *vocations*

The World Almanac is a useful reference by which to locate information about government, industry, commerce, world events, and sports. Pupils will profit from exercises in its use as well as instruction about it.

EXERCISE 18

1. Who is the governor of your state?
2. Who won the women's tennis championship of the United States last year?
3. How many people were killed by automobiles last year in the United States?
4. Who won the Pulitzer Prize for the best American novel in 1943?

Pupils should be given instruction in the use of the *Readers' Guide, etc.* Itself a monthly periodical, the *Readers' Guide* is an index to magazines. It has a bound volume once a year, and volumes which include several years. In the front of each copy is a list of magazines which are indexed alphabetically by the abbreviated name of the magazine. Pupils should learn that there are different ways of finding material in the *Readers' Guide*, as follows:

1. Articles are alphabetized under the *subject*, and the last name of the *author*
2. Stories are alphabetized under the *first word of the title*, and also under the last name of the author
3. Poems may be found under the heading *Poems* or under the last names of authors

A sample of entry from *Readers' Guide* on the subject "Russia" is given below:

Russia of the hour. J. B. Wood, Nat. Geog. M50: 519–98 N 26

"Russia of the Hour" is the title of an article by J. B. Wood in *National Geographic Magazine*, volume 50, pages 519–598, in the November issue of 1926. The same material will be found under the author's name *Wood, J. B.*

EXERCISE 19

1. What is the title of a novel by Ernest Hemingway?
2. In what recent issue of the *Saturday Evening Post* can you find an article about athletics?
3. Name three authors who have written recent articles on athletics.
4. Choose a subject of interest to you, and, using the *Reader's Guide*, find at least five recent articles on your subject. List the entries as found in the *Guide*.

Improvement of Vocabulary

Two closely related fundamental skills in reading are recognition of words and symbols and an understanding of the language used. Effective instruction in vocabulary building contributes to the pupil's understanding of what is read, to growth in expressing ideas both in oral and in written form, and to an understanding of ideas presented orally.

A. BACKGROUND EXPERIENCES

Pupils frequently fail to understand what is read because the vocabulary is not within their experience. Therefore, provision for common background experiences to enable pupils to understand many words before they meet them in reading about a problem or a topic helps in overcoming vocabulary difficulties. The following suggestions apply especially to slow readers:

1. Use these general guides for preparing pupils to read a selection:
   a. Provide concrete background experiences
   b. Use visual aids, such as maps, diagrams, charts, pictures, models, and motion pictures
   c. Use words in conversation and explain specific terms
2. Provide exercises giving specific helps for developing readiness to read a particular selection:
   a. Change the language of the text to one the pupils understand.
   b. Write difficult words in the lesson on the board. After each word, list the page on which it is found. In an in-

formal discussion, have pupils find each word and tell what it means.

c. Select difficult words from the lesson. After each word, write the page on which it is found. In another column write a word or phrase that has the same meaning.

B. DEVELOPMENT OF VOCABULARY

The emphasis in vocabulary building should be on meaning. In the best classroom practice, procedures for improving word recognition and pronunciation and for developing wider meaning vocabulary will be closely related. In this way, word meaning will be constantly emphasized. Specific exercises should be given for improving the mechanics of word recognition and pronunciation because ". . . comprehension cannot be raised to a high degree if the learner is struggling with the mechanics of the reading process."[2]

Although certain types of vocabulary drill are not always successful and the degree of improvement does not always justify the effort expended to produce it, the majority of research studies seems to justify well-motivated vocabulary training which grows out of the pupil's reading experience or other use of words.

The following suggestions, according to Ruth Strang, have proved to be of value:[3]

1. Note definitions which frequently follow the introduction of technical words. The definitions given in the text are often preferable to definitions found in a standard dictionary.
2. Check lightly unfamiliar words which are not defined in their context, and later look them up in a dictionary. Write each at the top of a small card. At the bottom of the card should appear a synonym, and in the middle of the card a sentence using the word, or a familiar word derived from or giving derivation to the unfamiliar one. These cards may then be used for individual practice. When the word is not immediately recognized, the "player" looks down to the "connecting link" in the middle of the card. If this does not bring about recall of the meaning, he must resort to the synonym or definition at the bottom of the card. Junior-high-school youngsters enjoy playing games with such cards and finding the words in new contexts. Adults find such a method of keeping up their recently acquired vocabulary useful because a knowledge of the range of literal meanings of a large number of words helps the reader to grasp its meaning in context.

[2] *A Preliminary Survey of a Reading Program for the Secondary Schools*, Bulletin 282. Harrisburg, Pennsylvania: Department of Public Instruction, Commonwealth of Pennsylvania, 1939, p. 32.

[3] Ruth Strang, with the assistance of Florence C. Rose, *Problems in the Improvement of Reading in High School and College*. Lancaster, Pennsylvania: The Science Press Printing Co., 1938, p. 84.

Throughout his reading experience, an individual tends to read about things more or less familiar to him. Each new bit of reading increases his fund of ideas, gives him new understandings and wider experiences, often vicarious, all of which builds up a certain ability to infer meanings.

When new words are encountered for the first time, great dependence is placed upon context clues. In fact, familiarity with ideas being expressed gives the reader his first clues to word symbols. In normal reading development, occasional unfamiliar words present little difficulty since meanings can often be derived from the otherwise familiar context. The more remote the subject matter from the reader's background of experience, the less able is he to anticipate or infer meanings. Thus, the poor reader with inadequate skill in word perception goes down under a too heavy load of unfamiliar words encountered in his reading.

Most of the instruction which is directed toward enlargement of students' vocabularies is based upon use of the dictionary. Instruction and practice in dictionary use are often carried to such a point that pupils feel helpless without a dictionary or, as a labor-saving substitute, a teacher who will define unknown words. Since, in practice, mature readers use context clues far more frequently than they use dictionaries in arriving at word meanings, it is highly desirable to give pupils some comprehension of the process involved and some training in applying it. All pupils need some help in this area and less alert ones must have intensive practice in it. To enrich the background and to choose material not too far above the level of the pupil's reading ability are first steps in specific training to use context clues as an aid to word recognition as well as to word meaning.

The next step might well be to help pupils become aware that words and meanings may be guessed, at times. Practice on familiar expressions will serve to awaken pupils to the realization that many words may be read without having been printed in the sentence. This is easily demonstrated by completing the following phrases:

Early in the......................	His one...........interest
As light as a	Flew in a straight ....

Other types of clues should be analyzed and taught specifically. Often an unfamiliar word is merely a synonym for a word previously used, as illustrated in the following two sentences:

> Today he tells the *property man* what he wants and tomorrow he finds the items waiting on the set. The *property custodian* has become the movie director's Santa Claus.

An unfamiliar word may be an antonym for a known word, for example:

Water is *seldom* found in the desert, but springs *frequently* occur in the surrounding hills.

Organized and systematic instruction on the use of these and other types of clues should form a part of the reading program throughout elementary- and high-school grades. Awareness of context clues and skill in using them are indispensable for independent and intelligent reading. Pupils must be able to use context clues in various ways:

a. In associating meaning with known word forms
b. In discriminating between words which are very much alike in sound and form but not in meaning
c. In checking on pronunciation derived from phonetic analysis
d. In determining which one of the various sounds of a certain vowel is appropriate in a given word.[4]

C. QUALIFYING WORDS

Common qualifying words are important to the meaning of a sentence, yet many pupils fail to understand the idea expressed in a sentence because they pass over the qualifying words. Common qualifying words include *many*, *no*, *more*, *most*, *less*, *few*, *only*, *almost*, *always* and *all*. Short phrases and clauses are frequently used in a qualifying manner and pupils should be trained to notice the way in which such phrases, as well as words similar to the ones listed above, change the meaning of a sentence. The following types of exercises have been found helpful in training pupils to notice how qualifying words or phrases change the meaning of a sentence.

1. Write on the blackboard sentences containing qualifying words or give them orally. Discuss with pupils the way in which the words affect the meaning of the sentence.
2. Write a group of sentences on the blackboard with the instructions to copy these sentences and draw a line through each qualifying word.

   EXAMPLE: There are *many* apples on the plate.

   a. After the sentences have been discussed and all pupils have drawn a line through each qualifying word, have them rewrite each sentence and substitute another qualifying word for the one used.

[4] William S. Gray and Lillian Gray, *Guidebook for Streets and Roads*. Chicago: Scott, Foresman and Company, 1941, p. 29.

b. Discuss the meaning of these rewritten sentences to show how qualifying words make distinct changes in the meaning of a sentence.

3. Write on the blackboard sentences containing qualifying words or phrases. Check the pupils' knowledge of how the words or phrases change the meaning of the sentence by having them answer yes or no to questions about the sentences.

EXAMPLE: The old Indian nearly always came to the trading post in the morning

QUESTIONS:

1. Did the old Indian always come to the trading post in the morning?
2. Did the old Indian usually come to the trading post in the morning?
3. Is it true that the old Indian seldom came to the trading post in the morning?

Oral discussion is a vital factor in all preceding procedures. It should be used freely.

D. WORDS COMMONLY OVERWORKED

Some words are so badly overworked that they have almost lost their specific meanings. They are the "maids of all work" and are used principally by the language beggars. High-school pupils need to be helped to overcome the tendency to use trite phrases and overworked words. The following exercises have been useful for this purpose.

1. Write on the blackboard from 10 to 15 sentences each containing the word "got." Have pupils substitute a verb with specific meaning for the overworked verb "got" in each sentence.
2. Have pupils develop a list of frequently overworked words, such as asked, awful, divine, fix, grand, great, keen, lovely, neat, nice, perfect, replied, said, swell, take, terrible, thing, want, wonderful.

E. FIGURATIVE AND OTHER NON-LITERAL LANGUAGE

How far the teacher can go in teaching junior and senior high-school pupils to understand the various forms of nonliteral writing depends on the same factors which limit teaching in other fields: the intelligence and cultural background of the pupils, the size of the class and the consequent ease or difficulty of conducting class discussions, the availability of good textbooks and of supplementary material, the rigidity of the course of study, and the teacher's own knowledge and love of literature. Every English teacher, however, should feel that he is remiss in his duties if he fails to open to his pupils the door to the infinite wealth of allusion, description, and suggestion which the intelligent writer and reader may enjoy.

Many teachers overlook the fact that figurative language is not confined to poetry, fairy tales and legends, and similar imaginative writing and limit their teaching of figures of speech to these rather limited areas, leaving largely untouched the much wider and more important fields of idiom, satire, irony, and the innumerable symbolically used words and phrases which appear in daily speech, in advertising, and in newspapers, books, and magazines. Pupils are left floundering in a sea of dimly or wrongly understood language. It is small wonder that they do not read more enthusiastically.

A brief consideration of sample passages from a newspaper, a textbook, and from ordinary conversation will show the necessity for teaching pupils to interpret this prosaic type of nonliteral language. The following samples may not appear to the average adult to be figurative at all because they are so familiar:

A thousand bills were thrown into the legislative hopper.
A chorus of protest arose throughout the land.
I almost died laughing.
The winning candidate swept the field.
The United States is a melting pot.
The enemy lines crumbled.

In junior high school it is probably better to explain figures of speech as they arise in regular class work than to present them "cold" as a unit of study unrelated to the rest of the work in literature, composition, and grammar. The teacher should scan carefully all assigned reading for phrases which might offer difficulty in interpretation and should himself bring them up for class discussion if one of the pupils does not do so.

At first, most of the initiative for such discussions will have to come from the teacher. Most pupils hesitate to admit their inability to understand the real meaning of something the surface import of which is clear. Only when they realize that adults, too, need help in interpretation will they bring their problems into the open. The teacher soon finds that sheer ignorance is the cause of many of the difficulties which pupils have. Biblical, historic, legendary, and artistic references can convey no meaning to those who lack a background of knowledge. "As strong as Samson" might just as well be "As strong as George" so far as many contemporary pupils are concerned. "Mars stalked the earth" creates confused astronomical impressions in the minds of pupils who have been deprived of the Greek myths.

Specific instances of this sort give the alert teacher an excellent opportunity to create in his classes an interest in reading some of the basic literature of our civilization. The classroom or school library should, of course, be ready to provide appropriate books for the pupil whose curiosity is thus aroused.

Lack of knowledge in other areas increases the difficulties of interpretation. "The log-roller lost his footing" was interpreted by a pupil as meaning that the man's foot had been amputated; the reader had no idea of the process of log-rolling. The acquisition of knowledge is, obviously, a never-completed process. The teacher can help himself to appreciate his pupils' shortcomings in this respect by thinking of the gaps in his own information.

It is an accepted principle of education that learning takes place best when the learner participates actively in the process. Thus pupils learn to understand the figurative speech of others when they use such figures themselves. At first, they may simply be asked to complete common similes. These are clichés to the adult, but not to the junior high-school pupil. The following list [5] of incomplete similes is suggestive:

black as	quick as......................
straight as	light as ....
wise as	clear as ....
brown as	sharp as......................
white as	sober as ....
busy as......................	hungry as ....
cold as	sly as ....
hard as......................	happy as ....

If some of the pupils' responses differ from the conventional ones which the teacher expects, these can be used as a point of departure for a discussion of the value of originality and vividness in figurative speech. The next step, of course, is to have some actual writing done by the pupils. The subjects assigned should be simple and of a nature to encourage the use of simile and metaphor. Short, carefully prepared compositions are preferable to long ones. Sample passages dealing with subjects similar to those assigned may be read to furnish pupils with ideas and inspiration. The best compositions may be read to the class, and particularly happy figures of speech may be pointed out and praised. It is easily understood that no public notice should be taken of the inevitable unsuccessful excursions into writing.

Bright pupils enjoy and benefit from learning the names of the

[5] Adapted from list in Frieda Radke, *Living Words*. New York: The Odyssey Press. 1940, p. 153.

various kinds of figures of speech and differences among them. However, merely learning to recognize and name them is a sterile exercise if it does not lead to understanding and appreciation.

Figurative language often offers the inexperienced and perhaps more literal-minded pupils some difficulty in comprehension. The junior high-school pupil can understand onomatopoetic words, alliteration, and similes, but the more complex aspects of figurative language should be developed at the eleventh- and twelfth-grade levels. At the outset the pupil must learn that figurative language occurs more frequently in poetry than in prose. He must be taught some of the basic distinctions between the two forms.

Prose	*Poetry*
1. No regular beat or rhythm	1. Definitely measured and rhythmical
2. No particular form	2. Definitely shaped and often divided into stanzas
3. Often low in emotional tone	3. Often concentrated and intense in tone
4. Usually involves facts and information	4. Usually involves feelings
5. Often detailed and precise	5. Imaginative and suggestive

Perhaps the best way to teach the pupil to interpret figurative language is by pattern. Once an easy pattern is established, the pupil can gradually learn to recognize the same type of pattern in his reading. Alliteration and onomatopoeia are so obvious they can be understood without difficulty. The more complex forms require examples, such as the following:

1. Simile (similarity)
   a. *Like* a cloud of fire
   b. My love is *like* a red, red rose.
   c. My heart is *like* a rhyme.
2. Metaphor (identification transfer)
   a. The moon is a ghostly galleon.
   b. The road is a ribbon of moonlight.
   c. Sarcasm is a dangerous weapon.
3. Personification (having the attributes of a person)
   a. . . . the jocund day, stands tiptoe on the misty mountain top.
   b. Now morning from her orient chambers came and her first footsteps touched a verdant hill.
4. Apostrophe (addressing the dead as living, or the absent as present)
   a. Phoebus, arise and paint the sable skies.
   b. Build me straight, O Worthy Master.
   c. Mother, come back from that echoless shore.
5. Metonomy (associating an object that is closely connected with the idea)

   a. The *pen* is mightier than the sword.
   b. Polly, put the *kettle* on and we'll have tea.
   c. A man should keep a good *table*.
6. Synecdoche (using a part to represent the whole)
   a. She gave her hand in marriage.
   b. I'll not lift a finger.
   c. Fifty sails were seen on the horizon.

The pupil can increase his enjoyment of the daily newspaper by learning to recognize both simile and metaphor as used so frequently in the headlines. He can have fun noticing the clever use of clichés in various radio plays and will discover that these clichés often are similes or metaphors. By training his ear to catch such clichés as "red as a beet," "bitter as gall," and "mad as a hornet," he can immeasurably improve his own speech and writing. Constant alertness on the part of the teacher and the pupil is necessary to enable the pupil to understand the great masterpieces. Nor can this be done in one semester; it must be part of a well-planned English program through the entire secondary school.

F. RETENTION OF NEW VOCABULARY

In order that words may become a permanent part of a pupil's vocabulary, word study must be vitalized for the individual through purposeful listening and reading so that vocabularies are enriched both for oral and written expression.

Extensive Reading. Wide and extensive reading is necessary if pupils are to develop rich vocabularies and wider interests in the world about them. Too often a pupil reads only one type of book — an adventure series, or radio magazines. Frequently, as pupils advance through junior high school, other interests take the place of reading; many pupils never read anything, even a magazine, unless required to do so by a teacher.

More extensive reading habits can be developed by the use of reading "ladders" in the case of the one-type reader; that is, suggestions of related books of wider interest or more mature nature. Books or magazine stories germane to the subject matter studied in class or to popular motion pictures, radio programs, and the like may be recommended. A classroom library, attractive displays, bulletin board, reading nook, are all helpful. The pupil should be given *time* to read. Sometimes, as a special treat, the teacher may read aloud a portion of a book from the library, stopping at some interesting point. Pupils will have to read the book themselves to find out the rest of the story.

The teacher himself will have to know books in order to provide a graded vocabulary load. A poor reader cannot acquire a good vocabulary and effective reading habits by being plunged into difficult reading material full of unfamiliar words. Second, the teacher must check the reading by discussion of the problem of the book, the characters, or the author and make use of the new words in conversation and in class.

> The most common way of improving one's vocabulary is through extensive and varied reading. The meaning of words is acquired through the recognition and use of words as parts of words of dynamic thought patterns. . . .
>
> . . . It is advantageous, however, for teachers to increase their students' acquaintance with words by using repeatedly in their conversation during a week several important new words in their field.[6]

Enlisting Pupils' Co-operation. Teachers should use a variety of procedures to (1) make the below-average pupils conscious of their need of knowing more words to meet everyday problems; (2) stimulate an interest in increasing vocabulary for the average pupil; and (3) to help pupils to overcome their adolescent tendency to censure those pupils who use their vocabularies more effectively than others.

Functional Vocabularies. The functional vocabulary is the vocabulary which the pupil uses to express himself in writing and in speech. Activities in which pupils of difficult levels of maturity may use this functional vocabulary are suggested below:

1. The *below-average* pupil may talk about actual experiences, such as home, school, and church activities; movies, radio programs, and community affairs. He may also write letters and fill out applications. In his writing, the pupil should strive for short paragraph development.
2. The *average* pupil may talk about various experiences gained through reading as well as through actual participation. His vocabulary should show increased maturity and his talks should show greater detailed observation than those of the below-average pupil. The average pupil should engage in considerable writing of an expository or narrative nature and should write letters.
3. The *above-average* pupil should be able to make deductions from listening and reading activities and should participate imaginatively in the experiences about which he is reading. The writing of above-average pupils should show maturity of thought and expression.

[6] Ruth Strang, with the assistance of Florence C. Rose, *Problems in the Improvement of Reading in High School and College.* Lancaster, Pennsylvania: The Science Press Printing Company, 1938, pp. 82–83.

Recognition Vocabularies. The recognition vocabulary is largely a listening or reading vocabulary. The *below-average* pupil will get general meanings only. He will read the vocabulary of current events. He will learn technical words largely through listening. The *average* pupil should work for more exactness in interpretation of thought through word study. The *above-average* pupil should approximate a more "ultimate" truth: *i.e.*, get implications. Reflection on subjects about which he reads may lead to participation in his chosen field.

Devices for Making Permanent the Pupils' Enriched Vocabulary. A variety of procedures may be used to help pupils incorporate words into their permanent vocabularies. The following suggestions are offered:

1. Teach pupils to discriminate between the various meanings of words and phrases. Suggestions for below-average, average, and above-average pupils are listed below:

Word	*Below Average*	*Average*	*Above Average*
root	The root of the plant is large.	The root word comes from Latin. Take the square root of four. A pig roots in the ground.	The root of all evil.
ordinary	The ordinary way of doing the home work all right.	It is a very ordinary procedure.	The ceremony was most ordinary.
pass	The pass is narrow. Pass the cake.	The hall pass is needed. He was passed to first base.	Things have come to a pretty pass!
ground	The apple fell on the ground. The meat is being ground.	This is the ground floor. This is made of ground glass.	He stood his ground. The ground swell is heavy today.
see	I see my way. I see a house.	I see what you mean. I shall come to see you.	I see my way clear. He shall never see death.

2. Teach pupils to learn new words from context and not alone from dictionary definitions:

Word	*Below Average*	*Average*	*Above Average*
hostile	My enemy is hostile.	He is a hostile witness.	He is hostile to my interests.

Word	*Below Average*	*Average*	*Above Average*
leg	The boy broke his leg.	The first leg of the journey is over.	He hasn't a leg to stand on.
propaganda propagandize	Do not listen to enemy propaganda.	To propagandize is unfair.	Propaganda is often a falsification of news.
object objective	Please pick up the object.	I object to your going to the party.	What is your ultimate objective?
proof	What is your proof of that statement?	We shall make a proof of the picture.	The proof of the pudding.

3. Have pupils listen to an auditorium program or a radio speech, listing unfamiliar words and reasoning out their meanings from the contexts.
4. Organize a vocabulary club in the classroom, members of which will be responsible for bringing in words from all subject fields and sharing them with the class.
5. Have pupils classify words for special study from a selected list, noting those foreign in meaning and those they may be using or may be taught to use in formal spoken and written English.[7]
6. Study words in *phrase groupings*, not as isolated vocabulary. Pupils and teachers should use them consciously in later discussions.
7. Increase vocabulary of meanings by learning new words through specifically purposeful meanings for written composition.
8. Point out for special study: (a) powerful verbs, and (b) colorful adjectives with fine discrimination of meanings, as they are discovered in reading
9. Use the "Word to the Wise" section in *Scholastic Magazine* as a weekly check.
10. Provide exercises on synonyms, with dictionary help.
11. Make vocabulary matching games for drill several times a term.
12. Have pupils deduce meanings of words from good oral reading by the teacher.
13. Have pupils analyze words through detection of familiar stems, prefixes, and suffixes.
14. Encourage pupils to be watchful for new words and their implications in wide and varied reading.

[7] William M. Tanner, *Correct English.* Vol. I. Boston: Ginn and Company. 1931, p. 408.

G. EXERCISES FOR IMPROVEMENT OF VOCABULARY

In addition to the suggested drills and exercises which have been given in connection with discussions on the various phases of improvement of vocabulary in the preceding sections, the following specific exercises for identifying and analyzing compounds, finding words within words, developing pronunciation from known parts of known words, and certain kinesthetic techniques may help to strengthen the program.

Compounds. Knowledge of the use of compounds and attention to their form is an excellent means of extending vocabularies. Exercises such as the ones given below are effective in this field.

1. Choose from a current reading lesson several solid compound words (not hyphenated) and write them on the board. Ask pupils to examine them for any unfamiliar parts. Point out that either part of each word may be used alone.
2. Let each pupil choose a compound word which he will separate into parts, using each part in a sentence. He then makes a third sentence in which he uses the compound.
3. Have pupils make sentences containing two or more compound words, for example, John's *workshop* was full of model airplanes made from *cardboard.*
4. Illustrate (when pupils are ready for it) the difference between the two big families of compounds: (a) the solids, as bookworm, roadbed; and (b) the hyphenated compounds, as long-eared, old-fashioned.

Finding Words within Words. As an aid to discovering similarities in word forms and, sometimes, word meaning, practice on identifying short words within longer words is helpful. Seeing that *management, carpenter, attendant, etc.,* contain familiar phonetic elements which are words, themselves, is often an awakening to the pupil who has had difficulty with word perception.

Practice in finding small words may be given in the following way: Pupils select from the context being read a list of long words. Small words within these words are then underlined. Caution must be used to prevent the identification of a small word which is not heard as the long word is pronounced; that is, it would be incorrect to underline *as* in *fashion.*

Developing Pronunciation from Known Parts of Known Words. Young and relatively immature pupils in junior high school may profit from some of the elementary techniques and exercises noted below.

1. Brief drills on consonant digraphs will facilitate recognition of known parts of words. Sight rather than sound should influence the recognition. List five to ten initial digraphs

on the board — bl, br, ch, cl, cr, fl, *etc.* After each one write, in parentheses, the remainder of a word — bl (ack); cl (ean). First see that pupils are familiar with the completed words, then ask them to see how quickly they can find additional words having the same beginnings, using a reading selection for the source.

2. Sentences including numerous digraphs offer a challenge. Give a sample sentence, as "The hunters blew *th*eir horns; the hounds *br*ayed, and the *ch*ase was on! The horses *cl*eared the fences, *cr*ossed the meadows and *sp*ed toward the *fl*eeing fox." Have pupils try writing sentences having two or more of the digraphs illustrated.
3. Common phonograms of three or four letters, especially end-phonograms, furnish worth-while association material. Well-rhymed poetry provides good patterns. Have pupils find pairs and mark the endings that rhyme.
4. Write a paragraph on the board containing many familiar word endings, something like this: "W*ake* up, J*ake;* you're an hour l*ate*, now. Sh*ake* yourself and d*ive* into your clothes. I'll dr*ive* you as far as St*ate* Street if your pride won't be hurt by a r*ide* in my old cr*ate*." Ask pupils to see whether they can outdo the teacher by bringing a similar paragraph of their own the next day.

Use of the Dictionary

For effective use of the dictionary, various knowledges, skills, and abilities are necessary. Although many teachers assume that use of the dictionary has been mastered previous to the junior high school, actual practice falls far short of this attainment. A rather complete list of skills and drills is given here but, as in all classroom work, the teacher of a given group must determine the needs of that group.

The immediate need of a pupil may be to learn how to pronounce a word that he must use in an oral report. The pupil may not be conscious that he has not acquired certain skills, but, if he has not, he can never master the pronunciation of words new to him, such as *aniline*, *antecedent*, *chronological*, *etc.* The exercises in this section indicate some of the various types of lessons that may be used to develop effective use of the dictionary.

A. ALPHABETIZING

Ability to write or repeat the letters of the alphabet in order, and in reverse order, too, is a necessary tool. Here is a little rhyme that will help pupils say the alphabet backward:

z y x and w v,
u t s and r q p
o n m and l k j
i h g and f e d c b a

EXERCISE 1

1. Put the following letters in alphabetical order:
   1. q, c, z, n, p, d, g, e, s, r.
   2. t, o, y, e, b, u, m, i, f, l.
2. Alphabetize the following in reverse order:
   1. t, u, x, o, l, c, f, j, w, b.
   2. g, i, m, p, k, r, l, y, n, s.

Ability to tell the letter that comes immediately before or after a given letter is necessary for quick and ready dictionary use.

EXERCISE 2

1. Write the letters that come just before and just after each of the letters listed below.

1.	......	s	......	7.	......	t	......	13.	......	h	......
2.	......	d	......	8.	......	c	......	14.	......	o	......
3.	......	r	......	9.	......	n	......	15.	......	t	......
4.	......	b	......	10.	......	u	......	16.	......	v	......
5.	......	l	......	11.	......	j	......	17.	......	m	......
6.	......	w	......	12.	......	q	......	18.	......	g	......

2. True-false exercise.
   EXAMPLES: *a comes before d — False*

1. m comes after n	6. q comes after p ......
2. t comes after s	7. n comes after o ......
3. h comes after i	8. u comes after v ......
4. g comes after f	9. w comes after x ......
5. c comes after d	10. k comes after j ......

3. Write the in-between letters.
   EXAMPLE: a (*b*) c

1. m ( ) o	6. o ( ) q	11. t ( ) v
2. f ( ) h	7. e ( ) g	12. l ( ) n
3. d ( ) f	8. c ( ) e	13. r ( ) t
4. x ( ) z	9. p ( ) r	14. i ( ) k
5. u ( ) w	10. s ( ) u	

4. Underline the letter which comes first in the alphabet.

1. s or t	5. c or e	9. q or e
2. q or r	6. y or u	10. f or d
3. l or m	7. n or l	
4. s or p	8. m or n	

Ability to list words in alphabetical order requires considerable practice, especially in junior high school.

EXERCISE 3

1. In the following list, each of the words begins with a different letter. Arrange them in alphabetical order. Number the words when you alphabetize them, and check the word as you place it in the new list. This procedure will save time when you are working with longer and more difficult lists.

seldom	pumpkin	royal
careful	football	appear
weather	northern	minute
1. appear	4.	7. ....
2. careful	5.	8. ....
3.	6.	9. ....

2. When you have a long list of words to alphabetize, you will probably find several words which begin with the same letter. You will wonder which word to place first in the list. You need to go to the second letter to find this order. Here is a list on which to try your skill in alphabetizing. Be sure to number the words in your final list.

geography	audit	great
plague	barren	foamy
animal	game	praise
freeze	payment	blade
broken	fame	aspire
queer	wondered	editor
housing	knock	jungle

EXERCISE 4

Arrange the names of your classmates in alphabetical order. Many of you will be secretaries or treasurers of organizations and will need this ability. Arrange the last names in alphabetical order. If two of the surnames are the same, then the first name determines which comes first in the list. If the first and last names should be the same, then the middle initial determines the order.

EXERCISE 5

Which word comes first? (Oral response) Number your paper from 1 to 10. Then write the word in each pair that appears first in the dictionary.

1. cast — case	5. empty — empire	9. album — alarm
2. piece — pierce	6. money — mold	10. captain — canvas
3. arrive — article	7. reship — restless	
4. choke — chunk	8. finger — fitting	

EXERCISE 6

Arrange the following groups of words in alphabetical order.

Group One

1. dairy	5. progress	9. native
2. cable	6. airplane	10. steel
3. harbor	7. plain	11. weather
4. foreign	8. lumber	12. until

Group Two

1. mold	5. earth	9. seed
2. herb	6. air	10. decay
3. cell	7. volcano	11. blossom
4. steam	8. fog	12. pest

Group Three

1. bought	5. dozen	9. dime
2. bank	6. divide	10. deposit
3. bill	7. dollar	11. during
4. both	8. divisor	12. different

Knowing the significance of the guide words at the top of the pages is important for skillful use of the dictionary.

EXERCISE 7

Notice the two words in heavy black type at the top of each page in the dictionary. These are called *guide words*. The guide word at the left-hand side of the page indicates the first entry to be found on that page, at the top of the left-hand column. The guide word on the right-hand side of the page indicates the last entry on the page, at the bottom of the right-hand column.

The following two guide words appear at the top of a page in a dictionary: LIKABLE — LIMIT.

Below is a list of words. Choose from this list the words that you would find on this page and write them in alphabetical order below the guide words. You will have six words.

1. lime	5. lighthouse	9. linden
2. lightness	6. limelight	10. limp
3. life	7. lighten	11. lilac
4. like	8. lily	12. limb

EXERCISE 8

Copy the three headings and column of words shown below. Then refer to the dictionary and fill in the outline in the same way that the first line is filled in. Remember to use the guide words whenever you look for words in a dictionary.

Word	*Guide Words*	Page
1. office	odd — office	424
2. mail		
3. settle		
4. king		
5. flood		
6. soil		
7. wreck		
8. traffic		
9. discover		
10. hill		

EXERCISE 9

Beneath each set of guide words below there are six words. Write on your paper the number of each word that can be found on the dictionary pages represented by these guide words.

Group One

Guide words: BENEATH — BERMUDA
Words to choose from

1. benefit	3. beg	5. better
2. bend	4. belong	6. berry

Group Two

Guide words: HESITATE — HIGHLANDS
Words to choose from

1. hew	3. highly	5. hero
2. hesitancy	4. hide	6. height

Group Three

Guide words: CLAIM — CONDITION
Words to choose from

1. commence	3. conditions	5. column
2. concert	4. complain	6. clad

B. PRONUNCIATION

The teacher should explain the various aids to pronunciation given by dictionaries, such as syllabication, accents, and respelling with diacritical marks or symbols. Explanations similar to the following, and exercises 10 to 16, will be found helpful in teaching pupils to use these aids.

Dividing a word into syllables is an aid to pronouncing it. A syllable is a part of a word which can be pronounced by a single impulse of the voice. Words in dictionaries are usually printed with separating marks or spaces between syllables. If the pupil can pronounce each syllable, he can pronounce the entire word. In each syllable there is always one sounded vowel, and a word, therefore, has as many syllables as it has sounded vowels. Two vowels do not occur in one syllable unless they are pronounced as one sound.

EXERCISE 10

Here are several words with only one vowel. Put a ring around each vowel.

1. kind	4. lock	7. hatch	10. help
2. talk	5. fish	8. long	11. then
3. told	6. witch	9. word	12. mind

How many syllables in each word of the above list?

EXERCISE 11

Some words or syllables have two vowels but they sound as one. In each of the following words, circle the two vowels that sound as one.

1. clean
2. eight
3. seat
4. coat
5. moon
6. bread
7. health
8. fruit
9. mound
10. seek
11. neat
12. foot

EXERCISE 12

The following list contains one-, two-, and three-syllable words. Circle the one-syllable words; underline the two-syllable words; underline twice the three-syllable words. If in doubt consult your dictionary.

1. dinner
2. purse
3. unhappy
4. strength
5. oratory
6. journey
7. stiff
8. fellow
9. handkerchief
10. struck
11. engine
12. volcano
13. stout
14. correct
15. parasol

Understanding of syllabication will simplify the process of dividing words at the ends of lines of writing or printing, or the setting of words to music. When a word has two or more syllables it may be divided between any two syllables. A word of one syllable is never divided.

EXERCISE 13

Following is a list of words having from one to three syllables. In the columns provided show the one or two ways in which they may be divided at the end of a line. If the word has only one syllable, write nothing in the column spaces.

Word	*First division*	*Second division*	*Word*	*First division*	*Second division*
1. symbol			7. rebuttal		
2. liberty			8. imbecile		
3. pout			9. example		
4. excavate			10. ludicrous		
5. horizon			11. scent		
6. brigade			12. schedule		

Dictionaries use accent marks after the syllables which should be stressed when the word is spoken. If there is more than one stressed syllable in a word, for example as in the word *mod′ i fi ca′ tion* two accent marks are used, one heavier than the other. The first syllable in this word is emphasized a little more than the next two syllables and thus is marked with a light accent; the fourth syllable is to be emphasized more strongly than any of the others and is, therefore, marked with a heavier accent mark. This is called the primary accent. The lighter accent is called the secondary accent. Some dictionaries use a double accent mark for the secondary stress.

EXERCISE 14

Divide the following words into syllables and give the accent mark as found in the dictionary.

1. vacation (va ca′ tion)
2. industry (in′ dus try)
3. chivalry
4. consolidate
5. infection
6. anemia
7. retaliate
8. triangle
9. incarnate
10. posture
11. companion
12. merino

Since the same sound in English may be represented by different letters and the same letters are sometimes pronounced in different ways, it is necessary for dictionaries to "respell" the words for pronunciation by printing them with different or specially marked letters or symbols which show how the syllables are to be sounded. The standard dictionaries differ in the alphabets they use for respelling, and a still different international system of symbols has been invented for transliterating the sounds spoken in foreign languages. Thus, it is well for the student to notice and become familiar with the system used by his dictionary.

The respelled form of a word is usually printed in parentheses directly after the word or near the beginning of the entry. Lines, curves, dots, and other marks, called diacritical marks, are added to the letters to show that the syllables are to be sounded in the same way as those in familiar key words which are printed, with the same markings, across the bottom margin of each pair of facing pages of the dictionary. Silent letters are usually omitted. Pupils should be able to pronounce all the key words correctly in order to use them for guidance in pronouncing unfamiliar or more difficult words.

modest (mŏd′ ĭst)	fetch (fĕch)	severe (se vēr′)
lately (lāt′ lĭ)	dreamy (drēm′ ĭ)	buckskin (bŭk′ skĭn)

The marks for the long and short sounds are easy to remember. A straight line over any vowel shows that it "says its own name," as in tāpe, ēqual, īce, ōpen, and ūse. A u-shaped curve over a vowel means that the vowel is sounded short, as in căt, gĕt, ĭt, hŏt, and nŭt. As the pupil works with a dictionary he will become familiar with all of the diacritical markings.

EXERCISE 15

Respelling of words help especially in the pronunciation of words that contain unusual combinations of letters. Look up the respelling of this list.

Word	*Respelling*	*Word*	*Respelling*	*Word*	*Respelling*
1. blight		5. aisle		8. cough	
2. phonics		6. dough		9. quickly	
3. eight		7. engine		10. conquest	
4. though					

EXERCISE 16

This exercise combines some practice in the use of diacritical marks and key words. Separate the words into syllables, using the diacritical marks and the accents, and list the key words that help you in pronouncing each word.

Word	*Syllables and diacritical marks*	*Key words with diacritical marks*
Example: preparation	prĕp ȧ rā′ shŭn	ĕnd, sofȧ, āle, ŭp
1. examine		
2. bungalow		
3. starfish		
4. cloister		
5. pencil		
6. athlete		
7. program		
8. sheriff		
9. valley		
10. quack		

Providing information on the correct spelling of words is one of the most important functions of a dictionary. Two spellings may be given for the same word. The first spelling is the preferred one, and those who wish to be as accurate as possible will use that form.

C. WORD ORIGINS

The basis of the English language is Anglo-Saxon, or Old English, which was spoken in England hundreds of years ago. To the short and simple words of everyday Anglo-Saxon life were added the literary words of the Norman-French court. Words from many other lands and tongues have been added and adapted until English may be said to be the richest language in the world. Latin, Greek, and French have contributed more than four-fifths of the adopted words.

In America we can trace the influence of the Indians in the place names of many of our rivers, states, counties, and cities. Iowa, which is bounded on the east by the Mississippi River and on the west by the Missouri, provides a good example of their effect. Hominy, papoose, and moccasin are words that have come from the American Indian.

The Spanish settlers of the southern and western borders brought in words that we did well to adopt, since they have helped to enrich our language. We commonly use the words canyon, coyote, hammock, rodeo, and lariat which are of Spanish origin. In the parts of California first surveyed under the Spanish and Mexican land system, the Spanish or Indian names then given to the land-grants have continued prominent among present-day place names. Examples of these are San Pedro, Puente, Atascadero, and Napa.

The influence of the French is also noticeable in our language, especially in place names. Lake Champlain, and the cities of New Orleans, Saint Louis, Marquette, and Joliet were named for French royalty, explorers and priests. Many widely used words like bureau, garage, depot, levee, cafe, and bicycle come from the French language. The following suggestions may give teachers ideas for developing interest in word origins, with resulting vocabulary enrichment.

1. Pupils will enjoy learning the life history of picturesque words, as chapel, bacteria, bonfire, curfew, derrick, kodak, and muscle
2. Explain the symbols used in an unabridged dictionary and show how to trace the derivation of words
3. Encourage the more interested pupils to become collectors of word origins and to keep notebooks on the subject
4. Ask pupils who are studying foreign languages to bring lists of words that have been taken over into English unchanged from those languages. Language teachers can supply illustrative material.
5. Show how the varied contributions and influences of Latin, Greek, German, Scandinavian, French, Spanish, and other languages have made English "the richest language on earth today"
6. Conclude the study by showing that language is composite and flexible because words are vital, living things
7. Make specific class, group, or individual assignments such as the following exercise

EXERCISE 17

1. Explain that the basis of our language is Germanic.
2. Show how the Germanic base was enlarged during the periods of Danish, French, Roman, Greek influences in England.
3. Make an intensive study of the life history and shift in meaning of some special word. Write a paragraph about the word, including its derivation, its original meaning, and the present meaning.
4. Compile a set of word families from such parent words as *scribe, graph, vis, dict.*
5. Mention some foreign words that have been borrowed unchanged from other tongues.
6. Give the Greek or Roman myths which explain the derivation of the words tantalize, psychology, mercury, vulcanize, colossal, siren.
7. Show how the influence of the study of Latin is seen in the Preamble to the United States Constitution. Contrast this classical style with

that of the Gettysburg Address and King James' translation of the Lord's Prayer.

8. List a number of current words that would have puzzled Washington and Lincoln. (Rayon, radio, vitamin, stratosphere, cinema, spirituals, transformer.)
9. List a number of words that have arisen during the war and that may become permanent. (Blitz, jeep, "Mae West.")
10. Name some common nouns and also some geographical names in California that are distinctly Spanish. Give the meanings. (Rodeo, patio, plaza, arroyo, Los Angeles, San Diego, Redondo.)

D. PREFIXES, SUFFIXES, AND STEMS OF WORDS

In most cases, instruction in the use of prefixes, suffixes, and stems should start informally, using an actual instance from whatever reading is being done as a starting point. Formal work in recognition of prefixes, suffixes, roots, and stems should be undertaken only after pupils have been led to understand how such study will benefit them.

The teacher should have his own lists of prefixes, suffixes, and roots so that he can be sure to introduce important ones.[8]

Instruction should begin with easy, obvious prefixes and roots. Suffixes are difficult, and should be left until later. Words which are familiar to pupils should be used first. Scientific terms are usually best. Everyone knows that a *motor* and an *automobile* both *move*, although in different ways. It is not hard to establish, *mot- mov- mob-* as a root meaning *move.*

The stem *terra-* meaning *earth*, is easy to teach. The word *territory*, *ter*rain, and *ter*restrial offer little trouble. On the other hand, a prefix such as *ad-* with its numerous variations (a, ac, ag, al, an, ap, ar, as, at) should not be presented until pupils have begun to acquire some facility in word analysis.

Long lists of words or syllables are apt to be discouraging, particularly to pupils who do not read well. It is much more important that a pupil understand the *method* of word analysis and know a few important examples well than that he have a full notebook.

Colorful, interesting illustrations should be used whenever possible. Pupils will remember that the word *pecuniary* is concerned with money if they know that it is derived from a Latin word meaning cattle, and that cattle were at one time a medium of exchange. Similarly, even the slower pupils will show interest in the information that the word *candidate* comes from *candida*, meaning white; that in Rome candidates for office wore white togas to show the purity of their intentions.

[8] Donald D. Durrell, *Improvement of Basic Reading Abilities.* Yonkers-on-Hudson, New York: World Book Company, 1940, pp. 202–203.

Exercises which provide practice in using prefixes, suffixes, and stems are given below. These exercises may be adapted to the needs of a particular class.

a. Prefixes

EXERCISE 18

1. Write words meaning
   a. paid before . . . .
   b. a view before, such as the advance showing of a motion picture. . . . . You will see that you have made new words by adding the prefix *pre* to a simple word.
2. Make a list of ten words that start with *pre.*

a.	f. . . . .
b.	g. . . . .
c.	h. . . . .
d.	i. . . . .
e.	j. . . . .

EXERCISE 19

Use the prefixes *ex* or *in* to make words with the following meanings:

a. goods sent out of a country . . . .
b. goods taken into a country . . . .
c. a person sent away from his native land . . . .
d. a pupil turned out of school for bad behavior . . . .
e. a foreign army entering our country . . . .

EXERCISE 20

Judging from the following words, what do you think the prefix *de* means? Write the meaning after each word. Use the dictionary, if necessary.

a. demerit . . . .
b. denounce . . . .
c. deprive . . . .
d. descend . . . .
e. decline . . . .

EXERCISE 21

The prefix *con* means *with* or *together*. You can see this prefix in the word *conductor*. A conductor is a person who goes along *with* (con) the passengers to *lead* (duc) them on the trip. *Underline* the prefix in the following words and tell what each means.

a. conclude . . . .
b. conform . . . .
c. condense . . . .
d. conduct . . . .
e. consists . . . .
f. connect . . . .
g. construct . . . .

Words beginning with *con* are common. How many can you list in three minutes?

Exercises similar to the preceding, using the prefixes *im*, *un*, *dis*, *etc.*, may be constructed.

b. Suffixes

A *suffix* is one or more letters or syllables placed at the end of a word to add to its meaning.

EXERCISE 22

Can you guess what the suffix *able* means by studying these words?

a. usable	d. lovable ....
b. teachable	e. portable ....
c. adorable	f. eatable ....

In these words, the suffix *able* means *that can be, able or deserving to be.* Therefore, the word *usable* means that which can be used or is capable of being used; a teachable person is one who *can be taught.*

EXERCISE 23

Separate the words listed above (Exercise 22) into root and suffix.

EXAMPLE: (a) use + able = usable (d)
(b) (e)
(c) (f)

EXERCISE 24

1. Add the suffix *ness* to each of the following words.
2. Give the meaning of the new word thus formed.
3. Use the word in a sentence.

a. cool ....
....
b. cranky ....
....
c. harsh ....
....

c. Stems

The stems or root words are the basic words before which prefixes may be placed and after which suffixes may be added to make new words of somewhat different meanings.

EXERCISE 25

By adding a prefix and a suffix, form two additional words from each of the following stem words according to the example at the top of the list.

Prefix	*Stem*	*Suffix*
*im*possible	possible	possibility
....	1. mature	....
....	2. pay	....
....	3. form	....
....	4. help	....

....	5. pass	....
....	6. suit	....
....	7. falter	....
....	8. perish	....
....	9. mount	....
....	10. cognize	....
....	11. doubt	....
....	12. friend	....

To encourage mastery of a wider vocabulary one author suggests making a 3″ × 5″ index card file. On each card is entered a prefix, suffix, or root (see sample card below).

> *re* — means *again, back.*
>
> review We will *review* the chapter.
>
> repeat They *repeat* the pledge.
>
> recede The tide *recedes. — etc.*

The teacher may arbitrarily assign prefixes, suffixes, or roots. Five sentences for each may be required for one day's work. These sentences need not be composed by the pupil. As he discovers words containing the assigned prefixes in his textbook or library book, he may record these words on his card, together with the sentences in which they occurred. Capitalization, punctuation, and spelling should, of course, be correct.

E. SYNONYMS, ANTONYMS, AND HOMONYMS

The more recently published reading books make provision for the study of synonyms, antonyms, and homonyms as important phases of reading.

Synonyms. Synonyms are words which express essentially the same idea but often have shades of difference in meaning. Even though they are alike in a general sense, they may have, in discriminating usage, special meanings or connotations. Pupils should note that dictionaries use synonyms in defining words. The following suggestions for preparation of exercises may be helpful.

1. Write in a column on the blackboard from a reading selection 10 difficult words which have simple synonyms. Write also, but in different order, one synonym for each of the 10 difficult words. Beside each word in the first column have the pupils write the synonym in a second column.

EXAMPLE:	*First column*	*Second column*
	labyrinthine	winding

This type of matching exercise can be used with antonyms.

2. Write sentences on the blackboard from a reading selection containing groups of words for which synonyms can be supplied. Underline the groups of words. For each underlined expression, pupils will choose an appropriate synonym, rewriting the sentences.

   EXAMPLE: *Little by little* he crept up the hill.
   Gradually he crept up the hill.

3. Choose an article from the reading material. Write on the blackboard a list of words chosen from the article. Tell pupils to rewrite this article, substituting synonyms for the words listed on the blackboard.
4. Write on the blackboard, or mimeograph, the following words, telling pupils to rearrange them into five groups of synonyms:

ample	conference	gathering	meeting	raw
abundant	congregation	green	proficient	specialist
assembly	crude	impel	profuse	thrust
authority	elbow	lavish	propel	unprepared
bounteous	expert	master	push	untrained

EXAMPLE: Group 1 — ample, abundant, bounteous, lavish, profuse

Antonyms. Antonyms are words which are opposite or nearly opposite in meaning. Knowledge of antonyms should aid pupils to become more accurate in expressing ideas. Dictionaries often give antonyms as well as synonyms in defining words. The following types of exercises are useful in studying antonyms.

1. Write on the blackboard, for word study, a group of 10 or 15 words. Have pupils write an antonym for each opposite it.

   EXAMPLE: abolish — establish

2. List 10 words to be matched with antonyms. Alongside each of these, write a group of five words, one of which is an antonym for the listed word. Pupils are to select the antonym from each group.

EXAMPLE: scrupulous — balanced, infirm, pompous, unprincipled, stupid
ANSWER: scrupulous — unprincipled

Homonyms. A homonym is a word having the same pronunciation as another word but differing in origin or meaning and often in spelling. Part of the difficulty for both slow and rapid readers in comprehending what they read is inaccuracy in the recognition of words which closely resemble others in spelling but differ from them in meaning. The following exercises are suggested for study of homonyms.

1. Mimeograph or write on the blackboard 25 or 30 sentences

to be completed by choosing one from two or more given homonyms.

EXAMPLE: 1. He was (aloud, allowed) to go early.
2. Electrical devices (lesson, lessen) work.

2. Mimeograph or write on the blackboard one word from each of 40 or 50 pairs or groups of homonyms. Have pupils copy these words on paper, writing at least one homonym for each, being sure to spell it correctly and know its meaning; then using the two in sentences.

EXAMPLE: 1. fete
2. doe
3. serial

ANSWERS: 1. fete — fate. I attended a religious fete.
The prisoner does not know his fate.
2. doe — dough. The doe protected her fawn.
The cookie dough is ready.
3. serial — cereal. The story is appearing as a serial in that magazine.
Oatmeal is my favorite cereal.

Reading Comprehension

A. RECOGNIZING CENTRAL IDEAS

A major skill in reading comprehension is the ability to recognize the main ideas in what is read and to distinguish them from the supporting details. The suggestions given here for helping pupils to develop the ability to select the central thought and subordinate topics are offered merely as provocators to other effective and more varied devices.

1. Select material within the range of the experience and interest and at the general reading ability level of the pupil. In the early stages, stories and pictures and other visual aids have a greater appeal and convey more clearly the themes and main ideas than do factual texts, which may be introduced later.
2. Use the title and paragraph or section headings as clues in discovering the chief thought.
   a. Have the pupils make questions for each heading. By making such questions for studying the section, the pupil has set up a purpose for his reading.
   b. Have the pupils invent their own titles for the material being read.
   c. Encourage pupils to write subject headings for reports and similar materials.

3. Have pupils read to discover the central thought by finding the key sentence and carefully following the thought from sentence to sentence. This not only helps pupils to grasp the main idea of the paragraph, but also to understand the author's plan. Oral reading is usually helpful in the first stages of finding key sentences and understanding the paragraph pattern.
4. Prepare a list of sentences that contain the idea expressed in a paragraph. Have the pupils select the sentence that best expresses the main thought of the paragraph.
5. Choose from material that is being read by the pupils several paragraphs that contain good key sentences. Write the key sentences on the blackboard. Have the pupils find the paragraph from which each was taken.
6. Provide a series of paragraphs each followed by several possible headings, one of them correct, one too inclusive, and one or two which are misleading or contain misstated facts. Have the pupils select the correct heading and give their reasons for their choice.
7. To help pupils understand the concept of reporting main ideas with brevity, the following exercises are good.
   a. Have pupils write telegrams conveying different types of messages.
   b. Train pupils to write one or two sentences as summaries of a motion picture, a selection from a book, a newspaper article, or a group discussion. This exercise also provides excellent training in expressing the author's ideas in the pupil's own words.

B. SELECTING DETAILS

The following suggestions are offered for training pupils to read for details.

1. Discuss the function of details as important additions to the central idea.
2. The detective approach of looking for clues and thinking about their relationship to the problem appeals to many pupils.
3. From an article in a current magazine or a section in a textbook, prepare a list of objective statements, varied in nature, such as are used in completion, multiple choice, and true-false tests.

EXAMPLE

Reference: Lester B. Rogers, Fay Adams, and Walker Brown. *Story of Nations*. New York: Henry Holt and Co. 1945. pp. 172–5.

Questions:

1. "Rome was well protected from pirates." True or false?
2. One slave constantly whispers this caution: "Remember thou art a ...." Supply the missing word to complete the thought.
3. "The laurel wreath is (golden or silver)." Choose the correct word.
4. List the following according to their order in the procession:

The trumpeters	The spoils of war	The prisoners
The senators	The oxen	The conqueror

C. FINDING FACTS

The ability to find facts speedily and to answer questions adequately and accurately are skills which are indispensable in the mastery of any subject. The pupil will use these techniques daily in getting facts from the newspaper, in locating data in the encyclopedia, in finding suitable definitions in the dictionary, and in drawing inferences and evaluating statements in a textbook in social studies, science, or English classes. Rapid reading or skimming or even slow reading may be the appropriate technique, depending upon the material and the objective.

The expert reader will probably first read the questions which serve as clues to the facts he is seeking. He will then read the material with energy and singleness of purpose, pursuing his search persistently until he has ferreted out the desired facts. When he thinks he has attained his objective, he will recheck with the questions to insure accuracy. Many textbooks supply helpful questions to direct the pupil in his study, but often the teacher will wish to formulate his own.

The teacher of reading may find suggestions in the following questions which may be used as fact-finding drills or as class exercises.

1. Finding a specific fact in a reference book.

REFERENCE: *The World Almanac*, "Aviation."
QUESTIONS: What was the increase in the number of fatal accidents in 1939 over those in 1935? Was there an increase or decrease in miles flown per fatal accident between those years? How much?

2. Interpreting the legend accompanying an illustration.

REFERENCE: Lester B. Rogers, Fay Adams, and Walker Brown. *Story of Nations*. New York: Henry Holt and Co. 1945, p. 263.
QUESTION: At the tournament, who occupied the box on the left?

3. Using the index.

REFERENCE: Rogers, *et al. Story of Nations*. p. 565.
QUESTION: To what Scandinavian country are we indebted for the idea of manual training?

4. Skimming to find word answers.

REFERENCE: Frieda Radke. *Living Words*. New York: The Odyssey Press. 1940. pp. 73–74.

QUESTIONS: 1. What serves better than fingers in the handling of postage stamps in a collection?
2. What is the best kind of stamp album for the amateur collector?
3. How many foreign stamps may be purchased for a dollar?

5. Getting specific information.

REFERENCE: Charles Dickens. *A Tale of Two Cities*.

QUESTIONS: 1. What three reasons were given by Charles Darnay, in his conversation with his uncle, for his intention to renounce his inheritance?
2. Give the date (the month and year) when the Dover mail coach toiled up Shooter's Hill.

REFERENCE: *Weekly News Review*. February 26, 1945, page 1.

QUESTION: At the Crimean Conference what decision was made as to who should represent each of the Big Three on the Board of Control of Germany after World War II?

6. Drawing inferences.

REFERENCE: Rogers, *et al*. *Story of Nations*. pp. 721–2.

QUESTION: In what respect is "The Christ of the Andes" a symbol of international fellowship?

REFERENCE: Charles Dickens. *A Tale of Two Cities*. Book II, Chapter VIII.

QUESTION: Who do you think was the man dangling by the chain under the carriage of the marquis?

D. RELATING SUBORDINATE DETAILS TO MAIN IDEAS

Understanding of the relationship of subordinate details to the main thought is necessary in order for the reader to comprehend fully what is read and studied.

Attempting to understand the designs of paragraphs in a selection will aid the pupil in thinking and will help him to improve both his comprehension and speed in reading. The pupil who has been trained to grasp the pattern of a paragraph or of a longer article will understand the true relationship of detail to main ideas. The following exercises help to develop this skill.

1. Select paragraphs or selections that describe details in chronological order.
   a. Have pupils list the steps of a process or a series of events in order. It is frequently helpful to indicate the number of steps.
   b. List the events of a story on the blackboard. Have pupils

rearrange these incidents in the order in which they occurred in the story.

2. Find selections that use *contrast*. Have the pupils divide a paper into two columns and then list in these columns the contrasting points that clarify the situation.
3. Find selections that use the *question and answer* pattern. Have the pupils list each question and beneath it write the important details that answer the question.
4. Select paragraph patterns commonly used in your subject field and train pupils to recognize them and to read them proficiently.
5. Relate reading and the study of the paragraph to speaking and writing by having the pupils use these common patterns in their own oral and written expression.

One of the most frequently used plans for organizing materials is the outline. The following suggestions are offered to assist teachers in guiding their pupils to develop proficiency in outlining.[9]

1. Use easy materials and short selections in teaching pupils the mechanics of outlining. The following steps may be followed in teaching pupils to make outlines.
   a. Teacher and pupils working together select the main topics
   b. Pupils, unaided, select the main topics
   c. Teacher and pupils select the main topics, leaving space for subheads. Teacher and pupils then fill in these subtopics.
   d. Main topics are selected by the teachers and pupils and are written on the blackboard. Pupils then fill in the subtopics unaided.
   e. Pupils write the main topics and subheads without help
   f. Pupils organize, in outline form, data gathered from many sources
2. Train pupils to find the main topics and to place them in outline form. Use books with paragraph headings.
   a. Have pupils read the paragraphs and discuss the headings. Suggest other possible headings and have pupils decide why the author selected the headings he used
   b. Match a given list of paragraph headings with numbered paragraphs
   c. Have pupils read a paragraph with this question in mind, "What is the main idea in this paragraph?" Write a

[9] Based on "How to Teach Pupils to Outline," *Teachers' Guide to Child Development in the Intermediate Grades.* Prepared under the direction of the California State Curriculum Commission. Sacramento: California State Department of Education, 1936, pp. 294–5.

number of suggested answers on the blackboard. Choose the best one.

3. Provide practice in filling in subtopics
   a. The teacher writes the main topics on the board or uses a text that has the main headings. Teacher and pupils then fill in the subheads.
   b. Have pupils skim other articles for more information and read carefully when additional material which is suitable for subheads is found. Add these new subheads. Do the same for new main topics.
   c. When pupils have gathered sufficient data, have them reread the complete outline and, if necessary, rearrange the order of the topics
4. Give instructions in making a standard outline form. Many secondary-school pupils do not know how to make an outline. Emphasize the fact that in a correct outline there must always be more than one item in the series under any subdivision. If there is an "a" there must also be a "b"; if there is a "1" there must also be a "2," etc. A commonly accepted outline pattern is the one given below.

OUTLINE PATTERN

I.
A.
1.
a.
(1)
(a)
(b)
(2)
(a)
(b)
b.
(1)
(2)
2.
a.
b.
B.
1.
2.
II.
A.
B.
etc.

5. Have pupils use this outline form in preparing and giving oral reports.

6. To develop ability to draw valid conclusions, have pupils use facts and ideas which have been organized in outline form, not only as a basis for an oral report or as an exercise in outlining a chapter, but also as the basis for drawing conclusions.
7. To check pupils' ability to make outlines, prepare lessons based on the following suggestions.
   a. List main points and subpoints consecutively. Have pupils copy these, indenting to show subordination of subtopics and writing correct numbers and letters in front of each point.
   b. List main topics and subtopics in mixed order and have pupils rearrange and number them
   c. List main topics with Roman numerals. List subtopics (all one value) with Arabic numerals. Have pupils organize subpoints under correct main points.
   d. Present short paragraphs of well-organized material and have pupils write main topics and specified number of subtopics
   e. Present part of a skeleton outline and have students complete it
   f. Have pupils outline a problem without assistance. Class discussion is valuable in checking a lesson of this type.

E. ASSEMBLING INFORMATION

The organization of notes into a coherent composition involves not only all of the reading skills but techniques of writing as well. Obviously, emphasis on this phase of the work is appropriate only for bright and mature pupils. The method of gathering information depends upon the purpose of the assignment. If the report assigned is to be short and informal, the reading of only one well-selected article may suffice and the notes may be brief. The first reading may be a rapid one. The pupil will then return to the article for a more thorough survey, taking notes on the data he wishes to use.

If the assignment involves a longer, more formal report, the pupil will find it desirable to go to the library for study. First, he will find what information is available and suitable by consulting such guides as a card catalog, the index, and the table of contents of books, the *Readers' Guide*, and an encyclopedia. After selecting from the references those that seem pertinent to his subject, he will proceed to read the articles and to take notes. The following suggestions for the taking of notes may prove helpful.

1. Use cards 3×5 inches or uniform half sheets of paper. Write on one side only.

2. Head each card with a single topic. Give the name of the author, the title of the book, and the pages.
3. Make notes brief but intelligible.
4. Develop a system of abbreviations of your own.
5. Do not copy the material word for word; try to summarize and state the author's ideas in your own words.
6. If you wish to copy an excerpt, you must give credit to the author quoted.

After this study has been completed, there comes the more complicated task of assembling the information given in the notes and of organizing the material into an article. Some such procedure as the following may be followed.

1. Reread your notes and decide on four or five main points.
2. Arrange the cards in piles, one pile for each of these main ideas.
3. Eliminate any irrelevant material.
4. Arrange the main points in an orderly sequence.
5. Arrange as subtopics the material of subordinate importance.
6. Make an outline, which is the blueprint of the article or composition.
7. Revise the outline, observing especially the proper sequence of the subtopics.

The construction of the composition is next. Suggestions follow.

1. Follow the outline.
2. Refer to your notes, but be careful not to copy the words of the author. Express his ideas in your own words.
3. Express your ideas as well as the author's.
4. Use footnotes when giving credit to an author.
5. In the conclusion of your composition you may give a brief summary of the main ideas, or draw your own conclusions.

An important part in the process of compiling a report is the preparation of a bibliography of reference materials to be consulted or to be recommended for further reading on the subject. The following form for a bibliography is suggested:

SUGGESTED FORM FOR BIBLIOGRAPHY

Article in Reference Book

"Advertising — United States." *Encyclopaedia Britannica*, Fourteenth Edition. 1929. Vol. I, pp. 200–205.

Book

Adams, James Truslow. *The Epic of America*. Boston: Little, Brown and Company. 1931.

Leonard, J. Paul, and Salisbury, Rachel. *Considering the Meaning*. Chicago: Scott, Foresman and Company. 1941.

Magazine Article

"Greece." *Time*, Vol. XIV. (January 8, 1945), pp. 25–28.

Thompson, Dorothy. "Freedom in Duty," *Ladies Home Journal*. Vol. LVIII. (July, 1941), pp. 6–10.

F. DRAWING INFERENCES AND FORMING CONCLUSIONS

While the teacher in a development reading program is always alert to all possible ways of encouraging the pupil to read, he must at the same time teach the pupil that not everything he sees in print is true. He must be taught to discriminate between mere statement and substantiated fact, between partial truths and the whole truth, between personal opinion and news.

The end product of education is all too often the acquisition of information; comparatively little stress is placed upon the use of this information. Few people deny the greatness of the philosophy and the literary quality of the Bible, of Shakespeare, of Homer, and of the other true classics, but how many readers really use the wisdom of these masterpieces as a basis for action in daily life? The application of information or learning, therefore, must be taught in the home and in the school.

The seventh-grade pupil as well as the high-school senior can be taught to draw inferences and form conclusions. The adolescent can be taught that what he calls his "good reasons" for certain actions are not actually his "real reasons." He can be taught that making excuses for his own shortcomings is a form of self-deception. He can be taught to see the difference between editorial opinion and news, between a half truth and a whole truth, and between propaganda and fact. He can be taught to question the source and completeness of his information; he can be taught to conceive of a subject in its entirety according to the organization inherent in the subject. The more able the pupil, the more important it is that he receive this guidance.

In talking with the pupil about a movie or book, the teacher can point out qualities of character that have led to the climax. He can teach the pupil that the plot is especially important when it reveals character. He can show how the setting is allied to the plot, and he can teach the pupil to enjoy outcomes that are appropriate even though they are not necessarily happy.

Through outlining, the pupil can be taught organization. Probably the seventh-grade pupil should learn to classify items first; then he might learn to outline factual material such as biographical accounts. In each succeeding grade the outlines can be made more complete and more perfect in form, and they can be about more abstract subjects. By the time he is graduated from senior high school, the average pupil should be able to make a three-margin outline about a current social problem, drawing his own conclusions. Such topics as ships, a ship, apartment houses, an apartment, automobiles, an automobile, factories, a factory, education, a school, housing, a home, and innumerable other topics offer several possible kinds of outlines. The pupil should be quick to see these possibilities and to apply the principles he has learned to more specific subjects.

Much in great literature is implied rather than stated directly. For instance, in *Les Miserables* the opening thirty pages are a treatise on man's inhumanity to man; indeed the whole story is that, yet nowhere in this novel does Hugo preach. In *A Tale of Two Cities*, the precept set forth in the fifteenth chapter of The Gospel of St. John is given dramatic force. In *Silas Marner*, the miser's redemption is hinted at in the incident of the broken water crock, and it is assured with the discovery of Eppie. In *The Keys of the Kingdom*, the contrast between the worldly priest and the self-sacrificing priest is full of implications for the reader. These points must be understood by the immature reader so that he may draw the correct inference. The pupil must also be encouraged to identify himself imaginatively with the chief characters of the story, the poem, or the play which he is reading. He must be one of the Knights of the Round Table, one of Robin Hood's men, one of Chaucer's pilgrims if he is to understand fully the implications of the author.

The enjoyment of poetry is dependent, to a large extent, upon the pupil's ability to interpret what is not expressed, but for the reader to supply from his own experience or imagination, or both. Note Edwin Markham's famous lines:

> He drew a circle that shut me out –
> Heretic, rebel, a thing to flout,
> But Love and I had the wit to win:
> We drew a circle that took him in.[10]

This quatrain, one commonly taught in American literature, is often quoted by pupils. Yet of what is the first circle composed? Why was the "me" shut out? How could Love win by drawing a second and supposedly larger circle? Each reader must answer these and other questions according to his experience and his imagination. His interpretation will change as the years bring him increased experience, knowledge, personal suffering, and understanding. The teacher can only inspire and point the way in drawing these inferences.

Pupils should be warned against false analogies. Because two

[10] Edwin Markham, *The Shoes of Happiness, and Other Poems*. Garden City, Doubleday, Doran and Company, 1915, p. 1.

objectives or two ideas have one or two points in common, the young pupil often assumes that they are alike in many or all of their aspects.

> Analogy reasons from particular case to particular case: if something is true of one thing, it is true of a second thing that resembles the first. It is a useful, easy, and dangerous form of reasoning. In a case like that the foregoing, dealing with something not susceptible to proof, with what one does not or can not know, one resorts to the nearest parallel within one's experience — what one does know.[11]

The pupil can learn to detect fallacious reasoning by analyzing statements like the following:

"Every cloud has a silver lining."
"It's a long lane that has no turning."

One of the best exercises for learning to think clearly, to draw correct inferences, and to make sound conclusions is précis writing. It is an excellent means of overcoming inaccurate and inadequate reading habits. The student learns concentration by following the line of reasoning of the author. If his attention wanders, this line of reasoning is broken. To make a précis is also a valuable exercise in analysis, for the student must discover and follow the writer's plan. He must keep the same tone, the same emphasis, and the same proportion as did the author. He must learn to differentiate between main ideas and illustrative details. He must recognize key words, and he must express the ideas in terms of his own. In general, a précis should be about a third as long as the original. Précis writing is useful in note-taking, in making book reports, in public speaking, in making committee reports, and in briefing. In fact, the pupil must realize that there is an almost universal demand for ability to condense knowledge and summarize facts. The following simple directions will aid the pupil in writing a good précis:

1. He must read the passage carefully to be sure that he understands it
2. He should reread the passage, selecting the main ideas in the order in which they are given
3. He should then select the supporting ideas for each main topic
4. He is next ready to write the précis in complete, well-balanced sentences — main ideas must be expressed in independent clauses; supporting ideas, in dependent clauses
5. He should revise for brevity by:
    a. Substituting words or phrases for clauses whenever possible

[11] Frank W. Cushwa and Robert N. Cunningham. *Ways of Thinking and Writing*. New York: Charles Scribner's Sons, 1938, pp. 365–66.

b. Using synonyms for long phrases
c. Replacing figurative language by literal expression [12]

The foregoing suggestions for helping the pupil to form inferences and to draw conclusions are in no sense complete. They should, however, serve as an introduction to some of the simpler problems of psychology and logic. The able senior pupil who plans to go to a university is eager to understand himself and his thought processes, but he must be warned that such work as can be studied in advanced high-school courses is, at best, only introductory. He should also be warned against pseudo-scientific psychologists and over-popularized personality specialists.

G. REMEMBERING WHAT IS READ

Using what they have studied will help pupils in remembering what they have read. Preliminary difficulties in the way of comprehension of a selection, such as vocabulary, having been cleared up, pupils can be taught how to take notes by finding central ideas, key words, or clues to the topic under discussion. If real interest can be gathered by bringing up a problem which gives pupils something with which to associate, compare, or contrast what they are about to read, they will be more likely to remember it.

> Mature students often take note rather than take notes. They prefer to gather information directly on a problem rather than to take notes on general reading in the hope that some day the facts recorded may come in handy. Adults . . . attempt . . . to incorporate the new ideas they gain from reading into the patterns of their thinking so that those ideas will later function in conversation, in the solution of problems, and in further reading.[13]

School can imitate real life if the teacher can make the problem clear, immediate, and interesting and then devise methods for having the pupils use information in an active and memorable way. If a series of questions to be answered precedes the assignment, the pupil usually skips over material until he finds the answers, unless, as in some types of reading matter, the questions can be so phrased that a critical reading of the whole selection is necessary in order to find the answer. Here again, the value of association in remembering can be taught by asking pupils to bring examples from their own experience, reading, or current events similar to what they have read.

[12] Adapted from Angela M. Broening, Frederick H. Law, Mary S. Wilkinson, and Caroline L. Ziegler, *Reading for Skill*. New York: Noble and Noble, 1939, pp. 196–97.

[13] Ruth Strang, with the assistance of Florence C. Rose. *Problems in the Improvement of Reading in High School and College*. Lancaster, Pennsylvania: The Science Press Printing Co., 1938, p. 49.

As has been said earlier, learning to write a précis is perhaps the most valuable technique by which pupils may acquire ability to comprehend and reorganize for themselves what they have read. The organization of facts helps the pupil both to see their relationship and to remember them easily. Hence, the making of outlines is useful in social studies and science classes. In these subjects, many pupils fail to remember the material they read because they merely skim instead of reading reflectively. Care in making the assignment, such as promoting reflective thinking by discussion before the reading, teaching pupils to read and understand directions before answering and, later, care in conducting exercises requiring critical interpretation of what they have read will improve their study habits.

H. FOLLOWING ORAL AND WRITTEN DIRECTIONS

People who live in a civilization which is as highly mechanized as ours must be able to follow directions quickly and accurately in order to earn a living, to use the machines which are a part of almost every home, and to preserve themselves from bodily and financial harm. Specific teaching, then, is essential in this field.

In the first place, the objective of the teaching must be made clear to the pupils. If they do not see *why* it is important to them personally to be able to follow directions, many of the exercises they will be asked to do will probably seem to be merely unreasonable, artificial chores devised by the teacher to keep them busy. On the other hand, pupils enjoy and profit from drills when they feel that these are contributing to their welfare.

Exercises such as those in the following paragraphs have proved useful in helping pupils learn to follow directions exactly. After obtaining class co-operation, the teacher should insist from the beginning that *no* mistakes can be allowed. The pupil must see that a very small error in adjusting a machine may mean the difference between danger and safety. The first directions to be followed may well be given orally:

1. John, open the third window from the left and walk down the middle aisle on the way back to your seat.
2. Write the date on the board, Mary; then write your first name over it and your last name under it.
3. Erase the third sentence on the East blackboard, Helen, and then bring me the first dictionary on the second shelf of the bookcase.

The first written exercises in the following directions should be simple:

1. Find a picture of an anchor in the dictionary. Write the num-

ber of the page on your paper. Draw circle around the number.

2. Draw as many short, up-and-down lines on your paper as you have fingers.
3. Write your first name. Under it, print the day of the week.

No more than ten sets of directions like the above should be given at one time. Young or slow-learning pupils probably should not get more than five at a time. The teacher must watch, when working with pupils of very limited ability, to see that the time devoted to the exercises does not exceed their span of attention.

After reasonable mastery of simple, oral and written directions, instruction in the performance of practical tasks should be given, even if the actual processes cannot be reproduced in an English class. Discussion will have to replace the baking of a cake, for example. However, the teacher of home economics may well use the same types of devices for improving reading in her classes.

Pupils will respond enthusiastically to requests that they bring in recipes, instructions for assembling model planes, and directions for mixing paint, using starch, and doing similar household jobs. Discussion of the possible results, both amusing and serious, which may follow a mistake in interpreting these instructions can furnish vivid examples of the need for accuracy.

One method of teaching pupils to be attentive to oral directions is to read to the class a short, simple passage of factual material. Warn the pupils that the paragraphs will be read only once. Then give simple questions that can be answered orally in one word. These, too, should be read only once. The first time such drill is tried, the results are likely to be appallingly bad. Usually the class asks for another chance at once. This time the pupils really listen, and the results are heartening to them and to the teacher.

Ten minutes a day for a week or so can profitably be devoted to this procedure. Then actual instructions can be given orally, in place of asking questions on material which has been heard by the class. Again, the directions should be given once only, since it is important to establish the habit of listening attentively.

It is better to spend a few minutes a day over a long period of time on such drill than it is to have a few long lessons and then drop the subject. The important objectives are to establish the correct attitude toward the following of instructions or directions and to give enough drill and practice to build habits of attention and accuracy. Much practice, in small doses, is usually the best way to accomplish both of these objectives.

Most of the books devoted to the improvement of reading have chapters on following directions, since it is a basic skill. Specific practice exercises are sometimes supplied. These are helpful in suggesting methods to the teacher, but most teachers will find it worthwhile to make their own drills, using materials which are interesting to the particular group of pupils for whom they are intended. Teachers of science, social studies, and fine and practical arts, all may use such devices to sharpen the attention and improve the reading skill of pupils in their classes.

I. DEVELOPING ABILITY TO READ CRITICALLY

For those pupils who can do so, it is important to develop the ability to read with discrimination. To help pupils learn to read critically, teachers should set up situations which the pupils feel have importance for them; should make them feel enthusiasm for wanting to know more about books, magazines, and newspapers; and should stimulate their curiosity and help to create in them a desire for enjoyment of reading and for analyzing what they read.

Teaching pupils how to select reading materials is one of the first responsibilities of the teacher who is trying to train pupils to read critically. Books should be selected for a variety of pupils' interests, both expressed and potential. Pupils should be encouraged to read books of all kinds selected for various reasons.

1. Some books for enjoyment only
2. Modern books which give a picture of the current scene
3. Books recommended by teachers and other pupils
4. Books by well-known authors
5. Biographies vitalizing various fields, like history and science
6. Books of vocational interest
7. Books by authors of other books which the pupil has enjoyed
8. Books that have been filmed recently
9. Books which bear a relationship to extracurricular activities

Magazines which are within the intellectual grasp of the individual and which are related to the curriculum and the pupil's interests should be recommended. The fields listed below are covered very well by current magazines.

Science	Music	Homemaking
Literature	Hobbies	Sports
Current events	Vocations	Arts and crafts
Travel		

To help develop critical analysis in magazine reading, the following questions may be useful guides.

1. What is the policy of the magazine?
2. Are the articles controversial?
3. Is the material presented simply and clearly?
4. Does the magazine give courageous opinions in politics and economics?
5. Do the articles help you to enjoy experiences vicariously?

The following standards for selecting newspapers may well be taught, and pupils should be encouraged to read newspapers regularly.

1. Is the paper dependable?
2. Is it accurate?
3. Is it fair?

To be able to form critical judgments of a newspaper, pupils may appraise it by means of answers to the following questions.

1. Does it cover the news adequately?
2. Does it cover the news in an interesting way?
3. Does it comment or editorialize in a fair way?
4. Does it serve the community?
5. Does it help to solve problems?
6. Does it entertain, amuse, and give you enjoyment?
7. What is its reputation for reliability?

In order for pupils to develop a critical point of view toward what is read, they should be trained to ask thoughtful questions about the book or selection read. They should be taught to interpret and evaluate the material according to their own personal points of view. The teacher should help them to analyze what is read in order to distinguish between what is true and what is false, and should help them to get the definite purpose, the correct meaning, and the broad view which may underlie the presentation.

J. INCREASING RATE OF READING

The following six suggestions are made to teachers who want to encourage pupils to increase their skill in this area.

1. Build an interest in reading
2. Encourage each pupil to read as much as he can
3. Help the pupils determine how rapidly they are able to read
4. Discuss the importance of rapid reading, and interest pupils in undertaking a program to improve their reading rates
5. Once or twice each week . . . hold timed reading practice periods
6. Help each pupil make habitual his improved rate of reading [14]

Various devices for timing reading and for charting the results may be found in textbooks devoted to improvement of reading skill. Most pupils do best when they can watch their progress and see the results of their efforts. Keeping of individual records seems to be a necessary part of any successful program. A few devices which are useful in helping the pupil to increase his reading rate are given below:

[14] From *Teaching Reading in the Secondary School*, Bulletin of the California State Department of Education, Vol. XII, No. 3, March, 1943, pp. 17–23.

1. Give the pupil an explanation of causes of slow reading rate, such as too brief eye-span, reversals, and bad habits in eye movement
2. The teacher may read aloud with the pupil, gradually increasing the *tempo* and, thus, forcing the pupil to read faster
3. Have the pupils follow by pointing with markers as the teacher reads aloud to the group
4. Teach the pupil techniques of skimming and finding main points
5. Insist on the elimination of vocalizing in silent reading (inner speech, lip reading)
6. Train pupils to develop reading rates appropriate to different types of materials read
7. Use timed reading drills. The following procedures for "timed reading" have been found to be effective in helping the pupil to read more rapidly, in training him to remember what he has read, and in improving his sentence structure and spelling.
    a. Select short, interesting materials. Mount on heavy cardboard as many different selections as there are pupils in the class who are reading at about the same level of reading difficulty. Number each card. Count the words. Prepare a short comprehension exercise on each selection. Type and paste the exercise on the back of the card. Prepare, if desired, a list of suggested answers. Type answer and place in a library book-pocket on the back of the card. Circulate the cards among the pupils in order, so that each pupil has an opportunity to use each card
    b. Ask the pupils to keep charts of their progress in terms of rate of reading and degree of comprehension. Have the pupil prepare one chart for rate and one for comprehension [15]
    c. Explain the purpose of the exercise and procedure
    d. Have the pupils prepare reports in this form:

Name	Date ....
Class	Period ....
Card Number	
1. I read .... words in .... minutes.	
2. My comprehension score was	

[15] An illustration of such charts will be found in *Teaching Reading in the Secondary School*, Bulletin of the California State Department of Education, Vol. XII, No. 3, March, 1943, p. 20.

e. Distribute the numbered cards in order
f. At the signal, "Ready, begin," have the pupils begin reading the selection
g. The teacher will write the time on the blackboard at the end of each quarter-minute, *i.e.*, ¼, ½, ¾, . . . *etc.*
h. When a pupil finishes reading, have him write on his paper the last figure written on the blackboard
i. Instruct the pupil to do the exercises found on the back of the card from memory. If there are questions to be answered, the pupil may be required to write the answers in complete sentences. In this way, the pupil is given practice in writing good sentences, and in spelling words correctly
j. When a pupil finishes the entire exercise, he may correct his exercise, if desired, and then read in a library book
k. When the teacher notes that all pupils have completed the exercise, he should correct the papers individually
l. Each pupil should be required to study the spelling of commonly used words which he misses, and to correct sentence structure if he has made errors

Some devices for the pupils to use which are helpful in improving comprehension of what is read are suggested below:

1. Getting the main idea in a paragraph and presenting the main idea in a sentence
2. Getting all ideas by answering specific questions
3. Getting ideas and rewriting them in one's own words
4. Supplying titles
5. Drawing inferences (Read, then answer question: "What conclusion do you draw?")
6. Following directions (for going, making, finding, *etc.*). Use a problem from a textbook and explain the solution step by step
7. Finding arguments for or against; finding cause and effect (the *why*, *how*, *what*)
8. Making or completing an outline
9. Reading simple diagrams, charts, and maps
10. Interpreting pictorial representation
11. Summarizing by sentences and outline
12. Listing details

Suggested Steps in a Reading Lesson

To provide for continuous development in reading commensurate with each pupil's level of maturity, emphasis must be placed upon improving reading instruction in both the elementary and secondary school. It is especially important that teachers of special reading classes or of retarded pupils in secondary schools follow sound procedures in planning reading activities for their pupils. Many excellent suggestions may be found in the teacher's manuals and workbooks written to accompany readers for pupils of the primary and intermediate grades. These suggestions may be easily adapted to meet the needs of classes in the junior and senior high school. To assist teachers in planning adequately the important parts of a reading lesson, some important steps are described below.

A. PREPARING THE PUPILS FOR READING THE LESSON

The teacher should help the pupils to build a background for understanding the concepts presented in the selection. Informal discussion based on the pupils' past experiences, pictures in the book or in the room, and other visual aids will prepare the pupils for the ideas found in the selection to be read. Such discussion also enables the pupils to become familiar with new words. As these words are used in the discussion, they may be written on the blackboard. In this manner, pupils associate particular meanings with the words.

In this preparatory step, specific purposes for reading the selection should be set up. This is in reality a "reading readiness period" during which a background for reading the story is established, unfamiliar words are presented, and definite purposes for reading are developed.

B. READING THE SELECTION THE FIRST TIME

In the first reading of the selection, the pupil should be directed to read as rapidly as possible to find the answers to questions about which his curiosity was aroused in the preparatory period. For the slower-learning pupil, the questions should be written on the blackboard. The more capable pupil probably will be able to read purposefully if he is encouraged to think about such questions as the following: What is the author's purpose? What is he trying to tell me?

C. REREADING A SELECTION

After the first reading of a selection, the slow-learning pupil should be given an opportunity to discuss the main points before he rereads it for a specific purpose. It is often a good plan to have the slow learner who needs help in overcoming the mechanical difficulties of reading reread the story orally. There should always be a definite purpose for the rereading. It may be to prove a point, to describe a person, or to select the main idea.

After the oral reading and group discussion of the selection, the pupil may be directed to do related practice at his seat. The related practice exercises should be written on the blackboard or duplicated. These assignments may include exercises similar to those outlined in preceding sections for using books, for improving vocabulary, or for improving comprehension. When the more able pupil has completed the first reading of a selection, he may be directed to reread the selection and do the related practice exercises before discussing the ideas gained in the first reading.

D. READING SHORT STORIES OR LIBRARY BOOKS

The above steps in preparing the pupil for reading a selection, reading the selection the first time, rereading the selection and doing the related practice exercises, are steps in the development of better reading habits through intensive study. The teacher should, however, use a variety of methods for building interest in reading and should encourage wide reading in many different fields.

Whenever the pupils complete the day's lesson, which should be short in the case of slow learners, they should be encouraged to read stories, magazines, or full-length books. In this way, pupils are helped to develop greater skill and interest in reading through both extensive and intensive reading.

E. PLANNING THE PUPILS' ACTIVITIES

In order to follow the steps outlined above, the teacher will find it necessary to plan carefully each reading lesson. Frequently, several days will be required to complete one short selection.

The preparation for reading the selection and beginning to read it may take one period. Completing the first reading and group discussion with oral reading may be included in the assignment for the second period. During the third period, the pupil may do the related practice. In the fourth period, the pupil may discuss the related practice exercises with the teacher and then read stories, books, or magazines.

The above divisions for the study of a selection are suggested as one possible way of planning the steps in the study of a selection. Obviously, no set rule or pattern can be set up for dividing the time spent on each step in studying a selection. However, the basic steps in teaching a reading lesson should be carefully followed in any program of systematic instruction to improve the reading of the pupil assigned to special reading classes or classes for the retarded pupil.

Summary

1. One of the objectives of classroom teachers is to provide continuous guidance in using the textbooks and references that pupils use in their classes. Practice lessons similar to ones suggested in this bulletin should be prepared to assist pupils in learning how to use effectively the materials of instruction.

2. Effective instruction in vocabulary building contributes (a) to the pupil's understanding of what is read, (b) to growth in expressing ideas in both oral and written form, and (c) to an understanding of ideas presented orally.

3. In vocabulary building, the emphasis should be upon meaning. It is, however, essential that difficulties of mechanics be overcome. Exercises for improving word recognition and pronunciation and for developing a wider meaning vocabulary should be developed by teachers. Instruction in these two phases of vocabulary development will, obviously, be closely related.

4. Guidance in using the skills essential to understanding what is read and studied in different subject-matter fields is the responsibility of each teacher in the school. The suggestions in this bulletin for improving techniques for recognizing the main ideas, finding details, finding facts, relating subordinate details to main ideas, assembling information, drawing inferences and forming conclusions, remembering what is read, and following oral and written directions may be adapted to the needs of a particular class by any teacher.

5. Pupils should be guided in their reading of books, magazines, and newspapers so that they will develop a critical point of view toward what is read. Ability to form critical judgments of articles in newspapers, magazines, or books is especially necessary for the citizens in a democracy.

6. Pupils should understand the importance of their reading rate, and teachers of the various subject-matter fields should guide pupils in developing a rate of reading suitable to the type of material being read and the purpose for which it is read. Emphasis should always be upon comprehension.

7. Developing more effective study-reading skills is only one of the basic aims of reading instruction, and at no time should the emphasis upon skills be such that interest in reading is killed. Separate specific steps in a reading lesson are suggested. The alert teacher will use a variety of methods to create a desire to read and to develop wide reading interests as well as to develop the ability to use study-reading skills efficiently.

PART SIX

Teaching Reading in the Content Fields

28. Teaching Reading in Science Classes

SCIENCE

Ruth Strang

Reading instruction is needed in every science class. This is true because there are special problems of reading science: the approach is different from reading fiction and many other kinds of material; there is a technical vocabulary to be mastered; and there are special problems to reading formulas, diagrams, directions. Second, effective reading in their science books will contribute to students' total reading efficiency. In this article we shall give a few glimpses into science classrooms showing how teachers are conducting successful periods of reading instruction.

How Do They Read?

With any new class the science teacher needs to know what his students are getting out of the books he expects them to read. Of course, he can get a general idea of their reading level from any standardized reading test that has been given. This is useful but it is even more useful to see exactly what is being communicated to different students by the authors of the science text and reference books used in his class. The results will surprise him.

This is the procedure one science teacher used. He selected a unit of two or three pages from the text that the students had not yet read. Since they all had copies of the book, he did not have to mimeograph the passage. He did, however, make copies of the questions on the passage for every student. The first question was a general one: What did the author say? The other questions were more specific ones on the main idea, the most important details, the technical vocabulary, and on generalizations or conclusions that could properly be derived from the passage. He also included several questions on the students' method of reading the passage.[1]

He gave this informal teaching-test the second day he met the class. He had told them on the first day something about the importance of science in the world today, the need for scientists, and the vocational opportunities to which his subject contributed. He also had explored with them their new science book — how it was organized, its special aids to understanding, the purpose of its various parts.

In introducing the informal test he gave simple directions to turn to page 205 when the signal to begin was given and to read, in the way they usually read a science assignment, until they came to the end of that section. When they had finished reading, they should look at the board and write the number they saw there: that would be the number of seconds they had taken to read the passage. (He would write the seconds as they passed in ten-second intervals.) Then, without looking back at the book, they were to write the answers to the questions.

After the class had finished this informal test, it was used for teaching purposes. The students exchanged papers and read and discussed the answers. The responses to the first question were most interesting. Some students gave only a few scattered facts; some were inaccurate in their reporting of details; some confused the main idea with illustrations of it; many were very poor in relating ideas and making generalizations, inferences, and applications; a few were able to state the author's thought clearly and in the proper sequence and also to see the significance of the passage as a whole.

As the answers were read, students discussed why some were good and some, poor. Those who had comprehended the passage well in a reasonable length of time were asked to describe their method of reading.

This informal test led to further instruction in how to read an assignment in science. In a few days the teacher gave a similar

[1] For more detail see Ruth Strang, Constance McCullough, and Arthur Traxler, *Problems in the Improvement of Reading* (Second Edition), pp. 258–60. New York: McGraw-Hill Book Company, 1955.

informal test to measure their improvement. Each student made a progress chart showing his reading speed and comprehension at the beginning of the year and improvement he had made.

How to Read More Effectively

Finding out how students in a given class read is not enough. All of them will profit by instruction in how to approach a science reading assignment. Instead of their usual haphazard, unreflective approach, they can be taught a more effective systematic method.

This same teacher, recognizing the students' need for instruction, devoted another period to how to read a science assignment. He began by giving them the assignment for the next day and asking how they would begin reading it. Then he said, "I have a short film today called, 'How Effective Is Your Reading?' [2] What help would you expect to get from it in studying science more effectively?" After their ideas were written on the board, the film was shown. It portrays a boy studying his science assignment, first thinking about what he already knows about the topic and why it is important to him; then skimming to see what the author is trying to do; then writing questions to which he wants to find the answers. He is then ready to read carefully. Finally, he checks his comprehension by reviewing and reciting. After showing the film, the teacher lets the class state in their own words the answers to their questions. To clinch some of the points, he showed the film a second time.

At the end of the second showing, he called for a group decision: "How many think we ought to study our assignment this way tonight — unless we have a still more effective method of our own?" He went further and let them take the first two steps in studying their present assignment: (1) survey what they already know and want to know and (2) skim and raise questions the book can answer.

Subsequently he gave less formal assignments, often in the form of problems to be solved or projects to be undertaken. They read at home for a "Science-News program" and for a Science Club in which they tried to find answers to $64 questions. But for a study-type of assignment in which the aim was, first of all, to find out what the author said, he referred back to this Survey Q3R method until they had mastered it and made it their own.

How to Build a Science Vocabulary

A comprehension of key words is essential in reading science material. The key words must be identified, their common mean-

[2] Coronet Instructional Films, Chicago, Illinois.

ings recognized, their special meanings as used in the science book illustrated.

One teacher used the simple device of writing on the board the key words related to the topic to be studied. One day the words were *temperature*, *thermometer*, *humidity*, etc. She wrote the words on the board and asked the students to share their experiences with these words. For example, with reference to *humidity* one youngster said, "I like to read the weather reports in the papers and always find out what the humidity is. If it's near 100 per cent on a hot day we feel very uncomfortable." Another said, "My mother is always complaining about the humidity, especially in August." With other words, whenever possible, the teacher had the substance to show them or demonstrated the process.

The students also made a class dictionary of the key words. Each student made one or more pages of this dictionary, giving the word, the dictionary pronunciation and definitions, several sentences using the word — these were often cut out from newspapers and magazines — and a picture, drawing, or diagram illustrating it, if possible. The students signed their name to the pages they had produced and vied with one another to make their pages the most interesting. In these ways the students gradually built a basic science vocabulary.

"The science texts for my grade are too difficult" is a common complaint of science teachers. Studies made by Mallinson and others [3] have confirmed teachers' impressions. There are, however, wide differences in level of reading difficulty among texts and even among sections of the same text.

The readability of these books could be improved in several ways — by relating a topic or problem to some real interest of the student, by improving the logical organization and sequence of ideas, by using less difficult nontechnical words, and by reducing the vocabulary load of technical words. In choosing books for his class the teacher should select those that best meet the above requirements. If the teacher is "stuck" with too difficult texts, he will have to give students more instruction in reading them with as much comprehension as possible and in building the necessary vocabulary. He will also try to supply easier supplementary reading.

How to Think Scientifically

Habits of thinking while reading science need to be developed. From concrete facts given in the text and reference books, first-

[3] G. G. Mallinson and Others, "Reading Difficulty of Textbooks for General Science," *School Review*, LX (February, 1952), 94–98.

hand experiences, and experiments described or demonstrated by the teacher or performed by the class, the students should learn to make sound generalizations about the physical world in which they live. To do this kind of thinking involves seeing relations among facts, following the author's line of reasoning, and testing the validity of the conclusions reached.

Another aspect of scientific thinking is the application of ideas gained from the reading of science to the world as they see it. With practice, students will gradually acquire the ability to apply what they read to real life problems. The skillful teacher creates conditions in which the student can move forward on his own in solving everyday problems.

The problem-solving method of reading is particularly important in science. Carter [4] described a science period in which the class was studying the causes affecting rainfall. The teacher first helped the students to read the rainfall maps in their texts to see where the rainfall was light and where it was heavy. Many questions were raised by this study of the maps: Why is there such a difference between the amount of precipitation on the western and the eastern slopes of the mountains? Why are the prevailing winds laden with moisture? Why does condensation take place? In addition to finding answers to these questions in science books, the students had the firsthand experience of seeing how moisture in the air condenses on a glass filled with 1 c.c. water. Many words such as *condensation*, *evaporation*, *relative humidity*, *water vapor*, took on additional meanings. Throughout this unit of study the students were encouraged to find facts through reading and observation and to use them in making inferences.

How to Encourage Free Reading

Children want to find out about science. Of their own accord, they frequently look up science topics. During school years they can acquire interests in reading science that persist throughout life.

One teacher asked her students to bring in clippings on science topics. They had a chance to read the most interesting to the class. All were put on the bulletin board under general topics. Those of permanent interest and value were filed by a committee for future reference.

Another teacher was fortunate in securing the co-operation of a librarian who had well-stocked shelves. When the class was studying a given topic, he asked the librarian to send in enough

[4] Homer L. J. Carter, "Reading, a Contributing and Concomitant Factor in the Study of Science," *School Science and Mathematics*, LIV (October, 1954), 567–70.

books on the topic so that each student might select one. Since a wide range of reading ability was represented in the class, the librarian chose books from third-grade to adult level. Part of a period the teacher spent in guiding the students' choice of books. The rest of the period they spent in free reading. After they had finished reading the books chosen, they discussed them in class.

While the students were reading independently, the teacher held individual conferences with students to see how they were reading, what difficulties they were meeting, and what they needed to do to improve their reading.

How to Achieve Personal Development Through Reading

The effective reading of science should result in people better able to cope with and contribute to the modern world.

In a tenth-grade biology class most of the students, ranging in age from thirteen to seventeen years, were behavior problems. The new teacher, unable to enlist their interest in his subject, began with their interests. They formed special interest groups, took field trips, and engaged in many other activities. In each of these activities they found they needed reading. Those who could not read or write effectively enough sought help in preparing and presenting the reports of their activities. The teacher gave instruction in word recognition skills as needed.

By the end of the year this "non-reading" group had filled a small bookcase with well-prepared, illustrated booklets, which they had made. They had written and produced a science play.

Evidence of the success of this program was shown in their higher scores on reading tests and in the favorable reports of their conduct. They remained in school and some took other courses in science.

In every class there is probably undiscovered science talent. It needs to be discovered and encouraged. Opportunities for its development, expert instruction and guidance, and the experience of success in the field are necessary for its fruition.

29. Helping Students to Read Scientific Material

SCIENCE

Homer L. J. Carter

In suggesting means of helping students read scientific material, it is the writer's purpose to discuss briefly (1) some essential reading skills, (2) the importance of background and mental content, (3) selection and adjustment of materials, and (4) some effective procedures.

Some Essential Reading Skills

The student working in any scientific field should know how to add words to his vocabularies. He should be able to read a chapter effectively, and he should know how to read for detail preparatory to the solution of a problem. It is the consensus of many leaders in the field that these skills should be acquired by the student as the result of a well-planned developmental program in grades three to sixteen, inclusive, in which each instructor has a contribution to make. The work should not be regarded as corrective or remedial processes in which only the reading specialist has a part. Instead each teacher should be responsible for the development of these essential skills in his classes. In brief, his problem is to teach his students how to study, a process closely associated with the teaching of reading.

The Importance of Background and Mental Content

Not all students can be expected to read effectively and well materials of a scientific nature. One of the first obstacles encountered is a lack of background and mental content. In the study of science, the student reads to secure meaning and he also makes use of meaning previously gained in order to read more effectively. Meaning, which is the product of certain physical and psychological factors, can be expressed by the formula: Meaning = Sensation × Mental Content.

Obviously, if either sensation or mental content is missing, there can be no meaning. The word "sine" can mean "the function of an angle," "without," or nothing depending upon the mental content of the reader. One sees and interprets with what he has seen and experienced. The student may *identify* and verbalize the concept "sine" but not *understand* its meaning and consequently he may fail to *evaluate* its significance and function. Amounts of mental content determine kinds and degrees of meaning. Obviously, meaning resulting from reading in any scientific field requires background and mental content and these in turn are built up by reading and experience.

Deficiencies in mental content are frequently due to a lack of both mental and emotional maturity. Individuals learn and adjust in accordance with their development or maturation. There is a positive relationship between intelligence and the ability to identify, understand, and evaluate facts. Mental content is the result of experience but in order to profit from this experience there must be a high degree of intellectual maturity. A lack of emotional maturity can also interfere with the acquiring of mental content, for many high-school and college students point out that scientific courses are difficult and consequently are to be avoided. This attitude does not contribute to the acquiring of background essential to the reading of scientific literature.

Selection and Adjustment of Materials

Materials are frequently not adjusted to the reading levels and interests of the student. In our schools of today children are promoted year after year irrespective of their reading skills and attainment. It is possible for a youth to find himself in the ninth grade and required to read from ninth-grade texts when his reading level is only that of a fourth-grade child. As he is promoted to junior- and senior-high school, he soon discovers that he cannot possibly do the reading that is required of him. In the process of selecting and using materials in science classes, it is necessary for the teacher to understand that the reading levels within any class may cover a range of three to five grades. Vocabularies of technical and nontechnical words should be considered. Furthermore, the teacher should take into account organization and clarity of material, style of writing, variety of illustrations, value of guided activities, and provision for individual differences. In general, a textbook with a glossary should be given preference over a similar book without one, providing that they are equal in other respects. Materials dealing with subject matter of a scientific nature but written simply and directly are available.

Developing Ability to Read in the Teaching of Science

In developing ability to read scientific literature, it is necessary to increase mental content, to develop adequate vocabularies, to increase skill in chapter reading and to identify essential details in problem solving.

Increasing Mental Content

In an elementary science class, for example, it may be the *aim* of the teacher to show causal factors affecting rainfall. The *materials* available are texts in elementary science, glass tubing, mercury, thermometers, Bunsen burner, a large dripping pan, and other equipment generally found in an elementary science laboratory. The *procedures* employed by the teacher in using these materials to accomplish the specific goal may be briefly summarized as follows.

The students can be asked to determine from the rainfall maps in their texts the amount of precipitation on both the western slopes of the Rocky Mountains and on the eastern slopes. The teacher can stimulate interest by asking the students to explain the marked difference between the amount of precipitation on the two slopes of the mountains. In solving this major problem, it may be necessary to ask: Why are the prevailing winds moisture-laden? What are the causes of ocean currents? Why do winds blow? Why are the prevailing winds from the West? Why does condensation take place?

The teacher can guide the students in a solution of these problems by a constant referral of the students to the various parts of their texts such as index, table of contents, and the various maps, charts, and illustrations made available by the authors of their texts. The students can be encouraged to ask questions of their books and read for answers. A barometer can be constructed and illustrations made of its use. Demonstrations of ocean currents can be set forth by making use of water in a large dripping pan covered sparsely with sawdust and with one corner placed over a Bunsen burner. A demonstration of condensation on a drinking glass filled with ice water can contribute to the solution of the major problem. Such terms as high and low pressure areas, air mass, altitude, condensation, convection, dew points, evaporation, Fahrenheit, front, isobars, isotherms, barometric pressure, water vapor, relative humidity, temperature, and velocity can be developed and illustrated by the instructor.

The teacher can show how to gather *facts* and how to use these facts in establishing *inferences*. Groups of students and individual students can be shown how to substantiate their inferences by careful reading of their texts and supplementary references. A critical evaluation of all inferences can be made. In this activity it is evident that mental content and ability to read can be developed simultaneously. The young student has been encouraged to add words to his vocabulary and to use his text and supplementary materials as he has participated in problem-solving activities. He has read to learn and he has learned to read.

Developing Vocabularies

Reading and spelling vocabularies can be developed if the student is taught to select from his textbooks and class discussions words which he needs to understand and use. Various forms of *contextual clues*, if thoroughly appreciated, will help him to determine meaning which can be verified by the *use of the dictionary*. A psychologically sound procedure making use of visual, auditory, kinesthetic, and tactual imagery can be employed. In this process, the student should look at the beginning and ending of words and observe phonograms within a word.

Structural analysis is helpful in the study of words, for meaning can generally be determined from a knowledge of prefixes, stems, and suffixes. The student can learn to pronounce the word subvocally, making certain that he associates each syllable with its corresponding sound and that the proper sequence of syllables is maintained. He should be expected to spell the word subvocally, paying careful attention to each syllable. He should be expected to write the word and then compare the word written with the word that he has selected for study. This process should be repeated until he can spell and write the word correctly.

In all instances, the student should be able to make use of the word in a complete sentence so that its full meaning is adequately expressed. Some students find it advisable to keep a list of words learned in this manner.

Reading a Chapter Effectively and Well

The teacher of science should demonstrate the manner in which chapter reading can be done effectively and well. A method widely used consists of having the student make a preliminary survey of the chapter by first reading the introduction and the conclusion. The author in the introduction has declared his intentions and in the conclusion indicated what he has accomplished in the chapter.

A preview of the main headings of the chapter gives the student some idea as to how the chapter is organized and an outline of chief points to be discussed. The student should be shown how to convert these main headings into questions and the advisability of writing each on a 3″ × 5″ card. For example, the heading "Weather Defined" can be changed to read "What is weather?" When this is done, the student should be expected to read for the purpose of answering each question. This provides purpose and motive for reading.

At this point the student should be taught to not only identify concepts but to understand them thoroughly in order that he may evaluate them and be able to arrange them in a proper sequence. Answers to the questions should be stated by the student in his own words and written on the card containing the question. The student then is ready to try and test his knowledge of the chapter by reviewing both questions and answers.

Reading for Details in Problem Solving

To develop skill in problem solving, especially in such areas as mathematics, chemistry, and physics, the student should learn to ask questions of his text and to read for detailed answers. He should ask what is to be found? What facts are known? What other facts are needed that are not included in the problem? What are the steps to go through for a solution? Can a picture or illustration be made of the conditions? What numerical quantities can be used in actually solving the problem? Is the answer reasonable? How can it be proved? This process involves identification of concepts, their interpretation and later their evaluation. The student is encouraged to ask questions and seek out his own answers.

In retrospect, it may be well to point out that vocabulary building, chapter reading, and reading for detail preparatory to problem solving are essential reading skills required by every student of scientific literature. The importance of background and mental content has been emphasized. It has been suggested that the selection of material is important to the science teacher. It has been shown how mental content can be built up by the teacher of science, and definite suggestions have been made for vocabulary building, chapter reading, and reading for detail in problem solving. These skills are both contributing and concomitant aspects of reading in the learning process.

30. Science

SCIENCE

Mary K. Eakin

Too frequently in the past, adults working with children and young people, whether as teachers, librarians or parents, have tended to regard fiction, and preferably fantasy or some form of folk literature, as the only type of reading that could be said truly to contribute to a child's personal development. Nonfiction, with the possible exception of biography, did not even classify as "reading," and often the junior-high-school student who read voraciously in the field of science, absorbing books that were considerably beyond his grade level and often even beyond his average reading level, would find himself under considerable pressure from the adults around him to abandon the newer *Skyrocketing into the Unknown* or *Men, Microscopes and Living Things* in favor of *Tom Sawyer* or *Treasure Island* or even, unhappily, "Evangeline."

The situation is fortunately changing, and today the reading of good books in the science fields is becoming accepted as being a desirable educational activity. Encouragement to read good fiction, whether modern or of the past, is, of course, still given, and it should continue to be given. But it is unrealistic to separate books into these two categories.

The whole idea that a child's personal deevlopment is somehow unrelated to what he does and learns in the classroom, or through class-directed activities, is giving way to a saner realization that anything a child does contributes, positively or negatively, to his personal development. And so today we can come to a conference on Reading and consider the matter of personal development through the reading of science books. Some of this change has, to be sure, come about as a result of the good writing that is now available in nonfiction books; writing that compares favorably in literary quality with much of the best fiction, old and new, to which children have access.

When we speak of personal development through the reading of science books, we are thinking primarily of the reading of supplementary materials rather than the reading of textbooks specifically assigned for classroom use. Such reading may grow out of an interest that starts in the classroom as a direct result of classroom work or of assigned readings, or it may be an interest developed spontaneously from browsing through a good library collection. Likewise the elements of personal development that result from such reading may relate to science learnings specifically or they may be of a more general nature, although these two areas will never be wholly discrete, since students themselves are not subject to division into neat and decisive categories within themselves. Let us look, then, at some of those elements of personal development that might reasonably grow out of a student's class-directed reading; always keeping in mind that such readings may be assigned readings that the student is expected to do as a required part of his work; additional readings suggested by the teacher to spur the gifted student on to greater achievement; reading to create a spark of interest in the less able learner; or reading that the student seeks out on his own with no incentive other than a personal desire to learn more about a subject that has been introduced in the classroom.

In order to identify these elements it might be helpful to look at some of the aims of a junior-high-school science program as those aims relate to the personal development of students. In the February, 1958 issue of *School Science and Mathematics*, J. B. Kelley identifies some of these aims, and I quote those that seem applicable:

1. "To help children develop concepts, principles, and generalizations which will be of value to them in understanding and solving their problems." As an example Mr. Kelley cites the development of concepts of environment that are based on "knowledge, insight, and reliable evidence rather than on superstition and faulty information." Many recent titles might be named that would satisfy this aim. Batchelor's *Superstitious? Here's Why*, for example, takes familiar superstitions of ancient origin and gives their history of development and present status of acceptability. Children are frequently startled to learn how many superstitions still exist; how many, in fact, they themselves subscribe to without conscious thought, and they may be stimulated to an examination of the origins of some of their beliefs and a questioning of their validity.

Hoke's *First Book About Snakes* is an interesting example of a book on a subject about which many myths have clung through the years. In his final chapter, the author sets forth a number of these old wives tales — that milk snakes milk cows; that a mother snake swallows her young to protect them from enemies; that a snake that has been killed does not really die until sundown, etc. — and gives the truth about each myth. Once a student has had some of his own superstitions disproved, he becomes better able to look carefully at other, similar statements and examine them for accuracy. Such a beginning, properly directed, can lead the student to an examination of beliefs in other areas, such as intergroup relationships, and can help to instill a habit of thinking before accepting generalizations of any kind.

Books such as Pough's *All About Volcanoes and Earthquakes*, or Zim's *Lightning and Thunder* can help a young person to understand some of the more violent manifestations of nature and to lose many of the fears that result from a lack of understanding of such phenomena. A growing number of science books in the area of nature study not only helps the reader to understand the plants or animals involved but also gives him an introduction to the life cycle in nature, balance in nature, elementary evolution and conservation.

Evans' *Why We Live Where We Live* and Scheib's *What Happened?* encourage the reader to look beyond the surface of his environment to see what causal relationships exist that may be linked to science.

2. "To help children develop intellectual honesty, cultivate scientific attitudes, become critical minded and willing to seek and act upon reliable evidence."

Science books, more than any other type, offer an opportunity for stimulating young people to question statements for evidence of proof. This may be done through a comparison of two books on the same subject, *i.e.*, some of the older science books in which it is stated categorically that man will never achieve space flight as compared with a book such as Poole's *Your Trip into Space;* or within a single book in which widely divergent theories on a subject, *i.e.*, the origin of the moon, may be stated, with the arguments for each theory presented clearly and objectively. Sometimes a hoax, such as that of the Piltdown man, can be useful in pointing up the fact that even books written in good faith may not be wholly accurate. In this connection, books of an historical nature, such as biographies of Galileo, Madame Curie, Benjamin Franklin, histories of medicine or of scientific discoveries, etc., can help to develop within the reader an awareness of how little of man's knowledge is static, proved beyond exception, and how even the seeming truths of today may be disproved by the discoveries of tomorrow. On the negative side we would wish to avoid giving children books in which simple demonstrations are said to "prove" something or other; or those that present a theory as a statement of fact or that state dogmatically that a problem is impossible to solve now or at a future time. Good science books will lead the reader to question what is before him and to attempt to find as much of the truth as is possible before making decisions.

Kelley's third aim may be omitted from our consideration since it is primarily achieved through participation in actual experiments in the classroom or through directed observations.

3. "To help children explore new avenues of interest which will lead to the satisfaction of achievement and discovery."

Reading in the field of science can open avenues of creativity and of discovery for the junior-high-school student. Although it is true that what the child of this level creates, what he discovers, has been created or discovered many times before, nevertheless, if it is a first experience for him and is carried through in an acceptable manner, then it becomes a real experience in creativity and encourages him to continue to develop his powers to the point where he may someday be actually making new discoveries. The better science books, therefore, will give the reader a solid basis of accurate facts, at the same time leaving something to his imagination or demanding of him some degree of participation. Thus Baer's *Sound* presents a problem, describes an experiment that will give an answer to the problem, but does not describe the results of the experiment. Books such as Ley's *Engineers' Dreams* and Poole's *Diving for Science* and *Today's Science and You* describe areas in which mankind has made partial achievement but where there are still major problems to be solved. Science books such as these do not satisfy the reader, but rather leave him with a host of unanswered questions that will spur him on to try to find the answers.

4. "To help children acquire those skills and techniques necessary to gain further information, such as reading science content with understanding. . . ."

We have long accepted the idea that a child's reading ability will affect his achievement in those classes where performance is based wholly or in part on reading. We also recognize that a child's interest in a subject can strongly affect his reading achievement, especially in that area. In the realm of science books, increasing numbers of titles are appearing that are useful for improving the junior-high-school student's reading skills by utilizing his interest in science. And, by the same token, as his reading skills improve, his ability to read with greater understanding of the field will be increased.

Children's books today are seldom specialized, and many science books lend themselves to use in broadening a reader's interests or experiences. For example, mythology is frequently introduced into science books. Lewellen's *Birds and Planes: How They Fly* makes use of the Icarus legend; Haber's *Our Friend the Atom* is built around the tale of the genie in the bottle. The reader who disclaims all interests except science may be enticed into reading other such myths and legends to find the scientific ideas represented in them and to consider how the myth might have been re-told in the light of present-day scientific knowledge. Plotz's *Imagination's Other Place* provides an experience with literature for the science-minded reader through its selection of poems about science and mathematics, most of them gleaned from the works of the world's greatest poets. Here, again, interest may frequently be sparked by a discussion of how the scientific principles expressed in the poem may agree with or differ from the principles as they are understood today.

For the student who needs no motivation to read, but who lacks an interest in science, books of science fiction, the poetry anthology just mentioned, biographies of famous scientists, popularized histories of medical and scientific discoveries, anthropology and archeology, may all be used to create an interest in the field.

5. "To help children develop social attitudes and appreciations needed in a democratic society."

Just as nations of the world can no longer lead an isolated existence, wholly independent of other nations, so scientists can no longer lead wholly isolated lives devoted entirely to research in pure science and with no awareness of the society around them. Many of the science books written for children and young people recognize this fact and make use of it. Thus we find that almost all books on nature, whether they be about plants or animals, rocks or weather, contain some material on conservation. It may be woven into the entire text or inserted as a separate chapter, but it is almost inevitably there.

Books on atomic energy usually stress the peace-time uses to which it has been or may be put, and, again, usually include some statement of the responsibility which people working in the fields of both pure and applied science have toward society as a whole in dealing with this force.

Summary

Books of science have the potentiality of contributing to the reader's personal development by encouraging him toward clear, accurate thinking; toward a greater understanding of the true nature of the world around him; toward a spirit of inquiry and creativity; toward the development of skills that will enable him to go on to greater heights of learning; toward a sense of responsibility toward society in his use of the knowledge that science opens to him.

The potentiality is there; its effectiveness will depend in large measure on the degree of access the student has to the materials and the kinds of guidance he is given in classroom and library to read widely and always with a thoughtful, open mind.

31. Teaching Reading, An Essential Part of Teaching English

ENGLISH — Ruth Strang

Some English teachers will say, "How can we find time to teach reading in addition to the literature that we have to cover?" Many of these teachers are providing incidental instruction in reading though they do not call it that. As evidence of this fact, I should like to report observations of selected English classes in two New York City vocational high schools.

Students' Views of the Reading Problem

Discussions with groups of students in these two schools indicated that they recognized the necessity for reading: to succeed in school, to get a job, to succeed in a job, to carry on a conversation, to be a good citizen. They also mentioned such practical uses as filling out blanks and applications; reading signs, directions, menus, and the like.

In reply to the question, "What do you read?" they spoke of newspapers, novels, and magazines. Some said it was easier to buy a thirty-cent paper-back book than to get a book from the library. Said one student, "The more you read, the better you read and the more you understand." In answer to the question, "What leads you to read?" one said, "Start with a hobby or interest; then you will want to read about it." Another said, "You read books recommended by friends; for example, *The Blackboard Jungle* — everybody was reading it."

When asked, "Why don't students read more and better books and articles?" they said that books are not presented to them in an appealing way; that students have a natural resistance to teachers who continually prod them to read; that students are allowed to waste time in their early years when they could be acquiring a taste for reading. One said quaintly, "A mind can take an awful lot of learning when it's young." The most able learners did not object to hard assignments, but they did criticize "assignments that are not well presented" and assignments "that are too cut dried, and do not make connections with the student's interests."

They suggested many sound methods by which teachers can help students to improve their reading:

Let students discuss books in class; point out the most interesting parts and study together the parts that are difficult to comprehend.

Check students' work more carefully.

Stimulate students to work hard and do their best; suggest voluntary reading in each subject. "If they're interested, students can find time to read," they said.

Make reading a pleasure.

Give students more choice; be more flexible about the number and nature of required books.

Personalize teaching — realize that some students are fast and some are slow. Break each class into groups; put together those who have certain difficulties; give them instruction and practice; let others read more widely and deeply.

Give students help early in high school; it's important to get started right.

Out of their own firsthand experience, these students had derived sound basic principles for the teaching of reading.

Reading Skills Taught in the English Classes

In the lessons observed, all the essential reading skills were taught in most cases incidentally or casually. Moreover, the teacher emphasized personal development through reading, and consistently maintained a point of view conducive to mental health. A few excerpts from the recorded observations will illustrate some of the procedures used in teaching basic reading skills.

Vocabulary building. In every class vocabulary building received attention in connection with the literature being read. Some teachers wrote on the board important unfamiliar words which the students would encounter in their reading. The students discussed the meaning of these words and gave examples of ways in which they had heard them used. A variation of this method is to have students skim an assignment to pick out words that they think may cause difficulty. Some social studies teachers spend a period or more to clarify a key concept. Other teachers encourage students to make a vocabulary-spelling file of important words, or to compile a picture-dictionary. Memorizing famous quotations is another way of giving meaning to certain words in context. By frequently introducing these new words in conversation, the teacher encourages the students to fix them in memory. Occasionally a teacher would interrupt the reading to study a particular word or phrase from a semantic viewpoint.

In some classes there were many students who had not acquired basic word recognition skills. Sometimes when these students met an unfamiliar word, the teacher would demonstrate methods for determining its meaning. In these groups there was need for more class instruction in these skills, and for word wheels, word games, and other devices to provide practice for individual students.

Understanding sentence and paragraph structure. Sentence and paragraph comprehension received attention in both reading and writing. The students would analyze a paragraph together, noting its general structure, the main idea, and the supporting details and illustrations. In writing paragraphs they had the experience of creating this kind of structure themselves. With longer passages, students were given practice in outlining or making a summary of the author's thought.

Locating information. In one class the teacher spent some time in teaching the students how to locate information, and how to scan material for specific information. This was done in connection with a unit in which each student chose a biography or autobiography and reported to the class on it.

The reading process from preview to review. A number of reading skills were involved in an approach to study-type reading — the Survey Q3R technic. First, the teacher related the assignment to the students' experience. For example, before reading one of Woodrow Wilson's speeches in a class where all the students had foreign-born parents, the teacher asked, "What would you say if you were to make a speech to citizens about to be naturalized?" Then the class skimmed the speech to see what questions it might answer. At home, they were to read, review, and recite what they had learned. By making the students aware of the effectiveness of the reading methods they were using, the teacher encouraged them to apply this method to other reading.

Interpretation and appreciation skills. Literary appreciation was emphasized in these English classes. Students were helped to recognize clues to plot and character development. For example, in a senior class which was reading *Macbeth*, the teacher asked: "What did you find in Act I that influenced Macbeth's decision to kill Duncan?"

Student: The witches' prophecy.
Teacher: How did that influence Macbeth?
Student: They told him he would be king.
Teacher: Had Macbeth ever thought of this before?
Student: Probably, but Shakespeare doesn't say.
Teacher: What else influenced him?

Student: Lady Macbeth.
Teacher: How?
Student: She said he didn't have any courage like a man.
Teacher: Do you think Macbeth would have killed the king if it hadn't been for Lady Macbeth? . . .

Later, discussing the scene following Duncan's murder, the teacher said: "Say in your own words what Macbeth is feeling."

Student: "I'm afraid to think of what I have done." Further discussion brought out various ways in which crime may affect the criminal — remorse, sense of guilt, fear of detection. This discussion was very close to the lives of some of these students.

In a freshman class that was reading a detective story, *Buttons*, the teacher asked, "What indications of the mother's character do you find?" The students pointed out details that showed that the mother hadn't let the son grow up, that she was a quick thinker but jumped to conclusions, and that she was jealous of her son's girl friend. Later, when the teacher said, "If the mother is overprotective, how might that affect Ernie?" one of the students remarked that "Children don't like it when the mother does all the thinking for them."

In a lesson on American documents (Patrick Henry's speech), the teacher encouraged feeling responses as well as intellectual appreciation by asking: "Why did you like that speech so much? How did it make you feel?"

Critical reading. The teachers of these classes gave considerable attention to critical reading and thinking. One teacher showed students the process of analyzing particularly difficult but important passages. For example, in studying the Woodrow Wilson speech previously mentioned the teacher said, "Wilson says, 'They came expecting us to be better than we are.' What does he mean by that? What did he want the immigrants to do about it?" Another teacher gave assignments that required the students to perceive relationships, draw inferences, or think imaginatively. For example, when the class was discussing the Wilson speech, the teacher made comments such as these:

"Did Woodrow Wilson really say that? Let's test your statement by the text. Be careful not to put ideas into the document that are not there. *First*, get the author's ideas accurately. Later you can speculate and read between the lines."

"You cannot understand a speech unless you know to whom, by whom, when, where, and why it was delivered. Read to find the answers to these questions."

"Can you be more precise in your statement?"

"Why is the oath of allegiance a very important part of the naturalization ceremony?"

Voluntary reading. In addition to making the students' school reading a rewarding, satisfying, and enjoyable experience, some teachers used special methods of encouraging students to continue to read outside of school. One teacher had a unit on biography in which each student chose his own book. Other teachers encouraged students to use the library and to buy certain high-quality paper-backs which they specifically recommended. By learning a few words each day in a high-grade newspaper, the students in one class gained an impetus to continue reading this newspaper.

Communication skills. These teachers also used various methods of encouraging more effective oral communication of ideas. One teacher gave students a detailed guide for making oral reports on a book they had read. After each report was given, the class discussed it constructively from the standpoint of content and method of presentation. This teacher also gave individual help to students with speech difficulties.

Oral reports of various kinds offer opportunities for students to learn from one another; they may interest one another in developing hobbies or in reading the books reviewed. Oral reports also help students to learn how to listen more selectively and creatively to radio and television. Practice in making oral reports helps students to read books accurately and creatively, while informal conversation about books, and talks on their own experiences, hobbies, or topics of particular interest to them are more closely related to real life situations. Other teachers suggested that their students give a simulated radio program such as Margaret Scoggin's "Young Book Reviewers," or a dramatized reading of a play or story.

To improve students' phrasing, one teacher occasionally reads aloud, while the class follows intently. From time to time she calls on a student to "be Jimmy" or to "read what the grandmother said."

Personal Development Through Reading

Many contributions to personal development and mental health were observed in the English classes in these two vocational schools. In introducing oral reports on biography and autobiography, the teachers related these reports to adolescents' needs for models and goals: rather than following any fad or popular person who comes along, adolescents do better to get acquainted with some of the real heroes described in literature.

In teaching *My Antonia*, the teacher first quoted from Thornton

Wilder's *Our Town*, which the class had read last year: "So all that was going on and we never noticed. . . . Do any human beings ever realize life while they live it?" Then they discussed how awareness is developed, and looked for examples of Jimmy's awareness of the things and people about him.

Constructive student-teacher and student-student relations underlie successful learning; learning takes place in a relationship. These classes furnished many examples of the ways in which the teacher helps to build students' self-esteem by finding something good in everyone's contribution to the discussion. For example:

"You went too fast for us! What you said came later in the story."

"Some of the things you mentioned are right. . . ."

"I think Dorothy started us on a good line of thought."

"You're getting 'warm.' " (Not exactly right but moving toward the solution)

"Yes, they *were* very religious people; we know this, but first we are trying to get the ideas in the document itself."

The teachers also sought to understand why a student had given an erroneous answer, instead of just saying, "Wrong." When a boy had given his explanation, the teacher said, "Now that you've pointed it out in your own words, I can see that you had the right idea." An atmosphere favorable to mental hygiene is created by teachers who clearly enjoy students and enjoy teaching, who show students that they want them to do their best, who are so skillful in teaching that students can learn without unnecessary failure. These teachers help students who do fail to view failure as an opportunity to learn.

A certain amount of routine and order in the classroom also has a good influence on mental health; it is especially welcome to students who have much confusion and disorder in their lives. When school work is related to students' life experiences, and when they have immediate opportunities to use their reading, the stage is set for effective learning.

Proportioning Time

It is hard to say exactly what proportion of time should be spent in appreciation of literature, or in understanding the printed word; the two processes are interwoven. The following allotment of time was suggested in one school:

Literature	35%
Special units — newspaper, movies, etc.	15%
Oral and written composition	30%

Correct usage and grammar	10%
Spelling	5%
Vocabulary	5%

These categories, of course, do not represent separate segments of instruction; one is appropriately introduced in connection with others. However, some such allotment of time allows opportunity to teach most of the essential reading skills in connection with the teaching of literature.

The question is not "Can English teachers find time to teach reading?" but "How can the essential language arts be taught in English classes?" It is probable that the majority of high school English teachers are now teaching reading more or less effectively in their literature classes. They need only to become more aware of what these skills are, how they may be taught to students of different backgrounds and abilities, and where to get appropriate materials of instruction as wide in range of appeal and difficulty as the reading interest and proficiency of the class.

32. How Can We Help Students Enjoy Literature?

ENGLISH Joseph Mersand

The enjoyment of literature has long been one of the most important objectives of teachers of English. In one of the earliest of those heavily annotated classics — that of Scott's *Marmion*, edited by Robert Morss Lovett in 1896, we read: ". . . Although *Marmion* is often used as a book for study, yet few books are read by the average pupil with more pleasure."[1]

B. A. Hinsdale, in one of the earliest books on methods in English (*Teaching the Language-Arts*, Appleton, 1896), concludes his chapter on "Teaching English Literature" with: "Teach the children of the land how to read, teach them what to read, and give them a love for what is good in English literature."[2]

[1] Edition published by Longmans, Green, New York, p. XXXI.
[2] *Ibid.*, p. 142.

Since the publication of Hinsdale's book, there have been more than fifty volumes [3] on the teaching of English, most of them dealing in one way or another with some aspect of teaching literature. In the many decades of publication of our council journals — *Elementary English*, *English Journal*, and *College English* — there have appeared hundreds of articles on the teaching of literature. What, then, can be said about the topic which has not already been said so much better by such master teachers as Dora V. Smith, Lou La Brant, Louella Cook, Robert Pooley, John DeBoer, and a host of others who have written so cogently and so eloquently on this subject?

Certainly there is no new magic formula which I can expound that would solve all our problems encountered as we teach literature. The best I can hope for is the expression of certain basic principles which have been found to be reasonably successful in these past sixty years since teachers have been searching for ways to enable their students to enjoy literature.

Let us begin with objectives. I quote those operative in my own school system in 1922 when I was a student in high school, because they were probably as good as any that were in use at the time and because I can recall quite vividly the texts, the procedures, and my own reactions and personal growth under these objectives. The English syllabus for the high schools of New York City, adopted in 1922 (which operated during my high-school days), states very clearly that:

> "The chief aim in the teaching of literature . . . is to get them to enjoy reading good literature and to desire to read more of it." Other things to be accomplished by the reading of literature were:
>
> 1. To deepen and enrich their imaginative and emotional life. The teacher should help the pupils to see their own lives and experiences reflected in the literature they read. He should in this way lead them to understand others and to arrive at a better understanding of themselves.
> 2. To cultivate high ideals of life and conduct.
> 3. To give a knowledge of books and the power to read them with appreciation.
> 4. To improve their power of self-expression by stimulating thought and by supplying information and models of construction.

These are noble objectives which many of us would consider valid today. Certainly, our curriculum makers of 1922 were inter-

[3] See Appendix I: Textbooks on English Methodology.

ested in fostering enjoyment through literature. Whether these objectives were realized in whole or in part by a large segment of the student body might make an interesting paper on another occasion. The matter of concern to us is how we English teachers in the high schools of 1959 with their heterogeneous student populations, coming from diverse backgrounds, so different in capacities, needs, and interests, can perform this all-important task. A few misconceptions must be cleared up before a positive program can be established.

1. We can no longer assume that students entering our high schools have the ability to read on their level. W. S. Gray has stated that, "Scores made on reading tests show that from twenty-five to forty per cent of the pupils who enter high school are reading below the ninth grade level." [4] In a recent testing program conducted in my own school, as part of a city-wide testing of reading competence of all entering ninth and tenth grade students, we learned that about one-third were reading below their grade level on the tenth grade, but (and this was much more encouraging) more than 46% were reading above their grade level. Almost 10% were already reading on the twelfth year level.

2. A necessary corollary follows from number 1. Teachers of English in high schools must stop bemoaning the situation mentioned above and blaming the teachers in the lower schools for failing to do their jobs. Rather they have the responsibility of maintaining the skills already acquired, providing remediation for skills undeveloped or underdeveloped, and guiding their students towards the mastery of the new reading skills necessary for high school work.

For example, after administering the 1100 tests and arranging for their correction, one of my tasks was to report to the entire faculty and to discuss the implications, not only for English teachers, but for every teacher in the school. The reading grade of every incoming student was recorded on his permanent record, and teachers of all subject areas were urged to familiarize themselves with these facts. Incidentally, the occasion offered me an opportunity to put in a plug for the teaching of reading by every subject-matter teacher as needs arise.[5]

3. The day of the "one-shot" classic is about over. We cannot assign, if we have any insight into adolescent psychology and learning, the next thirty-five pages of *Silas Marner* or *A Tale of Two*

[4] W. S. Gray, "Is Yours an Effective Reading Program?" University of Kansas Bulletin of Education, February, 1958, p. 47.

[5] See Appendix II: Report of Stanford Reading Tests administered at Jamaica High School, October 15, 1958.

Cities and expect a feverish search for the beauties of thought and expression of either George Eliot or Charles Dickens and any degree of growth — intellectual, emotional, or aesthetic — from such a search.

As far back as 1896, B. A. Hinsdale cautioned against excessive preoccupation with a few compositions.[6] Hence, those of us who warn against studying a classic to shreds are following in a tradition that is at least sixty years old. We are hardly pedagogical radicals or innovators.

4. We cannot afford blithely to ignore the fact that individual differences with respect to reading are here to stay like sex, baseball, and taxes. For any teacher to ignore differences in reading abilities, in interests, in rate of growth, and in possibilities of growth is to be teaching truly in the pedagogical dark ages. Individual differences constitute at once the major problem and major challenge in education today. Not that they did not exist in the "good old days" of the 1890's or the early 1900's. Teachers, because of the highly selective nature of the secondary population, could afford to ignore these differences with fewer dangers than today. Even if we wished to ignore the individual differences in our classrooms today, the four Horsemen of Retardation, Repetition, Boredom, and Poor Discipline would rear their ugly heads to remind us that they were present.

5. We cannot assume that growth will come automatically by exposure to literature, even to enthusiastic, over-bubbling exposure on the part of the teacher. A favorite cliché of poetry teaching when I began my career in the 1930's was "Poetry is caught — not taught." We want to be certain that what our students are catching are the right things about poetry and all other imaginative literature, not an aversion that will never be eradicated.

How many times have we been confronted by our successful returning graduates whom we thought we had taught to enjoy literature? Too often, even the most friendly will admit that they do not recall the classics over which you waxed so enthusiastically. And some who recall the classics — even with some degree of pleasure — will confess that they never read another book by the same author.

6. We cannot afford to cry defeat because of the onslaught of the mass media. Literature and enjoyment of literature have survived every holocaust since the burning of the library of Alexandria and will still be here long after the last TV antenna becomes only an object of historical interest. Rather than bemoan the impact

[6] *Op. Cit.*, p. 136.

of the mass media on our times in general and on our students' reading in particular, let us learn how to utilize them for our own advantage. All of the mass media — TV, radio, movies, magazines, and newspapers — have long had educational departments whose purpose is to demonstrate how these media can contribute to valid educational objectives. In the February 8, 1958, issue of the *Saturday Review of Literature*, Lester Walker in his article "Boom in Good Books" stated: "Part of the interest in good reading has been stimulated by an unexpected source: the movies."[7] Correspondence with Mr. Walker, *Publishers' Weekly*, the American Library Association, and the Public Library of Washington, D. C. confirmed the statement of Mr. Walker and elicited additional information about the stimulation of worthwhile reading through television.

7. We cannot stimulate enjoyment in others unless we enjoy literature tremendously ourselves, know a great deal not only about the great classics but also about the ever-increasing wealth of suitable adolescent literature, and learn how to apply that knowledge and enthusiasm in our classes.

8. We cannot do this in one lesson, one term, or even one high school course. Our own love for literature took a long time to develop. Let us not expect miracles overnight.

1. and 2. A Program for Stimulating Enjoyment of Literature

Accepting the fact that a large proportion of students entering high school are deficient in reading when they enter, each teacher of English (and other content subjects as well) must familiarize himself with the various ways of evaluating reading growth, the many reading skills subsumed under the term "reading," the techniques of providing remediation within the classroom, and the teaching of the new and advanced skills that are now required. This implies in-service training for the multitudes of high school teachers who have never taken a course in the teaching of reading or who have never even read a book on this subject. The field is now so rich that no high school English teacher can honestly maintain that he doesn't know where to get the information. The pages of such professional journals as *The Reading Teacher*, *The English Journal*, *The Journal of the N.E.A.*, and many others have a host of articles for those teachers who are genuinely interested. Let us stop complaining about the shortcomings of our colleagues in the lower echelons of the educational system, and do something ourselves about improving the situation.

[7] *Saturday Review of Literature*, February 8, 1958, p. 38.

I list only a few of the reading improvement books that have appeared in the past few years:

Evelyn Nielson Wood and Marjorie Wescott Barrows: *Reading Skills* (Holt, 1958).
Carol Hovious: *New Trails in Reading* (Heath, 1956).
Nila Banton Smith: *Be a Better Reader* (Prentice-Hall, 1958).
Paul Witty: *How to Improve Your Reading* (Science Research Associates, 1956); *How to Become a Better Reader* (Science Research Associates, 1953).

In addition there are at least seventeen books designed for college students who wish to improve their reading.[8]

3. The Passing of the Standard Classics

We must stop hoping that assigning a portion of a hallowed classic to every member of the class will result in comprehension, appreciation, enjoyment, or any noticeable growth. The teacher of literature in high school today must abandon his reliance on a dozen or so major classics in English literature as a *modus operandi.* As Dora V. Smith has cogently stated it: ". . . there is little place in high school teaching today for the old approach to the novel by having every pupil read the same book at a set pace of thirty-five pages a day. Some should finish such a novel in three days. Others lack the capacity to read beyond the second chapter." [9]

This implies that the teacher must know a great many books on various reading levels and must know the interests and abilities of each of his students. Whereas one student might not be ready to appreciate *Silas Marner*, he may find much to interest him in such books as: Carroll's *As the Earth Turns*, Walker's *Winter Wheat*, Gale's *Friendship Village*, Grayson's *Great Possessions*, Emery's *Mountain Laurel*, and Best's *One-String Fiddle.*[10]

In New York City, to implement the new course of study in senior high schools, a reading list of hundreds of books pertaining to the dominant theme "The Self-Reliant Individual" has been issued to each ninth grade teacher.[11] Similar reading lists and suggestions for integrated activities in the language arts will be issued soon to teachers in the tenth, eleventh, and twelfth grades to illustrate the annual themes:

Eleventh grade: The Individual, and the American Heritage
Twelfth grade: The Individual's Quest for Universal Values

Instead of building a literature course in senior high school on

[8] See Appendix III: Books on Reading Improvement for College Students.
[9] Dora V. Smith, "How Literature Is Taught in the Secondary Schools of Today," *Journal of the N. E. A.*, April 1951, p. 286.
[10] *Ibid.*
[11] Published by the Bureau of Curriculum Research, 130 W. 55 St., N. Y. C.

two classics a term, the teacher has a wealth of books both from the classics and contemporary authors to meet every taste, every stage of development, and every interest. The publishers of literature anthologies have given us fine examples of profusely illustrated, attractively printed, and intelligently edited compendiums of suitable materials for personal and social growth. Some of the following four-volume series certainly deserve careful study by our English teachers interested in fostering personal development:

Harcourt Brace's *Adventure Series*, Olympic Edition
Scott, Foresman's *America Reads*
Henry Holt's *Our Reading Heritage*
Houghton Mifflin's *Reading for Enjoyment*
Lippincott's *Reading for Life*
Ginn's *Good Reading*
Macmillan's *Literature*
American Book's *The Mastery of Reading*
Laidlaw's *Cultural Growth through Reading*
Heath's *Conquest*

These texts not only will open new worlds for our students, but for many teachers as well. The thematic or unit approach followed in these anthologies (and such reading lists as supplied by the New York City schools) will probably go much further toward our objectives of enjoyment than the careful analysis of a dozen standard classics, and nothing more.

4. Meeting Individual Differences in Reading

Part of this misconception of teaching only a few classics has already been corrected in the discussion of Point 3. If the teacher begins to realize that *Silas Marner* may be pleasure for some, but poison for others; that *Idylls of the King* will thrill some and chill others; that Burke's *Speech on Conciliation* may conciliate a few, but alienate the many; that *Much Ado about Nothing* may, alas, be taken quite literally by many in his class — then he has taken the first step on the long, hard road of recognizing individual differences within even the most homogeneously grouped class, and then doing something about them. Space does not permit me to summarize the studies made by the Commission of the National Council of Teachers of English on the provision for meeting individual differences in the teaching of literature. Reference must suffice at this time to Chapter 11, "The Challenge of Individual Differences," in *The English Language Arts*.[12]

[12] *The English Language Arts*, New York: Appleton-Century-Crofts, 1952, pp. 246–273; *The English Language Arts in Secondary School*, New York: Appleton-Century-Crofts, 1956, pp. 123–159.

The perceptive teacher who knows his students will understand which books out of the teeming multitudes on hand will contribute to Johnny's growth in understanding himself, to Mary's growth in sensitivity to poetry, to Henry's growth in understanding the ways of other people, to Loretta's growth in understanding her American Heritage. To all these and to other aspects of growth, books can contribute. The teacher should know them and know when best to bring the book and pupil together for maximum effect. The reading of an alert English teacher in high school never ceases.[13]

Does this mean that we must lower our standards as we attempt to provide for individual differences? That we must accept a comic book version of *Macbeth* instead of the real thing? That we must permit the sordid paperbacks which are found in so many stationery stores in our large cities? The answer is decidedly in the negative on *all* counts. Providing for individual differences does not mean descending to the lowest common denominator. Like the reverse of Gresham's law in economics, good literature will eventually drive out trash. A perceptive and well-read teacher armed with a multitude of books of interest to teen-agers is more than a match for the purveyors of paperback trash. There are many lists of excellent books which teachers can utilize. Some of them are listed in Appendix IV.[14]

Many teachers and administrators have accepted the need for individual conferences in teaching written composition. We are more and more coming to realize that the individual conference in enjoying literature is just as important. Lou La Brant in her *We Teach English* writes cogently about this important way to understand our children and to guide them to enjoyment of literature.[15]

5. The Fallacy of Growth by Exposure

If personal growth could be achieved by exposure alone, then our most developed young men would be attendants in library stacks or salesmen in bookstores. Exposure to good literature, however, is not enough. More has probably been written on the methodology of teaching literature than in any other subject in the high school curriculum. There are at least fifty textbooks on the teaching of English and almost every one has a substantial section devoted to literature. No teacher can honestly contend that he doesn't know where to get the information about teaching

[13] Arthur H. Parsons, Jr. "The Teachers' Need to Read," *Journal of the N. E. A.*, March, 1958, pp. 168–169.

[14] See Appendix IV: Lists of Recommended Books.

[15] Lou La Brant, *We Teach English*, New York: Harcourt Brace, 1951, pp. 242–248.

literature. Many of the publishers of literature anthologies mentioned earlier also provide substantial teaching guides for each of the volumes. The guidebooks to the Scott, Foresman series *America Reads* by such master teachers as William S. Gray, Robert C. Pooley, Irvin C. Poley, and others are over 300 pages in length and are in essence textbooks on how to stimulate growth through literature. Teachers' manuals by Harcourt Brace are likewise useful.[16]

Many teachers with the best intentions in the world fail to establish contact between the book taught and the student striving to grow up. Such an evanescent form as poetry has been particularly difficult to get across. Commenting upon the contrasting ways of teaching Amy Lowell's "Lilacs," Dora V. Smith indicates: "The old way of teaching was to begin with characteristics of Amy Lowell's poetry and stories of how she smoked a cigar or with definitions of free verse, examples of which were then sought in books. The new way is to help students realize how effectively poetry reveals what he himself has seen and felt and to discover something of the technic the poet has used. Then each pupil can read more poems by himself, under the teachers' guidance, finding what best meets his own need." [17]

There is no royal road to knowledge. There are many roads—probably as many as the youth before us. Too many of us think that the road which we took, and which led us to delight in literature is the one along which we must lead our youngsters. We must be on the alert to read new (and old) books which we can utilize in our reading-literature program. We must also be experimenting with, reflecting over, and evaluating the results of new methods of guiding our students to the understanding, appreciation, and response to a work of literature. Once that right contact has been made, the pupil is never quite the same. Flaubert spoke of *le mot juste* in describing his search for the perfect word to express his ideas. The teacher of literature should also search for *le methode juste* (if I may coin the phrase) to achieve the results outlined above. This is the reverse of the old-fashioned question-phrasing and daily mark-giving which is so unhappily associated with the literature experiences we have all had several decades ago.

6. Enlisting the Mass Media

Prophets of doom have been lamenting the effect of the mass media upon reading and reading habits of our population. At each

[16] See also *They Will Read Literature*, a Portfolio of Tested Secondary School Procedures; N. C. T. E., 1955.

[17] Dora V. Smith, *op. cit.*, p. 285.

stage, alert teachers of English have tried to utilize these media to strengthen their educational programs rather than attack them as Don Quixote's windmills were attacked. From Edgar Dale's *How To Read a Newspaper*, to the N.C.T.E. volume *Radio and English Teaching*, and the N.C.T.E. volume *Using Periodicals*, and the current guides to TV shows, we have many valuable procedures for utilizing the mass media. Rather than take away from reading time, many students have demonstrated that requests for books frequently rise when there has been a movie or TV version of a classic. The complete sellout of Stendhal's *Red and Black* after Floyd Zulli's lecture on *Sunrise Semester* is well known.

When such TV productions as *A Tale of Two Cities*, *Jane Eyre*, *Romeo and Juliet*, *Richard III*, *David Copperfield*, and other classics are produced live on TV or revived on film, the alert teacher can surely capitalize on them in presenting the literature program. Thus by means of comparisons and contrasts between the mass media and the literary work being discussed the teacher can open ever newer avenues toward enjoyment. No mass medium will ever take the place of reading, but it should be utilized profitably toward achieving the goal for which we are all striving. The novelty of a new medium wears off quickly. A love of literature which we instill lasts a lifetime.

The public library in Washington, D. C. informs us that:

"The production of *The Lark* aroused interest not only in the play but also in other books about Joan of Arc — as did the earlier stage production. Many viewers were prompted to read Shaw's *Man and Superman* and Shakespeare's *Romeo and Juliet* after seeing the plays. TV programs led readers to ask for Fitzgerald's *Great Gatsby* and other titles, Sherwood's *There Shall Be No Night*, and Lindsay's *Great Sebastians*." [18]

7. The Contagion of Personal Enjoyment

The testimony is so overwhelming that it is almost axiomatic that enjoyment in literature is contagious from teacher to student. How many teachers are still using books, not because they are themselves strongly moved by them, but because they happen to have a set (or somebody else's set of lesson plans); or because they can obtain three sets of these books for their three sections? When there are over 6,000 paperbacks in print and when the price is so low that few students will object to purchasing their own copies, need any teacher use a battered, torn and dirty set of *Tale of Two Cities* just because she has been teaching it for years and has a set of questions for each chapter?

[18] "Reading Trends for Year Ending June 30, 1957," p. 12.

No teacher should teach literature who is not herself fired with enthusiasm for it, is widely read in as many periods as she has time for, and is acquainted with the scholarship in the fields. Such a book as Lewis Leary's *Contemporary Literary Scholarship* should be read by each one of us! And how can we afford to neglect some of the 1,500 books published each year for children and adolescents?[19]

8. Enjoyment of Literature Is a Slow Process

Unless we were all precocious, we developed our love for literature and our burning desire to communicate it over a period of years. If we followed the traditional pattern, we did not enjoy *The Brothers Karamazov* or *War and Peace* before *Frank Merriwell* or the *Bobbsey Twins*. More likely, we all went through a period of reading what we now know to be little better than trash, until we began to see the light, the light that shone from the beacons of the great lighthouse-keepers of mankind, those authors who showed us the way out of the darkness of our own minds or limited environment into the clear light of self-knowledge and world-knowledge and all the satisfactions pertaining thereto. We are probably stirring more of our students than we presently realize. Time works many miracles on seeds properly planted. Let us at least be certain that we are not wasting our seeds, or planting them at the wrong time, or failing to nourish them properly.

As an indication of how gifted students themselves regard their development of enjoyment of literature, I have appended thirty-seven statements from students in a twelfth grade class. All have received 90% or above in English and have an I.Q. of 130 or above. Their comments on such subjects as the influence of their parents, friends and relatives, teachers, book reports, class discussions, television, and movies are revealing of the role that each of these factors plays in developing the ability to enjoy literature.[20]

APPENDIX I

Textbooks on English Methodology

Blaisdell, Thomas C. *Ways to Teach English* (1930)
Bolenius, Emma Miller. *Teaching Literature in the Grammar Grades and High School* (1915)
Bolenius, Emma Miller. *The Teaching of Oral English* (1916)
Carlile, Clark S. *38 Basic Speech Experiences: A Guide for Student and Teacher.* Second edition, 1954.

[19] David Dempsey. "Young Readers Made to Order," *New York Times Book Review, Children's Book Section*, November 2, 1958, p. 3.
[20] See Appendix V: What Some Gifted Students Think about Enjoyment of Reading.

Carpenter, George R.; Baker, F. T.; Scott, F. N. *The Teaching of English in the Elementary and the Secondary School* (1903)
Chubb, Percival. *The Teaching of English* (1902, 1929)
Clarke, Harold A., and Eaton, Mary P. *Modern Techniques for Improving Secondary School English* (1945)
Cohen, Helen Louise. *Teaching Modern Plays* (1924)
Craig, Virginia J. *The Teaching of High School English* (1930)
Cross, E. A., and Carney, E. *Teaching English in the High School* (1939, 1950)
Dakin, Dorothy. *How to Teach High School English* (1947)
DeBoer, J.; Kaulfers, W. V.; Miller, H. R. *Teaching Secondary English* (1951)
Fairchild, Arthur H. R. *The Teaching of Poetry in the High School* (1914)
Fries, Charles C.; Hanford, James H.; Steeves, Harrison R. *The Teaching of Literature* (1926)
Heffron, Pearl M., and Duffey, William R. *Teaching Speech* (1949)
Hinsdale, B. A. *Teaching the Language Arts* (1898)
Hook, J. N. *The Teaching of High School English* (1959)
Klapper, Paul. *Teaching English in Elementary and Junior High Schools* (1925)
La Brant, Lou. *The Teaching of Literature in the Secondary School* (1931)
La Brant, Lou. *We Teach English* (1951)
Leonard, S. A. *English Composition as a Social Problem* (1917)
Leonard, S. A. *Essential Principles of Teaching Reading and Literature* (1922)
Mahoney, John J. *Standards in English* (1923)
Marsh, George L. *A Teacher's Manual for the Study of English Classics* (1921)
Mirrielees, Lucia B. *Teaching Composition in High School* (1931)
Mirrielees, Lucia B. *Teaching Composition and Literature* (1937, 1943, 1952)
National Council of Teachers of English. *The English Language Arts* (1952)
National Council of Teachers of English. *Language Arts for Today's Children* (1954)
National Council of Teachers of English. *The English Language Arts in the Secondary School* (1956)
Parker, Roscoe Edward. *The Principles and Practice of Teaching English* (1937)
Pinto, Vivian de Sola. *The Teaching of English in Schools* (1946)
Pooley, Robert. *Teaching English Usage* (1946)
Raubicheck, Letitia. *Teaching Speech in Secondary Schools* (1936)
Robinson, Karl F. *Teaching Speech in the Secondary School* (1951)
Rosenblatt, Louise. *Literature as Exploration* (1938)
Seely, Howard Francis. *On Teaching English* (1933)
Seely, Howard Francis. *Enjoying Poetry in School* (1931)
Sharp, Russell A. *Teaching English in High Schools* (1924)
Smith, Reed. *The Teaching of Literature in the High School* (1935)
Stearns, Gertrude B. *English in the Small High School* (1950)
Stratton, Clarence. *The Teaching of English in the High School* (1923)
Tidyman, Willard F. *The Teaching of Spelling* (1919)
Trent, William P.; Hanson, Charles L.; Brewster, W. T. *An Introduction to English Classics* (1916)

Walch, J. Weston. *Successful Devices in Oral English* (1950)
Ward, C. H. *What Is English?* (1917)
Webster, Edward H., and Smith, Dora V. *Teaching English in the Junior High School* (1927)

APPENDIX II

Jamaica High School, Louis A. Schuker, Principal

RESULTS OF READING TESTS ADMINISTERED ON OCTOBER 15, 1958, BY THE DEPARTMENT OF ENGLISH

Test: Stanford Advanced Reading, Form LM, with special scoring table supplied by the New York City Board of Education

Students: September arrivals, divided as follows:

Term 1	110
Term 3	1048
Total	1158

RESULTS

Term 1 — 110 students:

High score — 12.9 reading grade equivalent
Low score — 3.4
Medians — 8.38 average reading grade equivalent, taking both parts of the test
7.7 Test 1 — paragraph meaning
8.3 Test 2 — word meaning

Advancement:

12.5	5 students	4.5%
12.0 plus	8 students	7.2%
11.5 plus	13 students	11.8%
10.5 plus	23 students	20.9%

Retardation:

8.5 minus	70 students	63.6%
7.5 minus	49 students	44.5%
6.5 minus	37 students	33.6%
5.5 minus	18 students	16.3%
4.5 minus	7 students	6.3%
3.5 minus	1 student	.9%

Term 3 — 1048 students:

High score — 12.9 plus
Low score — 3.3
Medians — 10.83 average reading grade equivalent, taking both parts of the test
10.45 Test 1 — paragraph meaning
11.11 Test 2 — word meaning

Advancement:

12.5 plus	99 students	9.4%
11.5 plus	357 students	34.0%

Retardation:

9.5 minus	383 students	36.5%
8.5 minus	235 students	22.4%

SOME REFLECTIONS BASED ON THE RESULTS

One-third of the incoming juniors are reading 1½ years above their level. Almost one in ten is reading 2½ years above level. Looking at the less brighter side, more than one-third are somewhat retarded. Over 22% are retarded 1½ years. The English Department has made the following provisions:

For the gifted students, honors and XH and a Journalism class, providing for 231 students.

For the retarded students, XG classes including 139 students.

It is obvious that there are many students reading above grade level who are in our normal classes. We have probably taken care of most of the severely retarded students in our XG classes this term.

Of the incoming freshmen, the following generalizations seem warranted:

One-fifth are reading at least one year above grade level. A far greater percentage is reading below grade level. Almost one-third of them are 2½ years retarded. We have one XG class, which probably takes care of the worst, but another remedial class would probably have been better.

In both the 9th and 10th year tests, the students did better on the word meaning part than on the paragraph meaning. In other words, their knowledge of words seems to be better than their ability to grasp thought in connected prose.

We are fortunate in having such a large percentage of good readers among the sophomore class, and recognition should be made of that fact not only by the English Department, but by all our colleagues. Teachers in all the subject areas can assist by challenging the reading capabilities of the brighter students, as well as assisting those who are less qualified by training in some of the basic reading skills pertinent to their subject areas.

APPENDIX III

Books on Reading Improvement for College Students

Altick, Richard D. *Preface to Critical Reading* (1947)

Brown, James I. *Efficient Reading* (1952)

Carter, Homer L. J., and McGinnis, Dorothy J. *Effective Reading for College Students* (1957)

Cosper, Russell, and Griffin, Glenn. *Toward Better Reading Skill* (1953)

Dallmann, Martha, and Sheridan, Alma. *Better Reading in College* (1954)

Glock, Marvin D. *The Improvement of College Reading* (1954)

Jones, Everett L. *An Approach to College Reading* (1955)

Judson, Horace. *The Techniques of Reading* (1954)

McCallister, James Maurice. *Purposeful Reading in College* (1942)

McCorkle, R. M., and Dingus, S. D. *Rapid Reading* (1958)

Miller, Lyle L. *Increasing Reading Efficiency* (1956)

Palmer, Osmond E., and Diederich, Paul B. *Critical Thinking in Reading and Writing* (1955)
Shaw, Phillip B. *Effective Reading and Learning* (1955)
Shefter, Harry. *Faster Reading — Self-Taught* (1958)
Stroud, James B., and Ammons, Robert B. *Improving Reading Ability* (1949)
Weber, Christian Oliver. *Reading and Vocabulary Development* (1951)
Wedeen, Shirley Ullman. *College Remedial Reader* (1958)

APPENDIX IV

Lists of Recommended Books

1. CLOTHBOUND BOOKS

Chambers, M. M., and Exton, Elaine. *Youth — Key to America's Future* (1949)
Eastman, Fred. *Books That Have Shaped the World* (1937)
Frank, Josette. *What Books for Children?* (1941)
Larrick, Nancy. *A Parent's Guide to Children's Reading* (1958)
Lingenfelter, Mary Rebecca. *Vocations in Fiction* (1938)
Logasa, Hannah. *Historical Fiction* (1958)
Munson, Amelia H. *An Ample Field; Books and Young People* (1950)
Strang, Ruth; Phelps, Ethlyne; Withrow, Dorothy. *Gateways to Readable Books* (1958)
Washburne, Carleton; Snow, Miriam; Morphett, Mabel. *The Right Book for the Right Child* (1942)

2. PAPERBOUND PAMPHLETS

Alstetter, Mabel F. *Children's Books for Seventy-five Cents or Less.* Washington, D. C.: Association for Childhood Education International (1950)
Beust, Nora E. *500 Books for Children.* Washington, D. C.: Superintendent of Documents (1940)
Carlsen, G. Robert; Alm, Richard S.; Hanna, Geneva. *Social Understanding through Literature.* Washington, D. C.: National Council for the Social Studies (1954)
Carr, Edwin R. *Guide to Reading for Social Studies Teachers.* Washington, D. C.: National Council for the Social Studies (1951)
Ciolli, Antoinette. *The Teacher in Fiction.* Brooklyn, N. Y.: Brooklyn College Library (1955)
Davis, Louise. *Recommended Children's Books* (1951, 1952, 1953, 1954, 1955, 1956, 1957). New York: R. R. Bowker.
DeBoer, John J.; Hale, Paul B.; Landin, Esther; Lohrer, Alice. *Reading for Living.* Springfield, Illinois: Department of Public Instruction (1953)
Dunn, Anita E.; Jackman, Mabel E.; Bush, Bernice C.; Newton, J. Roy. *Fare for the Reluctant Reader.* Revised edition. Albany: New York State College for Teachers (1952)
Durrell, Donald H., and Sullivan, Helen Blair. *High Interest Low Vocabulary Booklist.* Boston: Boston University School of Education (1952)
Kircher, Clara J. *Character Formation through Books.* Third edition. Washington, D. C.: The Catholic University of America (1952)

Lombard, Nellie Mae. *Looking at Life through American Literature.* Stanford: Stanford University Press (1944)

Rollins, Charlemae. *We Build Together.* Revised edition. Champaign: N.C.T.E. (1948)

Spache, George. *Good Books for Poor Readers.* Gainesville: The Reading Laboratory and Clinic of the University of Florida (1955)

3. ANONYMOUS BOOKLISTS

Adventuring with Books. Champaign: N.C.T.E., 1956.

Annotated Bibliography of Selected Books with High Interest and Low Vocabulary Level. Indianapolis: Indianapolis Public Schools, 1954.

Books for the Teen Age. New York: New York Public Library, 1954, 1955, 1956, 1957, 1958.

Books for You. Champaign: N.C.T.E., 1956.

Books for Young People. New York: New York Public Library, 1947, 1948, 1949, 1950, 1951, 1952, 1953.

Books We Like. Urbana: Illinois English Bulletin, February, 1955.

Current Books. Senior Booklist of the Secondary Education Board. Milton, Mass.: Secondary Education Board, 1956.

Paperbound Books in Print. New York: R. R. Bowker, 1958.

Starred Books from the Library Journal. New York: R. R. Bowker, 1953.

Your Reading, a List for Junior High Schools. Champaign: N.C.T.E., 1956.

APPENDIX V

What Some Gifted Students Think About Enjoyment of Reading

THE INFLUENCE OF READING

"Nevertheless, I might dare to say that through reading one grows far beyond his mortal years and one actually does become a little bit wiser in the ways of man. For every chapter, every page, every paragraph, and every line of a book bring to their reader a little bit of the truth that is in the world." — *Albert Chang*

INFLUENCE OF PARENTS

"My parents, being teachers, introduced me to books at an early age by reading to me such children's books as "Winnie the Poo." As I got older and began to learn to read, they read with me, helping me with the words I did not know." — *Bob Levy*

"My parents are both avid readers, and they belong to numerous book clubs. Within the walls of my house I have always been able to find interesting reading material and the encouragement to peruse through it."
— *Diane Kornblau*

"My parents provided me with a store of volumes from which to choose, and encouraged me to keep a small library of my own."
— *Helen Buckberg*

"My mother is an avid reader and so we occasionally discuss special books of interest. I am surrounded day and night by books, books, and more books which pleases me no end." — *Janet Blank*

Influence of Friends of Parents

"My parents' friends have influenced my habits as well. They have always looked upon reading as a social necessity, since books and ideas are a main topic of conversation." — *Carl Auerback*

Influence of Parents and Teachers

"Firstly, I believe that a person does not develop a love for reading. It is developed for him by his parents and teachers. If the parents help and greatly encourage the first awkward attempts of the student to choose and read a book, I believe that a gradual liking will develop." — *Gordon*

Conversation of Parents

"Their mention of good reading has also influenced me. It was the frequent mention of Thomas Wolfe that influenced me to make a term project of him and his works. When time permits I hope to read all of his works." — *Claus Engelhardt*

Influence of Parents' Oral Reading

"My parents read to me nursery rhymes, bedtime stories, and fairy tales among others. They would show me pictures and all this — because I was interested." — *Boykoff*

Discussions by Parents

"Now it is not uncommon for my whole family to read the same book and then sit down for an hour or two and discuss and analyze it." — *Bob Levy*

Reading of Parents

"My parents are avid readers of current periodicals, and consequently such magazines as "Scientific American," "Atlantic," "U. S. News and World Report," and "Harpers" are part of the decor of my home." — *Jeff Kroll*

Influence of Parents by Gifts

"At home my parents have greatly influenced my reading by their choice of books which they have presented to me — Dickens and Dostoevski to name two." — *Claus Engelhardt*

Books in the Home

"Reading has always been a part of our family life, so much so that there are bookcases in almost every room, and they're still not enough." — *Carl Auerback*

Influence of Friends and Relatives

"My friends and relatives also play an important role in my appreciation of literature. We recommend books to each other and by so doing, I have broadened my scope by learning to enjoy reading many types of books in many fields. By discussing various books with my friends, I get their reactions and interpretations and in turn give them mine. This leads to a greater understanding of the book and therefore to a much deeper appreciation of what is read." — *Bob Levy*

"My friends and relatives also played a role in my own development as a reader. In a relationship where one person admires another, it is only natural for the worshipper to emulate his ideal. If the second person happens to proffer an atmosphere of cultural dominance (reading, music, etc.) then we may expect his companion to absorb this." — *Donald Garren*

A Wholesome Diet

"In conclusion, I enjoy reading because I was fed a wholesome diet of good books when I was young, and had the good fortune of having inspiring English teachers in school." — *Jeff Kroll*

Introduction to the World of Books

"I also feel that an introduction at an early age to the world of books is quite advantageous. However, at this age (8–9) books must be chosen very carefully so that they will be of adequate interest to the adventuresome youngster." — *Donald Garren*

Early Inspiration by Teacher

"When I was in the third grade the teacher I had was a very intelligent woman. In the course of a lesson she would mention several facts about a book or a story she wanted us to read. However, she very rarely assigned the stories for home reading. The clues or facts she mentioned often interested the class so much that the next day the first topic of discussion more often than not was the story the teacher supposedly never assigned for homework." — *Kwarta*

Influence of Teacher

"I think it might also be very helpful, as it was in my case, for the teacher to make extra books available to the more avid students for use in their spare time." — *Gordon*

Influence of Teachers

"My teachers also influenced my reading to some extent. Although lower grade teachers did little to steer me to extra reading for they were more interested in teaching students to read, my fourth and fifth grade teachers set aside a few library periods where we were given a choice of books to read." — *Aaron Bleckman*

Influence of a Teacher

"Only recently has my interest in reading returned and I think this is due to my English teacher of last year. He stressed literature a great deal and made the required class interesting." — *David Berger*

The Effect of the Teacher's Oral Reading

"I do remember one teacher in elementary school who had a unique way of getting the class to read more. She would take time out of the class periods every once in a while, sit down and start to read aloud from some book. Whenever the story reached an interesting point she would stop and put the book away. The same book would never be taken out again. This caused many of us to get the book from the library and finish reading it ourselves. We read just for enjoyment and not for marks." — *Eric Bodow*

LESSONS IN LITERATURE

"Although I like to read I don't like the literature lessons the school gives. I don't like the phrases "teaching literature" or "teaching pupils to like to read." In my opinion a desire to read or an appreciation of literature cannot be taught; it can only be communicated from teacher to student. I don't think you can interest students in reading just by assigning them books to read and analyses to do. I have always hated to do written work such as analyzing books chapter by chapter, comparing characters, or explaining why I liked or disliked a book. I think the only proper way to appreciate a book is through discussion, led by a teacher who himself appreciates the book." — *Carl Auerback*

THE EFFECT OF REQUIRED BOOK REPORTS

"Whenever I was expected to read a book it was assigned as a book report. This developed hostilities against reading. I don't want to sound like a psychiatrist but I feel their idea of assigning books for reports at an early age is something that discourages reading. Each time a child would normally pick up a book and start reading he thinks that it is too much like work he had to do in school and puts the book down again."

— *Eric Bodow*

THE DANGER OF BOOK REPORTS

"In this connection I have one complaint. This is against book reports. True, a student should supplement his formal schooling with some extra reading but to make him write a report on the book, reading becomes a drudgery, all enjoyment is lost and the student gets very little out of what he has read. If instead, more books were read at home and then were discussed and analyzed in class the student would not lose interest and would benefit from the ideas of his classmates." — *Bob Levy*

THE EFFECT OF REQUIRED BOOK REPORTS IN JUNIOR HIGH

"During the next phase of my education, junior high school, my literary instruction consisted of a series of required monthly book reports. I recall reading the first fifteen chapters of *David Copperfield* as a class unit, and handing to my teacher a folder, prettily decorated, containing a summary of each separate chapter. We never discussed our opinions of the book, and were not encouraged to finish the book on our own."

— *Helen Buckberg*

NEW CLASSICS FOR OLD

"The teacher should not compel the reading of outdated novels, which no longer have the significance they had at the time of their original publication, such as *David Copperfield*, *House of Seven Gables*, and *Silas Marner*. The Board of Education should require novels of such contemporary authors as Dreiser, Hemingway, Steinbeck. Then high school literature would be more beneficial and more enjoyable." — *Jack Berenzweig*

DISLIKE OF THE HOUSE OF SEVEN GABLES

"Another of these extremely uninteresting novels was Hawthorne's *House of Seven Gables*. During the period of time when this novel was written it might have been interesting, but one century later, it does not belong on the required book list of a high school student." — *Jack Berenzweig*

Dislike of *Silas Marner*

"In high school I first encountered books which I did not enjoy. The first of these was *Silas Marner* by George Eliot. I have never found a more deterring novel for any student who is attempting to find a love for reading. In my opinion the only thing the reading of *Silas Marner* accomplished was to discourage me from indulging in any of the other works by Eliot."

— *Jack Berenzweig*

Class Discussions

"In Jamaica High School much of my desire to read was augmented by discussions of various books and authors. Criticisms by my classmates and teachers, as well, have introduced me to many books which I have enjoyed immensely, and I maintain that this is the best method of getting high school students interested in literature." — *Diane K.*

Required Reading a Block to Reading

"I enjoyed reading until I entered junior high school. Required book reports and the reading of certain books just didn't agree with me. I'm not sure that I know why, but I just seemed to rebel against the idea of having to read a book for school. My reading slacked off until I read only what I was required to read." — *Berger*

Liking vs. Disliking Books

"I developed a liking for reading because I never developed a dislike for reading. This may sound paradoxical. The only explanation I can give for this fact is that I never was assigned dull books to read in school. When Homer and Dickens were assigned, my teacher presented these works in such an enjoyable fashion that even they were a pleasure to read."

— *Jeff Kroll*

Forcing the Child to Read

"The child must not be forced to read, for if he is, he may develop an aversion for reading from which he may never recover."

— *Michael Gordon*

Influence of Library

"With the aid of library techniques taught in the seventh grade, the lock to the numerous volumes in public libraries was opened to us. In these buildings I never found it difficult to get lost among the written pearls of wisdom." — *Diane K.*

The Effect of Movies on Reading

"Movies have been instrumental in my selection of 'popular' novels. After viewing an interesting film I am often impelled to read the novel upon which the movie is based." — *Jack Berenzweig*

Television vs. Reading

"Another reason I would say for my developing the habit of reading is because television is not encouraged in my home. I am permitted to watch a few choice programs that have been approved and often selected by my parents." — *Jeff Kroll*

SUGGESTIONS FOR THE LIMITED READER

"Find out something that interests the student — romance, baseball, fate, etc. — and then dig up a book on the subject that is written in a manner pleasing to the tastes of the student." — *Greenhauf*

33. What Is a Good Unit in English?

ENGLISH

Richard S. Alm

It seems appropriate, in the opening issue of the school year, to emphasize unit planning. In this article, Dr. Alm, associate professor of education at the University of Hawaii, identifies criteria for evaluating teaching units in English.

What are the criteria of a good teaching unit in English? First, I must define some terms and explain my basic assumption in dealing with the topic. What are *criteria?* Standards by which one judges — in this particular instance, a unit of instruction in a class in English.

What is a *unit?* The curriculum-maker has many definitions for many kinds of units. In Volume III of the Curriculum Commission Series, *The English Language Arts in the Secondary School*, a unit is defined as follows:

> Varied activities in the language arts are developed around a central theme or purpose, clear and significant to the student. . . . [The unit] must be sufficiently broad to involve in some measure all four of the language arts and to permit each individual (1) to work in cooperation with his class and (2) to pursue certain special interests in a wide range of materials and experiences suited to his ability.[1]

My approach to this topic is based on this assumption: unit teaching is not only worthwhile, it is a highly desirable approach to the teaching of English.

[1] The Commission on the English Curriculum. *The English Language Arts in the Secondary School* (New York: Appleton-Century-Crofts, Inc., 1956), pp. 69–70.

Criterion No. 1

The good unit in English has some legitimate reason for being. At the outset I am introducing a subjective element. Philosophies about values certainly would not all agree. I am not trying to foist off my biases; instead I am declaring what mine are. I say that the study of the pronoun is not and cannot be a unit, nor a study of commas in a series, nor attention to the scansion of a modern poem. These activities may be labeled "units," but they have little substance; they are fragmentary and their importance is debatable.

The good unit, on the other hand, must deal with an idea, a problem, or a theme. The unit's reason for being is usually a synthesis of many things: the subject matter of the unit may be a part of our intellectual or aesthetic or creative heritage; the unit may center in students' interests; the unit undoubtedly will involve a study of specific skills and abilities; the unit may help students to achieve one of their developmental tasks[2] — as Havighurst and his University of Chicago associates use the term.

Critics of unit instruction in English frequently say, "You are stealing the stuff of social studies." My reaction is always: this depends primarily upon the state of mind of the English teacher. If you have been a scholar in history or geography or political science, you will look at such a unit as "Problems within America — Grade 11" in the Seattle Public Schools Unit Plan books for English teachers, and teach in one way. However, the English teacher looks at this unit title and material and realizes that through literature, he can make personal and real and significant the lives of people who live around us.

For example, think of cultural change or the impact of conflicting cultures on contemporary society. There is no better expression of this for high school readers than Jade Snow Wong's *Fifth Chinese Daughter*. In a study of man's quest for happiness, for fulfillment, for the good life, one might turn to Cather's *My Antonia*, Walker's *Winter Wheat*, Rolvaag's *Giants in the Earth*. Social studies? Never — not so long as the reading of literature is primarily a personal experience. This use of literature surely helps to give a unit meaning and significance.

Criterion No. 2

The good English unit has a sense of direction observable both by the teacher *and* the students. Not only should the class members know, in general, *where* they are going in a unit, they should be

[2] Havighurst, Robert. *Developmental Tasks and Education* (New York: Longmans, Green and Co., 1952).

aware of going there. *Objectives* is a much-battered word. We have in some courses of study too many objectives, lists that are so long that we may feel — "Everything is expected of us in every unit. What's the use! Skip the objectives. Go on to the activities." Thus, we may not know the *why's* of our doing, and our doing may be in vain.

But this sense of direction is vital to a good English unit; otherwise youngsters may, as they frequently do, merely mark time. Do you recall the convention program theme of the NCTE a few years ago — a line from Browning: "Man's reach should exceed his grasp." The unit that has many avenues within it, the unit that is many faceted is one that certainly will help youngsters to grasp a good deal and, what is highly important, to reach for more. After all, is not this the essence of the definition of an educated mind?

We have many examples in print of good units that reflect such a sense of direction. Any high school English teacher who has not read in *The English Language Arts in the Secondary School* the detailed description of a unit taught by Virginia Alwin should do so.

This *direction* involves two other problems: evaluation and the reactions of the participants. We must seek ways to evaluate in terms of where we are going and how. In addition, the work must give both teacher and student a sense of satisfaction in having gone a particular distance.

Criterion No. 3

The good unit reflects the interrelationship of the language arts and all aspects of it; the learning, the materials, the experiences must be related — honestly — to the unit theme. I interject "honestly" because often we merely rearrange the items in the window and call it a brand-new display.

In such a context I am reminded of Dora V. Smith's story of her visit to the class studying a unit entitled "This Air Age." The class was reading *Ivanhoe*. When questioned about the relationship of Ivanhoe to the unit, the teacher said, "Ivanhoe is a story of chivalry. We don't have knights today but aviators are our modern knights." Doesn't this logic remind you of Clarence Day's mother and her financial dealings with Father Day?

Writing activities should grow out of the development of the adolescent's intellectual and personal reaction to the theme of the unit. Here in a unit we find a logical base for explanation, assignment, motivation, example — all the elements of what Hitchcock [3]

[3] Hitchcock, Alfred. *Breadloaf Talks on Teaching Composition* (New York: Henry Holt and Co., 1927).

called the "pre-expression stage" in writing, the stage too often neglected, the crucial point in the writing experience of youngsters.

As I read Louis Zahner's "Composition at the Barricades" in the November 1959 *Atlantic*, I realized that the unit method of organizing instruction in the language arts provides a setting for the development of the language skills he wants. He does not talk about a unit and he may not recognize the possibilities of the unit; nevertheless, within the framework of the good English unit students can learn well the effective writing skills that Zahner believes are fast disappearing from American schools.

Criterion No. 4

Within a good English unit, the teacher focuses upon the learning activities necessary to accomplish the objectives of the unit. Unfortunately, summaries of units too often omit what I call the a-b-c'ing of the teacher unfamiliar with the unit approach. He reads a list of suggested activities and assumes that the students of his tenth-grade class will know this, or be able to do that. Without finding out the various stages of their development, the teacher assigns an activity, expecting it to be accomplished.

How many aimless class periods are spent in what is usually called "discussion"? What do we find? Routine and dull question-and-answer periods, domination by a few, silence from most, no sense of direction, poor or even no listening. Students must be taught how to discuss: how to lead, how to stimulate, how to react, when and how to ask questions, how to synthesize, how to summarize, the etiquette of participation. Again, to remind you of our central theme — what is a good unit? — the teaching of these elements of discussion must not be learned in isolation from ideas. One learns to discuss well when he listens well, reads wisely. Discussion is not just a matter of voice projection.

Last year, I sat with a State Language Arts Guide Planning Committee. The subject under discussion was the interrelatedness of language arts. One teacher of considerable reputation said, "I think you should ask the English teachers whether or not they want to include the teaching of speech in their classes." What stunning naïveté! How can one teach English well without attention at every point to *all* the aspects of the language arts?

Criterion No. 5

The good unit considers the individuals involved in the learning process. Youngsters — indeed, all people — learn at different rates, at different times, for different reasons, and surely to different degrees.

First, to illustrate one aspect of this problem. Activities must be possible of accomplishment, related to the background and development, the ability of adolescents. I have two examples of how some gifted children are today being challenged in language arts. In one large urban system within the last few weeks, a youngster spent considerable time one evening writing 109 adverbial-clause sentences. I trust that you recognize the subtleties here. The average child in that grade might be asked (although I am not sure why) to write ten such sentences. The gifted child, to exercise her talent, had to write 109!

Earlier in the fall the daughter of a librarian friend of mine was given an assignment by her English teacher. Remember now, the student had been identified as gifted. She was asked to write a paper dealing with the works of Ernest Hemingway. This girl, dealing with *A Farewell to Arms*, *The Sun Also Rises*, *For Whom the Bell Tolls*, and others, is twelve years old!

To cope with the variations among the individuals within a class, we prize the resource unit with its unlimited materials and more ideas than any one teacher can deal with in a reasonable length of time. The growing importance of these units is stressed in the U. S. Office of Education report, *English Language Arts in American High Schools*,[4] prepared by Arno Jewett. He notes, for example, that in more than half of the states which have printed courses of study, such bulletins are organized around resource units.

In specific areas of the language arts, how can we deal with great variations among individuals, tapping all resources and helping all youngsters to develop? The field of literature, for example, is so vast that certainly here one can find books for every interest, every taste, almost every stage of reading development. For a great variety of suggestions, read *Literature Study in the High Schools*[5] by Dwight Burton.

Criterion No. 6

The good English unit will carry within it an element of discipline. Involved here are the attitudes and the habits that influence students' language arts behavior. There must not only be a sense of direction in a unit — the development of an idea — the students must develop the vehicles whereby these ideas are expressed. One facet of writing, for example, is spelling. Think for a moment about the teaching of spelling. In spite of all that has been written about the subject, what are the chief approaches to teaching it

[4] Bulletin 1958, No. 13 (Washington: Office of Education, U. S. Department of Health, Education, and Welfare, 1959).

[5] (New York: Henry Holt and Co., 1959).

today? With or without graded spellers, teachers (1) provide a list of words on Monday (possibly in what is called a pre-test), (2) give a test on those words on Wednesday, and (3) administer a final test (for a grade) on Friday. The typical (unfortunately, usually the only) method of study is writing the word over and over again. Results: Possibly a 100 on Friday but no change of habit, no change of attitude. In spelling, teachers must help youngsters to develop both a spelling *consciousness* and a spelling *conscience*. Many errors are called "careless." What does that mean? It means for one thing that we do not demand careful habits of observation, year after year. It means that we are satisfied too often with less than a student's best performance.

In writing assignments that are a part of a good English unit, we must help each youngster to learn how to spell new words, to discipline himself to improve his spelling ability, to write and to rewrite carefully, to proofread automatically.

Criterion No. 7

The good English unit will give the learner new, increased, and fresh perspectives about himself in relationship to the unit theme. Gerald Green, in *The Last Angry Man*, says, "The most overwhelming fact of the twentieth century is the assault on the public ear and eye, the incessant, relentless avalanche of useless information." [6] Green was not referring to the ear and eye of the youngster in the English classroom, but well might he have done so. Much discussion goes on *about* language and literature, but this is a pallid substitute for actual experiences in writing, reading, speaking.

Joseph Mersand has said that we must get some commitment on the part of each student. He must be *involved*, and the degree of involvement will influence his learning and his retention of that learning. Involvement in a piece of writing or in reading a novel will certainly change the student's perspective about the experience. Within a good English unit, the alert teacher will find opportunities to provide diverse experiences with several of the language arts.

In summary, then, these are my criteria: the good unit deals with a subject that is worthwhile; it has direction; it is honest in its presentation; it focuses on learning activities inherent within it; it considers the individual students involved; it means a disciplining of talents; it means broader horizons for the student. Now what are these criteria? Certainly they are characteristics of good English teaching regardless of how it is organized. In fact, the criteria are probably standards for good teaching in any area.

[6] (New York: Pocket Books, Inc., 1959), p. 481. (Originally published by Charles Scribner's Sons, 1957.)

To remind you of my own personal persuasion, one that I share with countless others: the unit is a highly logical vehicle for teaching the kind of English program we want, one that is significant for all children, one that embraces the teaching of all the language arts in a context that has far more meaning than a day-by-day series of fragmentary lessons, or a page-by-page analysis of a textbook. We want — in short — for our labors in the English class the kind of development in our students that only we who teach English can give.

34. The Problem of Reading Instruction in Mathematics

MATHEMATICS John R. Clark

While on an automobile tour not long ago, I went into a stationery store one evening to do some shopping. The only persons in the store were three boys, in the rear, doing, or attempting to do their homework in mathematics. One of the boys, evidently the son of the proprietor, came forward with a polite "Sir, may I help you?" After completing my purchases, I said, "What are you boys doing?" One replied, "Our math problems, Sir. We're stuck. Could you help us?"

I expressed my interest and accompanied them to the rear. One of the boys handed me the text (of which I was an author) and said, "We're having trouble with problem four."

"Will you read it aloud to me?" I asked. The boy pronounced the words unusually well, but with such obvious lack of comprehension of the nature of the problem that I commented: "Your reading doesn't help me to understand the problem." I pointed to another boy. "Will you read it?" His reading revealed no better interpretation than did that of the first boy. The third boy then volunteered to read it aloud. His reading indicated quite clear comprehension of the thought and meaning of the problem, and brought forth from the other boys an "Oh! I see. I get the point."

After treating in a similar manner the other problems in the assignment, the boy on duty remarked: "Sir, may I ask you a question? What is your occupation? I know you aren't a teacher, but I can't figure out what you do."

I replied that I lived on a farm in Pennsylvania and spent a great deal of time thinking about mathematics.

Then I asked, "How could you tell I wasn't a teacher?"

"I knew you weren't a teacher," he answered, "because you didn't tell us anything."

Without revealing any more about myself, I took leave of the trio with the remark, "In Pennsylvania the boys who read well, who interpret the ideas in their problems, have very little trouble with mathematics. Reading isn't just saying words. It's seeing the ideas behind them. Reading is very much like thinking."

Many junior high school boys and girls do have difficulty in reading their textbooks in mathematics. This paper proposes those procedures for teaching reading which the author has found effective with most pupils, excluding only those whose mental, emotional, or physical conditions render them "clinical cases."

Levels of Reading Ability

We know that junior high school pupils in mathematics classes vary greatly in their ability to read the explanations and problems in their textbooks. For some pupils, reading at best consists of mere saying of words, with little or no comprehension. They dislike reading. Obviously they require more of the oral developmental, experiential type of instruction which is currently so effectively employed in many elementary schools.

At the other end of the scale are those pupils who, independently, are able through reading to modify old concepts or to acquire new ones. They are capable of reading for a degree of depth, difficulty, and range greater than that of the average mathematics text. Unless challenged by reading content appropriate to their capacity, they are likely to lose interest in the subject. If effectively challenged, they will be able to become outstanding thinkers. In this group we are most likely to find our future leaders in science and mathematics.

Then there is the large middle group of readers at whose level most of us direct much of our teaching and our writing. In this, group we find various kinds of reading disabilities — mental-physical, and emotional. Specialists in reading have made significant contributions to the classroom teacher, looking toward correction and prevention of such disabilities.

The purpose of this paper is to suggest instructional procedures to benefit, in varying degrees, learners at all levels of ability and achievement, both in mathematics and in reading.

Objectives of Mathematics Education

Before considering further the place of reading in our mathematics classrooms, we must have a large measure of agreement concerning the major objectives of mathematics education.

For our purpose here we shall assume, not argue, these major objectives. Stated very briefly, they are (1) learning to reason, to think one's way through a problem situation (quantitative, of course) to find a response that has not previously been learned, and (2) learning to compute and to estimate, once the reasoning has disclosed the operations required to bring forth the wanted results.

But reasoning requires ideas, concepts, meanings. Reasoning is rearranging or relating the ideas in the problem situation so that the "what is wanted" is seen as a consequence of the "what is known." Thus, reasoning presupposes knowledge of the concepts. Hence, we have as an *instrumental objective* the teaching of the fundamental concepts inherent in the number system. (Recently we have been calling these ideas or concepts the *meanings* of mathematics.)

We may say, then, that we are greatly concerned with instruction in the concepts of our field, in order that the learners may be able to "think about," to "reason about" significant problems in their experience.

Experience has taught us that in the initial stages of instruction in each new concept we should rely upon *oral* rather than *written* communication. We *explore*, *say*, *hear*, *discuss*, *talk about* the problem. We experiment, discover, explain, listen, use illustrations, and develop. We build new meanings and modify old ones, we generalize, and particularize. We introduce new symbols, and new words in context. All the while, the teacher records these new words and symbols on the chalkboard and calls attention to their spelling and formation. The learners use them in sentences and enter them in their "New words" or "New symbols" lists.

These symbols and words, such as *circle*, *diameter*, *circumference*, *ratio* and π (*pi*), illustrate the technical vocabulary of mathematics. They, the technical vocabulary, are unique and indispensable. We are saying that their meanings and inter-relationships are more effectively learned at the outset through oral discussion, experimentation, and informal verbalization than through reading. But there comes a time when it is to the learner's advantage to be able to supplement, if not replace, the oral with the written expression. He must be able to read, to comprehend thought communicated through written sentences. Reading, of course, helps the pupil to establish and clarify concepts which he has acquired through more direct experience.

Making and Reading Mathematical Generalizations

Let us continue our discussion of the concepts of *circle*, *circumference*, *diameter*, *ratio*, and *pi*. As a result of the informal, developmental, discussion type of teaching, the pupil will have participated in the making of such generalizations as:

1. The circumference of a circle is a little more than three times its diameter.
2. When we divided the length of the circumference of a circle by the length of its diameter, we got a quotient of about 3.
3. We called the "quotient of the circumference divided by the diameter" the *ratio* of the circumference to the diameter. Ratio means quotient.
4. We agreed to call the ratio or quotient *pi*. It's the same for all circles.
5. We also found that the diameter is about one-third of the circumference.

These, and other observations about the concepts of *circumference*, *diameter*, *ratio of circumference to diameter*, and *pi*, are prerequisites for reading. They constitute a kind of mathematical reading readiness. The teacher prepares learners *for* reading!

After this careful preparation, most learners may be expected to be able to read and respond successfully to such written questions and statements as the following (presumably found in the textbook or supplied in other written form):

1. The circumference of a circle is about how many times as long as its diameter?
2. Jack measured the diameter of a circle, and decided that it was 12.2 inches. He wanted to find its circumference. To do so, would he have to measure it? Why not?
3. Is *ratio* a sum, a difference, a product, or a quotient?
4. To find the ratio of circumference to diameter (when both are known) would you divide the diameter by the circumference, or divide the circumference by the diameter?
5. Make a sentence using the words *circumference*, *diameter*, and *pi*. What is the subject of your sentence?
6. Complete the sentence: To find the circumference when the diameter is known, ...
7. Complete the sentence: To find the diameter when the circumference is known, ...

Problem Analysis Leading to Reading and Solution of Problems

In the circle-circumference-diameter-ratio-pi illustration, we have been concerned with learning leading to reading generalizations with comprehension. We shall now consider the analysis of the so-called verbal problem, leading to its reading and solution:

"Find the rate of discount on a six-dollar pair of skates that sold for four dollars." To solve the problem, the learner (the reader) must bring to the problem a galaxy of previous learnings. These include:

1. *Marked price, selling price, discount,* and *rate of discount.* Without these concepts, there can be no real reading, even though the words may be pronounceable and spellable.
2. Moreover, the reader must know the *relationship* between (a) the concepts of marked price, selling price, and discount, and (b) the rate of discount, discount, and marked price.

Obviously the particular data in the above problem are relatively unimportant in comprehending the problem, and are necessary only for computing the numerical answer.

Thus, as we said previously, before the learner can be expected to read with comprehension the above problem, before he is ready to read it, he must realize that discount means "marked price minus selling price," and that *rate of discount* means "*discount compared with marked price by division.*"

Guidance or help in the reading of the problem is almost, if not wholly, equivalent to guidance in the reasoning required in solving the problem. This may be facilitated by such questions as:

1. What is the problem? (Finding rate of discount.)
2. What do you have to know and do to find rate of discount? (Know discount and marked price; and then divide discount by marked price.)
3. Does the problem tell you the discounts? (No.)
4. What must you know and do to find the discount? (Know marked price and selling price; and then subtract selling price from the marked price.)
5. Does the problem tell you the marked price and the selling price? (Yes, six dollars and four dollars; so the discount is two dollars.)
6. Now that you know the discount and the marked price, what did you say you must do to find the rate of discount? (Divide the discount by the marked price.)

The reader must be in possession of the concepts of marked price, selling price, discount, and rate of discount. He must be prepared to read, i.e., to sense the ideas denoted by the words and phrases of the verbal statement. With this preparation, the reading (getting the thought) is possible.

To emphasize the ideas or concepts in reading a verbal problem, we often have the problem read and paraphrased, naming only the big ideas. Thus, in our rate of discount problem the pupil might paraphrase as follows: I paid so much for an article which regularly sold for so much; I got a discount of so much; I have to find the rate of the discount.

We are insisting that reading in mathematics, whether of generalizations or problems, implies analysis, recognition of ideas and the relationships among them. In a sense, reading is thinking, relating what is wanted to what is given. It should be obvious by now that in the writer's opinion, the ability or inability of the pupil to *read* mathematics exposition and problems with comprehension and discernment is determined to a great degree by the clarity, depth, and range of his mathematical concepts. Good readers are those who have the conceptual equipment necessary to recognize the mathematical ideas connoted by mathematical words, phrases, and symbols. Poor readers are those who are deficient in this conceptual equipment. Remedial reading is closely equivalent to relearning or improved learning of the ideas. The pupil whose understandings are relatively immature will of necessity be a relatively poor reader. We improve his reading by clarifying his understandings, by reteaching, by moving him at a slower pace, by providing more experiences with ideas.

Now let us consider what reading difficulties may be encountered in a group of verbal problems. What opportunities for growth in reading may be provided?

1. Meaningless technical words or phrases may appear in one or more of the problems. If so, they, the problems, should be omitted from the assignment. In this case the teacher or textbook will have violated the accepted principle that verbal problems should apply *previously learned concepts*.
2. The non-technical vocabulary may be inappropriate or above the reading level of the class, or some members of the class. In this case the problem should be read aloud by one or more good readers, after which the word or phrase may be modified, or replaced.
3. The sentences may be too long. Here the teacher may have the pupils suggest ways of revising them to make them more readable.
4. The problem may contain insufficient data for its solution. If so, this fact should be recognized by the class, with a resulting agreement as to what action should be taken to supply the missing needed data.
5. A problem may contain irrelevant or unneeded information. In fact, some problems of this type are desirable. Identification of such information makes for purposeful reading.

Characteristics of Mathematical Reading

Reading in mathematics is distinctive in three important respects:

1. The vocabulary of mathematical reading is probably more limited and more exacting than that of any other subject area. Its words and symbols are characterized by a high degree of precision of meaning. Its sentences are succinct. The flow of thought is sequential. Such words and phrases as *since, therefore, consequently, put-together, take-apart, compare, by definition, by assumption,* and the like, call for keen discernment. The learner's reading rate is necessarily slow. There is no such thing as "skimming." Every word, phrase and symbol must be digested. The reader becomes disposed to ask himself, "What does this mean? How are the ideas related? In which direction do I go now? Is the statement always true?" In this reading-thinking process, explanations and problems may need to be read several times for full comprehension.
2. The symbolic or shorthand language of mathematics cannot be read intelligently until the symbols have meaning. This symbolic language can have meaning only by skillful association with less symbolic and more meaningful language.

For example, to read with insight such symbolic expressions as $a \div b$, $\frac{a}{b}$, $b\sqrt{a}$, the pupil must have the concepts of partition and comparison division. Interpreted as partition, the verbalization of each algorism is: "Some number *a* is to be separated into some number *b* of equal parts." Interpreted as comparison division, the verbalization of each is: "How many *b*'s are there in *a*?" or "*a* is what part of *b*?"

Effective reading of such expressions as $y = 2x + 3$ presupposes the concepts of *variable, equality, multiplication,* and *addition.* The expression states that "two numbers are so related that one of them is always 3 more than twice the other."

Thus, as in the reading of word symbols, the reading of mathematical symbols demands of the reader the possession of the concepts and the relationships among them.

3. Reading simultaneously improves and widens language usage and mathematical understanding. Textbooks are written in terse, concise, and correct statements. Pupils must be taught to appreciate those various and equally correct ways in which mathematical thought is expressed. For example:
   (1) The commission at the rate of 5% on sales of $1600 is (a) 5% of $1600, or (b) .05 × $1600, or (c) $1600 multiplied by .05, or (d) the product of .05 and $1600, etc.
   (2) The number of yards in a mile (5280 feet) is (a) the quotient of 5280 feet divided by 3 feet, or (b) equal to the number of times

3 feet is contained in 5280 feet, or (c) may be computed by dividing 5280 feet by 3 feet, etc.

(3) The area of a rectangle 4 feet wide and 6 feet long is (a) 4×6 square feet, or (b) 6×4 square feet, or (c) $4 \times 6 \times 1$ square feet, or (d) the product of its dimensions (in feet), etc.

The stating and reading (with comprehension) of such varied, equivalent, and equally correct ways of thinking and expression, deepen insight. Practice in re-casting in other equivalent language, statements found in the text, is rewarding.

High Level Maturity in Reading

It will be apparent that up to this point we have proceeded upon the assumption that the teacher has played the major role in the instruction. She has employed reading, to be sure, but chiefly as a follow-up, as a continuation, extension and enrichment of the oral, developmental instruction. She has prepared the pupil for reading by making sure that he has the conceptual background prerequisite to the reading. However, the teacher believes that the pupil should become increasingly able to learn through his reading, and become less and less dependent upon her. Eventually the pupil should become able, through his reading, to sense and clarify the ideas, get new ideas, and see the relationships among them. Through critical study of what he reads, he can become his own teacher. At this mature level, reading will have become the open sesame to mathematical insight.

A colleague of mine ingeniously and effectively promotes this kind of teaching. One of his pupils reads (and reports to the class) textbook A's treatment of a topic, such as Area. Another pupil reads and reports on textbook B's treatment of the same topic, and so on for several other texts. On other topics, other pupils read and report. The teacher's assumption is that pupils *can read*, and that they derive profit and pleasure from the reading and from the sharing and comparing of their learning experiences.

Conclusion

1. In order to be able or to be ready to read, most pupils require an oral, exploratory, experimental, developmental, discussion type of teaching designed to build and enlarge the concepts and generalizations. During this period the essential oral and written vocabulary becomes familiar and meaningful.
2. Following the above procedure, pupils having no special disabilities are able to read with comprehension statements and questions about the topics just developed. Emphasis is upon the recognition of ideas and the relationships among them.

3. After verbal problems have been read they should be paraphrased or re-stated so that the mathematical ideas appear in bold relief. This facilitates the reasoning leading to their solution, and at the same time aids the poor reader.
4. Mathematical reading is highly specialized. The person best equipped to guide the reader is the mathematics teacher, who conceives of the teaching of reading of mathematical ideas as an integral part of the learning in his field. Mathematics teachers, however, need the guidance of "reading specialists" in the prevention and correction of deep-seated reading disabilities.

35. Improving Comprehension of Mathematics

MATHEMATICS

Mary C. Austin

Improving comprehension skills in mathematics typically requires attention to the activities or processes of developing concepts, building comprehension skills, and reading related materials. Each of these will be discussed briefly.

Developing Concepts

The teacher of mathematics must plan to build an understanding of the language of mathematics and the ability to translate it, for the specialized vocabulary is frequently a communication barrier for students. More and more teachers are realizing that without adequate understanding of the vocabulary of mathematics, learning of the mathematical principles and techniques is impossible.

In mathematics, each new unit of study is built on those that have preceded it; hence, difficulties in concept development are cumulative. Junior and senior high school teachers find it helpful to make a pretest of terms basic to the course — concepts which have been introduced at earlier levels in the sequence of mathematics courses. When the results of the pretest have been tabulated, the teacher knows which technical terms need to be presented to the entire class, to small groups, or to individuals. The students themselves can work on their individual needs, test each other, and gradually acquire the essential terms.

In the development of concepts in mathematics, emphasis is rightly placed upon understanding general vocabulary (e.g., *consecutive*, *depreciation*, *invested*, *exceeds*) as well as upon the technical vocabulary of mathematics. Special attention should be directed also to two types of words: (1) those whose mathematical meaning is different from their general meaning (*root*, *improper*, *rational*), and (2) those whose mathematical meaning is more precise than the general meaning (*opposite*, *direction*, *similar*). To ensure good comprehension, teachers need to make an analysis of both the general and the specialized vocabulary which their students will encounter in the present course and then provide definite opportunities for introducing these terms. *The Teacher's Handbook of Technical Vocabulary* [1] may be consulted as an initial guide in the construction of such a list.

Since meanings are based upon experience, mathematics teachers should develop needed meanings through experience *before* making an assignment. Pupils who have a clear understanding of the concepts represented by 7, 3, 7^3, 343 and = will have no difficulty when they read that $7^3 = 343$. They know that the expression 7^3 means that 7 is to be taken three times as a factor and that related to this expression are the ideas of "base" and "exponent," which are technical mathematical terms. How were these terms learned effectively?

Fawcett [2] points out that thoughtful teachers prepare students to read with understanding by providing experiences wherein a factor is repeated, such as $7 \times 7 \times 7$. Once students understand the concept of the use of a number as a factor a given number of times, they are introduced to the symbolism which expresses this concept concisely. When the pupils describe this symbolism, they speak of a little number above, and to the right of, another number and are glad to replace this awkward expression by giving the appropriate names to these numbers. Increased comprehension, rather than confusion, is the result when these students read in their textbooks during the preparation of their assignments that "an *exponent* is a small number written to the right of, and a little above, another number, called the *base*, to indicate how many times that number is to be used as a factor."

[1] Luella Cole, *The Teacher's Handbook of Technical Vocabulary.* Bloomington, Illinois: Public School Publishing Company, 1940.

[2] Harold P. Fawcett, "Nature and Extent of Reading in Mathematics," *Improving Reading in Content Fields*, p. 28. Supplementary Educational Monographs, No. 62. Chicago: University of Chicago Press, January, 1947.

Wherever possible, the teacher should explain the appropriateness of the mathematical term or symbol. In some instances an analysis of the word may be helpful. *Per cent* can be related to the familiar word *cent*, the hundredth part of a dollar. *Monomial*, *binomial*, *trinomial*, and *polynomial* can be associated, respectively, with *monologue*, *monopoly*, and *monocle; bicycle*, *biped*, and *biennial; tricycle*, *triangle*, and *tripod; polygon*, *polychrome*, and *polyped* to indicate the meaning of the prefixes.

Stimulating students' interest in the origin of words may also contribute to their understanding and enjoyment of mathematical terms. The word *calculate*, for example, was derived from Latin in the days when the old Romans used stones to compute their transactions. *Calculus* was originally a stone used in reckoning, while *calx* (limestone) was the type of stone used at that time.

Building Comprehension Skills

Adequate comprehension in mathematics is based upon knowledge of vocabulary and upon an awareness of the contributions of each word, phrase, or sentence to the solution of the problem. But good comprehension requires more; it necessitates visualizing the problem as a whole, selecting data essential to the solution of the problem, arranging the facts selected in proper order for use in solving the problem, and recalling fundamental mathematical principles and applying them. With these demands being made upon the reader, it should come as no great surprise to anyone that helping pupils learn to read mathematical problems intelligently is still one of the most troublesome instructional problems in the teaching of mathematics.

Successful teachers have found three techniques particularly helpful in improving comprehension skills: (1) helping students build good problem-solving procedures; (2) helping students adjust their rate of reading to their purposes; and (3) helping students read with the purpose of later using the ideas gained.

Many students reach high school without having established good problem-solving techniques. Early in the school year the teacher should determine which students need special instruction in this area. Practice in reading and solving problems orally as a group, or with individuals, may then be carried on with specific attention devoted to having the pupils answer questions similar to the following: (1) What do we need to find? (2) What facts are given in the problem? (3) What steps are necessary for a solution? and (4) What is a reasonable answer? With frequent exercises of this type, students will begin to use this approach to problem solving in their own study.

In mathematics, students must be guided to understand that their speed of reading needs to be adjusted to both the material being read and to their purposes for reading the material. Bond [3] suggests that the reader read rapidly for general impression in an arithmetic or algebra problem, that he then read to put the facts into proper relationship with one another, and then read to check the organization of relationships. The first reading is more rapid obviously than the following readings but at a much slower pace than for narratives. The succeeding readings where attention is centered on details of relationship and organization should be deliberate and intensive.

Teachers can help students learn to read mathematics with a purpose. Certainly a basic principle in the development of comprehension is that students will find meaning in what they read only if they are looking for it. By the type of assignment given, teachers can encourage the kind of purposeful reading which leads to better comprehension. Students should be told what they should know, understand, and be able to do upon completion of their reading.[4] The following directive to students is illustrative of the type which may be used as a class activity or in making an assignment: [5]

> *Reading for Sequence or Outline.* Steps in an experiment or problem: Using the example of a mathematical process, make two columns on a sheet of paper; list in one column the steps required for solution in your own words and in order; in the second column translate these steps into mathematical symbols. Placing a sheet of paper next to these lists of steps and symbols, work a problem of the same kind step by step according to your description in the lists.

Other examples of directives which call attention to reading skills are given on subsequent pages in *Problems in the Improvement of Reading.*

The Survey, Q (Question), 3 R (Read, Recite, Review) method which is recommended for students as they read chapters in their other textbooks can become an equally effective approach in mathematics. Students should decide what the purpose of each assign-

[3] Guy Bond and Eva Bond, *Developmental Reading in High School*, p. 188. New York: The Macmillan Company, 1941.

[4] Kenneth B. Henderson, "Methods of Increasing Competence in Interpreting Reading Materials in Arithmetic and Mathematics in Grades Seven to Fourteen," *Improving Reading in All Curriculum Areas*, p. 162. Supplementary Educational Monographs, No. 76. Chicago: University of Chicago Press, November, 1952.

[5] Ruth Strang, Constance McCullough, Arthur Traxler. *Problems in the Improvement of Reading*, Second Edition, p. 178. New York: McGraw Hill Book Company, Inc., 1955.

ment is before beginning their reading. As they read, they should formulate and answer questions pertaining to this purpose. At the end of each section, they should stop for a mental review in their own words of what has been read. Selective rereading of "hazy" parts of the assignment and locating strange words or symbols in the dictionary or in other parts of the textbook should follow. If, in addition, students read with the deliberate intent of being able to recall the material, their study will be rewarded with deeper understanding and retention.

Teachers can help students read with the purpose of later using the ideas they have gained in other ways also. By having frequent tests which demand application of understanding of mathematical principles, instructors give opportunities which require repetition of the material during and after learning. Numerous other opportunities should be provided for students to use the ideas gained through reading: reproducing mathematical data in discussions, explanations, and answering questions; gathering mathematical data for increasing general information, such as population and travel data; and giving mathematical information to others — data pertaining to weather, distances, household quantities, and current business trends.

Reading Related Materials

In the past, wide reading was practically nonexistent in mathematics courses. Today, however, in order to improve pupils' reading in mathematics, the teacher must be concerned with the building of interest and purpose in reading in this field. Through wide reading in mathematics, interest may be heightened and competence increased. Wide reading also opens the door to a closer correlation with work in science, industry, and everyday life.

While the preparation of supplementary materials in quantity has not attracted authors and publishers to any great extent, many good materials are available. By making more and better use of the materials for wide reading that do exist, perhaps the situation will gradually be remedied. An excellent bibliography may be found in the *Chicago Schools Journal Supplement.*[6]

Teachers who wish to achieve the objective of wide reading in mathematics will plan their work to include the following steps: (1) Review the mathematics courses to find places where time may be saved from content without neglecting the essentials; (2) Select a few topics in connection with which wide reading may be done; i.e., a bibliography including the history of a topic, biographies

[6] "Mathematical Teaching Aids," *Chicago Schools Journal Supplement* for January and February, 1954.

of mathematicians, and more extended writings or articles related to certain topics or units in the texts; (3) Locate these references, examine and evaluate them, and distribute them to the pupils; (4) Give the pupils time to use these materials and time to discuss the ideas they have gained.

Current articles frequently demand an understanding of mathematics. A profitable activity which leads to a deeper appreciation of the role of mathematics in our modern culture is the collection by students of recent materials containing mathematical ideas. As students explain the examples they have procured, critical reading, mathematical insight, and use of mathematical data are being promoted.

36. Interpreting Materials in Arithmetic and Mathematics in Grades Seven to Fourteen

MATHEMATICS

Kenneth B. Henderson

Speaking generally, the process of reading is the same whether the student is reading English or mathematics. The symbols, whether they are English words or mathematical signs, serve as cues to the ideas which are to be communicated. As the student reads, he interprets the symbols and uses the ideas they represent to accomplish a certain purpose. As in reading English, so in reading mathematics, the two chief causes of reading difficulty are (1) not knowing what the symbols mean and (2) not knowing, or being confused about, the purpose of reading.

Helping Students Build Concepts

One can hardly discuss the improving of reading, whether in mathematics or in any other subject, without considering the problem of helping students build clear and correct concepts; for, when a student reads, his understanding of what he reads is a function of the meaning of the symbols he encounters.

There appears to be a sequence which a teacher can follow whether he seeks to have students develop new concepts and symbolize these with words or mathematical signs or whether he extends the meanings the students have previously attached to certain symbols. The first step in this developmental sequence is to provide the students with a selected and organized set of experiences with things or ideas already meaningful to them.

In a trigonometry class, rather than directing students to memorize the definitions of the sine, cosine, and the other trigonometric functions, each student might be told to construct right triangles of various sizes all having the same acute angles. Then each student would be asked to measure the sides of each triangle and to find the value of such ratios as the side opposite one of the acute angles to the hypotenuse, the side adjacent to the angle and the hypotenuse, etc., for each triangle. When the results of the experiment are summarized, it should be evident that, accepting the existence of error of measurement, the values of the various ratios apparently depend only on the size of an angle and not on the size of a triangle. The teacher then should suggest that the students test this hypothesis to see whether it can be proved true for *any* (and hence every) right triangle. This not only deepens the students' knowledge of proof and of the propositions of plane geometry but also ties more associations to the concepts they are building.

Research evidence seems to indicate that it makes little difference in developing concepts whether the teacher begins by stating the name of the concept to be developed (for example, "measurement" or "percentage") or whether he does not announce the subject of the study (as in the trigonometry class) but directs the students' experiences in such a way that the concept evolves. However, the amount, kind, and organization of the experiences that the teacher provides for the students make a great difference.

The second step in helping students build concepts is to get them to intellectualize or talk about the experiences. The purpose of this is to enable them to abstract the common elements involved. For the students doing the measuring, the teacher's questioning should bring out that measurement (notice the generalization) consists in (1) selecting a unit of measure having the same property as the magnitude to be measured and (2) comparing it with the magnitude to be measured. In the trigonometry class mentioned before, the students should be made aware of what they have found: that the ratios are a function of the size of the angle and are invariant as to the size of the right triangle in which the angle is situated.

If a new concept is being developed rather than an old one extended, the third step is at hand. This consists in indicating the symbol which we are accustomed to use to represent the concept. If possible, the teacher should explain the appropriateness of the symbol. This is easy to do for symbols like those for logarithmic and trigonometric functions. It is harder for the symbols like Δx and $f(x)$, for it must be pointed out that these symbols do not mean x multiplied by Δ or x by f. In some cases an analysis of the word or symbol is helpful. *Per cent* can be tied to the more familiar word *cent*, the hundredth part of a dollar. *Monomial*, *binomial*, and *trinomial* can be related, respectively, to *monologue*, *monogram*, and *monocle; biped*, *bicycle*, and *bicuspid;* and *tricycle*, *triangle*, and *tricolor* to indicate the meaning of the prefixes. The "ratio" in *ratio*-nal numbers may help students remember the fundamental property of these numbers.

The final step in the concept-building sequence is again to provide situations in which the students have to use, and see the significance of, the symbol and the idea or ideas it represents. Such experiences in applying their knowledge provide both the students and the teacher a chance to see whether the concepts are clear, for the test of understanding is the ability to use them in new situations. In addition, these experiences further broaden and deepen the concept.

In summarizing, improving students' reading in mathematics is directly dependent upon helping them establish clear referents for the symbols they use. This process arises in experience and returns again to experience for verification. In no other way can meaning be given to symbols.

Checking on Meaning of Symbols Presumed to be Known

Not only must the mathematics teacher help students build new concepts and extend some of the concepts they formerly had, but he must also continually check on the preciseness of the meaning that the students have for the various symbols they use. At times these symbols will be words like *formula*, *power*, and *parallelogram*. At other times they will be mathematical signs like $\surd$, %, and π. In every case the teacher must assure himself and the students that the referents (ideas which the symbols call to mind) are correct and precise.

Checking on what a student means by the symbols he uses can be done by questioning him. The explanation he gives should indicate whether his idea is clear or fuzzy. This questioning should be penetrating enough to satisfy the teacher and the other students.

This procedure should be started in the first few days the class meets. The teacher should explain why this is being done and that it is not an attempt to embarrass or punish any student who is not clear as to what a symbol means. Then if the teacher checks up on good and poor students alike and is objective and patient in reteaching when lack of clarity is apparent, many of the students will gradually take on this procedure and use it on themselves in their own study.

When concepts are vague, it is sheer delusion to continue "covering ground" and trying to build new concepts on the quicksand of the old ones. Imagine continuing to talk about *functions* — linear, quadratic, and trigonometric, and their representation by an English statement, a graph, a table of related values, or perhaps by an equation — when the students do not have a clear idea of *function* to start with. If teachers are to take seriously what other teachers, college professors, and employers say about the vague ideas of some students, it should be apparent that it is not possible to go too far back in the students' knowledge in checking their ideas. Junior high school students should be checked on such elementary concepts as subtraction, division, fraction, and place notation and the symbols for these. Senior high school students should be checked on their understanding of the meaning of the ratio, per cent, proportion, coefficient, exponent, and logarithm and the symbols for these ideas, in addition to the ones mentioned for the junior high school students. Scarcely anything a teacher does has so much value as this continual check, reteach, check later, reteach if necessary, check-again procedure in the classroom.

Helping Students Understand Purpose of Reading

How a person reads depends on why he is reading. If he wants to get specific information, he reads differently from the way in which he reads if he wants to understand and be able to make use of this understanding later on. Since reading is dependent upon the reader's purpose, his reading will be ineffective to the extent that the reader is confused about why he is reading or to what end his acquired knowledge will be put. This suggests two things that mathematics teachers should do when they make assignments, be these daily, weekly, or at the beginning of a unit of study. Students should be told what they should know, understand, and be able to do upon the completion of their reading. They should also be given suggestions concerning how to read so as to attain these objectives. This attempts to establish principles which will transfer as the students face the same purposes in new contexts.

There is an old adage that what a person *does* speaks so much more loudly than what he *says* that one cannot hear what he says.

Placing this in the context of the present discussion, it is rather ineffectual continually to preach understanding what is read and yet, by the assignments and tests, encourage imitation of sample or type problems which require little reading. As Trump points out, "Because our goals are too frequently set in terms of the objective skills to be mastered or problems to be solved, the child decides that he can skip the presentation and come at once to what he considers the assignment, namely, the practice work."[1] And when teachers use sets of problems all of which are solved the same way, they fail to encourage discrimination in reading. The carelessness in reading that this tends to teach may even transfer to other reading situations.

Students do a lot of reading of verbal problems. These problems are preformulated. They almost always contain data which are both necessary and sufficient. The solution of this kind of problem sets certain purposes for the student in his reading. He must ascertain what is to be found and what is given and must infer the nature of the functional relationship between these sets of data.

If students are given only preformulated problems to solve, they will not learn to read for such purposes as determining which variables are relevant and which can be quantified, what simplifying assumptions must be made, how accurate and representative the data are, and what the nature of a satisfactory solution is. Reading for these purposes is important. Most of life's problems that lend themselves to mathematical analysis come to us unstructured. Consider, for instance, a family deciding whether they should buy a home freezer, rent a cold-storage locker, or continue relying on their refrigerator. If they do as they should — read the literature related to the problem — they will have to read for the purposes mentioned above. Would that their mathematics teachers had taught them how to do this as well as how to attack unstructured problems of this kind!

One further point should be made. Research evidence indicates that, if a student reads with the deliberate intent of being able to apply later what he learns, he will read in a manner that will reflect this purpose. Teachers can help students to this end by suggesting that, before they start to read, they first decide what they are supposed to learn through the reading. Then as they read, they can ask themselves questions relative to this purpose. This will keep them actively attentive. A further suggestion is that

[1] Paul L. Trump, "Types of Reading Development Needed in Mathematics," *Improving Reading in Content Fields*, p. 57. Compiled and edited by William S. Gray. Supplementary Educational Monographs, No. 62. Chicago: University of Chicago Press, 1947.

they go back in the textbook or use the dictionary to find what strange words or symbols mean and that they stop at the end of their reading and tell themselves in their own words what they have read. Vocalization or reading aloud difficult ideas or passages is sometimes useful in fixing the ideas. We all use this reinforcing technique. These and other suggestions will help the students develop effectiveness once they have accepted the purpose.

How can a mathematics teacher induce this "set" in students? Probably the most effective way, assuming the students are motivated, is frequently to use tests which demand application of understanding. To students, tests are an operational definition of the teacher's objectives. They direct the students' study. Hence, if tests reward study which aims at understanding and application of understanding rather than mere memorization, it may be expected that the students will take on this purpose in their reading and study.

Implications of the Distinctive Nature of Mathematics

Mathematics as a language is very concise. Think how much information is packed in the relationship $A = \frac{1}{2}h(b + b')$. Think also how crucial the decimal point is in the statement, "Multiply the number on line 5 by .24."

As a consequence of this conciseness, it is at times necessary to advise a fast reader to slow down when reading mathematics symbols. The ability to skim in reading, an ability which is very useful in some contexts, is usually out of place in mathematics. A fast reader or one who is skimming could, for example, easily miss the prime attached to the second b in the formula above or the decimal point before the 2.

Careless readers also have to be shown that missing even one word or a sign often changes the entire meaning. The answer to $\sqrt[3]{8}$ is different if one misses the index number. And if the student has been working per cent of decrease problems, his "set" may make him miss the prefix *in-* in the next problem which says, "Find the per cent of increase." Reading mathematical subject matter usually demands slow and attentive reading. This should be pointed out to students early in their study of mathematics.

Finally, there are special kinds of reading to be done in mathematics. Students are expected to read formulas, tables of related values, and graphs. This requires special training. They should be taught, first, to find the subject or title. This sets the formula, table, or graph in context. They should ascertain what the variables are, what they mean, and what their units of measure are, if any. Since formulas, tables, and graphs describe functional relations, students should read these with an eye as to how the variables are related. Finally, in the case of graphs and tables, they should be able to read pairs of related values if this is the nature of the graph or table. Sufficient practice leading to the formation of guiding principles in the reading of formulas, tables, and graphs should help students improve in this aspect of their reading in mathematics.

37. What Are the Responsibilities of Social Studies Teachers for Teaching Reading?

SOCIAL STUDIES

Mabel Rudisill

We shall approach the question of the responsibilities of social studies teachers for teaching reading by analyzing (*a*) the skills an effective student uses as he reads and studies various types of social studies materials, and (*b*) the role of social studies teachers in helping him attain these skills. Let us take a student who is highly mature with reference to the techniques, attitudes, and habits of thinking which he employs in reading and study. An analysis of the processes he uses will reveal the goals toward which we should work.

Our hypothetical student has established effective basic reading habits. With each fixation of the eyes he perceives a group of words as an idea, which, with preceding and succeeding ideas, he structures into larger thoughts. He varies his rate of reading and his thought processes according to the type of material and his purpose for reading. He has learned that the difference in effective rates is not so much in the visual work of word recognition as in the kind of thinking required.

He knows that to comprehend printed material, the reader must be able to recognize words and understand their meanings. In this respect social studies materials offer unusual difficulty. Some of this difficulty arises because their vocabulary is extensive and specialized. Much of the vocabulary deals with ideas and events which are remote in time and in space. For such concepts, our student has had little help from his personal experience. Even when the vocabulary deals with today's institutions and events, the concepts involved are likely to be complex and abstract.

Our student has learned that if he applies common meanings to certain words in his regular vocabulary, he may have misleading images and referents. He has found, for example, that *foreign ministers* do not preach, that *watered stock* refers neither to water nor to animals, and that the *iron curtain* contains no metal drapery.

At each step his teachers, if they are professionally competent, have reckoned with the abstractness of social studies concepts. They have anticipated vocabulary difficulties, giving attention to both pronunciation and meaning. They have utilized existing backgrounds of experience as a basis for developing understandings, and they have used pictures and concrete activities for filling gaps in these experiences. They have helped pupils to learn to use contextual clues for inferring meanings, and to check such inferences by reference to the glossary or dictionary. In the case of words with multiple meanings, they have guided pupils in judging which of several dictionary definitions best states the meaning of the word as used in the particular context.

Let us analyze further the skills used by a highly successful student. From them we can deduce the responsibilities that the social studies teacher has for teaching reading.

First, let us watch the student's use of the textbook. He *does* use a textbook. He values it because it gives a concise, systematic, comprehensive, organized treatment of the subject. He has learned that the text must be supplemented with wide reading from a variety of materials. But it stands as a basic core, an organized framework within which ideas from other sources can be woven and evaluated. Of course the facts and concepts from the basic textbook are likewise examined in comparison with those from other textbooks and sources.

How then does the ideal student deal with this book? He studies it; he reads it to understand ideas, to organize related content, to remember significant facts. To this task he applies basic principles governing effective learning. He studies with a purpose; he studies with intent to remember; he organizes ideas; he stops at intervals for self-recitation; he reviews. Specifically, he surveys or previews the chapter, noting the title and the headings of major subdivisions. He does this for an over-all view and to identify and center his attention on the author's main problem and his general organization. The student considers these problems and sub-problems in relation to problems previously studied. He pauses to recall what he already knows on the subject.

Before beginning the reading of one section or subdivision in his text, the ideal student scans the material to discover the main question which the author is attempting to answer. He notes the major sub-problems. Usually, he does this by noting the boldface or italicized headings. If there are no such headings, he does it by skimming. He recalls the question which the author is attempting to answer and reads to find the author's answer to his question. As he goes along he identifies the main points and the supporting points; he distinguishes between major ideas and illustrations of these ideas; he distinguishes between the relatively important and unimportant content; he subordinates or discards irrelevant matter.

After a section has been read in this manner, he recalls first the main points, then the supporting points, and finally the important details. He now skim-reads the material he has just recited to ascertain that he has made no serious omissions in his recall. He attacks succeeding sections in like manner. At the end of the chapter, he reviews it as a whole for a grasp of the total organization and a review of the important ideas.

During the process described above, our ideal student gives special attention to place names and unfamiliar words. If an unknown place location or physical feature is crucial to understanding, he refers to a map. Other unfamiliar words he first studies in context. Whether he checks their pronunciation and meaning from the glossary or dictionary at this time or waits until later depends upon whether the term is the key to understanding the basic idea. When charts and tables are referred to in the text, he studies them. He identifies in them the facts to which the author has referred. He studies the additional facts given in these charts and tables and evaluates the author's point of view and conclusions in the light of these facts. He considers whether the facts are sufficient to support the author's conclusions or whether they point to different conclusions.

Our student has been taught to supplement information from the text with facts from other sources. He refers to a variety of reference materials: atlases, encyclopedias, yearbooks, other textbooks. He uses skimming techniques for locating particular items in lists and in connected discourse. He compares facts from these sources with those of the textbook. He is alert to discrepancies and, when they are found, he checks the qualifications of the authors and the sources of their data. He judges which facts are most likely to be valid.

The above description has assumed that the student is using a basic textbook. He may use many sources. Obviously, he does not need to use the text as a basic source of information as he seeks to collect, organize, and summarize data on one particular problem.

The teacher is responsible for teaching her pupils the use of tables of contents, indexes, and lists of tables, charts, graphs, and maps in dealing with their own textbooks. This is done when there is need to locate specific items and when additional training is needed.

Rather than referring students to certain books, pages, and paragraphs, the teacher trains students to use these sources independently. She consistently helps students to judge which kinds of reference books are most likely to contain certain kinds of information.

The social studies teachers instruct their pupils in how to use maps and globes. They teach the meaning of special symbols when they are needed. They have pupils convert lines, dots, colors, shadings and other symbols with their accompanying keys and legends into ideas of direction, distance, location, topography, climate, production, and transportation systems. They teach that maps and globes are indispensable aids and that some ideas are not adequately conveyed through verbal presentations. Maps and globes are unique tools of the social studies. The need for detailed training in their use is generally recognized. The needed skills and the techniques for teaching them have been well presented in a number of sources (8, 9, 11).[1]

The materials with which our ideal student has dealt so far are highly condensed, quite abstract, basically factual. How are they made meaningful? How are they converted from dead to living matter? How do they become significant in his daily living? Of course the alert social studies teacher is using many means of making concepts concrete and personal. Among these are other types of reading materials.

Our student is a reader of the literature of biography, fictional biography, and historical and geographical fiction. He reads for enjoyment, and he reads as a student of the social studies. His teachers have carefully guided him into literature related to the topic being studied. They know that one's concepts must be clarified, refined, and enriched by experience in varied concrete situations. The usual person reads historical fiction primarily for the characterization and plot; but he incidentally acquires some conception of the geographic, economic, social and political conditions and some insight into the beliefs and feelings characteristic of the time and place.

On the other hand, our mature social studies student is more

[1] Bibliographical references are listed on pages 408–409 at the end of this article.

critical and perceptive. He has been taught to differentiate between the factual and the fictional. His social studies teacher has encouraged him to be alert to the details of the historic or geographic background in which the characters move — their manner of living, the impact of events on their lives; the influence of location, topography, and climate; and the relation of these factors to the events of the time. The student questions whether the situation or condition of the principal characters is typical or is atypical for the time or the place. He guards against allowing a strong emotional experience with an atypical situation to distort his view of the whole. He guards against allowing the atypical to symbolize for him the typical.

In connection with units of work, teachers have made available varied narrative and fictional accounts. They have provided materials with different levels of reading difficulty so that all students can find some to read independently with pleasure and profit. Teachers have discussed with their students the related fictional materials they were reading. Inevitably, with contributions from different sources, discrepancies in facts or concepts are found among the various fictional presentations. Discrepancies are found also between them and textbook accounts.

Such disagreements lead to joint teacher-pupil problem solving: to rereading material for more exact interpretation, to recognition of the significance of qualifying phrases, sentences, or paragraphs; to investigation of the author's background and his scholarly reputation; to development of criteria for judging what was intended as factual and what was intended as fictional; to judgment as to whether the setting or the condition was general or unusual; to drawing conclusions as to the most probable realities.

The genuine student of the social studies keeps abreast of current events; he is conversant with the arguments on both sides of controversial issues; he himself is beginning to grapple with problems of citizenship. Today, he has many sources of information or of misinformation; many sources for ready-made opinions. But along with the other sources, he is a reader of current materials — newspapers, magazines, books. He needs all the reading skills employed in the effective reading of other social studies materials, plus other skills. He has a greater need for suspended judgment and critical evaluation. The writer who attempts a fair, complete, and impartial analysis of a current issue has a difficult assignment. The reader's assignment is likewise difficult.

With the newspaper, our highly mature, hypothetical student reads headlines to determine which topics to follow up. For superficial interests, the first several paragraphs suffice. For deeper interests, he skims the article to locate facts in relation to the writer's generalizations. He questions whether these facts harmonize with, and whether they are adequate to the writer's generalizations. He is familiar with more than one newspaper. He has discovered whether the interests of the publisher and owner are revealed in the selection of the news, as well as the treatment of what is selected.

This exceptional student has regular contact with a variety of magazines, and he uses the *Readers' Guide to Periodical Literature* to locate other articles on his special interests and problems. Among the articles selected on the basis of titles, he often skims to locate the particular portions which directly apply to his problem or interest. Often, he merely skim-reads an article for the author's main thesis and general point of view. This he is able to do if the subject is familiar and the style is direct. As he does this he notes whether the author supports his point of view with facts or with opinions.

But our student knows that it is not the writer alone who must be objective. He knows that as a reader he must strive for an objective point of view. He knows that research has shown: (1) that the reader with preconceived attitudes and opinions tends to remember those facts that support his own point of view, and not to remember those that oppose it; (2) that the biased reader tends to interpret the facts to support his own point of view, whether it is pro or con; and (3) that he tends to accuse the author of prejudice because he himself holds an opposite prejudice (3, 10). Our student therefore attempts to withhold judgment until all the facts are in, and until they are weighed. He tries not to over-generalize from isolated cases.

But he does not remain forever in this state of balance; he does not hold to a fence-straddling position. Issues must be resolved; decisions must be made; action must be taken. One should not merely view the action; one should participate in the action, whether to restrain or to promote. Therefore, to generalize rightly and to draw conclusions soundly are the final acts.

Good social studies teachers have assumed responsibility for teaching pupils that the reader's first obligation, regardless of his personal opinion, is to understand the author's meaning. They teach their pupils to judge which of several statements are factual or opinion and to judge the validity of assumptions; they teach pupils to examine the adequacy of evidence given in support of opinions; and they teach pupils to discover the fallacies in their own hasty conclusions (7). The ideal student learns to read and think in these ways.

The attitudes and the skills needed for effective reading are not simply or quickly acquired. With training and experience, they develop in depth and power and in widening areas of application. It is difficult to say that at any given level any one of them is begun, or that any one of them is completed. Where the junior high school teacher can begin to develop pupils' reading abilities depends upon pupil skills, interests, and previous training. At whatever point that may be, the junior high social studies teacher can make a vital contribution.

REFERENCES

1. Anderson, Howard R., Marcham, Frederick G., and Dunn, Seymour B. *An Experiment in Teaching Certain Skills of Critical Thinking*. Journal of Educational Research, 38:241–51, December 1955.
2. Carpenter, Helen, ed. *Skills in Social Studies*. Washington, D. C., Twenty-fourth Yearbook of the National Council for Social Studies, 1954.
3. Crossen, Helen J. *Effect of the Attitudes of the Reader Upon Critical Reading Ability*. Journal of Educational Research, 42:289–98, December 1948.
4. Gainsburg, Joseph C. *Critical Reading Is Creative Reading and Needs Creative Teaching*. Reading Teacher, Vol. 6, No. 4:19–26, March 1953.
5. Glaser, Edward M. *Experiment in the Development of Critical Thinking*. Teachers College Contribution to Education, No. 843. New York, Bureau of Publications, Teachers College, Columbia University, 1941.
6. Horn, Ernest. *Methods of Instruction in the Social Studies*. New York, Charles Scribner's Sons, 1937.
7. Jewett, Arno. *Detecting and Analyzing Propaganda*. The English Journal, 29:105–15, February 1940.
8. Kohn, Clyde F. *It's Wise To Build Map-reading Skills One Step at a Time*. NEA Journal, 42:488–89, November 1953.
9. ———. *Interpreting Maps and Globes, Skills in Social Studies*, Chap. 8. Washington, D. C., Twenty-fourth Yearbook of the National Council for the Social Studies, 1954.
10. McCaul, Robert L. *The Effect of Attitudes Upon Reading Interpretation*. Journal of Educational Research, 37:451–57, February 1955.
11. Parker, Edith P. *Learning to Read Maps, Adapting Reading Programs to Wartime Needs*. Gray, William S., comp. and ed., Supplementary Educational Monographs, No. 57:167–71. Chicago, University of Chicago Press, December 1943.
12. Robinson, Francis P. *Effective Study*. New York, Harpers, 1946, p. 11–33.
13. Rowlands, Louise C. *Promoting Reading Competence in Content Fields: in Junior and Senior High Schools, Classroom Techniques in Improving Reading*. Gray, William S., comp. and ed., Supplementary Educational Monographs, No. 69:138–42. Chicago, University of Chicago Press, 1949.

14. Rudolph, Kathleen B. *The Effect of Reading Instruction on Achievement in Eighth-Grade Social Studies.* New York, Bureau of Publications, Teachers College, Columbia University, 1949.
15. Sawyer, Richard P. *A Reading Teacher in the Social Studies Class.* Social Education, Vol. XX, No. 8:264–368, December 1956.
16. Strang, Ruth, McCullough, Constance M., and Traxler, Arthur E. *Problems in the Improvement of Reading.* Second edition. New York, McGraw-Hill, 1955.
17. Whipple, G. W. *Vocabulary Development: Social Studies.* Education, 71:564–66, May 1951.

38. Materials for the Unit Plan in Social Studies

SOCIAL STUDIES

Jean Fair

A unit plan implies that students are to organize some wholeness or unity out of many aspects of their experiences. A unit plan usually calls for the development of several kinds of behavior, understanding, beliefs and attitudes, interests, skills, and thinking, in content areas appropriate for individual students. The topic or problem on which the content is centered is frequently, although not necessarily, structured in some other fashion than that of the conventional subject field. Since a unit plan is usually expected to organize several weeks of student time, some careful decisions must be made about definitions of, and priorities among, objectives, with mere coverage for its own sake ruled out. Student purposes take on great importance, and materials and experiences need to have maximum meaning. Learning activities must be chosen with an eye to what students are to learn, and these activities must be ordered to facilitate organization of experiences.

Materials to Promote a Variety of Objectives

Let us turn to the kinds of reading materials required in a unit plan of study. It is obvious that we shall need a wide variety; no one book is likely to permit the development of the several kinds of behaviors appropriate for the purposes of a particular group of students. Textbooks are useful for giving information about, and understanding of, topics and problems. Many teachers and students limit what can be learned by relying almost exclusively on such books. Others go to the needless trouble of finding the necessary discussions in a cumbersome variety of sources, when equally useful, and sometimes more suitable, treatments could be found more efficiently in classroom textbooks. The helpfulness of textbooks is increased when several are available and when students free themselves of the mind-set that textbook information can be used only in the organizational structure of the textbook itself.

Still, textbooks alone are not likely to be sufficient. Students also need encyclopedias appropriate for their reading ability; reference books, from the common almanacs to the less often used, but frequently more efficient, *Statistical Abstracts* (U. S. Government Printing Office), maps, atlases, gazeteers, biographical dictionaries, and the like; pamphlets; magazines suitable for readers of different abilities (to be saved over a period of years to increase sources); and books. We are all aware of the variety of sources which promote understanding.

However valuable these may be, they are usually not the most useful materials for involving students' feelings and so developing meaningful understandings, attitudes, and interests. Novels can help here. Consider, by way of illustration, Lewis' *Young Fu of the Upper Yangtze* (Winston, 1937) and Pearl Buck's classic, *The Good Earth* (World Publishing Co., 1952), for a unit dealing with China. Short stories are helpful; how valuable in a study of civil rights is a story such as Shirley Jackson's "The Lottery." [1] Plays are useful, for example, Miller's *Death of a Salesman* (Viking, 1949), for showing the values of modern society. Titles from biography and poetry will occur to all of us. We sometimes forget, however, the non-fiction articles and books. Think of the power of "The Blast in Centralia No. 5" [2] in a problem unit on how to improve conditions of labor; John Hersey's *Hiroshima* (Knopf, 1946) in a topical unit on World War II or a problem unit on what to do about national defense; or James Michener's *The Bridge at Andau* (Random, 1957) in a study of present American policy toward Europe. There are classic documents, too: Webster's "Reply to Hayne," Bryan's "Cross of Gold" speech, and many more. A collection of such materials, while not sufficient in themselves, do represent a needed type.

[1] Shirley Jackson, "The Lottery," *Fifty Great Short Stories*, pp. 175–85. Edited by Milton Crane. New York: Bantam Books, 1952.

[2] John Bartlow Martin, "The Blast in Centralia No. 5," *Harper's Magazine Reader*, pp. 38–89. New York: Bantam Books, 1953.

Many of these can be used also for the development of abilities in critical and creative thinking. Textbooks should be used to obtain comparisons of authors' points of view and for documents, graphs, and tables for interpretation. However, students will frequently need materials, other than textbooks, specifically chosen to permit questions like these: "What is the problem discussed?" "To what kind of audience does the author intend to speak?" "What are his assumptions or conclusions?" "Is his argument consistent?" "Are his facts relevant, accurate, and adequate?" "How does this interpretation compare with that interpretation?" "What difference does it make whether we adopt one or the other interpretation?" "What other solutions are possible?"

For able students, several sets of materials are particularly useful in units on American history. The Amherst series of "Problems in American Civilization" (Heath), which range over many significant problems (for example, "Slavery as a Cause of the Civil War" and "Loyalty in a Democratic State"), help students define problems and analyze and compare arguments in both contemporary statements and interpretations by later historians. Similar remarks might be made about Leopold and Link's *Problems in American History* (Prentice-Hall, 1952) and other excellent collections. Somewhat less difficult are the three pamphlets dealing with American foreign policy toward China, Russia, and Germany, recently published under the auspices of the North Central Association of Colleges and Secondary Schools (Science Research Associates, 1957). The series in the yearly "Reference Shelf" (H. W. Wilson) on such problems as federal taxes and national defense can also be mentioned. Such materials as these, which offer help in defining problems and choosing among alternative solutions, are particularly valuable in unit plans where individuals or small groups are working on aspects of a problem independently.

Students will need what we often call "documents." Some of the classics ought not to be overlooked. The *Declaration of Independence* and Number Ten of *The Federalist Papers* are easily available arguments for some units. Analyses of contemporary materials, such as quotations from Churchill and Hitler, may be needed in a unit on the origins of modern war. Eye-witness accounts are helpful when properly criticized or skimmed for a point of view. While there are fewer such accounts suitable for world-history units, a wealth of such material is available to us in other areas. Moreover, accounts of current events are readily obtained from newspapers and magazines.

Controversy is inherent in almost any meaningful social-studies unit, whether the content comes from the past or the present.

In a unit on problems of improving law and justice, the concepts of justice embodied in Hammurabi's Code can provoke controversy when applied to cases of modern wrongdoing. Contemporary materials from books, magazines, and newspapers will be needed both for units on recurring issues in human affairs and for those dealing with specific present-day problems. Articles in magazines of opinion and editorials will be integral parts of plans for a unit; they are to be criticized, evaluated, and compared, and used as statements of alternatives in decision-making.

Graphs and tables, too, are helpful, particularly when they encourage interpretation. Those of the National Industrial Conference Board, "Road Maps of Industry" (The Board, New York), a regular and easily obtained series, fit into many units dealing with recurring issues. They present enough data to compare trends, question predictions, and check the accuracy of many other materials.

Students will need, then, materials which allow the development of a range of behaviors in content flexibly structured to meet their particular purposes.

Meaning in Materials

Young people must also have meaningful materials, for they cannot organize what does not carry meaning. I will do little more here than call attention to the use of audio-visual materials and the study aids, pictures, and the like found in textbooks and pamphlets. We might help students by taking advantage of many excellent television programs which can contribute meaning to the reading materials used. Picture magazines, both those current and those saved from past years, are useful at many ability levels.

Some special mention may well be made of the kind of pamphlet material which contains enough of what we may call "case material" to put meaning into often empty generalizations. The "Life Adjustment Series" (Science Research Associates), by way of example, includes more than fifty titles, some at two maturity levels, on such topics as *Relations with Parents*, *Leisure Time*, and *Unions*, which are of particular use in problem units dealing with the family, recreation, working, and the like.

Documents like the Magna Charta can often be rewritten by able students and used by the less able in units such as one centered on the growth of democratic government.

Life magazine has done some heavily illustrated series on general topics, such as "The World's Great Religions" (Time, 1957), which, by drawing matters together, promote meaning in topics of broad sweep. Cartoons like Burr Shafer's "Through History with J. Wesley Smith," which have appeared frequently in the *Saturday Review*, can clarify, in a memorable way, the meaning of many an important point.

Relationships Among Materials

Students also need materials selected with particular reference to the organization planned for in the unit. To develop, within a unit centered on the American West, the generalization that frontier life influenced the growth of American democracy, students might read a variety of novels for pictures of western life and compare them in group discussions. Just any novels set in the West will not do; students need those which actually present pictures of democratic living. Rölvaag's *Giants in the Earth* (Harper, 1927), for example, contains enough material for students to work from; Willa Cather's *Death Comes for the Archbishop* (Knopf, 1927) does not, even though this book has much merit in itself and may be useful in other kinds of units. To enable students to discuss the control of wealth, excerpts taken from the writings of Jefferson, Hamilton, Byran, Mr. Dooley, Andrew Carnegie, and Franklin D. Roosevelt must be carefully selected; selections from just any of their writings and speeches will not do. Teachers and students are often bewildered about the use of a variety of reading materials in group learning activities, partly because the variety of materials gathered have only a tenuous connection with the hoped-for organization.

Moreover, students need enough materials to arrive at sound conclusions. Learning activities sometimes have not borne fruit because students have not read enough. Concretely, the weekly current-events paper or even two or three well-selected pieces of material may be insufficient to permit students to apply the concept of the balance of power, which has been developed, let us say, in an international relations unit in a panel discussion on "Should We Revise NATO?"

Reading materials must be capable of fitting into some sort of sequence within the unit. Some materials are first rate for the beginnings of units; think of the power of Irwin Shaw's short story "Preach on the Dusty Roads" [3] for raising questions about citizens' responsibilities in foreign affairs. We have already mentioned the value of materials which define problems. While controversial materials may also be used to raise questions and to define problems, students are not likely to be able to analyze and interpret the reading until they have had opportunities to read

[3] Irwin Shaw, "Preach on the Dusty Roads," *Best American Short Stories of 1943.* Edited by Martha Foley. Boston: Houghton Mifflin Co., 1944.

materials which give them information and understanding. The excellent chapter on the Constitution in Bragdon and McCutchen's *The History of a Free People* (Macmillan, 1954) is usually more suitable for developing understanding in a unit on the development of American government than for the beginning or the concluding activities. Materials to be interpreted or skimmed for a point of view very often fit best after students have some information and understanding. Maps are likely to be most useful, too, when students are developing understanding, although I can think of times when they might be used as summary materials. Teachers will be wise, also, to consider as reading materials the sources which enable students to locate the information they need. Forum discussions are useful for comparing points of view, generalizing, and summarizing.

Moreover, our unit plans need to permit sequence among units within a course and, for that matter, among courses. If students in a course on problems of democracy are to relate various concepts of democratic method, some collection of such materials as Stuart Chase's short article, "Zoning Comes to Town"; [4] a more difficult article, "A New Attack on Delinquency," [5] and Vern Sneider's *Teahouse of the August Moon* (Putnam, 1951) will be useful. An article like Kouwenhoven's "What's American about America?" [6] is fine material for extracting common elements from several kinds of American-history units.

Concluding Statement

There is a wealth of reading material for the kinds of unit plans that high-school students need. Some clear ideas of what the students need materials for and some imaginative thinking help both teachers and students to find them.

[4] Stuart Chase, "Zoning Comes to Town," *Reader's Digest*, LXX (February, 1957), 129–33.

[5] John Bartlow Martin, "A New Attack on Delinquency," *Harper's Magazine*, CCI (May, 1944), 502–12.

[6] John Kouwenhoven, "What's American about America?" *Harper's Magazine*, CCXIII (July, 1956), 25–33.

PART SEVEN

Examples of Secondary School Reading Programs

39. About Successful Reading Programs

Margaret J. Early

Who teaches reading in the secondary school? A study of current programs indicates that the answer seems to be the English teacher and the special reading teacher. Who *should* teach reading in the secondary school? The varied answers to this question emphasize the *if's*, *and's*, and *but's* that riddle any discussion of a balanced reading program at the secondary level. Authorities agree that every teacher should be a teacher of reading, but they point out that this desirable goal is far from being achieved, largely because subject-matter teachers lack training in reading methods. When the need for adequate reading instruction is felt, administrators and teachers look for leadership from the English department or a reading coordinator in organizing an all-school program in which every teacher adjusts his reading assignments to the range of ability in his class and teaches the reading skills necessary for understanding his subject.

Reading programs vary according to the size of the school, the type of community, the abilities of the pupils and their needs now and in the future, the curriculum offered, the attitudes and skill of the teachers, the size of the staff, and the consultant help available. No one pattern can be described as "most likely to succeed." Furthermore, experience with reading programs in the high school is still extremely limited. Most of those reported in the literature are fairly recent developments, and few practices have been evaluated in objective experiments. Promising practices and trends on trial are the most that can be reported at this early stage.

Nevertheless, even in this dawn of reading at the secondary level, light is available from two sources: sound theory and practical experience. Administrators and teachers in the planning stage of program development can find useful guidance in (1) the recommendations of reading specialists and (2) the experiences reported by those who are now trying out various schemes. This paper will summarize findings from these two sources.

The All-School Developmental Program

If the various types of reading programs that have been suggested by competent authorities or tried out in actual practices were arranged according to comprehensiveness of approach, at the top of the ladder would stand the all-school developmental program. Such a program provides for:

1. Continuous instruction in reading skills from kindergarten to grade twelve for *all* pupils
2. Integration of reading skills with other communication skills: writing, speaking, and listening
3. Specific instruction by subject-matter teachers in *how to read and study* in their special fields, using the basic reading materials of their courses
4. Cooperative planning by all teachers so that skills will not be overlooked or overstressed
5. Adjusted reading materials in all subjects for slow, average, and superior students
6. Guidance in free reading
7. Emphasis on the uses of reading as a source of information, as an aid to personal and social development, and as a means of recreation
8. Corrective or remedial instruction for seriously retarded readers
9. Measurement of growth in skills by means of standardized and informal tests; study of students' application of techniques in all reading tasks
10. Evaluation of the uses of reading through study of the amount and quality of voluntary reading; study of effect on achievement in all school subjects; effect on percent of drop-outs

Behind each of these requisites lies a tangle of problems that makes it clear why the *all-school developmental program* is "easier said than done." For example, numbers 1, 3, and 4 imply that teachers at all grade levels and in all subject areas not only must understand how human beings grow in their ability to read, but that they also must have the technical know-how to contribute to this growth. The implications of the second criterion are equally intense. Teachers must see reading, not as an isolated tool, but as one phase in the complex process of communication. Understanding the nature of language and agreeing that education in any field, no matter how specialized, is dependent upon skills of communication are basic planks in a platform for reading improvement. But teachers who have achieved a philosophic understanding of their responsibility to teach reading still need to know how to translate that understanding into action.

Involved in the fifth criterion of a total program are issues that go much deeper than those involved in how to teach reading. A thorough-going reconsideration of the offerings of the content fields is preliminary to achieving an all-school developmental program in reading. Too often subject-matter teachers look upon a reading program as a means of bringing every pupil up to grade level. They think that instruction in reading should make it possible for all pupils to use the textbook around which their courses are built. Or, as they decide to discard the single-textbook method, they look for easy vocabulary materials that present the same concepts as the standard text, and they are disappointed when they find none. It is questionable whether teachers have the right to ask for low-vocabulary materials in their subject fields until they re-examine the concepts they include in their courses of study and decide whether the same concepts remain when complex topics are rewritten in easier vocabulary and sentence structure.

The remaining criteria carry heavy implications, too. Numbers 6, 7, and 10 point to the ultimate purpose of all reading instruction: promoting wider use of reading. Fundamental though specific skills are to the reading process, a program which focuses only on skills is severely limited. Broadening the program to include enthusiastic attention to the uses of reading demands the active participation of all the faculty in building the resources of school and classroom libraries. It brings the librarian to the fore in this phase of the program.

The inclusion of number 8 suggests that even in the best developmental program there will be some students who need more specialized individual instruction than can be provided in the regular secondary classroom. Provision must be made for students who, for reasons other than low mental age, have disabilities that can be diagnosed and treated.

Evaluation of a total program in all its aspects is implicit in the last two criteria. Accurate interpretation of the results of standardized tests presents a problem to many teachers. A still more complicated lesson for teachers to learn is how to build reliable informal tests and keep accurate observations of the less tangible evidences of reading growth.

Some of the ten criteria presented here demand from teachers new understandings of the role of language and of their responsibilities toward its development. Out of these understandings must come fundamental changes in course offerings. All of the criteria demand the learning of new teaching techniques. Changes in attitude, in methods of teaching, and in curricula evolve slowly. Since a realistic all-school developmental reading program must wait upon the carefully reached decisions of committees of teachers in each content field, it is easy to see why temporary, compromise plans have been initiated in most schools that have attacked the reading problem.

Compromise Programs

In an attempt to provide systematic instruction in reading before a total program has been fully developed, many secondary schools offer special classes in reading (see references). In some cases these classes are additions to the regular curriculum. Frequently they are labeled "developmental" to show that they provide for all pupils — slow, average, and superior — at a given grade level. Sometimes they are called "corrective" when they are designed for students with specific reading disabilities. When individual or very small group instruction is provided for retarded readers, the program is sometimes designated as "remedial," although this term has fallen into disrepute because it carries unattractive connotations.

In place of the regular English course, corrective classes sometimes are offered for a semester or two. This type of program is different in objectives and organization from the type described next.

Another common approach, especially in smaller schools, is to charge English teachers with the responsibility of developing the reading skills of all students as part of the regular English courses. Occasionally, especially in the junior high school, the teaching of reading is a specific area of instruction within the core course or, as in one laboratory school, an integral part of a problem-centered core (25).

Emphases differ and variations occur within these patterns, but essentially these four types — the special reading class, the substitute English class, instruction within the regular English class, and developmental reading as part of the core course — are the practices commonly recommended and followed.

SELECTING STUDENTS AND SCHEDULING CLASSES

Whenever the program is less than "total," decisions must be made as to how students will be selected, how classes will be scheduled, and who will teach them.

The easiest type of program to plan is the reading-within-the-English-class. There is no need to schedule extra classes and no additions need to be made to the staff. Instead of the selection of some students for special classes, the problem becomes that of grouping all the students for English classes. In large high schools where administrative grouping is feasible, the recommendations of Gray (6) can be considered. He suggests developing a program around the needs of five types of readers in the following manner:

Needlessly retarded readers, comprising those students who read far below the level of their ability and have no recognizable handicaps, should have intensive instruction adjusted to their specific needs, preferably during first-semester English.

Handicapped readers, those who have retarded language and speech development, limited backgrounds of experience, serious emotional disorders, and disturbing parental relations, should be grouped together in special English classes limited to ten or fifteen students.

Mentally retarded or *slow learners* are most effectively helped in language arts classes adjusted to their respective levels of advancement and rates of learning.

Superior students, in regular classes, should be challenged by differentiated assignments.

Students of average ability, making normal progress in reading, should continue to receive reading instruction within regular classes.

Decisions must be made as to the placement of and emphasis on skills in a course of study for reading-within-the-English-class. One example of a four-year sequence is that suggested by Davison (3):

Grade 9. Flexibility of rate; reading for various purposes; reading of charts, maps, graphs, etc.; locational skills; recognition and use of simple sentence patterns; development of a two-level outline.

Grade 10. Organizational skills with emphasis on recall; vocabulary building; use of reference materials; skill in following directions.

Grade 11. Summarizing from several sources; note-taking; analysis of patterns in paragraphs; techniques involved in problem-solving.

Grade 12. Critical reading.

The principal limitation of such a sequence is that it seems to parcel out instruction over the high school years, whereas a sounder procedure is to practice and maintain all the important reading skills during the entire span of years. Critical reading, for example, should not be postponed until the senior year.

Reading-within-the-English-class is a satisfactory beginning. A cooperative administration will provide for in-service training, an effective evaluation program, and for growth beyond the English department as efforts are made to coordinate skills instruction in other content areas.

Reading classes that are an extra for all pupils raise the question of how to find time in an already full schedule. Corrective classes, restricted to the students most in need, raise problems of identifying and selecting these students. Solutions to these problems are suggested in the descriptions of programs below.

The shortcomings of any program which is less than total are evident. Even when instruction is provided for all pupils, provision for the transfer of skills to the content fields is usually unsatisfactory. Classes that are corrective or remedial in nature are emergency measures. They do nothing to raise the quality of reading instruction throughout the school. It should be remembered, however, that the four types of programs described here as compromise plans are intended as stages of development along the way to the all-school program.

Examples of Existing Programs

In the remainder of this paper, very brief descriptions of promising programs will be given. Other excellent programs are described in books by Simpson (8), Blair (1), and Strang, McCullough, and Traxler (9). At the end of this paper is a list of schools whose programs are described in available sources.

In an effort to obtain up-to-date information on present practices as well as suggestions for setting up programs in grades nine to twelve, a questionnaire was sent to 293 senior high schools in thirty-four states in the spring of 1956.[1] These schools do not represent a random sampling. Many were selected because leads from various sources suggested that programs might be in operation. Returns from 147 schools responding to the questionnaire give an indication of the types of programs in current use:

[1] The writer is indebted to Miss Ruth Viox, secondary school reading consultant in Kenmore, N. Y., for the use of information from this study.

Reading taught in:	*No. of Schools*
English classes only	32*
English and special reading classes	19
Special reading classes only	10
No program for reading instruction	86

* Includes schools where English is part of core.

Questionnaires from the eighty-six schools reporting "no program" expressed a need for a program; some described beginning steps or future plans; some indicated that reading is taught by individual teachers.

PROGRAMS WITH READING COORDINATOR

In systems where a secondary school reading consultant is available for leadership and direction, strides are being taken toward the desirable objective of an all-school program. Cities like Philadelphia (34), St. Louis (9), and Detroit are creating valuable patterns for total organization of large systems.[2] The Detroit program, in operation since 1944, looks to all teachers to accept responsibility for teaching reading skills in their special fields. At the present time, reading is taught in all literature classes. A few classes have combined literature and social studies with emphasis on reading. Some special reading classes are offered in place of literature periods. To schools embarking on new programs, the coordinator offers the following suggestions: secure, first of all, cooperation of the administrative staff; look for skilled elementary teachers of reading; reduce class load; acquire plenty of materials; provide in-service help to teachers.

Coordinating a reading program in a central school district presents problems comparable to those found in city systems but peculiar to a different geographical setting. In Valley Stream, New York, a corrective program for retarded readers was set up seventeen years ago. Today, in the two six-year high schools, corrective and developmental services and a summer reading school are available. The program is staffed by a district reading coordinator and three full-time reading teachers working through a Reading Laboratory. In September, all new entrants, students referred by staff members, and students formerly in corrective classes are given the Gilmore Oral Reading Test. Priority for corrective work goes to students of average mental ability in critical need of help in word analysis. Students with problems in the areas of meanings, study skills, and rate of reading (in that order) are

[2] Information from Miss Viox's study.

accepted in the Reading Laboratory as far as scheduling permits. Students come to the laboratory during study periods at least twice a week. Groups vary in size from one to twelve. Instruction terminates at any time that the reading teacher feels sufficient progress has been made. Generally poor achievers in reading spend at least a semester in the laboratory; others with specific weaknesses spend from ten to twenty sessions. No credit is given.

In building the developmental program, the reading coordinator and consultants are working with all teachers in the following ways: (a) discussing the school-wide testing program; (b) giving demonstration lessons in the classroom; (c) visiting classrooms to evaluate progress of former Reading Laboratory pupils; (d) helping teachers to organize reading groups within the classroom; (e) evaluating materials in all subject-matter areas; (f) constructing or supplying instructional materials; (g) helping to build classroom libraries. The summer reading program serves as a workshop for teachers who participate, and an in-service course in reading is offered almost every year (39).

Laying the groundwork for a developmental program by providing continuous in-service training is the major objective, too, in a small city system such as Norwalk, Connecticut. At the present time, reading is taught as part of the core program in the junior high school, and in the senior high school all subject-area teachers are responsible for the skills needed in their courses. In addition, two special reading classes are offered: one for retarded and one for superior readers. Set up as regular English classes, they meet five times a week for fifty-minute periods. Students are chosen on the basis of standardized test results, class achievement, teacher judgment, and data from cumulative records.[3]

ENGLISH WORKSHOP

Coordinated by the supervisor of language arts, the program in language arts in the Oakland, California, schools emphasizes reading as one phase of communication. Accordingly, the plan provides for (1) attention to specific reading skills and technical vocabulary in all academic classes; (2) developmental reading in English classes, with emphasis on guided reading for pleasure and personal growth; (3) English workshop classes for retarded readers. Selection of students for the workshop classes is based on a difference of one year or more between reading age and mental age and on recommendations of teachers and counselors. These classes meet one hour daily for one semester as a substitute for English. Success of the workshop program, which is now in its fourth year of opera-

[3] *Op. cit.*

tion, is based on excellent in-service training that has included a four-week summer workshop for teachers (33).

COMBINED ATTACK IN SMALL SYSTEM

In a small New York State high school (Gouverneur), an English teacher became the reading consultant six years ago. Beginning with "corrective" and "efficiency" classes, the program now includes reading instruction for all students in grades seven to twelve in the English class where twenty minutes each day are given to skills instruction and directed reading. In addition, corrective classes are scheduled in grades seven to nine for pupils of average to superior ability reading two or more years below grade placement. In grades ten to twelve the "efficiency classes" are open to superior students (eightieth percentile or above in intelligence). Emphasizing efficient reading and study skills, this course is organized around centers of interest. Students are introduced to twenty-one fields from which they select five for specialization. In this growing program, experiments are now under way in three other aspects: an experimental core class in the seventh grade; a reading homeroom in the eighth grade; and reading clubs meeting twice monthly in both the junior and senior high school.[4]

LABORATORY PROGRAMS

A dramatic initiation of an all-school program began in Indianapolis as an experiment in improving speed, comprehension, and interest in reading through laboratory methods. In each of eight high schools a reading laboratory is equipped with workbooks and readers, the Iowa Reading Training Films, and twenty "shadowscopes" (a type of pacer). A specially trained director is in charge of each laboratory. Scheduling varies from school to school, but in general, students work in the reading laboratory for at least one period a week as part of their regular English courses. In one school, the program was concentrated in a three-week period of daily classes with results that warrant continuation of this plan. Evaluation of the program during the first year, when control groups were set up, showed consistent gains in speed and comprehension for the experimental groups. The Indianapolis program in the spring of 1956 was reaching 21,998 students in grades nine to twelve (24).

In Eugene, Oregon, a laboratory or workshop course is open to all high school students as an elective. Any student who wishes to improve his reading may apply. Since class size is limited to twenty, and only three classes are offered, some students are placed

[4] *Op. cit.*

on a waiting list. In the opening week the Iowa Silent Reading Tests are given. Each student corrects his own test, and the nine parts are explained and discussed as a method of self-analysis. Each student works on his own self-improvement plan. When common needs are recognized students may work in teams. A folder of work accomplished serves as a record of achievement and as the basis for conferences with the teacher (18).

Conclusion

This review of current practices in secondary school reading programs was drawn from the replies to 147 questionnaires in a recent study and from descriptions of more than thirty programs appearing in the professional literature since 1940. The following conclusions seem justified:

1. No school claimed to have achieved a total developmental program.
2. Very few schools have attempted to achieve an all-school program by a direct attack on the reading skills in each academic area.
3. Most important to the development of a total program is a coordinator who can provide in-service training for subject-matter teachers.
4. "Developmental programs" (in the sense that reading instruction is offered to all students) are generally confined to the English department.
5. Most schools feel the need for remedial or corrective classes to care for the most seriously retarded readers, but few are satisfied with just a remedial or corrective program.

The variety of existing programs is evidence of a vigorous effort to "do something" about reading problems in the secondary school. There is a growing conviction on the part of secondary school personnel that teaching reading is their job. Specific steps are being taken to prepare whole faculties for assuming this job. In the meantime, needs of students are being met at least in part by emergency measures that will either disappear altogether or become very minor aspects of the *all-school developmental program.*

Bibliography

1. Blair, Glenn M., *Diagnostic and Remedial Teaching* (New York: Macmillan Co., 1956).
2. Bond, G., and Bond, E., *Developmental Reading in High School* (New York: Macmillan Co., 1941).
3. Davison, E. B., "Co-ordinating Basic Instruction and Guidance in Reading in the Content Fields in Junior and Senior High School,"

Conference on Reading: Basic Instruction in Reading in Elementary and High Schools (University of Chicago Press, 1948), pp. 210–14.

4. Dolch, E. W., "A Remedial Reading Program for a High School," *Methods in Reading* (Champaign, Illinois: Garrard Press, 1955).
5. Fay, Leo C., *Reading in the High School*. No. 11 in series, "What Research Says to the Teacher" (Washington, D. C.: Department of Classroom Teachers, American Educational Research Association of the National Education Association, 1956).
6. Gray, W. S., "How Can the Poor Reader in the Secondary School Be Rescued?" *Bulletin of the National Association of Secondary-School Principals*, 36 (April 1952), pp. 129–35.
7. Niles, Olive S., "Organizing and Administering a 12-Year Developmental Reading Program, Part 2," in *The Road to Better Reading* (Albany: Bureau of Secondary Curriculum Development of the State Education Department, 1953).
8. Simpson, E., *Helping High School Students to Read Better* (Chicago: S.R.A., 1954).
9. Strang, Ruth; McCullough, C.; and Traxler, A., *Problems in the Improvement of Reading*, Second Edition (New York: McGraw-Hill, 1955).
10. Witty, P. A., and Brink, W. G., "Remedial Reading Practices in the Secondary School," *Journal of Educational Psychology*, 40 (April 1949), pp. 193–205.

Descriptions of Secondary Reading Programs

Arlington Heights, Illinois

11. Snap, Alfred, "The Reading Program in the Arlington Heights Township High School." See Simpson (8), pp. 116–117.

Birmingham, Alabama (Ensley High)

12. Sechriest, E., "Program for the Improvement of Reading of School Youth," *Bulletin of the National Association of Secondary-School Principals*, 35 (March 1951), pp. 56–62.

Boone, North Carolina

13. Wey, Herbert and Graff, Margaret, "Let Us Help Them Learn To Read," *Bulletin of the National Association of Secondary-School Principals*, 37 (November 1953). See also Simpson (8).

Bradford, Pennsylvania

14. Sprague, S. H., "Bradford Program of Reading Instruction," *Clearing House*, 19 (January 1945), pp. 293–95.

Burlington, North Carolina

15. Linnemann, C. C., "Program for the Improvement of Reading of School Youth," *Bulletin of the National Association of Secondary-School Principals*, 35 (March 1951), pp. 48–56.

Clinton, Iowa

16. Jones, Nellie F., "A Motorized Reading Project in Clinton High School, Clinton, Iowa," *The English Journal*, 40 (June 1951), pp. 313–19. See also Simpson (8).

Dubuque, Iowa

17. Hill, M. K., "Organizing the Reading Improvement Program in the Secondary Schools of Dubuque," *High School Journal*, 39 (November 1955), pp. 106–111.

Eugene, Oregon

18. Beacon, R., and Gillett, L., "The Eugene Reading Program," *High School Journal*, 39 (December 1955), pp. 185–188.

Evanston, Illinois

19. Bland, Phyllis, "A High School Developmental Reading Program," *The Reading Teacher*, 8 (February 1955), pp. 146–152.

Floral Park, New York

20. Lyons, Anita, and Campbell, Lillian, "Reading Programs for Retarded Readers of Average Ability," *High School Journal*, 39 (November 1955), pp. 112–117.

Germantown Friends School, Philadelphia, Pennsylvania

21. Bond, George W., "A Program for Improving Reading in the Secondary School," *School Review*, 60 (September 1952), pp. 338–342.

Gillespie, Illinois

22. Moon, J. V., "We Tackled Our Reading Problem," *Education*, 36 (April 1948), pp. 212–214.

Highland Park, Illinois

23. Perry, Harold J., "The Developmental Reading Program in the Highland Park High School, Highland Park, Illinois." Simpson (8), pp. 122–127.

Indianapolis, Indiana

24. Leamnson, G. F., "Indianapolis Produces Better Readers," *School Executive*, 74 (December 1954), pp. 64–67.

Muncie, Indiana (Laboratory School of Ball State Teachers College)

25. Toops, M. D., "Core Program Does Improve Reading Proficiency," *Educational Administration and Supervision*, 40 (December 1954), pp. 494–503.

New Haven, Connecticut

26. McGrath, Eleanor, "We Tackled the Reading Problem," *Journal of Education*, 130 (September 1947), pp. 190–191.

New York City

27. Lazar, May (ed.), *The Retarded Reader in the Junior High School*, Publication No. 31 (Bureau of Educational Research, Board of Education, City of New York, 1952).
28. Wilman, M. C., "Reading in the Upper School," *Volta Review*, 48 (November 1946), pp. 673–675.

Newton High School, Newtonville, Massachusetts

29. Rideout, Edith M., "The Growth of the Reading Clinic in the Newton High School, Newtonville, Massachusetts." See Simpson (8), pp. 128–135.

North Adams, Massachusetts

30. Patterson, W. G., and Brown, M. B., "Students Evaluate Their Course in Developmental Reading," *Clearing House*, 30 (December 1955), pp. 199–201.

Oak Park, Illinois

31. Dehl, Kermit, "Reading Improvement Service in the Oak Park and River Forest High School, Oak Park, Illinois." See Simpson (8), pp. 118–121.

Oak Ridge, Tennessee

32. Capehart, B. E., and McKeehan, R., "A Junior High School Reading Program Adjusted to Individual Needs," *High School Journal*, 39 (December 1955), pp. 172–177.

Oakland, California

33. Gustafson, Myrtle, "Practical Plan for Helping Retarded Readers in Secondary Schools," *California Journal of Secondary Education*, 30 (April 1955), pp. 196–199.

Philadelphia, Pennsylvania

34. Cushman, C. Leslie, and Green, Rosemary, "Philadelphia Schools Attack the Reading Program," *Nation's Schools*, 51 (May 1953), pp. 52–55.

Phoenix, Arizona

35. Jensen, Ralph, and Clark, Van D., "A Developmental Reading Program: Description and Evaluation," *High School Journal*, 39 (December 1955), pp. 178–184.

Providence, Rhode Island

36. Saylor, G., "Developmental Reading Program for Secondary School Pupils," *Educational Leadership*, 5 (January 1948), p. 282.

Rochester, Minnesota

37. Glendenning, M., "Improved Reading Program in Rochester Junior High School," *The English Journal*, 36 (December 1947), pp. 513–518.

Seattle, Washington

38. Slocomb, H., "Committees Build a Seattle Course of Study," *Clearing House*, 22 (March 1948), pp. 428–430.

Valley Stream, Long Island

39. Robinson, H. A., and Udall, R. M., "All-School Reading Program," *High School Journal*, 39 (November 1955), pp. 91–96.

Wausau, Wisconsin

40. Swenby, Clifford, and Zielsdorf, Margaret, "A Remedial Reading Program in a Senior High School," *School Review*, 59 (September 1951), pp. 350–357.

Windsor, Connecticut

41. Crockett, S., and Niles, O. S., "Developmental Reading Program on the Secondary Level," *Education*, 67 (April 1947), pp. 516–520.

40. Reading in the Junior High School

Mary Clifford

Exactly what outcomes should a junior high language arts teacher strive for in a reading program? What materials, activities, and methods should she use? Is she a basic reading skills teacher, a literature teacher, or is she both? Does she alone have the responsibility for all reading instruction in the upper grades?

These are the questions. The answers? There are no "either-or" answers as school programs, classes, individuals in classes, and teachers will forever vary. (Thank goodness!) However, after due consideration, I have arrived at the following conclusions which to me seem reasonable and workable. The ideas presented herein are not original. They are my interpretation of the theory and methods I have read about, heard discussed, seen used, and practiced.

First, what is "reading"? Let us say that it includes, "Those complex processes involved in the interpretation of the printed page and in the effective use of books. Reading includes not only the ability to pronounce the words of a passage and to reproduce the ideas presented but also the ability to grasp the full import of these ideas after reflection, consideration of their worth, and clarification of their meaning." [1] Yes, we teach a big, broad subject!

Why carry out a definite program in junior high reading? At least four valid reasons are: (1) all upper grade students need some help in developing specific reading skills; (2) there are general reading abilities which profit from direct instruction; (3) the average reading of adults in the United States is still only around the middle and upper elementary school level, which indicates that more effort needs to be spent in adequate teaching of reading; and (4) reading habits and tastes of young people may be improved through sound instruction.

[1] Gertrude Whipple, *Reading in the Intermediate Grades*, Research Bulletin of National Conference on Research in English, No. 9 (Chicago: Scott, Foresman, 1941), p. 8.

If goals are targets in whose direction we aim, where shall our reading instruction arrows point? Might not we guide our students in the acquiring of basic skills of reading, in a background of word meaning, in the ability to adjust methods of reading to a particular purpose, in the acquiring of a variety of reading interests, in the habit of using good taste in choosing books and selections for reading, in the habit of demanding an understanding of what is read, in the habit of interpreting, evaluating and reflecting upon what is read, and in independence in the application of reading to the meeting of goals? [2]

It's a big order! Where do we start? First, we should find the extent, nature, and causes of individual differences. Much information may be gleaned from a testing program, school records, and personal observation. Causes to look for are intellectual factors, language abilities, physical conditions, personality disturbances, interests and motivation, and environmental and instructional factors. A good "Getting Acquainted" unit can give the teacher an idea of the student's understanding and appreciation of literature, his interests, powers of concentration, rate of work, independence and initiative, personality adjustment, and physical problems, such as eye strain, hearing loss, and fatigue factors. Some of the items I include in such a unit are: a book program, in which the pupil brings sample books, magazines, and papers from home, and tells the class about them; a period during which I read short sketches of family or school life as a springboard leading to the writing of papers or the telling of stories on topics such as "The Most Fun I've Ever Had with My Family," "Brothers and Sisters Are Sometimes Fun," and "Things My Parents Won't Let Me Do"; a period of browsing among class magazines and books; a period of common silent reading and subsequent discussion of an easy selection of great interest to the students during which I observe the pupil's facial expressions, attention, and contributions as an indication of appreciation and comprehension; and, a short time in which I have each child read aloud one or two paragraphs, where I note the number of words missed, mistakes on beginnings and endings of words, words omitted, substitutions, insertions, repetitions, and mispronunciations, and then ask a few well placed questions. (Ordinarily, comprehension is not sufficient if a student misses more than one out of twenty words.) If the above procedures indicate that a student's reading is seriously retarded and well below what could be expected for his mental

[2] Guy Bond and Bertha Handlan, *Adapting Instruction in Reading to Individual Differences* (Minneapolis: University of Minnesota Press, 1948), pp. 3–4.

ability, then I refer him to the remedial reading teacher for special help.

After we have acquired a working knowledge of the child, then what specific factors should we consider in instruction? A first factor is readiness for reading. We should: make sure students have the skills and habits necessary for the reading at hand; stimulate interest by relating the particular reading to pupil experiences or by arousing curiosity; build a background of ideas or concepts that will occur in the reading; provide a mental set in terms of the author's mood or purpose; and, help students arrive at the purpose for which they are reading a particular selection. Perhaps, readiness is most easily provided for in unit plans of instruction where the selections will be related to a theme. For example, I sometimes use a unit on mystery stories around Hallowe'en. Readiness is acquired through discussions of favorite ghost and mystery stories on television and radio, the time of year and day these mysterious happenings occur, the types of places where they occur, the words used to describe objects, places, and sounds connected with mystery, and the elements of nature at this time of year that lend themselves to mystery and "spookiness." To provide readiness for a poem such as De La Mare's "The Listeners" in this unit, I tell the students the poem has an atmosphere of mystery, that it concerns a traveler knocking at a door, and ask them to listen while I read it to see if they can discover who the traveler might be, and why no one answers.

A second specific factor to be considered is vocabulary development. Most authorities say that vocabulary is best developed through wide and varied reading. Using the unit theme approach, we should have a rotating classroom library made up of books related to the theme being currently studied in the basal reading texts, or of books especially related to the pupils' interests at the time. The teacher will need to help students select books which have factors of interest for them, and which are on their reading level. I think the following interest summary is very helpful:

> The special factors which arouse boys' interest in reading materials, as revealed by the current study, are: adventure (outdoor adventure, war, scouting), outdoor games, school life, mystery (including activities of detectives), obvious humor, animals, patriotism, and male rather than female characters. Unfavorable factors for boys are: love, other sentiments, home and family life, didacticism, religion, the reflective or philosophical, extended description, "nature" (flowers, trees, birds, bees), form or technique as a dominant factor, female characters.
>
> For girls the favorable special factors are: adventure without grimness (mild outdoor adventure, games, school life, detective and other

mysteries), humor, animals, patriotism, love, other sentiments, home and family life, male and female characters. Unfavorable factors: grim adventure (including war), extended description, didacticism, form or technique as a dominant factor, and "nature" (flowers, trees, birds, bees).[3]

For teacher planning for rotating classroom collections, and for individual guidance in book selection, the following bibliographies could be used:

Reading for Living: An Index to Reading Materials. Illinois Curriculum Program (Bulletin 18), John J. DeBoer *et al.*, 1953. (Circular Series A, No. 51. Supt. of Public Instruction, Springfield, Illinois.)

Reading Ladders for Human Relations (revised and enlarged edition). Margaret M. Heaton, Helen B. Lewis. American Council on Education, Room 110, 1785 Massachusetts Avenue, N.W., Washington 6, D. C., 1955.

Your Reading: A Book List for Junior High School. National Council of Teachers of English, 704 S. Sixth St., Champaign, Illinois.

Character Formation Through Books: A Bibliography. Compiled by Clara J. Kirchner (revised and enlarged edition). Catholic University of America Press, Washington 17, D. C., 1952.

Gateways to Readable Books. Compiled by Ruth Strang, *et al.* New York: H. W. Wilson Co., 1952.

If it is impossible to arrange for a class library through existing school facilities, books might be borrowed from the town or state library or students might bring books from home to make up a collection. In junior high, students should be able to select their own room librarian, make their own rules for using the collections, and manage their own checking-out system.

In addition to wide reading to further vocabulary development, each student should keep a notebook of new words met in his reading with their definitions. Class exercises in using the dictionary and analyzing strange words, and exercises in which pupils list one type of words in a selection such as the beautiful, technical, or obsolete words are good, because they lead to development of critical reading and a better understanding of the way our language operates. Occasionally motivation devices can be profitably used. To give dictionary training, to aid in learning how to skim, and to gain word meaning, a dictionary relay may be employed. For this, a dictionary is given to each row of students. Then a list of words, one for each pupil in each row, is exposed on the blackboard. As soon as the first pupil finds a word and its definition, he hands the dictionary to the one behind, and so on until the dictionary is passed through the row. When the first row finishes, each person

[3] George V. Norvell, *The Reading Interests of Young People* (Boston: D. C. Heath Co., 1950), p. 6.

gives his definition to the class. If one misses, the opportunity goes to the second row. On successive occasions, pronunciation, derivations, or right definition for a particular context could be stressed. For smaller group work in vocabulary, two interest-arousing devices are vocabulary bingo and crossword puzzles. Vocabulary bingo is effective with small groups of low-ability students. The cards with words to be learned are given out, and players cover words known as they are called. When a row is covered, the player calls "bingo," but must define correctly every word in his row before he's pronounced winner. For good students, crossword puzzles worked either individually or in small groups are worthwhile.

A third factor to be considered in junior high instruction is the work-type or study skills. In general, these skills are: defining a specific purpose for reading, adjusting reading methods to a particular purpose, comprehending what is read, locating information, selecting and evaluating information, using information, and remembering what is read. These skills need to be taught and retaught by each teacher in the system as they pertain to his particular subject, and purpose at hand. It would be wise for faculties to devote some meetings to the listing of specific study skills needed in various subject areas, and to denote ways in which these skills are being taught and reinforced in each. In language arts class, the main study skills have to do with the reading of literature with a capital "L," and the reading of magazines and newspapers. However, through well-planned work, practically all study skills can be strengthened. For individual and group help, the teacher's manual and workbooks accompanying basal reading texts give appropriate exercises; cumulative files of *Practical English* [4] reading exercises may be used; and, exercises from books such as Paul Witty's *How to Improve Your Reading* [5] can be adapted to class work. Aspects for which the language arts teacher is particularly responsible are the use of the dictionary, encyclopedia, card catalog, readers' guide, and "the book."

A fourth factor in the program is the development and guidance of interests and tastes. In an article, "Behind Reading Interests," in the January, 1954 *English Journal*, George Carlsen states that young adolescents need assurance of their status as human beings, assurance of their own physical and psychological normality, and in later years, need role playing. He says they satisfy these needs

[4] *Practical English* (Scholastic Corporation: 33 West 42nd St., New York 36, New York).

[5] Paul Witty, *How to Improve Your Reading* (Chicago: Science Research Associates, 1956).

through reading. If a teacher is to guide in the satisfaction of these needs, in reading discussions, she should help students pull out the attributes in books and stories common to them — the anger, frustration, insecurity, moments of elevation, responses to beauty — and get students as far as possible to tell similar instances in their own lives or ones they know. For example, in animal stories, talk about the way the animal solved his problems. Then, if the animal can do these wondrous things, how much more can man do with his superior powers! In adventure stories, talk about the situations in which men find themselves, and emphasize the characteristics of the men that helped them through great difficulties. In hero stories, discuss the qualities of the heroes, and compare them with ordinary men. What makes people do these things? How much were the heroes themselves responsible for their own achievements?

Dora Smith [6] in her discussion of the functions of literature in the elementary schools says that literature is meant to give delight, to give a heightened quality to familiar experience, to broaden experience and deepen understanding, to open up to young readers the common culture of children, to offer an escape from the humdrum activities of daily life, and to help boys and girls develop standards of aesthetic appreciation. She says love of the beautiful in God's creation, and the appreciation of form and ideas can not be learned by rote or handed out ready made. It is only developed, now in this setting, and now in that, until gradually it becomes a part of the very being of the reader himself. We teachers must remember this.

Some ways to encourage a variety of reading interests are: the use of devices such as "My Reading Design" [7] or "The Cumulative Reading Record";[8] bulletin board displays planned and made by students; teacher-made annotated book lists; dramatizations of scenes, or characters from books; and puppet shows based on books. Also, my students sometimes compile their own annotated bibliographical cards or book lists, and give reviews of new books, or of books of interest to the class at the moment.

A sixth specific instructional factor is enrichment activities which involve creative reading and the related language arts. The enrichment activities should evolve around the classroom library and magazine table filled with current magazines of interest to students.

[6] Dora Smith, "Literature and Personal Reading," *Reading in the Elementary School*, Forty-eighth Yearbook of the National Society for the Study of Education, Part II (Chicago: University of Chicago Press, 1949), pp. 205–209.

[7] G. O. Simpson, *My Reading Design* (North Manchester, Indiana: "The News-Journal," 1946).

[8] National Council of Teachers of English, *The Cumulative Reading Record* (Champaign, Illinois: National Council of Teachers of English, 1956).

Plenty of time for reading should be allowed during the class period. Records, slides and films, as well as radio and television programs should be used to stimulate interests, and to illustrate common ideas presented in different media. (For me, the *Practical English* teacher edition section, "Listenables and Lookables," is helpful in pointing out programs which would be suitable for tie-in with class work. Also, in the students' edition, some work is given to correlate with the major literary presentations of each winter season on television.) Choral reading with accompanying dramatizations is a popular activity in junior high. Ballads and humorous or narrative poems, such as "The Singing Leaves" and "Jonathan Bing" which have marked rhythm and repetition, lend themselves well to this.

The correlation of literature with holidays is important at this level. Other school departments emphasize the seasons in planning programs and projects; language arts will become a "dead" subject unless we too make efforts to supplement our program with the best literature having to do with the season. Again using a unit on mystery stories, occurring around Hallowe'en, an illustrative activity is the dramatization of the radio version of "The Legend of Sleepy Hollow," in the form of a tape-recorded production. The original story can be reviewed by a class member or teacher, the dictionary used to establish pronunciation of characters' names, and the play first read to gain insight into how it could be dramatized. Criteria for choosing a cast can be drawn up by the class. For discussion of criteria for casting, I use questions such as these: What kind of person is Katrina? What kind of voice should she have? What kind of expression will she use? What kind of teacher, lover, party-goer, and man is Ichabod? How many different scenes is he in? How will his personality be shown in each? After allowing time for oral practice at home, class try-outs can be held. The class may choose committees for the dramatization, for the securing and playing of records for background music, and providing sound effects. Parts of several class periods may be spent in group work, and the climax will come in the recording of the play for class playback, for other classes, or for outside groups.

At Christmas, I use unit plans similar to the ones described in the November, 1955 *English Journal*. Records, poems, plays, stories, current television and radio production can be correlated, and the whole unit spiritedly ended by the telling or reading of original Christmas stories on the day before vacation. The teacher may find good anthologies of seasonal materials appropriate for this age group listed in the "Children's Catalog."

A seventh factor in reading instruction is evaluation. In evaluating reading we should judge the student continuously from day to day by the way he contributes to discussions, his written reactions, and his zest for the reading period. Through questions on basal reading lessons, we can determine his comprehension, interpretations, and application of ideas from reading to other situations. Periodically, standardized tests can be used to compare achievement in the measurable aspects.

Undergirding all seven of these specific factors of upper grade instruction is the concept that the improvement of, and growth in reading abilities and skills need not be divorced from the reading of literature with a capital "L," and that reading is a continuous, life-long process involving the total personality. What activity in the public school curriculum can contribute more to an adolescent's all-around development than the "reading of good Literature"?

To summarize, good teaching of reading in the upper grades is characterized by: flexibility of procedure; increasing independence of students; increased amounts of committee work; varied attacks on new words — adapting rate and methods of reading to a variety of materials — thoughtful consideration of ideas gained in reading; close relation to other curricular and co-curricular activities, especially language arts; and a favorable reading atmosphere in the classroom.

Isn't this a rather comprehensive program? Yes, it is. Involving much work? Oh, yes. Is it worthwhile for both teacher and students? I think so.

PART EIGHT

The Effectiveness of a Reading Program

41. Ideas on Evaluation

M. Jerry Weiss

Who really knows how to evaluate a teacher, a student, or a program?

Roma Gans, Professor Emerita of Teachers College at Columbia University, once told a story concerning two students and the grades she gave them. To a young man, she gave a "B"; to a young lady, an "A." Several months after she had had these students in class, she accepted invitations to visit them at their new teaching posts.

She told how the former "B" student conducted his class and said he was a "marvelous young man — his students loved him." He showed much initiative, was creative and resourceful, was working out all kinds of projects with his students. It was thrilling to watch him in action. "And to think I gave him just a 'B'."

At the other school Miss Gans was somewhat disappointed. The teacher was not nearly as imaginative as her class reports and the "A" grade might have indicated.

Dr. Gans then asked the following question: "How do you ever *really* know who deserves what?"

If so experienced and astute an observer as Dr. Gans can question the validity of teacher evaluation, it is no wonder that other evaluation failures, involving both students and programs, come readily to mind.

I once had the opportunity to conduct a special summer workshop for teachers who were interested in exploring new methods for handling reading problems. A number of children had been accepted to serve as laboratory students for the teachers.

One of the workshop participants, a school administrator, told me he was most interested in what we were doing. He concluded our discussion by saying, "Oh, we don't have *any* reading problems in our schools. Whenever we find any reading difficulties, we just change our reading books."

I was dumfounded. A number of teachers in his school system had assured me they had no scarcity of problems in their reading program, and four of his teachers, enrolled in the workshop, had discovered that changing the texts did not help at all.

The following failure in evaluation is of a somewhat different nature. A friend of mine, a principal, had attended a special workshop on testing programs in the school. He was so impressed by his new-found knowledge that he immediately instituted sweeping changes in the curriculum. "If we are to have standards, then we must be objective! Standardized tests will show how successful and effective our teachers really are."

The teachers became frightened by the new testing system. Their own judgments were ignored — the tests would tell all. Before long they stopped teaching children and started teaching to pass the tests. Passing the tests was the ultimate goal, the sign of the superior teacher. The creative, imaginative, resourceful teachers left. The remaining teachers were dominated by a system of tests that undermined all sense of purpose and value not only in their reading program, but in the total school program as well. Much of the program was devoted to studying sample exercises based on previous examinations.

My friend had learned something about testing but had not learned how to evaluate — his one-sided approach led him astray. My friend's staff could have told him about those important aspects of learning that his tests — important as tests are — could not possibly measure. They could have told him, for example, that his tests did not recognize effort, initiative, creative thinking, attitudinal and behavioral changes — the very qualities and conditions which the teacher alone could best judge, on the basis of experience with the individual student.

If anything, this demonstrates again that evaluation is a job for the total faculty and that tests, if used, furnish only one part of a composite answer. Teachers and administrators, acting together, should determine the objectives of a program.

Once the objectives have been thought through, the reading teacher, or the person responsible for coordinating the reading program, might very well draft four letters which explain the general plans of the reading program to (1) administrators, (2) teachers, librarians, guidance staff, etc., (3) parents, and (4) students. Each person needs to understand what the program is attempting to do and what his area of responsibility is for the successful development of the program.

Throughout the year, checks can be made to see how those involved are meeting their responsibilities. The coordinator should then assemble the data to get the answers to the following questions:

1. Is the program doing all that it set out to do?
2. Are our objectives helping *each* child to grow *in* his reading and *through* his reading?
3. Do we have adequate materials for all to fulfill their responsibilities in developing the objectives?
4. Are we using the most effective procedures for implementing the objectives?
5. Have we adequate methods of communicating and recording the results of our reading program?
6. What changes in the program are necessary to better serve each child for his growth in reading?

As the program has progressed, some objectives may have been found unsuited for the students. Modifications must be made, since the success of the program is measured by its effectiveness in serving those students. Evaluation is, thus, a painstaking and continuous process.

There are no "pat" answers in evaluation. A reading program, for example, permeates the entire curriculum and can be evaluated only in the total framework. To evaluate a student's reading, one should examine the complete pattern of his reading experiences. How does he perform in each of his classes? What new skills has he attained? How effectively does he use these skills? What new insights and values has he gained through his reading? What new attitudes has he formed? How has his behavior changed as the result of his learning? Does the student find adequate practical reward and pleasure in reading so that he will continue to read throughout his lifetime?

Each teacher's records can reveal the results of teacher-constructed tests; the types and quality of projects developed by students, individually or in groups; the number and kinds of books each student is reading; the individual progress being made in specific skills; etc. These play a distinct part in the evaluation process.

Through the teacher's records and his personal observations much can be learned about the state of the reading program — where it is successful, and where it faces problems. The teacher can see which students are responding and — just as important — which students are not. He must find out the reasons for the difference in response. Only then can he decide what changes have to be made.

I have become somewhat wary of the traditional "A," "B," "C," method of recording and reporting student progress. Too many students, parents, and administrators do not understand what the symbols actually represent to the teachers who gave them. What does a "C" in reading actually mean? I believe we need to move away from this type of grading and encourage teachers to record more accurately through detailed written statements what a student's strengths and weaknesses are and what progress is being made by the student to improve himself. Granted that this will require more work on the part of the teacher, but perhaps by periodical interviews with parents such reports can be cut down to four times a year. Carbon copies of these reports will become a permanent part of each student's records and will be passed on from grade to grade and from teacher to teacher. This method insures greater continuity in the evaluative process.

A group of teachers I had in class one summer developed this list of areas "for consideration in evaluating reading."

1. Effort
2. Enjoyment (as shown by interests and attitudes)
3. Independence in selection of books read
4. Number and types of books read
5. Skills (word attack)
6. Vocabulary
7. Comprehension
8. Improvement of individual as compared with own former level
9. Questioning mind — active reading — critical thinking
10. Interaction with other students
11. Creativity (projects)
12. Class participation
13. Study skills

They listed three "suggested means of evaluation":

1. Self-evaluation — check lists, written comments, etc.
2. Personal interviews with each student
3. Tests

This list covers the important elements in a reading program fairly well. As long as *all* teachers participate and comment on the strengths and weaknesses of the program, a meaningful evaluation can be achieved.

Self-evaluation by each student is also important and should be stressed. Since reading is an extremely personal process, only the reader really knows what he is getting out of it. Consider the following comments made by seventh and eighth grade pupils to their reading teachers (I am indebted to Kenneth Sohmer of Bald Eagle Nittany High School, Mill Hall, Pa., and to Mrs. Carol Oswald of Junior High School, Bellefonte, Pa., for these comments):

1. Reading is a way of an author to tell his feelings. It is a way to tell about people, places, and things. It is also a way to learn important things and a way to pass time. In some cases it is interesting to read and learn new words. If we didn't have books, newspapers, etc., we wouldn't be able to learn about history and some important things going on in our nation, town, and surroundings.

I think reading is a necessary thing in life, without it we couldn't teach new things about foreign countries and learn about space, the earth, and many other things. Although I don't do much reading, I have learned a lot of new things.

2. From reading you can find out a great many things. Its sort of a school by itself. You can learn history, geography, almost anything from reading. There is no limit to reading. I think you can learn a great many more things from reading than you can from all the teachers put together, because they learned from books in the first place, so why don't we just read it in the first place? People talk about not having enough teachers, well, I think we need books a lot more because for enstance, in our English class, we have these literature books and half of them don't even have all the stories in them. I love to read all the poems and stories in the book but half the time I have to share, and the girl I share with, is awful selfish because she always takes the book. And anither thing, some people don't even know how to read. Why? Because we don't have enough books and teachers thats why.

I love to read. One day I spent almost a whole afternoon in our county library reading about things. When I went home, my mother asked me what I had learned, and I told her some things even she didn't know. I guess I should read books that I will really learn something from but I just read for fun most of the time, like Nancy Drew Mystery Stories, Calling All Girls, Ice Skating Books, Hardy Boys, and love stories sometimes but I don't like them when ther'e mushy. Ugh!

3. I like reading because it gives me an interest in the world I live in and the world of long ago and what it was like.

I like reading because it gives me a feeling I am not alone.

4. I think reading is a very useful subject. We can use books to help

us in other subjects. Another thing is we all don't have to read the same book.

I like reading because we can go in, pick up a book and start reading it until the period is over. I also like reading because I like to make projects for the books.

5. Reading is a form of communication. In my opinieon it is very nesseary, not only as a form of enjoyment but at business. Most of my scientific knowledege has been because of books. I have always enjoued reading very much of course I never liked school. But I would rather read Aku Aku (the story of easter Island) than listen to our math teacher (which I often do) There is some printed matter which isent worth the powder it takes to blow it up.

6. I like to read because I learn a lot that I didn't know before. I think it is fun to read.

I like to read but I don't like to make reports.

7. I really never thought of what reading meant to me. I got interesting in reading from watching T. V. programs and wanted to find out more about the program so I started to look in different books and found many interesting views on the subject. I think in my own mind that reading a book is a lot better than a summer's play or swim. If I had a chance and had the money I would see to it that every person and every family in the United States should have a brand new set of books. I think they help the average person in school alot more than T. V. or radio would.

8. Reading is interpreting something that is written. By reading you learn many things about people and the things around us. If you did not know how to read you would not know very much. In school we learn by reading.

I like reading very much except for some school books. I like to read true adventure books. By reading I learn what is happening in other parts of the world. I like to read hot rod stories because maybe I will be a race car driver.

9. Reading means that you learn more words and more about books. I don't care what kind of books I read just so they are interesting. I like the books about people who are already dead.

My attitude in reading class should be acting in a nice way and being quiet. And I should read instead of talk to my neighbor. I shouldn't act loud but silent and listen to the teacher.

10. Reading is a study of words. I think we need reading every day, because we must read signs, bills and papers every day, and we must be able to read them to understand what they are or mean. Our reading progress depends upon weather we like to read or not. If we like to read it will be very easy to learn — but on the other hand if we don't like to read it will be very hard for us to learn but I think reading is. People say you couldn't bake a cake without math but you couldn't even read the directions on a cake mix box if you couldn't read. I don't agree with the statement "One picture is worth a thousand words — you have to read and find out what is in the picture!

11. Reading means to me something to do when there is something no good on TV. But I like it. I am not very good at it. But good enough.

My attitude toward reading as would thing is not very good. It gives me something to do. I do not read any more than I have to. As you would think. But it is the best that I can do.

12. Reading to me is very interesting. The kind of books I like best are about presidents and inventors. I do not like fiction books very well but I do like non-fiction books very much.

I like to read very much. I am not a fast reader but I liked the books I read so far. Reading class is one of my best subjects.

13. Reading is truthfully increasing your vocabulary, but every time I open a book I don't think of that. I don't think, "Boy I'm going to increase my vocabulary. When I open my book I think of wonder what's next. I talk very little about reading. I don't want to sound conceated but I some times have to talk down to others. There is only one boy in our class who does really get along with me. He and I do enjoy the same things. He and I are on what I consider the same level in reading. He and I get along very well. I personally like science fiction and adult books. But people can't understand that these kids that like SO–CALLED–TRASH — not for the trash but for reading sake.

14. When I can read I enjoy reading. In non-fictional books I sometimes read information that is later some use to me. On a stormy day when its lightning and you shouldn't use the T. V., Radio or Stove I read. Sometimes I read funny parts in a book then tell them to my family.

Reading is exciting. I like history stories the best. Reading isn't just anouther subject reading is an important interest. You shouldn't just take reading grantent. You can make reading lots of fun.

15. I did not like reading until I came to this school. I like my reading teacher. It will help me with my education. It will help me when I get a job.

16. I enjoy reading when I can choose my own book. But when someone tells me to sit down and read a certain book, I get bored. I like mystery books best because they are exciting.

17. Reading is how well somebody reads an article, book, magazine, paper, etc. It's a ability which some people receive when they are young. Reading habits develope more and more as a person reads more.

I have never liked reading because of one reason. When I was in the early grades of Elementary School, I only read when I had to do so for homework. Today it is practically the same. Now when I read something, I hardly get anything out of it without reading it a couple of times. My brothers are practically the opposite, they read it once and they know it. My brothers read a book one night that would take me at least three nights. I had reading class once in high school. That did not influence me one bit to like reading. I think pupils should have it at least two years of high school. It would help them read a little bit.

18. Reading doesn't mean very much to me because I like the outdoors and good fresh air. I can't compel myself to stay in and read. Another thing I never did much reading when younger and therefore don't know

some things like other kids do. Jest one more thing when in earlier grades we never had vocabulary or any thing like that, that makes reading hard for me and this is why I dislike reading. Once I fource myself to read a book I didn't like, and that didn't help at all.

In spite of an occasionally negative response to reading, the ease of relationship between these two teachers and their students is excellent. A good number of the students show quite a sense of perspective regarding the general values and the practical uses of reading. Others reveal how they have enjoyed the teacher's help when they had problems, especially problems connected with skill or enjoyment in reading.

Through assignments such as those which led to these comments, the teacher can see what a child is interested in, how he is using his reading, and what problems he still has, and then can arrange student interviews to make further plans. These students are honest enough to tell a teacher what they really think of him and his program. A wise teacher will ponder the message.

The administrator of a school also has an extremely important responsibility, not only in participating in the evaluation process, but also in acting upon the results where they point toward deficiencies in the program. He should encourage recommendations from his staff and help with the scheduling and budgeting problems that arise. He knows that a reading program requires a variety of books and other materials and should not try to pinch pennies when a need for such supplies is indicated.

The administrator should make sure that his reading teachers are qualified to teach reading and that they have time to work with other teachers in the school. He should encourage and plan in-service training courses for his staff so the entire faculty can take a more active, responsible part in implementing the objectives of the total school reading program. This is particularly crucial since most secondary school teachers coming from college have no idea what a reading program is. The administrator must accordingly plan programs and workshops where they learn the essentials of reading for application within their content fields.

Such in-service training might very well begin with the establishment of a reading committee. At least one representative from each department in the school — as well as the school librarian, the guidance counsellor, the school psychologist, and a parent — should be on the committee. The reading teacher or a reading consultant can advise the committee on ways of implementing objectives and handling special reading problems. The committee can observe special demonstrations in the teaching of reading in all content areas. The demonstrations might stress specific methods of teaching word-attack skills, comprehension, speed, critical and creative reading, etc. The committee might be instrumental in reviewing and selecting new materials for more effective teaching.

Committee members would carry new ideas back to their classes and also share them with their own department members.

Membership on the reading committee should change yearly so as to involve more faculty members and acquaint them with ideas and methods for more effective teaching.

At times a youngster may need a special service, such as psychological help, to overcome a reading problem. The administrator should arrange for such help as soon as possible. If there is no regular school psychologist, perhaps a special fund can be established to provide for one on a part-time basis as emergencies arise.

The administrator can be the "check person" to make sure of order and articulation in developing a total school reading program from kindergarten through the twelfth grade. By working with other administrators and teacher committees, he can design the program that will best serve the students, the community, and the school. He is a key person in the school's public relations and can make sure that parents and other interested persons understand what the school's reading program is and how it is being developed. Unless these functions are satisfied, the evaluative process exists in at least a partial vacuum.

By the same token, the guidance counsellor, the school medical team of doctors and nurses, and the librarian are all part of the school reading program and of the evaluation process. Their ideas and suggestions should be seriously weighed.

Evaluation, like teaching itself, is a total school job. It is a continuous, cooperative job that tells teachers, students, and administrators what is working and what is not. The ideas presented here reflect the opinions and activities of many people whose primary aim is to find out what sort of program will best develop the reading skills and make reading an intelligent, lifetime habit.

Bibliography

Part I

A list of books, journals, and special publications on the teaching of reading.

All Teachers Can Teach Reading. Plainfield, N. J.: New Jersey Secondary School Teachers' Association, 1951.

Anderson, Irving H., and Dearborn, Walter F. *The Psychology of Teaching Reading.* New York: Ronald Press, 1952.

Austin, Mary C. *The Torch Lighters.* Cambridge: Harvard University Press, 1961.

Austin, Mary C.; Bush, Clifford L.; and Huebner, Mildred H. *Reading Evaluation: Appraisal Techniques for School and Classroom.* New York: Ronald Press, 1961.

Bamman, Henry A.; Hogan, Ursula; and Greene, Charles E. *Reading Instruction in the Secondary Schools.* New York: Longmans, Green and Company, 1961.

Berry, Elizabeth. *Guiding Students in the English Class.* New York: Appleton-Century-Crofts, 1957.

Betts, Emmett A. *Foundations of Reading Instruction.* New York: American Book Company, 1954.

Blair, Glenn M. *Diagnostic and Remedial Teaching* (Revised Edition). New York: Macmillan Company, 1956.

Bond, Guy L., and Tinker, Miles A. *Reading Difficulties: Their Diagnosis and Correction.* New York: Appleton-Century-Crofts, 1957.

Bond, Guy L., and Wagner, Eva Bond. *Teaching the Child to Read* (Revised Edition). New York: Macmillan Company, 1950.

Botel, Morton. *How to Teach Reading.* State College, Pa.: Penns Valley Publishers, 1959.

———. *Teaching Word Attack by the Discovery Technique.* State College, Pa.: Penns Valley Publishers, 1960.

Bullock, Harrison. *Helping the Non-Reading Pupil in the Secondary School.* New York: Bureau of Publications, Teachers College, Columbia University, 1956.

Buros, Oscar K. (Editor.) *The Fifth Mental Measurements Yearbook.* Highland Park, N. J.: Gryphon Press, 1959.

Burton, William H.; Baker, Clarabelle; and Kemp, Grace. *Reading in Child Development.* Indianapolis: Bobbs-Merrill Company, 1956.

Carter, Homer L. J., and McGinnis, Dorothy J. *Learning to Read.* New York: McGraw-Hill Book Company, 1953.

Causey, Oscar S. (Editor). *The Reading Teacher's Reader.* New York: Ronald Press, 1958.

Center, Stella S., and Persons, G. *Teaching High School Students to Read.* New York: Appleton-Century-Crofts, 1937.

Center, Stella. *The Art of Book Reading.* New York: Charles Scribner's Sons, 1952.

Cleary, Florence Damon. *Blueprints for Better Reading*. New York: H. W. Wilson Co., 1957.

Darrow, Helen Fisher, and Howes, Virgil M. *Approaches to Individualized Reading*. New York: Appleton-Century-Crofts, 1960.

De Bernardis, Amo. *The Use of Instructional Materials*. New York: Appleton-Century-Crofts, 1960.

DeBoer, John J., and Dallmann, Martha. *The Teaching of Reading*. New York: Henry Holt and Company, 1960.

Dever, Imogene. *Positions in the Fields of Reading*. New York: Bureau of Publications, Teachers College, Columbia University, 1956.

Dolch, Edward W. *A Manual for Remedial Reading* (Second Edition). Champaign, Ill.: Garrard Press, 1945.

———. *Methods in Reading*. Champaign, Ill.: Garrard Press, 1955.

———. *Psychology and Teaching of Reading* (Second Edition). Champaign, Ill.: Garrard Press, 1951.

Durrell, Donald D. *Improving Reading Instruction*. Yonkers, N. Y.: World Book Company, 1956.

Ephron, Beulah K. *Emotional Difficulties in Reading*. New York: Julian Press, 1953.

Fay, Leo. *What Research Says to the Teacher: Reading in the High School*. Washington, D. C.: Department of Classroom Teachers and American Educational Research Association of the National Education Association, 1956.

Fernald, Grace M. *Remedial Techniques in Basic School Subjects*. New York: McGraw-Hill Book Company, 1943.

Figurel, J. Allen (Editor). *New Frontiers in Reading*. International Reading Association Conference Proceedings. New York: Scholastic Magazines, 1960.

———. *Reading for Effective Living*. International Reading Association Conference Proceedings. New York: Scholastic Magazines, 1958.

———. *Reading in a Changing Society*. International Reading Association Conference Proceedings. New York: Scholastic Magazines, 1959.

Gates, Arthur I. *The Improvement of Reading*. New York: Macmillan Company, 1947.

———. *What Research Says to the Teacher: Teaching Reading*. Washington, D. C.: Department of Classroom Teachers and American Educational Research Association of the National Education Association, 1953.

Gordon, Edward J., and Noyes, Edward S. *Essays on the Teaching of English*. New York: Appleton-Century-Crofts, 1960.

Gray, Lillian, and Reese, Dora. *Teaching Children to Read* (Second Edition). New York: Ronald Press, 1957.

Gray, William S., and Larrick, Nancy (Editors). *Better Readers for Our Times*. International Reading Association Conference Proceedings. New York: Scholastic Magazines, 1956.

Gray, William S., and Rogers, Bernice. *Maturity in Reading: Its Nature and Appraisal*. Chicago: University of Chicago Press, 1956.

Gray, William S. (Editor). *Basic Instruction in Reading in Elementary and High Schools*. Chicago: University of Chicago Press, 1948.

———. *Improving Reading in All Curriculum Areas*. Chicago: University of Chicago Press, 1952.

———. *Improving Reading in Content Fields*. Chicago: University of Chicago Press, 1946.

———. *Promoting Growth Toward Maturity in Interpreting What Is Read*. Chicago: University of Chicago Press, 1951.

Harris, Albert J. *How to Increase Reading Ability* (Fourth Edition). New York: Longmans, Green and Company, 1961.

Heilman, Arthur W. *Principles and Practices of Teaching Reading*. Columbus, Ohio: Charles E. Merrill Books, 1961.

Hester, Kathleen B. *Teaching Every Child to Read*. New York: Harper and Brothers, 1955.

Hildreth, Gertrude. *Teaching Reading*. New York: Henry Holt and Company, 1958.

Hovious, Carol. *Suggestions for Teachers of Reading, Grades VII to XII*. Boston: D. C. Heath and Company, 1939.

Hunnicutt, C. W., and Iverson, William J. *Research in the Three R's*. New York: Harper and Brothers, 1958.

Jewett, Arno (Editor). *Improving Reading in the Junior High School*. Washington, D. C.: Department of Health, Education, and Welfare, Bulletin No. 10, 1957.

Journal of Developmental Reading. Department of English, Purdue University, Lafayette, Ind. ($3.50 a year — $3.00 to teachers.)

Kottmeyer, William. *Handbook for Remedial Reading*. St. Louis: Webster Publishing Company, 1947.

———. *Teacher's Guide for Remedial Reading*. St. Louis: Webster Publishing Company, 1959.

Laird, Charlton. *Thinking About Language*. New York: Rinehart and Company, 1959.

Larrick, Nancy (Editor). *Reading In Action*. International Reading Association Conference Proceedings. New York: Scholastic Magazines, 1957.

Larrick, Nancy. *Your Child and His Reading — How Parents Can Help*. New York: Public Affairs Committee, 1959.

McKee, Paul. *The Teaching of Reading in the Elementary School*. Boston: Houghton Mifflin Company, 1948.

McKillop, Anne S. *The Relationship Between the Reader's Attitude and Certain Types of Reading Responses*. New York: Bureau of Publications, Teachers College, Columbia University, 1952.

McKim, Margaret. *Guiding Growth in Reading*. New York: Macmillan Company, 1955.

Metropolitan School Study Council. *Five Steps to Reading Success in Science, Social Studies and Mathematics* (Revised Edition). New York: Metropolitan School Study Council, Teachers College, Columbia University, 1960.

National Council of Teachers of English, the Commission on the English Curriculum. *The English Language Arts in the Secondary School*. New York: Appleton-Century-Crofts, 1956.

National Society for the Study of Education. *Reading in the High School and College*. Forty-seventh Yearbook, part II. Chicago: The University of Chicago Press, 1948.

———. *Development In and Through Reading*. Sixtieth Yearbook, part I. Chicago: University of Chicago Press, 1961.

New Practices in Reading. Seventeenth Yearbook. Washington, D. C.: Department of Elementary School Principals of the National Education Association, 1955.

Newton, J. Roy. *Reading in Your School*. New York: McGraw-Hill Book Company, 1960.

New York City Board of Education. *Reading, Grades 7, 8, 9: A Teacher's Guide to Curriculum Planning*. Brooklyn, N. Y.: Board of Education, 1959.

New York State Education Department. *The Road to Better Reading.* Albany, N. Y.: Bureau of Secondary Curriculum Development, The State Education Department, 1953.

Norvell, George W. *Reading in the Secondary School Program.* Albany, N. Y.: The University of the State of New York Press, 1952.

Penty, Ruth C. *Reading Ability and High School Drop-Outs.* New York: Bureau of Publications, Teachers College, Columbia University, 1956.

Pooley, Robert C. (Editor). *Perspectives on English.* New York: Appleton-Century-Crofts, 1960.

Preston, Ralph C. *Teaching Study Habits and Skills.* New York: Rinehart and Company, 1959.

Price, Jacob (Editor). *Reading for Life.* Ann Arbor: University of Michigan Press, 1959.

Robinson, Helen M. (Editor). *Clinical Studies in Reading, II.* Chicago: University of Chicago Press, 1953.

———. *Corrective Reading in Classroom and Clinic.* Chicago: University of Chicago Press, 1953.

———. *Evaluation of Reading.* Chicago: University of Chicago Press, 1958.

———. *Materials for Reading.* Chicago: University of Chicago Press, 1957.

———. *Oral Aspects of Reading.* Chicago: University of Chicago Press, 1955.

———. *Promoting Maximal Reading Growth Among Able Learners.* Chicago: University of Chicago Press, 1954.

———. *Reading Instruction in Various Patterns of Grouping.* Chicago: University of Chicago Press, 1959.

———. (Editor.) *Sequential Development of Reading Abilities.* Chicago: University of Chicago Press, 1960.

———. *Why Pupils Fail in Reading.* Chicago: University of Chicago Press, 1946.

Rothney, John W. M. *What Research Says to the Teacher: Evaluating and Reporting Pupil Progress.* Washington, D. C.: Department of Classroom Teachers and American Research Association of the National Education Association, 1955.

Russell, David H. *Children Learn to Read* (Second Edition). Boston: Ginn and Company, 1961.

———. *Children's Thinking.* Boston: Ginn and Company, 1956.

Shepherd, David L. *Effective Reading in Science.* Evanston, Illinois: Row, Peterson and Company, 1960.

———. *Effective Reading in Social Studies.* Evanston, Illinois: Row, Peterson and Company, 1960.

Simpson, Elizabeth A. *Helping High School Students Read Better.* Chicago: Science Research Associates, 1954.

Stewart, L. Jane; Heller, Frieda M.; and Alberty, Elsie J. *Improving Reading in the Junior High School.* New York: Appleton-Century-Crofts, 1957.

Strang, Ruth M., and Bracken, Dorothy Kendall. *Making Better Readers.* Boston: D. C. Heath and Company, 1957.

Strang, Ruth M., and Lindquist, Donald M. *The Administrator and the Improvement of Reading.* New York: Appleton-Century-Crofts, 1960.

Strang, Ruth M.; McCullough, Constance M.; and Traxler, Arthur E. *The Improvement of Reading* (Third Edition). New York: McGraw-Hill Book Company, 1961.

Strang, Ruth M. *Reading and the Junior High School Teacher*. Bulletin No. 12. Middletown, Conn.: Department of School Services and Publications, Wesleyan University, 1959.

Teaching Reading in High School. Kansas Studies in Education, Vol. 10, No. 1. Lawrence, Kans.: University of Kansas Press, February, 1960.

The English Journal. Publication for secondary school teachers. Champaign, Ill.: The National Council of Teachers of English, 508 S. Sixth Street. $4.00 a year.

The Reading Teacher. Publication of the International Reading Association, 5835 Kimbark Avenue, Chicago, Ill. $3.50 a year.

Tooze, Ruth. *Story Telling: How to Develop Skills in the Art of Telling Stories to Children*. Englewood Cliffs, N. J.: Prentice-Hall, 1959.

Traxler, Arthur E., and Jungenblut, Ann. *Research in Reading During Another Four Years*. New York: Educational Records Bureau, 1960.

Traxler, Arthur E., and Townsend, Agatha. *Another Five Years of Research in Reading*. New York: Educational Records Bureau, 1946.

———. *Eight More Years of Research in Reading: Summary and Bibliography*. New York: Educational Records Bureau, 1955.

Traxler, Arthur E. *Ten Years of Research in Reading*. New York: Educational Records Bureau, 1941.

Veatch, Jeannette. *Individualizing Your Reading Program*. New York: G. P. Putnam's Sons, 1959.

Vernon, M. D. *Backwardness in Reading*. London: Cambridge University Press, 1957.

What We Should Know About High School Reading. Champaign, Ill.: National Council of Teachers of English, 1958.

Wilborn, Lee J.; Alexander, Nelle; and Bracken, Dorothy Kendall. *The Improvement of Reading in Secondary Schools*. Bulletin No. 540. Austin, Texas: Texas Education Agency, March, 1953.

Witty, Paul, and Kopel, David. *Reading and the Educative Process*. Boston: Ginn and Company, 1939.

Witty, Paul, and Ratz, Margaret. *A Developmental Reading Program for Grades 6 through 9*. Chicago: Science Research Associates, 1956.

Witty, Paul. *Reading in Modern Education*. Boston: D. C. Heath and Company, 1949.

Wolfe, Don M. *Creative Ways to Teach English: Grades 7 to 12*. New York: The Odyssey Press, 1958.

———. *Language Arts and Life Patterns: Grades 2 through 8*. New York: The Odyssey Press, 1961.

Woolf, Maurice D., and Woolf, Jeanne A. *Remedial Reading: Teaching and Treatment*. New York: McGraw-Hill Book Company, 1957.

Yoakam, Gerald A. *Basal Reading Instruction*. New York: McGraw-Hill Book Company, 1955.

Part II

A list of articles on reading and reading in the content fields.

Alm, Richard S. "The Utmost Need," *The English Journal*, 46 (November, 1957), 470–474.

Barbe, Walter. "A Study of the Reading of Gifted High School Students," *Educational Administration and Supervision*, 38 (March, 1952), 148–154.

———. "Measuring Reading Comprehension," *Clearing House*, 32 (February, 1958), 343–345.

Beard, Richard L. "Reading Habits and Interests," *High School Journal*, 39 (January, 1956), 207–212.

Bell, Max. "Speaking of Figures, We Must Find Ways of Meeting the Language Arts Needs of Mathematics Students," *California Teacher Association Journal*, 52 (May, 1956), 32f.

Berry, June. "Letter to a New English Teacher," *Clearing House*, 34 (February, 1960), 343–345.

Betts, Emmett A. "Reading as a Thinking Process," *National Elementary Principal*, 35 (September, 1955), 88–96.

———. "What About Phonics?" *Education*, 75 (May, 1955), 547–559.

Brown, Carl F. "Developing Reading Skills through Literature and Social Studies," *High School Journal*, 36 (October, 1952), 12–16.

Brown, Clyde M. "Reading in Science as a Means of Improving the Junior High School Program," *Science Teacher*, 21 (November, 1954), 281–283.

Budish, B. E. "Business Education Instructor Also Teaches Reading," *Journal of Business Education*, 30 (November, 1954), 68–70.

Campbell, W. E. "Reading Can Be Improved," *The Bulletin of the National Association of Secondary School Principals*, 40 (November, 1956), 42–48.

Capehart, Bertis E., and McKeehan, Rollin. "A Junior High School Reading Program Adjusted to Individual Needs," *High School Journal*, 39 (December, 1955), 172–177.

Carlsen, G. Robert. "Behind Reading Interests," *The English Journal*, 43 (January, 1954), 7–12.

Carter, Homer L. J. "Reading, A Contributing and Concomitant Factor in the Study of Science," *School Science and Mathematics*, 54 (October, 1954), 567–570.

Covell, Harold M. "Reading and the Social Studies," *Social Education*, 21 (January, 1957), 14–16.

Cushman, C. Leslie, and Green, Rosemary M. "Philadelphia Schools Attack the Reading Problem," *Nation's Schools*, 51 (May, 1953), 52–55.

Dale, Edgar. "The Problem of Vocabulary in Reading," *Educational Research Bulletin*, 35 (May 9, 1956), 113–123.

———. "The Reading of Magazines," *Education Digest*, 20 (December, 1954), 22–23.

Dallmann, M. "Help with the Social Studies," *Grade Teacher*, 75 (April, 1958), 30–31.

Davis, L. R., and Davis, Jacqueline. "What Principals Should Know About Remedial Reading," *Clearing House*, 29 (January, 1955), 298–300.

DeBoer, John J. "Individual Differences in Reading Instruction," *High School Journal*, 39 (October, 1955), 8–13.

Eagle, Edwin. "The Relationship of Certain Reading Abilities to Success in Mathematics," *The Mathematics Teacher*, 41 (April, 1948), 175–179.

Eller, William. "Essentials of Critical Reading," *High School Journal*, 39 (November, 1955), 66–70.

Harrison, Lincoln J. "Teaching Accounting Students How to Read," *The Journal of Business Education*, 35 (January 1, 1960), 169–170.

Hinds, Lillian R. "Melvin Regains His Self-Respect," *Education*, 81 (October, 1960), 115–118.

Hull, Mae P. "One Hundred Ways of Improving Reading," *High Points*, 38 (October, 1956), 5–16.

Hunt, J. T. "Reading: The High School's Problem," *High School Journal*, 36 (October, 1952), 2–6.

Jacobs, Leland B. "Individualized Reading Is Not a Thing!" *Teachers College Record*, 59 (March, 1958), 319–329.

Jensen, Amy Elizabeth. "Attracting Children to Books," *Elementary English*, 33 (October, 1956), 332–339.

Jensen, Lisbeth J. "Fostering Interest in Reading," *The English Journal*, 42 (October, 1953), 367–370.

Johnson, Donovan A. "The Readability of Mathematics Books," *The Mathematics Teacher*, 50 (February, 1957), 105–110.

Johnson, Eric W. "Stimulating Reading in Junior High School," *The English Journal*, 48 (February, 1959), 68–76.

Keesler, Earl R. "Vocabulary in Plane Geometry," *The Mathematics Teacher*, 35 (November, 1942), 331.

Kerchner, Nelle F. "Reading in the Secondary School," *The English Journal*, 34 (June, 1945), 329–333.

Leary, Bernice E. "Improving Reading Skills in Mathematics and Science," *High School Journal*, 36 (October, 1952), 17–21.

Leighty, V. E. "How Slowly Do They Read?" *The English Journal*, 45 (May, 1956), 257–260.

Letton, Mildred C. "Diagnosis of Reading Problems in High School," *High School Journal*, 39 (October, 1955), 40–43.

Levine, Isidore N. "Solving Reading Problems in Vocational Subjects," *High Points*, 41 (April, 1960), 10–27.

Mallinson, George G. "How to Use the Textbook in Science Teaching," *School Science and Mathematics*, 53 (November, 1953), 593–600.

Mallinson, George G., and Others. "The Reading Difficulty of Textbooks for General Physical Science and Earth Science," *School Science and Mathematics*, 54 (November, 1954), 612–616.

———. "The Reading Difficulty of Some Recent Textbooks for Science," *School Science and Mathematics*, 57 (May, 1957), 364–366

Maney, Ethel S. "Literal and Critical Reading in Science," *Journal of Experimental Education*, 27 (September, 1958), 57–64.

McCullough, Constance M. "Teaching Creative Reading," *Journal of Education*, 136 (April, 1954), 200–203.

McDowell, Kyle C. "The Teaching of Reading in the Junior High School," *The Bulletin of the National Association of Secondary School Principals*, 38 (December, 1954), 36–39.

McGuiness, A. E. "Reading Guidance in the Junior High School," *Wilson Library Bulletin*, 28 (April, 1954), 682–685.

Parker, Don H. "The Multi-Level Approach to Meeting Individual Differences in Reading," *High School Journal*, 39 (January, 1956), 247–252.

Porges, Irwin. "Mathematics Motivated Through Science Fiction," *School Science and Mathematics*, 56 (January, 1956), 1–4.

Reeves, Ruth E. "Planning a Literature Program for the Junior High School," *The English Journal*, 48 (October, 1959), 374–381.

Robinson, Helen M. "Qualifications for Teachers of Remedial Reading," *School Review*, 63 (September, 1955), 334–337.

Rose, Frances. "Improving Reading Skills," *Library Journal*, 76 (September, 1951), 1398–1401.

Russell, David H. "Reading Disabilities and Mental Health: A Review of Research," *Understanding the Child*, 16 (January, 1947), 24–32.

———. "Reading for Critical Thinking," *California Journal of Elementary Education*, 14 (November, 1945), 79–86.

Schubert, Delwyn. "Better Reading: Everyone's Job," *High School Journal*, 37 (January, 1954), 117–118.

———. "Formulas for Better Reading in Mathematics," *School Science and Mathematics*, 55 (November, 1955), 650–652.

———. "Science Teachers: What You Can Do to Help Your Students to Read More Efficiently" *Clearing House*, 30 (October, 1955), 83–84.

———. "The Word Reader, His Plight and What Can Be Done," *Clearing House*, 29 (December, 1954), 221–222.

Sheldon, William D. "Can We Improve Reading by Using Mechanical Devices?" *Education Digest*, 21 (September, 1955), 45–47.

Siegelbaum, M. "Mental Health and Remedial Reading," *High Points*, 36 (February, 1954), 66–70.

Smith, Belle W., and Hearn, Arthur C. "A Mathematical Attack on the Reading Program," *School Science and Mathematics*, 55 (June, 1955), 483–486.

Smith, Nila B. "Planning for a Total Reading Program in the High School," *High School Journal*, 43 (November, 1959), 58–70.

Strang, Ruth. "Illustrative Reading Programs," *High School Journal*, 36 (October, 1952), 22–27.

Thomas, E. L. "Critical Reading Laboratory," *Education Digest*, 25 (May, 1960), 45–47.

Tormey, Mary K. "Reading Factors in Clerical Training," *UBEA Forum*, 5 (February, 1955), 14–16.

Totten, W. Fred. "Words as a Basic Factor in Understanding Algebra," *School Science and Mathematics*, 56 (March, 1956), 230–233.

Traxler, Arthur E. "Remedial Reading Today," *School Review*, 61 (January, 1953), 17–24.

Wagner, Guy. "Toward Better Reading in the High School," *Midland Schools*, 72 (May, 1958), 19f.

Weiss, M. Jerry. "The Individual *Is* the Secondary School Reading Program," *TAB Memo to Teachers*, Scholastic Book Services (January, 1960), 1f.

Zamchick, David. "The Battle of the Book: Slow Learner," *Clearing House*, 33 (September, 1958), 41–43.

Part III

Some Suggestions on booklists.

Books for the Teen Age, 1960. New York: The New York City Public Library (Fifth Avenue and 42nd Street), 1960.

Bracken, Dorothy Kendall. "Easy Reading Material for High School Students," *The Reading Teacher*, 7 (April, 1954), 236–239.

Burton, D. L. *Literature Study in the High Schools.* New York: Henry Holt and Company, 1959.

Carpenter, Helen McCracken. *Gateways to American History.* New York: H. W. Wilson Co., 1942.

Chandler, S. C. "Science Books for the High School Library," *School Science and Mathematics*, 57 (November, 1957), 593–594.

Committee on the Junior High School Book List. *Your Reading.* Champaign, Ill.: National Council of Teachers of English, 1960.

Committee on the Senior High School Reading List. *Books for You.* Champaign, Ill.: National Council of Teachers of English, 1959.

Dawson, Mildred A., and Pfeiffer, Louise. *A Treasury of Books for the Primary Grades.* San Francisco: Howard Chandler, 1959.

Dunn, Anita E.; Jackman, Mabel; and Bush, Bernice. *Fare for the Reluctant Reader.* Albany, N. Y.: Teachers College, State University of New York, 1952.

Fenner, Phyllis. *Proof of the Pudding.* New York: John Day Company, 1957.

———. *Something Shared: Children and Books.* New York: John Day Company, 1959.

Frank, Josette. *Your Child's Reading Today* (Revised Edition). Garden City, N. Y.: Doubleday and Company, 1960.

Goldenson, Robert M. *Helping Your Child to Read Better.* New York: Thomas Y. Crowell Company, 1957.

Heaton, Margaret M., and Lewis, Helen B. *Reading Ladders for Human Relations.* Washington, D. C.: American Council on Education, 1955.

Hill, Margaret Keyser. *A Bibliography of Reading Lists for Retarded Readers.* State University of Iowa Extension Bulletin No. 37. Iowa City: State University of Iowa, 1953.

Hunt, J. T. "Easy and Interesting Fiction for the Handicapped Reader," *High School Journal*, 39 (April, 1956), 378–385.

———. "Easy Non-Fictional Materials for the Handicapped Reader," *High School Journal*, 39 (March, 1956), 322–332.

Larrick, Nancy. *A Parent's Guide to Children's Reading.* New York: Pocket Books, 1958.

———. *A Teacher's Guide to Children's Books.* Columbus, Ohio: Charles E. Merrill Books, 1960.

Lawson, Russell D. "The Effective Biology Library," *The American Biology Teacher*, 22 (May, 1960), 290–292.

Norvell, George W. *The Reading Interests of Young People.* Boston: D. C. Heath and Company, 1950.

———. *What Boys and Girls Like to Read.* Morristown, N. J.: Silver Burdett Company, 1958.

Panush, Louis. "New Books for the High School Science Shelf," *School Science and Mathematics*, 54 (May, 1954), 371–376.

Paperback Review. New York: (101 Fifth Avenue), 1960.

Paperbound Books in Print. New York: R. R. Bowker Company (62 West 45th Street).

Spache, George. *Good Books for Poor Readers* (Revised Edition). Champaign, Ill.: Garrard Press, 1960.

Strang, Ruth; Phelps, Ethlyne; and Withrow, Dorothy. *Gateways to Readable Books* (Third Edition). New York: H. W. Wilson Co., 1958.

Sullivan, Helen Blair, and Tolman, Lorraine E. *High Interest—Low Vocabulary Reading Materials*, a Selected Booklist in the *Journal of Education*, Vol. 139, No. 2. Boston: School of Education, Boston University, December, 1956.

Tooze, Ruth. *Your Children Want to Read*. Englewood Cliffs, N. J.: Prentice-Hall, 1957.

Weber, J. Sherwood (Editor). *Good Reading*. New York: Mentor Books, 1959.

Weiss, M. Jerry, and Others. *The Use of Paperbound Books in the Nation's Schools*. Champaign, Ill.: National Council of Teachers of English, 1960.

Note: A letter sent to any publisher, hard-cover or paperbound, requesting a complete list of titles will bring a prompt reply. You can also request your name to be placed on the mailing list for notification of new titles as they become available.

Part IV

Some suggested materials for use in the secondary school reading program.

One of the most important parts of a substantial reading program is a good classroom library made up of a wide variety of titles and subjects. One way of starting a good library is to investigate the many titles available in paperbound editions. *Paperbound Books in Print* (listed in Part III) is a good source of information, as is checking the catalogues of the different companies.

For another source, check *H. W. Wilson Standard Catalogue of Books for the High School Library.*

Most of the materials listed below are useful for developing skills in reading and in handling reading problems in the content fields.

Adult Education Readers. Pleasantville, N. Y.: Reader's Digest Educational Department.

American Adventure Series. Chicago: Wheeler Publishing Company.

Baker, William D. *Reading Skills*. Englewood Cliffs, N. J.: Prentice-Hall, 1953.

Bear, Robert M. *How to Get the Most Out of Your Textbooks*. New York: The American Textbook Publishers Institute, 1957.
Botel, Morton, and Smith, Margaret H. *Multi-Level Reading Activities*. State College, Pa.: Penns Valley Publishers, 1959.
Botel, Morton (Editor). *Interesting Reading Series*. State College, Pa.: Penns Valley Publishers.
Cuomo, George. *Becoming a Better Reader*. New York: Rinehart and Company, 1960.
Dale, Edgar. *How to Read a Newspaper*. Chicago: Scott, Foresman and Company, 1941.
De Vitis, A. A., and Warner, J. R. *Words in Context*. New York: Appleton-Century-Crofts, 1961.
Dolch, E. W. *Dolch Reading Games*. Champaign, Ill.: Garrard Press.
Farquhar, William W.; Kramboltz, John D.; Wrenn, C. Gilbert. *Learning to Study*. New York: Ronald Press, 1960.
Funk, Wilfred, and Lewis, Norman. *30 Days to a More Powerful Vocabulary*. New York: Pocket Books, 1942.
Funk, Wilfred. *Six Weeks to Words of Power*. New York: Pocket Books, 1953.
Gates, Arthur I., and Peardon, Celeste C. *Practice Exercises in Reading*, Books III, IV, V, VI, Types A, B, C, D, for each book. New York: Bureau of Publications, Teachers College, Columbia University, 1944.
Goodman, Roger B., and Lewin, David. *New Ways to Greater Word Power*. New York: Dell Books, 1954.
Gray, William S., and Others. *Basic Reading Skills for Junior High School Use*. Chicago: Scott, Foresman and Company, 1957.
Greene, A. *Word Clues*. Evanston, Ill.: Row, Peterson and Company, 1951.
Hovious, Carol. *New Trails in Reading*. Boston: D. C. Heath and Company, 1956.
Johnson, Eleanor M., and Others. *Modern Readings*, Books I, II, III. Columbus, Ohio: Charles E. Merrill Books, 1946–1947.
Life Adjustment Booklets. Chicago: Science Research Associates.
McCall, William A., and Crabbs, Lelah Mae. *Standard Test Lessons in Reading*, Books A, B, C, D, E. New York: Bureau of Publications, Teachers College, Columbia University, 1950.
Monroe, Marion; Horsman, Gwen; and Gray, William S. *Basic Reading Skills for High School Use*. Chicago: Scott, Foresman and Company, 1948.
Morris, William. *It's Easy to Increase Your Vocabulary*. Garden City, N. Y.: Dolphin Books, 1961.
Murphy, George, and Others. *Let's Read*, Books 1, 2, 3, 4. New York: Henry Holt and Company, 1953–1955.
Parker, Don H., and Others. *Reading Laboratory, College Preparatory Edition*. Chicago: Science Research Associates, 1959.
———. *Reading Laboratory, Elementary School Edition*. Chicago: Science Research Associates, 1959.
———. *Reading Laboratory, Secondary School Edition*. Chicago: Science Research Associates, 1958.
Preston, Ralph, and Botel, Morton. *How to Study*. Chicago: Science Research Associates, 1956.
Reader's Digest Reading Skill Builders, Grades 2 Through 8. Pleasantville, N. Y.: Reader's Digest Educational Department.
Robinson, Francis P. *Effective Study* (Revised Edition). New York: Harper and Brothers, 1961.

Russell, David H., and Karp, Etta. *Reading Aids Through the Grades*. New York: Bureau of Publications, Teachers College, Columbia University, 1951.

Shaw, Philip. *Effective Reading and Learning*. New York: Thomas Y. Crowell Company, 1956.

Shefter, Harry. *Faster Reading — Self-Taught*. New York: Pocket Books, 1958.

———. *6 Minutes a Day to Perfect Spelling*. New York: Pocket Books, 1954.

Simpson, Elizabeth. *SRA Better Reading Books, 1, 2, and 3*. Chicago, Ill.: Science Research Associates, 1951.

Simpson, G. O. "My Reading Design," *The News Journal*, North Manchester, Ind., 1945.

Smith, Nila B. *Be a Better Reader Series*. Englewood Cliffs, N. J.: Prentice-Hall, 1958–1960.

Strang, Ruth, and Others. *Study Type of Reading Exercises* (College Level). New York: Bureau of Publications, Teachers College, Columbia University, 1951.

———. *Study Type of Reading Exercises* (High School Level). New York: Bureau of Publications, Teachers College, Columbia University, 1956.

———. *Teen-Age Tales Series*. Boston: D. C. Heath and Company, 1954–1958.

Uni-Kits Brochure. New York: Uni-Kits (59 Pearl Street), 1960.

Weiss, M. Jerry. *Guidance Through Drama*. New York: Whiteside, 1954.

Witty, Paul. *How to Become a Better Reader*. Chicago: Science Research Associates, 1953.

———. *How to Improve Your Reading*. Chicago: Science Research Associates, 1956.

———. *Streamline Your Reading*. Chicago: Science Research Associates, 1949.

Wood, E. N., and Barrows, M. W. *Reading Skills*. New York: Henry Holt and Company, Inc., 1958.

Note: No effort has been made to list all of the workbooks and reading texts available at this time.

Many teachers make their own materials and games. Some use commercially prepared games such as Anagrams and Scrabble; many use cross-word puzzles. Quite a few report use of audio-visual materials, such as reading accelerators and pacers, tachistoscopes, movies such as those prepared by Coronet Films, etc. However, research reveals quite a controversy over the ultimate success of machine-powered programs. (This writer would prefer spending the money on one or two machines and most of the other funds going into a variety of materials and trade books for building a good curriculum library of resource materials for a total school reading program.)

Other books in this bibliography, such as *Gateways to Readable Books*, include much more detailed descriptions of materials currently available.

College Preparatory Reading List

Compiled by Mrs. Cordelia Smith, Young People's Librarian, Lucas County Library, Maumee, Ohio, and M. Jerry Weiss, The Pennsylvania State University.

(Selections from the reading lists used in several preparatory schools and colleges)

The number or numbers following the title correspond to the appropriate number given each publisher of paperbacks and appear in the directory at the end of the list. (Titles have been checked in the Winter, 1960–61, edition of *Paperbound Books in Print.*)

Adams	*The Henry Adams Reader* (1)
Anderson	*Winesburg, Ohio* (2)
Austen	*Emma* (3; 4; 5)
Austen	*Pride and Prejudice* (4; 5; 6; 7; 8; 9; 10)
Austen	*Sense and Sensibility* (4; 7; 10)
Benét	*Stephen Vincent Benét: Selected Poetry and Prose* (8)
Blackmore	*Lorna Doone* (11)
Boswell	*Life of Samuel Johnson* (7 [abr.]; 16)
Bowen	*Yankee from Olympus* (3)
Brontë	*Jane Eyre* (4; 5; 8; 10; 11; 13; 14)
Brontë	*Wuthering Heights* (4; 5; 6; 8; 10; 13; 14)
Buck	*The Good Earth* (11)
Bunyan	*Pilgrim's Progress* (8; 11)
Butler	*The Way of All Flesh* (4; 6; 8; 10; 14; 15)
Byrd	*Alone* (16)
Byrne	*Messer Marco Polo* (6)
Carroll	*Alice's Adventures in Wonderland* (4; 6; 14; 17)
Carson	*The Sea around Us* (14)
Cervantes	*Don Quixote* (10; 11 [abr.]; 13; 14 [abr.]; 18)
Chaucer	*Canterbury Tales* (6; 8; 13; 18; 19)
Chute	*Ben Jonson of Westminster* (2)
Chute	*Chaucer of England* (20)
Chute	*Shakespeare of London* (20)
Clemens	*A Connecticut Yankee in King Arthur's Court* (6; 22)
Clemens	*Huckleberry Finn* (4; 5; 6; 7; 8; 13; 14; 21)
Clemens	*Life on the Mississippi* (3; 22)
Clemens	*Tom Sawyer* (4; 6; 13; 14)
Conrad	*Heart of Darkness* (7; 14; 23)
Conrad	*Lord Jim* (3; 5; 8)

Conrad — *The Nigger of the Narcissus* (7; 23)
Conrad — *Victory* (1)
Cooper — *Last of the Mohicans* (4; 5; 6)
Cooper — *The Spy* (4; 24)
Cousteau — *The Silent World* (11)
Crane — *The Red Badge of Courage* (4; 5; 6; 7; 8; 10; 14)
Cronin — *The Citadel* (3)
Cronin — *Keys to the Kingdom* (3)
Curie — *Madame Curie* (11)
Day — *Life with Father* (11)
Defoe — *Moll Flanders* (4; 5; 8; 10; 11)
Defoe — *Robinson Crusoe* (4; 11)
De Kruif — *Microbe Hunters* (11)
Dickens — *David Copperfield* (5; 7 [abr.]; 11)
Dickens — *Great Expectations* (4; 6; 8)
Dickens — *Oliver Twist* (4; 11)
Dickens — *Pickwick Papers* (6)
Dickens — *Tale of Two Cities* (4; 6; 10; 14)
Dostoevski — *The Brothers Karamazov* (7 [abr.]; 10; 13; 14; 23)
Dostoevski — *Crime and Punishment* (3; 7; 9; 13)
Douglas — *The Robe* (11)
Doyle — *Sherlock Holmes* (4; 13; 25)
Dreiser — *American Tragedy* (7)
Dumas — *The Three Musketeers* (13; 26)
Edmonds — *Drums along the Mohawk* (3)
Eliot — *Adam Bede* (4; 8; 11)
Eliot — *Middlemarch* (5)
Eliot — *Silas Marner* (4; 6; 7; 14)
Fast — *Citizen Tom Paine* (3)
Ferber — *Cimarron* (3)
Ferber — *So Big* (27)
Fielding — *Joseph Andrews* (3; 4; 8; 10; 28)
Fielding — *Tom Jones* (10; 23; 29)
Fitzgerald — *The Great Gatsby* (30)
Franklin — *Autobiography* (4; 5; 6; 8; 10; 31)
Gaskell — *Cranford* (4)
Goldsmith — *The Vicar of Wakefield* (4; 11)
Guthrie — *The Big Sky* (11)
Hardy — *Far from the Madding Crowd* (4; 8; 15; 17)
Hardy — *The Mayor of Casterbridge* (4; 8; 10; 11; 17)
Hardy — *The Return of the Native* (4; 6; 8; 14; 17)
Hardy — *Tess of the d'Urbervilles* (4; 5; 6; 10; 17)
Hawthorne — *The House of the Seven Gables* (4; 6; 7; 8)
Hawthorne — *Scarlet Letter* (4; 5; 6; 7; 8; 10; 14; 21)
Hemingway — *For Whom the Bell Tolls* (30)
Hemingway — *The Sun Also Rises* (30)
Hilton — *Lost Horizon* (11)
Homer — *Odyssey* (10; 13; 14; 33)
Homer — *The Iliad* (3; 10; 13; 14; 28 [shortened version]; 32)
Howells — *The Rise of Silas Lapham* (4; 5; 8; 10)
Hudson — *Green Mansions* (3; 9)
Huxley — *Brave New World* (3)
James — *The American* (7; 8; 9)
James — *Daisy Miller* (7; 9)

James	*The Portrait of a Lady* (5; 10)
James	*The Turn of the Screw* (7)
Joyce	*Portrait of the Artist as a Young Man* (2)
Kipling	*Captains Courageous* (3)
Kipling	*Kim* (7)
Koestler	*Darkness at Noon* (14)
Lawrence	*Sons and Lovers* (2; 14)
Lewis	*Dodsworth* (7)
London	*Call of the Wild* (11; 14)
Marquand	*The Late George Apley* (9; 11)
Marquand	*H. M. Pulham, Esq.* (3)
Marquand	*Point of No Return* (3)
Maugham	*Of Human Bondage* (11 [abr.]; 23)
Melville	*Billy Budd* (3; 20; 21)
Melville	*Moby Dick* (4; 5; 7; 8; 10; 11 [abr.]; 14)
Melville	*Omoo* (4)
Melville	*Typee* (3; 20; 21)
Meredith	*The Ordeal of Richard Feverel* (10)
Monsarrat	*The Cruel Sea* (11)
Nordhoff and Hall	*Men against the Sea* (11)
Nordhoff and Hall	*Mutiny on the Bounty* (11)
Parkman	*The Oregon Trail* (14)
Paton	*Cry the Beloved Country* (30)
Pepys	*Diary* (34 [abr.])
Poe	*Tales* (4; 5; 6; 7; 8; 10; 14; 21)
Reade	*Cloister and the Hearth* (6)
Remarque	*All Quiet on the Western Front* (29)
Sandburg	*Abraham Lincoln* (7)
Scott	*Ivanhoe* (4; 6)
Scott	*Quentin Durward* (4)
Sienkiewicz	*Quo Vadis* (3)
Steinbeck	*Grapes of Wrath* (2)
Steinbeck	*Of Mice and Men* (3; 21)
Stevenson	*Kidnapped* (4; 6; 7; 13; 14)
Stevenson	*Treasure Island* (4; 6; 13)
Swift	*Gulliver's Travels* (4; 5; 6; 8; 10; 14; 21)
Tarkington	*The Magnificent Ambersons* (22; 27)
Tarkington	*Seventeen* (3)
Thackeray	*Henry Esmond* (4; 10)
Thackeray	*Vanity Fair* (8; 10; 11; 23)
Thoreau	*Walden* (4; 5; 8; 10; 14; 21)
Tolstoi	*Anna Karenina* (3; 13)
Trollope	*Barchester Towers* (3; 4; 8; 10)
Voltaire	*Candide* (3; 13; 19; 20)
Wells	*The History of Mr. Polly* (5)
Wharton	*Ethan Frome* (30)
Wilder	*Bridge of San Luis Rey* (6)
Wister	*The Virginian* (11; 25)
Wolfe	*Look Homeward Angel* (30)
Wren	*Beau Geste* (35)

Plays

(From the reading lists of preparatory schools and colleges)

Anderson	*Elizabeth the Queen* (36)
Anderson	*High Tor* (36)
Anderson	*Mary of Scotland* (36)
Anderson	*Winterset* (36)
Chekhov	*The Cherry Orchard* (3; 9; 13; 21)
Euripides	*Medea* (12; 14; 32)
Goldsmith	*She Stoops to Conquer* (18; 19; 37)
Ibsen	*A Doll's House* (3; 7; 10)
Ibsen	*Enemy of the People* (3; 8; 9; 10)
Ibsen	*Ghosts* (3; 8; 10)
Ibsen	*Hedda Gabler* (7; 8; 9; 10; 13)
Ibsen	*When We Dead Awaken* (1; 37)
Ibsen	*The Wild Duck* (3; 7; 8; 9; 13)
Miller	*Death of a Salesman* (2)
O'Casey	*Juno and the Paycock* (17)
Rostand	*Cyrano de Bergerac* (3)
Shaw	*Androcles and the Lion* (13)
Shaw	*Arms and the Man* (3; 13; 14)
Shaw	*Caesar and Cleopatra* (7; 13)
Shaw	*Candida* (7; 13)
Shaw	*Devil's Disciple* (7; 13)
Shaw	*Major Barbara* (13)
Shaw	*Pygmalion* (13)
Shaw	*Saint Joan* (13)
Sheridan	*The Rivals* (4; 18; 19; 37)
Sheridan	*The School for Scandal* (4; 18; 37)
Sophocles	*Oedipus at Colonus* (12; 13; 14; 32)
Sophocles	*Oedipus Rex* (6; 12; 13; 14; 19; 32)
Synge	*Playboy of the Western World* (23)
Synge	*Riders to the Sea* (23)
Wilde	*The Importance of Being Earnest* (3; 4; 8; 13; 18; 21)
Wilder	*Our Town* (3)

Directory of Paperbound Publishers

1. Anchor Books, 575 Madison Avenue, New York 22, New York.
2. Compass Books, 625 Madison Avenue, New York 22, New York.
3. Bantam Books, Inc., 271 Madison Avenue, New York 16, New York.
4. Dolphin Books, 575 Madison Avenue, New York 22, New York.
5. Riverside Editions, 2 Park Avenue, Boston 7, Massachusetts.
6. Washington Square Press, Inc., 630 Fifth Avenue, New York 20, New York.
7. Dell Publishing Company, Inc., 750 Third Avenue, New York 17, New York.
8. Holt, Rinehart and Winston, Inc., 383 Madison Avenue, New York 17, New York.
9. Universal Library, 1107 Broadway, New York 10, New York.
10. Modern Library College Editions, 457 Madison Avenue, New York 22, New York.
11. Pocket Books, Inc., 630 Fifth Avenue, New York 20, New York.
12. Oxford University Press, Inc., 417 Fifth Avenue, New York 16, New York.
13. Penguin Books, Inc., 3300 Clipper Mill Road, Baltimore 11, Maryland.
14. New American Library of World Literature, Inc., 501 Madison Avenue, New York 22, New York.
15. Premier Books, 67 West 44th Street, New York 36, New York.
16. Ace Books, 23 West 47th Street, New York 36, New York.
17. St. Martin's Library, 103 Park Avenue, New York 17, New York.
18. Barron's Educational Series, Inc., 343 Great Neck Road, Great Neck, New York.
19. Appleton-Century-Crofts, Inc., 35 West 32nd Street, New York 16, New York.
20. Dutton Everyman Paperbacks, 300 Park Avenue, South, New York 10, New York.
21. Viking Paperbound Portables, 625 Madison Avenue, New York 22, New York.
22. American Century Series, 104 Fifth Avenue, New York 11, New York.
23. Vintage Books, Inc., 457 Madison Avenue, New York 22, New York.
24. Hafner Library of World Classics, 31 East 10th Street, New York 3, New York.
25. Popular Library, Inc., 355 Lexington Avenue, New York 17, New York.
26. Pyramid Books, 444 Madison Avenue, New York 22, New York.
27. Avon Book Division, 959 Eighth Avenue, New York 19, New York.
28. W. W. Norton and Company, Inc., 55 Fifth Avenue, New York 3, New York.
29. Crest Books, 67 West 44th Street, New York 36, New York.
30. Charles Scribner's Sons, 597 Fifth Avenue, New York 17, New York.
31. American Heritage Series, 153 West 72nd Street, New York 23, New York.
32. University of Chicago Press, 5750 Ellis Avenue, Chicago 37, Illinois.
33. Galaxy Books, 417 Fifth Avenue, New York 16, New York.
34. Harper Torchbooks, 49 East 33rd Street, New York 16, New York.
35. Permabooks, 630 Fifth Avenue, New York 20, New York.
36. Harvest Books, 750 Third Avenue, New York 17, New York.
37. Dramabooks, 104 Fifth Avenue, New York 11, New York.

Contributors

(Figures refer to numbered selections in the text)

1. M. Jerry Weiss, Jersey City State College. 2. Anne McKillop, Teachers College, Columbia University. 3. Miriam Aronow, Board of Education of the City of New York. 4. David H. Russell, University of California at Berkeley. 5. Marshall Covert, Highland Park High School, Highland Park, Illinois. 6. Earle W. Wiltse, District High School Superintendent, Park Ridge, Illinois. 7. Nancy Larrick, Quakertown, Pennsylvania. 8. Marjorie Seddon Johnson, Temple University. 9. George D. Spache, University of Florida. 10. Paul Witty, Northwestern University. 11. Marvin D. Glock, Cornell University. 12. Dorothy Bratton, Mattoon High School, Mattoon, Illinois. 13. Bulletin of the National Association of Secondary School Principals. 14. Phillip Shaw, Brooklyn College. 15. Edwin Mingoia, University of California at Berkeley. 16. Ruth C. Penty, Battle Creek, Michigan.

17. Dwight L. Burton, Florida State University. 18. George E. Murphy, Pennsylvania State University. 19. Paul A. Wagner. 20. Charles G. Spiegler, Food Trades Vocational High School, New York City. 21. David V. Curtis. 22. E. Elona Sochor. 23. Richard Corbin, Hunter College High School, New York City. 24. Charles B. Huelsman, Jr., Miami University, Oxford, Ohio. 25. Roma Gans, Teachers College, Columbia University. 26. Kansas Studies in Education. 27. Bulletin of the National Association of Secondary School Principals. 28. Ruth Strang, Teachers College, Columbia University. 29. Homer L. J. Carter, Western Michigan University, Kalamazoo, Michigan. 30. Mary K. Eakin, Iowa State Teachers College, Cedar Falls, Iowa. 31. Ruth Strang, Teachers College, Columbia University. 32. Joseph Mersand, Jamaica High School, New York City. 33. Richard S. Alm, University of Hawaii.

34. John R. Clark, New Hope, Pennsylvania. 35. Mary C. Austin, Harvard University, Cambridge, Massachusetts. 36. Kenneth B. Henderson, University of Illinois, Urbana, Illinois. 37. Mabel Rudisill, Duke University, Durham, North Carolina. 38. Jean Fair, Wayne State University, Detroit, Michigan. 39. Margaret J. Early, Syracuse University, Syracuse, New York. 40. Mary Clifford, J. W. Eater Junior High School, Rantoul, Illinois. 41. M. Jerry Weiss, Jersey City State College.